SimPolitics

Information Policy Series

Edited by Sandra Braman

The Information Policy Series publishes research on and analysis of significant problems in the field of information policy, including decisions and practices that enable or constrain information, communication, and culture irrespective of the legal siloes in which they have traditionally been located as well as state-law-society interactions. Defining information policy as all laws, regulations, and decision-making principles that affect any form of information creation, processing, flows, and use, the series includes attention to the formal decisions, decision-making processes, and entities of government; the formal and informal decisions, decision-making processes, and entities of private and public sector agents capable of constitutive effects on the nature of society; and the cultural habits and predispositions of governmentality that support and sustain government and governance. The parametric functions of information policy at the boundaries of social, informational, and technological systems are of global importance because they provide the context for all communications, interactions, and social processes.

A complete list of the books in the Information Policy series appears at the back of this book.

SimPolitics

America's Quest to Solve Politics with Computers

Fenwick McKelvey

The MIT Press
Cambridge, Massachusetts
London, England

The MIT Press
Massachusetts Institute of Technology
77 Massachusetts Avenue
Cambridge, MA 02139
mitpress.mit.edu

The MIT Press would like to thank the anonymous peer reviewers who provided comments on drafts of this book. The generous work of academic experts is essential for establishing the authority and quality of our publications. We acknowledge with gratitude the contributions of these otherwise uncredited readers.

This book was set in Stone Serif and Stone Sans by Westchester Publishing Services. Printed and bound in the United States of America.

Library of Congress Cataloging-in-Publication Data

Names: McKelvey, Fenwick author
Title: SimPolitics : America's quest to solve politics with computers / Fenwick McKelvey.
Description: Cambridge, Massachusetts : The MIT Press, [2026] | Series: Information policy series | Includes bibliographical references and index.
Identifiers: LCCN 2026001063 (print) | LCCN 2026001064 (ebook) | ISBN 9780262053198 paperback | ISBN 9780262053204 epub | ISBN 9780262053211 pdf
Subjects: LCSH: Political participation—United States—Computer simulation—History | Election forecasting—United States—Methodology—History | Voting research—United States—Methodology—History | Politics, Practical—United States—History | United States—Politics and government
Classification: LCC JK1764 .M3938 2026 (print) | LCC JK1764 (ebook) | DDC 323/.0420973—dc23/eng/20260226
LC record available at https://lccn.loc.gov/2026001063
LC ebook record available at https://lccn.loc.gov/2026001064

EU Authorised Representative: Easy Access System Europe, Mustamäe tee 50, 10621 Tallinn, Estonia | Email: gpsr.requests@easproject.com

Contents

Acknowledgments

Writing acknowledgments for a book that started ten years ago feels like its own history. Eduardo Galeano wrote, "I believe in memory not as a place of arrival, but as a point of departure—a catapult throwing you into present times, allowing you to imagine the future instead of accepting it." Memories spring back—books unwritten and those moments of insight—so the acknowledgments become a chance to be with everyone again that was there in its making.

The book began at Toronto Metropolitan University back in 2010 when I chanced upon Richard Charltand's 1972 book, *Computers and Political Campaigning,* with its cover of a computer on a podium. That book clashed with then-present discussions of computers in political campaigns.

My time at Toronto Metropolitan University was formative for the book's early questions. Credit goes to my supervisor, Greg Elmer, for sending me to the Personal Democracy Forum, exposing me, in retrospect, to the highs of American optimism around computers in politics. I was also thankful to attend the Politics: Web 2.0 international conference co-organized by Andrew Chadwick, where I am grateful to Ganaele Langlois and the rest of the Infoscape Research Center for shaping an enduring interest in technology and politics. A lot of what I wanted the book to be comes from another committee member, Robert Latham, who told me to read Karl Deutsch and think about systems. Also, I thank Kenneth Werbin for introducing me to Paul Edward's Closed World. Big thanks to Luke Simcoe, Brady Curlew, and Zachary Deveraux for the lasting friendships and shared interests.

For too brief a time, I had the privilege of starting to look into the early history of political campaigns and computers at the University of Washington. Thanks to Phil Howard for this opportunity and the early support on a much larger research project. I'll never forget the bookshelf in his office. Katy Pearce and Jessica Beyer were two of the most special people I met in Seattle and were great company as I started this journey. Daniel Kreiss, who served in a rather abstractly described postdoctoral research committee, really inspired me to go back and start to piece together this history and connected me with key references in the book, including Bob Blaemire. I started a few interviews, but my conversation with Robert G. Meadow stands out. I still remember talking with him and looking out at Puget Sound with such excitement that there was a history to tell. He also sent me a box of books that has become a treasured part of the book's archive. My time in Seattle lasted eight months, but it's a place I still feel a connection to.

By 2013, I started a new job and new life at Concordia University. Another book delayed this project until 2019, when I could return to it during my first sabbatical. Thanks to everyone in Montreal and Concordia who sustained this project. Colleagues at Concordia include Stefanie Duguay, Rachel Berger, Martin French, Peter Van Wyck, Charles Acland, Jason Lewis, Joshua Neves, Elena Razlogova, Alessandra Renzi, Mia Consalvo, Bill Buxton, Elizabeth Miller, and Marc Steinberg, who was so gracious in giving me feedback on the book proposal. A special thank you to Bart Simon for the mentorship and ever-present comradery.

I also want to acknowledge the many tremendous graduate researchers that have contributed to the project. Scott DeJong and I nearly wrote another book about political games. Thanks to Colleen McCool, Luciano Frizzera, Robert Marinov, Jill Piebiak, Maggie Macdonald, Natalia Balska, and Anna Sigrithur Houston for help on the book production and my great AI cohort—Nick Gertler, Saskia Kowalchuk, and Meaghan Wester. This book, like the last one, would not have been possible without Robert Hunt—your book is next.

That the book took shaped during the COVID pandemic meant the original plan of on-site archival research turned into a lot of emails and dead ends. My deepest gratitude to all the archivists and librarians who shared their time responding to my overly broad requests. Thanks to Daniel Kreiss, Jessica Baldwin-Philippi, and Dave Karpf for some of the Zoom meetups. Your scholarship and friendship have always been a driving inspiration for this project. You also all had the privilege of watching live when I discovered that Jill Lepore was writing a book on the Simulmatics Corporation. Also, a special thanks to Jill Lepore, who very generously helped answer some requests during this project. Thanks to Joy Rohde for being such a fantastic historian and great company as the scale of the book expanded past just American campaigning to the global project of computer simulation. Her supported early on helped make this book possible.

Thanks to Kevin Driscoll and Lana Swartz, Robert Gehl (for introducing me to situational analysis), Kate Dommett for her encouragement, Thomas Streeter, Molly Wright Steenson, Lucy Suchman, Andrew Clement, Fabian Ferrari, Sun-ha Hong, Stephanie Dick, Luke Stark, Sara Bannerman, Chris Parsons, Chris Salter, Orit Halpern, Paul Edwards, Joanna Redden, past and present Data + Society members (especially Robyn Caplan), Joan Donovan, and Alice Marwick, Beth Coleman, Gabriella Coleman, Niels ten Oever, Markus Elias Ramsauer, Sophie Toupin, and Theo Lepage-Richler. Thanks to my colleagues at Groupe de Recherche en Communication Politique (GRCP), including Frédérick Bastien, Thierry Giasson, Colette Brin, Alex Marland, and Mireille Lalancette, and to fellow technology and politics researchers, including Colin Bennett, Andrew Clement, Sara Bannerman, Heidi Tworek, Chris Tenove, Elizabeth Dubois, and Taylor Owen. Thanks to all the members of the Shaping AI team, including Christan Katzenbach, Donato Ricci, Michael Castelle, and Noortje Marres. Finally, un grand merci to Jonathan Roberge for the friendship, the collaborations as well as the encouragement for believing in this project.

Variations of the book have been worked out in a few key talks, notably the Politics of Algorithms panel at the 2012 Society for Social Studies of Sciences, the 2018 Cultural Life of Machine Learning preconference at the Association of Internet Researchers (especially Jonathan), and the 2024 Society for the History of Technology. A few public talks also gave me the time to elaborate my work in detail. Thanks to Nanna Bonde Thylstrup and Louise Amoore for the chance to give a public talk for the AI Reuse and various talks at the Milieux Institute and to Emily Klancher Merchant and Myron P. Gutmann for organizing The IT of Demography at the University of Colorado, where I presented my early work on the Claritas Corporation. I am deeply grateful to the History of Media Studies Working Group for the opportunity to speak, especially for the support, inspiration, and guidance from Jeff Pooley, Dave Park, and Peter Simonson. Finally, at the last stages, the Media History Research Center helped me make some final clarifications and hone my introductions.

To all interviewees and people who helped me with the project, especially Richard Chadwick, Murray Fishel, Robert Meadow and Phil Schrodt, without your insights and generosity this project would have not been possible. Thanks to Sarah McPhee for the kind words at the end of the project. Aure Shrock helped me in the last stages of pushing a draft into a manuscript; their advice was essential to the book's final form. Thanks to That-Ben at the Mac Repository, Paul McJones for his patience, and the WZB for their help with the Micro-GLOBUS. Access to archival materials was made possible by Scott at Micro-Scott, NDG's best computer store.

Publishing with the MIT Press has always been a life goal. I am honored to have been able to work with Gita Devi Manaktala, Rashmi Malhotra, and Suraiya Jetha at the MIT Press. I want to give a special thanks to Sandra Braman. The book, for better or worse, is the thing I have worked hardest on academically thanks to Sandra's care and support. Her autodidact scholarship is an inspiration in this book and all my work.

This book has been graciously supported by an Early Career Grant from the Fonds de Recherche du Québec, the Social Sciences and Humanities Research Council, and the Aid to Research-Related Event grant from Concordia University.

This book was written through the love and support of my family—Jillian, Wallace, and especially Harriet, my party machine, all of whom I love without end.

Series Editor Introduction

Sandra Braman

The brilliant poet Larry Eigner, who had paraplegia, titled one of his books *Anything on Its Side*. It included a poem about what his home and yard looked like from the ground where he lay, calmly and otherwise unhurt, after his wheelchair fell over. Fenwick McKelvey's fascinating and revealing book *SimPolitics* so effectively rereads political science and other literatures of recent decades that it leaves this author, who has been reading in these areas since the 1980s, feeling as if I am lying on my side on the ground looking at work I thought I knew from a new perspective.

Research for the book *SimPolitics* required genuinely archaeological digs on voter and international system simulations from the 1960s through the 1980s. McKelvey found ways to run programs designed for operating systems no longer in use, read through archives to learn what those commissioning and making simulations were thinking, and dug up material such as manuals—one of which ran almost a thousand pages. The amount of technical and material effort involved, as well as that which was scholarly and conceptual, was substantial, requiring originality and expertise in its pursuit and inspiring the thought that it might be useful in future to include archaeological methods sections in such works so that others can learn "how to."

Some of the news thus learned is good. In 2011, the Pew Center found eight types of voters; in 2021, they found nine. Experientially, many living in highly polarized societies might report they experience only two. Thus, it is refreshing to learn that in 1959 one of the first efforts to analyze US voters found 480 types. Indeed, seeing the sense of the possibilities of political nuance that the many facets used by designers of voting models, games, and simulations give provides one hope regarding possible voter, and voting, futures under contemporary conditions. Authors rarely discuss the deontology of their work—why they do what they do—but in this case McKelvey does let the reader know that, in fact, providing hope was among the goals of the book.

It also provides a sense of lost innocence for those who are otherwise thinking about what the tools of a company like Palantir provide governments. McKelvey lets us know what those who commissioned and those who built simulations wanted to achieve, what was done with the results, and critiques that were levied. Uses were often rhetorical. The fact that voter simulations were consulted at all may have been more important than the data produced, at least rhetorically, in some election campaigns. In 1951 CBS contracted with Remington Rand to use its computer to forecast election results, but a mock-up of it was on set on election night because the real one was far too large to bring into the studio. (Many organizations as late as the 1980s were including computers in their budgets for rhetorical purposes, to indicate that they were "up to date"; as someone hired first as a temporary secretary, in the late 1970s I built a database for the industrial relations unit of an eight-location, three-state steel company that had bought one without knowing what it would actually be used for.)

Support for the development of simulations ran in both directions—computers aided politicians, and the support of politicians helped legitimize the use of computers. It is classical that political scientists were largely excluded from the development of simulations of political systems during the 1970s, when so many were being built. And it is delightful to learn about the 1958 development of a precomputer precursor to *Pong*. The work is filled with generative gifts for future work by other scholars.

The book is theoretically strong and conceptually rich. Importantly, McKelvey distinguishes among three types of computational citizens, each with a different type of agency—cybernetic citizen, rational actor, and data chimera. He distinguishes imaginaries, general understandings about the nature of the world, from models that provide static simplified pictures of that world and the prototypes that then operationalize the models, making them active. "Recursive" causality is used because, McKelvey says, he "cannot locate an exact beginning to the computational imaginary of politics" (p. XXX).

The issues raised here have moved on. The broad diffusion of networked computing after the Internet became available in 1993–1994 to anyone for any purpose yielded a concomitant rise of various types of simulations and gaming by a growing number of entities exhibiting varying levels of formalism. Increases in bandwidth and computational capacity meant these could become increasingly complex while taking ever-larger amounts of data into account. In the 1990s, when people were first able to link data across space and time, they began to see patterns never before visible, strongly affecting what went into simulations. Big data and, now, AI in the wild make the situation more complex again by orders of magnitude.

SimPolitics provides just the foundation we need for today and what is yet to come. Details about specific simulations and games tell us not just about how voters, on the one hand, and political systems, on the other, were imagined, but also how they were modeled and then acted upon. They tell us a great deal about the ways in which these different modes of human activity provide affordances for and affect each other. McKelvey raises the biggest questions of all about how thinking about politics computationally provides the affordances for different types of agency. The lenses, intellectual tools, and insights he offers are as valuable for thinking about the contemporary environment as they are for mining what we can from the key period he analyzes in such detail. And I confess that reading the book is also a lot of fun.

1 From 480 to 538: The Origins of the Computational Imaginary of Politics

How did simulating politics with computer modeling become so "routine," as scientist Dan Rockmore claimed in a 2024 piece? Reflecting on modeling for *The New Yorker*, Rockmore elaborated that "we model everything, from elections to economics, from the climate to the coronavirus."[1] Political systems have become *just* another system to be modeled. The same techniques that predict the weather can be applied to elections just as well. Rain, however, does not read the weather report as people do the news. Modeling politics—whether national or international—*should* be different and more difficult.

Modelling politics can be a "far-out" idea. Orrin Clotworthy began his article, "Some Far-out Thoughts on Computers," hoping these machines could see the hidden patterns that eluded human intelligence:

> **Question:** What does the size of the next coffee crop, bullfight attendance figures, local newspaper coverage of UN matters, the birth rate, the mean daily temperatures or refrigerator sales across the country have to do with who will next be elected president of Guatemala?
>
> **Answer:** Perhaps nothing. But the question is not a frivolous one.[2]

Clotworthy saw coffee, bullfighting, and birth rates as inputs that, when properly interpreted by a computer, might predict voter behavior in Guatemala or the United States. Clotworthy sought another kind of computer science: a political science to predict the actions of voters and foreign leaders alike. His ambitions are clear: "What is proposed is to bypass the voter himself in this analytic process, looking beyond him for the reasons underlying his decisions."[3] Computers would explain voters' behaviors better than people themselves. By suggesting that computers could find meaning in random data, Clotworthy illustrates a widespread hope about politics' computability: There are patterns in the data found only by machines that could make politics more stable and predictable. Clotworthy admits that "mass cause-and-effect relationships are more elusive for people than for molecules," but undaunted by this difficulty, he continues, "they must be there, somewhere, and scholars are looking for them."[4]

Clotsworthy's "far-out" thoughts sound recent, but are old. He published his ideas in 1962 in CIA's classified peer-reviewed journal, *Studies in Intelligence*.[5] Clotworthy was a CIA analyst. His "far-out thoughts" are now routine. When the CIA declassified his article in 2013, a Bloomberg headline dubbed it "The 1962 CIA Paper That Predicts the Big Deal with Big Data."[6] Amid a long and ongoing discussion of the impact of artificial intelligence (AI), big data, or social media in politics, my book contributes something a little different: a history.

SimPolitics traces a genealogy of the breakdowns between the political and computational from Clotworthy's time until the late 1980s, tracing the roots of what I call a *computational imaginary of politics* in the United States. For over six decades, the public has been promised that computers are a tool that will revolutionize politics nationally and internationally. Political change is easily imagined through *or* because of computers. Indeed, ample scholarship has demonstrated the close link between computer systems and political systems in US politics. My book adds to this story by piecing together how programmers, consultants, academics, and political scientists alike have built simulations to win campaigns, predict coups, and render politics as legible as a spreadsheet—as easy as predicting your next song. The cases I discuss in this book's pages come from the parallel efforts to simulate voters and international relations in the United States.

A history of the computational imaginary of politics might read at first glance like a history of techno-solutionism, or what Meredith Broussard calls techno-chauvinism.[7] Technology seems like a solution to every problem—a chauvinism that lets technological experts claim to be knowledgeable enough to solve the world's most vexing problems. Marginalized, poor, and racialized populations often become the targets of technological experiments as well as the problem to be solved.[8] That is a particularly American tradition with a long history.

From the electronic to the digital sublime, American culture has dreamed of technological solutions, of "brave new worlds" that promised a utopia through technology.[9] The late Vincent Mosco situated the technological sublime as an enduring American quality that spanned from the telegraph to the early Internet hype preceding the first dot-com crash. That faith, to Mosco, often leads to a historical amnesia, as if the latest gadget will fix the shortcomings of the last one. Mosco captures the promise and ambiguity of this cultural faith in technology's utopian promise: "The positive visions of the technological sublime may have succeeded in winning popular support for railroads, for steam, for electricity, and for nuclear power. And many would say that on balance those technologies (particularly the first three) created more good than harm. Nevertheless, society has also paid an enormous price for their promises in lives and resources sacrificed to realize impossible dreams."[10] Like Mosco, my goal is to push past stark judgements about computational politics as just "good" or "bad." Public debate seems caught between hope and fear that computers will lead to utopian or dystopian futures. The hype and backlash feel almost cyclical; computers become an object of public revelry or revulsion every few years. On a 2013 cover of *The MIT Technology Review*, computing and "big data" were portrayed as the path to political salvation (Bono appeared on the cover). Five years later, Barack Obama's 2012 election was a distant memory, Donald Trump had won the presidency, and the September 2018 issue asked the inverse question: How could democracy be saved from technology?[11] The same questions endure.

SimPolitics offers new critical directions to explore the computational imaginary of politics beyond just hope and fear. I explore the imaginary's political dimensions—ways to describe its facets and scale—drawn from a careful study of the history of political simulation. I don't argue that this history determines our present; rather, it offers concepts and problems still relevant today. My goal is to provide an account of the computational imaginary of politics that recovers its multitudes and potentials. I draw inspiration from feminist theorist Louise Amoore's ethicopolitics of AI. Amoore proposes strategies to study of computation and politics by "reopening the multiplicity of the algorithm, digging under the stories, and attending to the branch pathways that continue to run beneath the surface."[12] In practice, strategy means acknowledging the stories and partiality of models and prototypes—trying to take up what is unspoken yet present. For computational imaginaries, Amoore's strategies mean looking at multiplicities and investigating which models and prototypes might be forgotten or missing but nonetheless remain important and influential.

Uniting Voting Politics and International Relations

The computational history of voting politics and international relations remains scattered across fields and is often forgotten at the start of each wave of technology. To unearth this history, *SimPolitics* navigates decades of high-tech research and on-the-ground computing applications. This book traverses research in national and international politics to understand how computers were imagined and built to solve the political problems of the United States at home and abroad.

Simulating politics with computers had consequences. Computers evolved into political tools, which also configured their users. What does it mean to investigate a "computer's view" of a political campaign or the world? How does the computer's interfacing change the politician, the party, or the expert's understanding and relationship to political power?

Figure 1.1 illustrates the kinds of mutual configuration of users and computers happening in this book—less as an explanation than a way for me to describe the task ahead. The arrows describe a reflexivity, recalling Katherine Hayles, where thinking about politics *with* computers changed how practitioners understood politics *as* computational.[13] As historian of science Peter Galison noted of early simulations, "Bit by bit (byte by byte), computer designers deconstructed the notion of a tool itself as the computer came to stand not for a tool, but for nature itself."[14]

The computational imaginary of politics is a socio-technical discourse that shapes lay understandings of political behavior, validates proposals

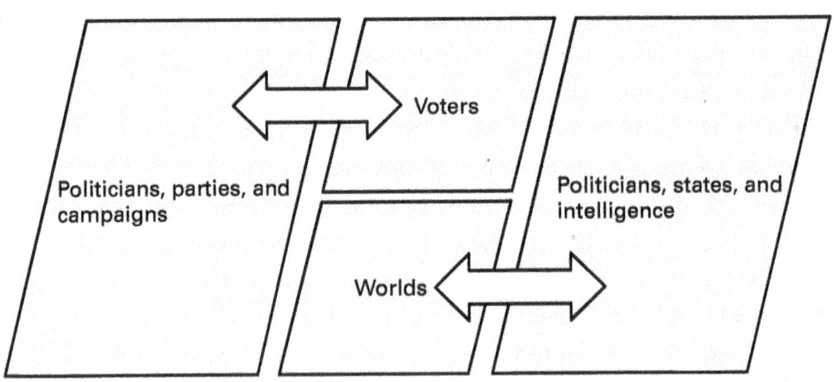

Figure 1.1
The trading zone of the computational imaginary of politics.

for political innovation, legitimates prototypes, and produces desires for political futures through the recursive interaction between political institutions and contemporary computing. I say "contemporary" because prior history has shown how theories of political behavior worked themselves out in relation to mainframe and personal computing. That is, different forms of computing changed this imaginary, and still does. "Political institutions" refers to the parties, publishers, and firms oriented around elections and party infrastructure. As a nod to Chris Kelty's concept of recursive publics, I invoke "recursive" because I cannot locate an exact beginning to the computational imaginary of politics. Instead, I found a loop that recursively built on the innovations in modeling worked out through prototypes.[15]

As a research program, the computational imaginary focuses on cultural not technical change. Politicians and international relations practitioners could speculate, imagine, and practice politics by thinking with and using computers. Following philosopher Gilles Deleuze the influence of computation on politics is not explicitly technological. That is, for Deleuze, computation's influence does not stem from the idea "that machines are determining" but rather "because they express those social forms capable of generating them and using them."[16] In other words, as computers started to model politics, politics began to model computers. My history explores the first breakdowns between computer systems and political systems in the United States, pressure points when the elements started to fuse. My hope is that these beginnings help us to discover new directions for thinking about how to combat the current allure of Vincent Mosco's digital sublime in our current era of AI and "big data."

This book foreshadows today's imaginaries at work in technology-intensive political campaigning and the geopolitical importance of cloud computing globally. Domestically, Daniel Kreiss has shown how successive political campaigns have become prototypes for future campaigns to mimic, turning campaigns toward greater emphasis on their digital operations.[17] The turn has become seen as an imaginary that shapes how campaigns think of themselves and their work. Jessi Baldwin-Philippi astutely notes a similarity to what David Beer terms the data imaginary in her research on political campaigns' data operations. Baldwin-Philippi notes that data-driven campaigning emphasizes the revealing, panoramic, and prophetic aspects of the data imaginary.[18] In other words, the promise of data-driven campaigning is to win elections—a promise that sells software and consulting services cycle to cycle by leveraging a belief that better data offer superior insight into the nature of politics and a campaign's success. Globally, Phil Howard has described a similar importance of digital infrastructure to the international order, part of how regional blocks imagine and action their power, or what he calls a "pax technica."[19]

The computational imaginary of politics developed as the US research community turned to computers to create a new generation of digital models of world and electoral politics. These efforts built on prior, predigital investment in the prowess of the scientific method, quantification, and statistics to solve social problems as well as the growing influence of applied mathematics.[20] So the computational imaginary has deep roots, but the era of modern and high modern social science encouraged experimentation and adoption of new digital computers in politics.[21] Even before political scientists started tinkering with punch cards and primitive processors, cybernetics, systems engineering, and Cold War thinking imbued the computer with a daemonic intelligence that might solve political problems.[22] This belief justified budgets and eventual experiments with newly accessible digital computers after the arrival of UNIVAC, the first digital computer, in 1952. Efforts were slow and computers never solved politics, but practitioners of political simulation were not dupes or naive. Rather, the computer, too, was a work in progress—a prototype of something better, even as it continued to fail.

The result was an awkward parallel effort to know the minds of American voters with greater computational detail and to understand the world at greater scales of computational abstraction. Computer simulation seemed to match American ambitions; as Anna Tsing writes, "Under American hegemony, bigger was always better."[23] New techniques and computational methods allowed for this expansion in the computational imaginary. The same people applied the same methods to both domestic and international politics. Just as the American government turned to computers to guide its nuclear strategy and foreign affairs, domestic politicians and consultants looked to computers to better address the American voter. As Clotworthy wrote his far-out thoughts, Winthrop Rockefeller, a grandchild of tycoon John D. Rockefeller, had been collecting voters' names in Arkansas. These names ended up running one of the first IBM machines, which was tasked with giving Rockefeller insights about his ultimately successful 1966 campaign for governor of Arkansas. For one of the first times, the computer tracked, targeted, and contacted voters through direct mail.[24] Studying America's domestic efforts with computing at the same time as its international applications produces just such a strange mix of the mundane and realpolitik.

Computer simulation promised to not only solve politics but afford its simulators a computational legitimacy. Clotworthy's work on computers at the CIA stressed the importance of computing's strategic foresight, while pacifists turned to computer simulation to outwit "war hawks." Institutional desires—from governments and political parties—framed the research agendas and funding contexts for simulation around management and control. Computers and computer simulation became constructed as tools for American politicians, parties, policymakers, and government institutions. Specifically, I examine prototypes that confronted the complexity of simulating politics.

Institutions eased the blending of computers and politics through the progressive tradition of technocratic liberalism.[25] Political scientist Theodore J. Lowi noted that "modern social science and modern government have common origins in liberal thought."[26] These common origins favored rational decision-making because, as Lowi continues, "there was no objective way to determine which moral among all moral codes was the source of virtue."[27] Social sciences provided processes to fix this conundrum. Computation, "cyborg science," and other forms of Cold War rationality offered new forms of technical judgment to solve enduring political projects. Liberal institutions, in short, were primed to consider computers as the latest solution to the unresolvable moral challenges of politics.

The computer became a political target in the late 1960s. Anti–Vietnam War protestors marched in the streets and burned punch cards to oppose academics building computers for wartime service. Researchers could smell the tear gas from their labs, while critics saw computers as a tool of a new "Big Brother."[28] They had a point. Academic computing labs around Cambridge, Massachusetts, were either working on the war directly or more obliquely as they simulated counterinsurgencies and foreign crises. Clotworthy's "far-out thoughts" were becoming mainstream. He posed his question, "Who will next be elected president of Guatemala?" eight years after the agency backed a coup in Guatemala.

But even critics turned to computers. Student activists at Columbia University in 1969 understood the close links between computer simulation and military strategy, enough to make their own simulations. Wargamer Jim Dunnigan explained in the Columbia student newspaper that his simulation "Up Against the Wall, Motherfucker": "is as close to a computer-assisted simulation as you can get without using a computer. Why the computer? The computer keeps the books. It handles the details. An operations research simulation looks at an event to be simulated as a 'system' which has 'movable parts' and is oriented towards an 'objective.' . . . Thus one immediate benefit you obtain from social simulations is a defining or [*sic*] objectives, or at least possible objectives."[29]

Dunnigan's aspirations for his simulation are telling. Even as the computer was known to be integrated into the US war efforts, it still held the possibility of being a tool for counterculture as well. Such diverse applications remain a testament to the computer's unique status as a postwar trading zone for politics.[30]

Importantly, my history offers the needed depth to parse a computational image of politics in the United States. I argue that there was not one computational turn in politics but many. Comparable histories of political cybernetics in Chile and the USSR have demonstrated the multifaceted political impact of computing and made me more interested in the uptake of computing in politics in the United States.[31] Here, I take inspiration from Paul Edwards's writing on the relationship between the postwar development of computing and the attendant discourse about computational technologies. He argues that a closed-world discourse "supported the visions of centrally controlled, automated global power at the heart of the American Cold War politics."[32] Extending his argument, I argue that there were multiple "closed worlds" beyond the confines of the military-academic complex. The long promise of technocratic governance has let the politics of computing in America often be overlooked. Edwards himself supports that argument in his turn to comprehensive "mathematical simulation models of global dynamic processes," including world dynamic models or system dynamic models and, more famously, his work on climate modeling.[33] What I emphasize here is the political differences between computer simulations.

The fracture between computer simulations restores the conflict in computer simulation. The digital sublime or techno-solutionism can suggest that technology offers a singular approach—one ideal way to model politics with computers. That thinking omits the political conflict in simulation. As the seminal Louise Amoore writes about artificial intelligence today, there is a faith in the technology to provide a universal account. Amoore continues, "a claim that promises a general resolution of difficult problems across *technical computational* and *political* paradigms: an AI model that draws upon a structure of 'how the world works' in order to respond to an input it had *never encountered in training*; and a political model that is always capable of action in the face of the *unencountered situation*."[34]

I find, instead, that there are many ways to model politics with computers, and these approaches conflict. That might be evident today (as made clear by influential social scientist Scott E. Page in his expansive review of modeling in social applications.)[35] However, I am interested not in conceptual differences in modeling but in political differences.

The computational imaginary is marked by deep political differences. Democratic theorist Chantal Mouffe suggested a clear and helpful distinction between politics and the political: "By the political, I mean the dimension of antagonism which I take to be constitutive of human societies, and by politics, I mean the set of practices and institutions through which an order is created, organizing human coexistence in the context of "conflictuality" provided by the political."[36] She suggests there is no naturally correct moral or technical answer to what the political implications of computing are. To restate my claim in Mouffe's terminology, I focus on computer simulations of *politics* in hopes of understanding the *political* within the computational imaginary of politics. Encouraged by Louise Amoore's ethnopolitical strategies discussed above, my histories offer critical questions to probe the multiplicities and partiality of the computational imaginary to recover a sense of the political. My goal is neither to prove nor disprove these theories but to open the possibilities of understanding the consequences and the possibilities of a computational imaginary of politics.

Dominant Approaches to Researching the History of Computation in US Politics

The two main approaches to researching the history of computers and US politics have been developed in political communication and the history of the social sciences. This book draws from both these fields, adding to a small but growing literature about the history of American political communication, as well as debates about the consequences of computers on social thinking and research. Specifically, this book takes a similar interdisciplinary approach as two recent books on computational history. First, historian Jill Lepore's book *If Then* offers a detailed account of the Simulmatics Corporation, a company I also discuss in depth, which employed the kinds of researchers described by Orrin Clotworthy.

Simulmatics has been discussed for its influence on John F. Kennedy's 1960 presidential campaign and the war effort in Vietnam, and Lepore's book exceptionally unites its national and international facets. Her compelling synthesis highlights how the behavioral sciences promised to better manage foreign and domestic populations simultaneously.[37] My book does not reproduce her scholarship but instead traces the broader political effects of Simulmatics and others working under the postwar computational imaginary. My two-part structure gets direct inspiration from media scholar Charlton D. McIlwain. In his book *Black Software*, McIlwain presents a compelling history of how software was used by and against Black Americans. McIlwain contrasts how Black technophiles turned to computers just as the Simulmatics Corporation offered computational explanations of Civil Rights Movements to government elites. Where McIlwain looks at two sides of computing in America so productively, I look at two applications of computer simulation—voters and worlds—to introduce a productive tension as well as to understand the global ambitions of a computational imaginary of politics in the United States.[38] Inspired by Lepore and McIlwain, I balance national and international perspectives on the frictions around computers and politics.

This book also fills in the backstory of more recent technology-intensive and data-driven campaigning. Communications scholar Daniel Kreiss argues that we are in an era of technology-intensive campaigning, "where parties and campaigns have invested considerable resources in technology, digital media, data, and analytics to not only keep pace with these changes, but also actively shape technological contexts and define what twenty-first-century citizenship looks like."[39] Across two books that track the evolution of technology-intensive campaigning by the Democratic and Republican parties, he emphasizes that technology adoption is not straightforward. Even when successful, institutional and financial constraints mean that campaign technologies break down and must be rebuilt, requiring a reconsideration of the nuances of technology-intensive campaigning. Kreiss's arguments have become even more persuasive in subsequent US elections that demanded even more data-driven campaigning.

Following both the hype and the rhetoric, political communication scholar Jesse Baldwin-Philippi defines "data-driven campaigning" as having two main features: "targeting, or deciding which messages go to what potential voters at what time during the campaign, and testing, or empirically measuring how well messages perform against one another and using that information to drive content production and further targeting."[40] As an example of "digital citizenship," Baldwin-Philippi argues that email messaging exemplifies contemporary party-voter relations' reliance on data to identify voters, craft messages, and implement what David Karpf calls "digital listening" that converts feedback from voters into campaign strategy.[41] Data-driven campaigning is also a theme in Eitan Hersh's research on the impacts of political data on campaigns, in which he looks at the early efforts of the Democratic Party to create a shared database. His skepticism about the effects of "big data" on politics informs my own caution in approaching technology as deterministic.[42] My book aims to offer a prehistory of technology-intensive campaigning tracked by these scholars over the last several decades.

Several books chronicle simulation or technology in political communication before the 2000s.[43] Phil N. Howard studied the first generation of digital consultants in US politics in his landmark *New Media and the Managed Citizen*. He introduced the consequences of computers replacing voter feedback, which he called "thin citizenship."[44] These political actors were part of a longer history of the professionalization of political campaigning enabled by the adoption of computers to demonstrate expertise.[45] Sasha Issenberg offers the most complete history in *Victory Lab*, which tracks the efforts to introduce science to the study of campaigns. Issenberg rightly notices that early political science found practical application on the election trail.[46] All these histories help explain the rise of the computational imaginary of politics that I elaborate on but also remain disconnected from parallel efforts in the history of the social sciences.

My interest in models, computing, and politics is also situated in histories of the social sciences and genealogies of the media. As I discuss in the next chapter, these histories complement extant political communication literature by emphasizing the concurrent investment in computers to address another political need: US security in the Cold War. Propaganda scholars and defense intellectuals during the Cold War turned toward new digital computer technologies as part of a behavioral revolution to enhance the science of international relations and US strategy.[47] This period was marked by what Paul Erikson and his coauthors describe as a "Cold War rationality" that operated "by emphasizing the divergence between actual human reasoning and standards of formal rationality such as logic and Bayesian statistics, [behavioral psychology] implicitly reinforced the normative authority of the latter."[48] Cold War rationality is not a singular way of thinking, and learning about its variations in this book shows us how to think of computational imaginaries as having regularities and irregularities.

Cold War rationalities may draw from game theory, systems theories, cybernetics, policy modeling, data sciences, future sciences, and computational social sciences. These histories complement studies of the changing craft of political campaigns by exposing the discursive and cultural shifts in the sciences, industry, and government that legitimated computers as producing societal knowledge. Historian Joy Rhode, for example, looked broadly at the changing nature of the Cold War social sciences. Her primary interest was in how the computer became imbricated in efforts to better render and track global politics. Whereas the political histories above focused only on political applications in the United States, Rhode clarifies that these efforts happened simultaneously in global politics. My efforts bridge a disconnect by simultaneously considering domestic and global simulations.[49]

The pairing of these two literatures is productive in several ways. First, they provide a way to attend to the parallel efforts to adapt and develop computing for political purposes at home and abroad. Second, they similarly direct attention to lived accounts and the practical applications of computing to define the computational epistemologies and governmentalities of politics. Finally, these twin histories elaborate on how American investment in computing has been tied to the pursuit of power and influence, whether by winning the votes for the next campaign or successfully predicting the world's future. In other words, as I discuss, this book's twin history helps to provincialize US-based efforts to develop computer simulation in contrast to what was happening in Europe, Latin America, and Africa.[50]

Chapter Overview

The book explores the multiplicities within and beyond the computational imaginary of politics. Figure 1.2 illustrates how the book's structure relates

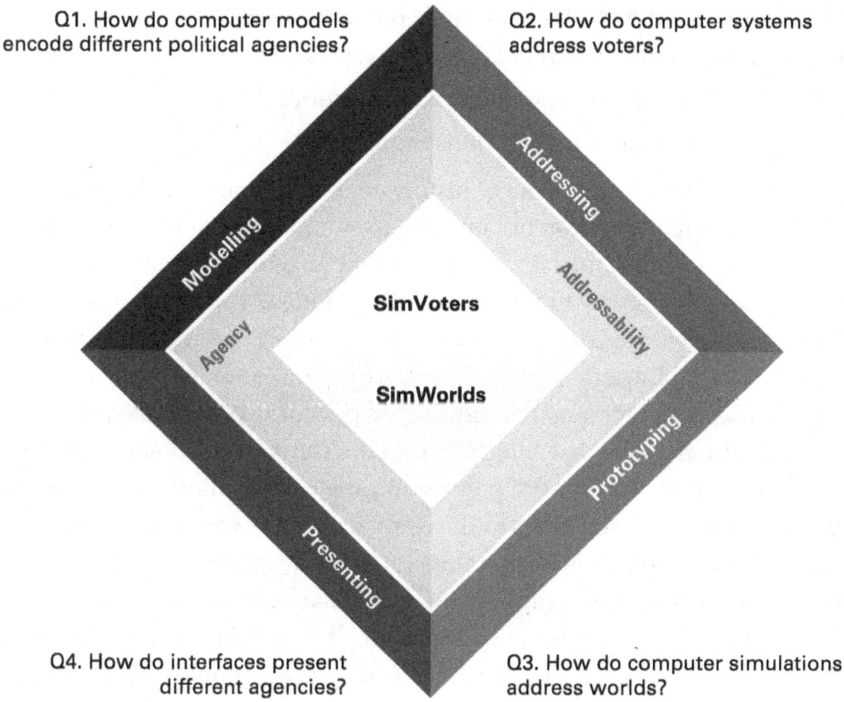

Figure 1.2
Exploring the computational imaginary of politics.

to key questions. The book's two parts—"SimVoters" and "SimWorlds"—capture the national and international political problems (respectively) that computers were used to try to solve in the United States. Each part elaborates on the situations where a computational imaginary of politics emerged in America. My situation is the context of computing and its relation to politics in postwar America.[51]

Agencies and addressability are my two main concepts if SimWorld and SimVoters are my situations. I use these two concepts to offers concepts to explore the computational imaginary of politics. The four main chapters represent intersections of each situation and concept. Each chapter elaborates on and expands on this situation through discourse analysis, interviews, and archival research to tell part of a history and elaborate one of my four key questions. These questions, as I explain, are

Q1. How do computer models encode different political agencies?

Q2. How do computer simulations address voters?

Q3. How do computer simulations address worlds?

Q4. How do interfaces present different agencies?

These questions, emerging out of history, remain relevant today. They don't explain a complete history but rather look at moments of intense pressure that provide insights into the computational imaginary of politics.

"Agencies" refers to the ways of acting, and in computer simulations "agencies" refers to certain behaviors of simulated voters and worlds. At a time of talk of agentic artificial intelligence and automated governance, agencies expose how computer simulations present their simulated elements with certain agencies that influence how we think about them, a reflexivity between how we simulate politics and the computational imaginary of politics. "Agencies" also refers to the relationships between how simulations *present* their modeled worlds to its users. The term "present" draws from Lorraine Daston and Peter Galison, who noted that with computer simulation "the camera and the tweezer had merged."[52] Representation, or showing, Daston and Galison argue is different from presentation, or showing and doing. Certainly, researchers and funders desired simulations of the world that could be actionable. Closing this utility gap speaks to a second concept, how computer simulations related to their so-called real world.

Addressability, as I discuss at length, involves the delicate relationship simulators had to balance to ensure that their computer worlds matched the political systems they sought to model.[53] If models become too abstract, they might present something of a hyperreality. Addressability relates a lot of current debates about scale. Scalability, Anna Tsing writes, is "the ability to expand—and expand, and expand—without rethinking basic elements."[54] But scalability is not quite right, as scale emphasizes an "expansion-oriented world" when computer simulations tried to be more detailed and more global.[55] Election forecasting, for example, progressed by claiming to have more detailed data or more precise voter models. World simulations, using the same behavioral models, improved by claiming to predict national behaviors, sometimes forecasting decades into the future. My interest concerns how the computational imaginary legitimated some gazes as complete or somehow less partial than other accounts of the world, a problem of addressability.

The first part of the book, "SimVoters," looks at the applications of computers in US electoral politics. Specifically, I start by examining politics and political research that inspired interest and investment in what was then experimental computer technology. To lay the foundation for what enabled computers to enter politics and the study of political systems, I discuss an early computer simulation of politics: William McPhee's macroscope. Through this project, he applied early theories of political behavior sympathetic to computer modeling, and it anticipated the demand and funding for better predictions of election outcomes.

Chapter 4 asks, *How do computer models encode different political agencies?* The chapter introduces and compares the agencies of three idealized voter models, which I call cybernetic citizens, rational agents, and digital chimeras. Each claimed to describe how voters behaved, but not in a compatible way. Voters could not be cybernetic citizens and rational agents simultaneously. Furthermore, cybernetic citizens emphasized active voters, whereas digital chimeras treated voters as largely static. These different agencies shaped and stabilized different political theories of how American voters led to the fundamental tensions that animate this book.

Chapter 5 tracks the integration of computational approaches into elections post-1960, a history that has led to the digital politics industry today. The gradual spread, investment, and adoption of computers into campaign practices posed a fundamental challenge—keeping virtual voters in sync with real ones. The chapter poses a second question: *How do computer simulations address voters?* To answer, chapter 5 elaborates the concept of addressability, which allows for a deeper discussion of the relationship between the imaginary and practical politics, or in the words of later chapters, how the simulated system corresponds to its referent system.

The book's second part—"SimWorlds"—explores concurrent efforts to model world politics, beginning with 1959's Simple Diplomatic Game. Designed as a toy, the game foreshadowed decades of building computational prototypes that simulated world politics. Chapter 6 sets up the promise and problem of computer simulation of world politics.

Chapter 7 explains how computer simulation became preferred over more experiential human-led simulations in world politics. Chronicling this evolution raises a third question: *How do computer simulations address worlds?* I argue that computer simulation can and was shaped to offer a specific gaze—a gaze like Donna Haraway's famous "god's eye view" in politics, which remains a major selling point for political simulations of world politics today. That might apply as much to the promise of looking into the minds of American voters, but it's readily apparent in the desire to present a simulated globe thought to be a valid proxy of the real world.

Chapter 8 returns to how my voter models—cybernetic citizens, rational agents, and digital chimeras—were applied to *world* politics. I identify attempts to use all three to model international relations, but I focus on the tensions between a cybernetic approach and its emphasis on world systems versus the antecedents of agent-based modeling through rational choice applications. These different simulations present their worlds and their users with different agencies. Looking at two key cases, the chapter asks, *How do interfaces present different political agencies?* The implication is that ways to imagine politics with specific programs create vantage points—god's eye views—with specific agencies of how the world behaves and how users interact with these worlds. The tension elaborates an important sense of the political in the computational imaginary of politics: how the computer simulations present forms of agency in their simulated worlds that matter for both how their users understand themselves and their worlds.

Finally, I look at the fringes of the simulation community in chapter 9. In contrast to the first part's conclusion, I look at what remains outside these histories instead of what endures. I explore alternative simulations to analyze how activists, gamers, and crossover intellectuals like Buckminster Fuller tried to find new ways to model, build, and represent world systems. Both existed contemporaneously with political computer simulations and yet consciously undermined the instrumentalism of both rational agents and cybernetic systems.

My hope is that this book recovers the political in the computational imaginary of politics. The book concludes by examining the facets of computational imaginaries at work in contemporary popular and academic discussions of computing and then looks at what we might learn from the forgotten ideas and possibilities of other systems. American political elites have been thinking with computers for a long time; asserting this history patches a flaw in debates that so often feel like they are starting from nothing. Computers have been promising to revolutionize politics since their inception, and without understanding what has and has not changed, we remain in a halting state: never able to see politics as already computational, never able to close this loop and begin another.

2 Models, Prototypes, and Imaginaries

"It matters what ideas we use to think other ideas (with)."[1] This quote, attributed to Marilyn Strathern by Donna Haraway, sums up my interest in computer simulation and politics. From growing up playing political simulation games to studying the craft of building political databases, I have observed how people have thought with and through computer simulations to imagine politics. What I have developed is my own approach to understanding how computer simulations shape, reflexively, a political imaginary through two critical concepts I explore in this chapter: models and prototypes.

What is a computer simulation? A computer simulation combines a working theory or model of a noncomputational system encoded in an interactive computer program. A computer simulation is a model and a prototype, but what that means for politics, for reality, can get philosophical fast.

There is broad, interdisciplinary literature on computer simulation. Opinions range from a romanticism found only in the natural world to a paranoia about what's real from science fiction thrillers. Computer simulation can be doubted as not being "real." At the farthest ends is a growing debate about whether mathematics is socially constructed such that no simulation can ever be real.[2] Or maybe our whole lives are a simulation. The "simulation hypothesis" argues that all of reality is, in fact, a simulation.[3] The hypothesis is a modern equivalent to the riddle of how many angels can dance on the head of a pin, something never answered and endlessly debated. As a start, these slight exaggerations illustrate the big differences in studying computer simulation.

A key theme in the literature questions how computer simulations are a *particular* model of reality.[4] How is a computer simulation different from a mathematical description, or even a myth. One of the ways to approach a computer simulation is to address its core assumptions, its model. Social scientist Scott E. Page begins his acclaimed comparative study of the field by defining models generally as "simplifications of the world."[5] The model is an abstract simplification, as I discuss later in this chapter. Scott E. Page is clear that all models are "wrong because they simplify."[6] His observation is a practical one, leading him to advocate for a multiple-model approach. But the acknowledgment drives a lot of the research on computer simulation, trying to understand the consequences of a particular model in being *wrong*.

"Bias" is the best word to encapsulate differences over how much a computer simulation is wrong and by how much. Instrumental answers, like Page's, look to recognize and compensate for bias in computer simulations like biases in any other simplification. A more ideological critique calls into question the ways that code and models might hide political decisions or reify social power. Mathematician Cathy O'Neill made famous the phrase "weapons of *math* destruction" to call out the discriminatory efforts of bias in justice and education systems where abstraction masks racial and social inequity.[7] However, de-biasing itself might be the problem. Media theorist Wendy Chun argues that being "race-free" does not mean "racism-free." Without specifically attending to the discriminatory problems of modeling, Chun stresses, so-called unbiased models only make matters worse.[8] Chun's concerns about the hidden politics of computer modeling are the most relevant to me and my interest in this specific link between computer simulation and modeling. But how do these political assumptions become hidden in modeling? How can the origins of bias be discovered? I propose a unique approach focusing on models, prototypes, and imaginaries, that builds on past approaches to studying computer simulations.

Studying Computer Simulation

At least four approaches to studying the development of computer simulation are relevant here: cultural studies, media studies, lab studies, and approaches best labeled as histories of the cyborg sciences or media genealogies. Cultural studies and sociology track how popular culture, social structures, and institutional cultures become encoded in computer simulation. The enduring politics of Silicon Valley, for instance, perpetuates what sociologist Ruha Benjamin calls the "new Jim code."[9] Cultural theorist Neda Atanasoski questions cultural and social definitions of what counts as human to understand how racism and sexism can strip bodies of humanity, easing their automation and simulation.[10] I keep these approaches with me to interpretate the Cold War America situation—not to judge but to help make their assumptions strange and tangible.

Anthropologies focus on how big concepts make their way into a few lines of code by studying modelers in the lab.[11] Stefan Helmreich describes Sante Fe Institute researchers studying how to build artificial life. Their perspectives translate "first nature," or given nature, into a socially constructed "second nature," what Helmreich calls "silicon second nature," which are "rule-ordered human constructions . . . meant to mirror first nature."[12] I have less access to simulations-in-the-making, but in my interviews I have tried to understand how researchers found political rules to code into their simulations. These approaches so far help me appreciate the situated knowledges of researchers whose own biases and perspectives informed the construction of computer simulations often presented as objective and scientific as well as the specific context of work and funding.

Media studies emphasizes the epistemic consequences of computer simulation, or how modeling politics with computers changed both computers and politics.[13] Media theorist Peter Krapp defines computer simulation as "a set of practices"—or cultural techniques—"by which modeling, emulation, and serious play are constitutive in how we comprehend and relate to our mediated situation."[14] Katherine Hayles helps me to clarify this exchange; she calls it reflexivity: "the movement whereby that which has been used to generate a system is made, through a changed perspective, to become part of the system it generates."[15] Hayles, first, spurred me toward thinking about the reflexivity found in computational theories of the mind and the liberal nature of disembodied reason. Comparatively, the computer as a system actualized desires to model society, elections, and worlds as systems, producing a reflexivity that stabilized computing and politics as knowable, controllable, and malleable. The implications can be profound. Media theorist Claus Pias recognizes that computer simulation was "an epistemic shift of considerable magnitude."[16] Pias speculates that the shift shapes social theory today, concluding that we "are dealing with a theory design that could only emerge because computer simulations have worked precisely in this way."[17] Extending Pias, past computer simulations of politics might shape the political theory we have today. How might history be more central to the study of computer simulation?

Diverse histories of science have questioned how computer simulation became a legitimate and accepted social epistemology. As I discussed in the last chapter, these genealogies track the politics of expertise that let computing have a growing influence in society.[18] Economist historian Phil Mirowski describes an overall shift toward computational modeling as the dawn of the cyborg sciences.[19] As Mirowski asked how economics became a cyborg science, I ask the same question about political science—though political science became a cyborg science slower and more unevenly than economics. As I develop in the subsequent chapters, these efforts were far from homogeneous in their computational thinking, with game theory, rational choice, cybernetics, and system dynamics all offering competing approaches to the turn toward computer simulation.[20]

All these approaches complicate the relationship between reality and simulation such that neither is entirely second or first nature. The closest I have come to a clear answer is how historian Alain Desrosières describes statistics as being real and made up all at once—that "the paradox is that although these two statements are incompatible, it is nonetheless impossible to give a different answer."[21] The result for living with this paradox is accepting the reflexivity of simulation and reality.

Whereas studying the relationship between computer simulation and reality has been a general question, I am only focused on the political aspects—hence my focus on the computational imaginary of politics. That specificity has been difficult to enforce, as on the international side, I have had to weigh how much scholarship to include on war forecasting or ecological systems—phenomena also deeply political. My logic has been to focus on the express modeling of political matters, not economic or ecological systems. That is, in this book, I focus on computer simulations *of* political systems, not the wider field of simulations *for* political systems. For example, I examine the Globus political simulation instead of its many comparable models, including the more influential *Limits to Growth* models. The *Limits to Growth* simulation was political in that it was designed for policymakers, but it did not *simulate* political systems in its code. By contrast, Globus positioned itself as the *only* global simulation that included a political subsystem.

Politics make the paradox of simulation and reality more complicated because it's already made up even before computers. Politics differs from the behavior of atoms or even the behavior of populations to the statisticians studied by Desrosières. Democracy is an empty space according to theorist Claude Lefort.[22] So where others can debate computer simulations in general, I focus on simulations consequence for political imaginaries.

Political Imaginaries and Politics

"Imaginaries" is a term for institutional and individual practices that imagine and realize ways of life. Canadian theorist Charles Taylor's modern social imaginaries offered "ways in which people imagine their social existence, how they fit together with others, how things go on between them and their fellows, the expectations that are normally met, and the deeper normative notions and images that underlie these expectations."[23] Modern social imaginaries stress the quotidian, the shared beliefs behind social interactions. These everyday specifics of imaginaries are important to me, and yet I see these habits repeat in different moments: how, across time and space, campaigns, and most broadly, political conditions, computers get so entangled with politics. Socio-technical imaginaries, developed by Sang-Hyun Kim and Sheila Jasanoff, offer a way to address these broader, institutional practices. These imaginaries are "collectively held, institutionally stabilized, and publicly performed visions of desirable futures, animated by shared understandings of forms of social life and social order attainable through, and supportive of, advances in science and technology."[24] Their future-oriented, institutionally stabilized version of imaginaries offers a good addition to Taylor, leading me to look at both how individuals thought of politics with computers and the wider institutional contexts that enabled a political imaginary linked with computation.

The computational imaginary has powerful policy and political effects. Most relevant here is Stephanie Ricker Schulte's analysis of the influence of the film *War Games* on policy. In the 1983 film, Matthew Broderick plays a boyish hacker who hacks into the US nuclear arsenal, which is controlled by the supercomputer WOPR. Much more playful than HAL 9000, WOPR is commanded by Broderick to play what the boy thinks is the game *Global Thermonuclear War*, only to set off a real showdown with the USSR. American news coverage toyed with the possibilities of the film, helped popularize the still-experimental Arpanet, and led Congress to draft some of the US's first antihacking laws. As Schulte notes,

> The irony was that although *War Games* advocated an antiregulation, antimilitary, antigovernment hacker ethic mode of laissez faire cyberspace, the film was ultimately used to fear-monger about global destruction and used to lobby for controlling measures over cyberspace. The film made it visually imaginable that a teenage hacker could access military weaponry, even by mistake, and bring the world to the brink of destruction. This example, fictional as it was, proved a powerful tool for the policy makers who were looking to demonstrate that government control over the internet was a matter of national security.[25]

That a teenager perpetrated the hack recast the problem of technological regulation as a parental one. Schulte continues that "policy makers used the film and its discursive engagement to not only push arguments for policies that taught youths 'appropriate' computer use, but also to cast this regulation as democratic and not repressive."[26] The film punctuates so much of the significance of imaginaries, particularly imaginaries about politics. Furthermore, the film captures the whole rather strange setting of this book, where a movie about war games is better known than actual war games.

The computational imaginary of politics matters to the study and history of governmentality. Schulte's is just one example of how politics and computing intertwined publicly. The conceptual shifts that enabled a computational imaginary of politics reimagined theories of governance. To Foucault, governmentality tasked science with addressing the problem of governing populations, a categorization that both worlds and voters fit into.[27] Foucault emphasizes that governmentality is a general trend that includes specific forms that produce distinct types of power. Sovereignty, discipline, control, and biopower might be the best-known forms, but I subscribe to the idea that the entanglement of computing and computational theory was itself a significant advent in governmentality. Their intermingling led to marked changes in the business of government and practical politics as described in the following chapters.[28] Communication policy scholar Sandra Braman offers a detailed account of how changes in government, governance, and governmentality led to an *informational state* premised on "manipulating the informational bases of instrumental, structural and symbolic power."[29] Similarly, I am indebted to media historian Orit Halpern and to Louise Amoore, who astutely questions how logics of artificial intelligence have coproduced different visions of societal order and governance.[30] Following them all, thinking about politics computationally was not just a thought experiment—it changed how politics was imagined, so the shifts that I describe next aid in recognizing the growing influence of platforms and AI in society on our political imagination today.

From the broad problem of governmentality, my project focuses on the local history of computer simulation applied to political problems in the United States. To do so, I need to introduce my two key subjects of the book: models and prototypes. Thinking up computational models of politics and building these models into working prototypes informed and transformed the computational imaginary of politics. It might sound a bit cliché now to describe technology as society made durable, but models and prototypes are moments when politics is made computable and when there is a breakdown between political and computer systems that reflexively changes senses of both. Prototypes contribute to the performance and actualization of these visions of proper politics. Both become central to the study of the computational imaginary of politics.

Models: Big Science, Microworlds

Many of the people found in this book describe their work as model-building, whereas I see my project more as model hunting.[31] But how do I know what I am looking for? Defining a model is slippery because of its breadth. Modeling is used for everything so much so that modeler Erica Thompson wrote a popular book titled *Escape from Model Land*, calling for more literacy in the biases of models.[32] Herein lies the initial debate as to how these simplifications matter, as well as the practices of the simplification of modeling. Many of the developers encountered in this account describe their programs as something of a miniature cosmos, a microglobe, or fictional US states. The model allows these miniatures; it is the opposite of the imperial map imagined by Jorge Luis Borges that becomes so detailed that it replaces the territory it once represented.

One central figure in global political modeling, Harold Guetzkow, described the outcome of modeling as "an operating representation in reduced and/or simplified form of relations among social units by means of symbolic and/or replicate component parts."[33] Models, to Guetzkow, were abstractions. They are never natural, and the ways voting is modeled are as political as who's on the ballot. Throughout the book, I trace debates about what to abstract, what to include, what to leave out, and why politics should be understood computationally.

I am looking for what models do, how they actualize political imaginations. While writing, I have kept Haraway's definition of a model with me: "A model is a work object; a model is not the same *kind* of thing as a metaphor or analogy. A model is worked, and it does work. A model is like a miniature cosmos, in which a biologically curious Alice in Wonderland can have tea with the Red Queen and ask how this world works, even as she is worked by the complex-enough, simple-enough world. Models in biological research are stabilized systems that can be shared among colleagues to investigate questions experimentally and theoretically."[34] They are not simply definitions. Winning a political campaign or predicting the next coup are very specific motivations to use computer modeling. Modeling, in short, could become a political act. Here, I am reminded of a quote attributed to Buckminster Fuller: "You never change things by fighting the existing reality. To change something, build a new model that makes the existing model obsolete."[35]

Models can guide action in many ways. Page discussed above suggests that models can be used to reason, explain, design, communicate, act, predict, and explore.[36] The predictive promise of a model primes the reception of computer simulation. Early computer simulations helped predict atoms to build the devastating hydrogen bomb, or H-bomb (otherwise known as the superbomb to its opponents who built the earlier atomic bomb).[37] Much of the excitement about computer simulation came from its predictive capacity. Historian Jenny Andersson evocatively relates the emergence of postwar futurology, or future studies, which inspired significant investment in the computer simulations.[38] But models also change how we think.[39]

My interest in models focuses on the historical moments of analogy between computer systems and political systems. Phil Mirowski compellingly describes how postwar economists modeled their field after John von Neumann's automata theory (as opposed to Herbert Simon's computational thinking, which stands out to me as a path not taken). In doing so, economics mimicked computer science.[40] Prominent political scientist and figure in this book Karl Deutsch turned to the physical diagrams of circuits to describe his concepts of how a government works. These moments are deeply political even if framed as technical debates.

The literature on modeling often conflates its conceptual and practical functions—a problem for computer simulation that is at once conceptual and theoretical because you could describe politics as computational as well as work out how these models worked through computation. The difference is subtle but helps frame some of the debates in the field. Computer simulation is one of three forms of modeling according to philosopher of science Michael Weisberg. The other two are concrete models that can physically stand in for real-world systems and mathematical models that translate physical systems into abstract, mathematical formulas.[41] Weisberg acknowledges significant debate about whether mathematical and computational models should be separate, but for me the difference is between the model and how that model works in the world—how to distinguish between gravitational as a theoretical model and building an orrery to mimic how planets circle the sun. Computer simulation is both conceptual, a way of describing politics as working like a computer system, and functional, another turn that turns that model into computer code. I use the concept of the prototype to study this second step.[42]

Prototypes: Models Realized

Prototypes put models in motion. Whereas a model is a nebulous, conceptual thing—a way of sensing and thinking—a prototype is tangible. The prototype, in short, materializes a model. It is the other side of the relationship between model and materiality. Lucy Suchman, Randall Trigg, and Jeanette Blomberg define the prototype in design as "an artefact with particular performative characteristics."[43] Following Karen Barad, they maintain that the prototype performs as "a tangible, but also provisional, apparatus—an object that reconfigured material and discursive practice in an accountably relevant way."[44] The prototype, then, is not an output or a materialization of a model but a way of working with a model that entangles humans and machines and that, in the case here, informs both the model and the prototype. The prototype works "as a reflexive probe into the practical materializations that configure new technological objects."[45] Most of the prototypes in this book attempted to simulate voter behavior or international relations—attempts that importantly built on existing political models. The prototype *performed* the model computationally, foregrounding researchers' and consultants' expectations for computers as well as the practical limits of early computers. Many of the projects here were the first use cases of computing in politics, advancing how, in keeping with the provisional quality of a prototype, certain models and approaches to computing proved useful to politics.

The prototype is a necessary concept for my history, as often I find prototypes first and then explore their underlying models. My early efforts to write this book started by looking at early computer games—*Balance of Power, Shadow President,* and *President Elect*—to see if these popular computer simulation games contained a model of politics. (They did not, which partially explains how this book came to be).[46]

The computer is by no means the only way to prototype models. Thinkers like Buckminster Fuller or William Gamson and movements like New Games or the World Order Models Project tried more analog formats to prototype their more idealistic visions of politics. The choice to prototype with computers mattered. Tracing the development of epistemic virtues around scientific observation, Lorraine Daston and Peter Galison emphasize the prevalence of observation and visual cultures, creating an enduring link between modes of seeing, optical media, and accountability at the expense perhaps of auditory or performative theories of knowledge.[47]

Computer simulation is a specific kind of prototyping.[48] A computer simulation is a prototype of a computational model of politics to run as a computer program. Computers are as important to prototyping as they are to modeling. The computer is a specific medium for prototyping. Like an orrery, a computer simulation puts a model into motion; yet it is not a physical equivalent. The computer prototype works out the model in a distinct computational space. Computer programs can be changed; variables can be updated. "The digital computer," says Heyck, was "the modeler's muse."[49] Computers eased and encouraged prototyping political theories. To give an example from what's ahead, I discuss William McPhee and the Simulmatics team, best known for advising the 1960 Kennedy campaign. Building on his past survey research, William McPhee developed a model of voter behavior that he set in motion in a campaign cimulator, the first computer program I have found that predicted voter behavior outside election night forecasting. Simulmatics built on McPhee's prototype to advise the Kennedy campaign and to later market as their "people-machine." This people-machine relied on McPhee's voter model and put it in action to set expectations about how people should behave, a foresight the firm tried to sell, as well as claiming it to be a kind of future research. For the most part, Simulmatics failed, so even though the firm expressly tried to be prototypical, it mostly fell short but nonetheless maintained great hopes for computing.

Prototyping helps make the model's predictive function more tangible. My introduction to the term "prototype" came from Daniel Kreiss and Fred Turner. Kreiss most directly addresses the link between prototypes and politics in his seminal research into the development of technology-intensive campaigning beginning in the early 2000s. The prototype, Kreiss writes, is "a model for future campaigns, and a set of claims about the world that are actionable for practitioners."[50] In other words, building a complex campaign assemblage—data, experts, code, and servers—involves understanding both present possibilities and future opportunities. Kreiss emphasizes that prototype status is awarded to campaigns retroactively, imbuing them with legitimacy as an exemplar for campaigns. Obama's first presidential campaign, to Kreiss, was a classic prototype: Everyone wanted to mimic its success. Fred Turner describes prototypes as looking forward and backward at once. Prototypes in Silicon Valley "belong to a way of looking at the world in which individuals constantly remake themselves, in which they test themselves against the world, and, if they find themselves wanting, improve themselves."[51] Turner's emphasis on remaking helps me think about a specific claim found throughout this book: that models made into prototypes could be predictive. I like this flexibility in the term "prototype" being at once a way to put knowledge in motion, to make a play for legitimacy, and more immediately, to be a way to "test the world" that, especially in the case of rational choice theory, found the world wanting.

The prototype's performative qualities influence models in unpredictable ways and change the model's own internal meaning. Games help me elaborate this last point. Games, especially computer games, are a common prototype found in local elections and world politics. Games enroll humans to play with models' scripts and codes. James Coleman, a quantitative sociologist, made games to explicate his theory of voters as rational agents. Coleman enjoyed watching the games play out, seeing his miniature worlds in motion. Coleman was not the only one to prototype models with games. Other game-makers, like the developers of Buckminster Fuller's *World Game* and the New Games Movement, eschewed completion, looking "to imagine and perhaps to create a new social order" through cooperation and emergent play.[52] There is then a significance to how a prototype sets a model in motion, or as Turner asks at the end of his discussion of New Games, "What kinds of politics are we playing at?"[53] What kinds of politics are presented by prototypes? Without prototypes, models might be too static, leaving the computational imaginary as the sum of a few computational approaches to politics. Instead, prototyping helps me emphasize how trial and error, experiments with computers, contributed to a computational imaginary of politics.

The Iceberg of the Computational Imaginary of Politics

These three concepts—models, prototypes, and imaginaries—inform the work of this book, serving to distinguish different instances and their changing influence. Models are a way to think with computers. Prototypes put models into action as experimental computer programs. Computational imaginaries are coproduced by models and prototypes.[54] Together, these efforts contributed to a larger sociotechnical imaginary of politics as computational, and they help answer my book's three objectives as seen in figure 2.1. Let me conclude with an example.

Stuart Bremer was one of the leading world modelers in political science, influential for leading the GLOBUS Project that I discuss later in the book. Part of a rush by governments and scientists to invest in computer modeling, GLOBUS was part of political science's response to this modeling boom of the 1970s. Lasting a decade, GLOBUS was a massive undertaking involving then high-performance computing, top figures in the field, and a massive synthesis of international relations research. At such a time, Bremer might have expected that explaining the computer simulation would be easy. Instead, he found himself in a spot much like me. GLOBUS was hard to explain—how could Bremer distinguish the computer code from the theory from the overall idea of the project? I'll use Bremer's own explanation of GLOBUS to illustrate my book's theoretical approach: how the study of models and prototypes informs the components of a computational imaginary of politics.

In Bremer's introduction to a book explaining the team's choice when designing GLOBUS to be "multinational and multidisciplinary," he offered an analogy to an iceberg. "The tip, which is the smallest and most visible part, is the computer [program]; near the waterline is a large base area upon

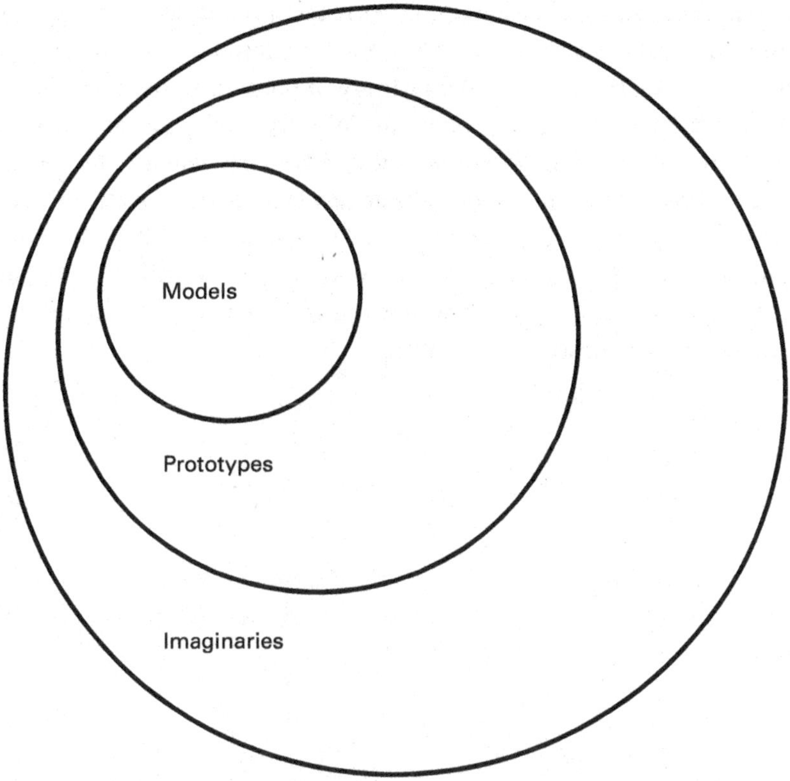

Figure 2.1
Nested concepts of models, prototypes, and imaginaries.

which the computer [program] is based. Below this and invisible to all but a few is the large mass which supports all of the above: this corresponds to the GLOBUS project."[55] Bremer's analogy includes the computer program, the theory behind it, and a larger vision of the computability of politics that helped attract funding for the project.

Putting it in my terms, Bremer first discusses his *prototype*, the GLOBUS program. He defines the prototype as the tangible part built from a more conceptual *model*, the waterline. GLOBUS instantiated a working theory about how best to study, to think about, and to interact with the international order. The base of the iceberg becomes the multitude of influences and theories that support the model and the prototype. That base is the larger imaginary surrounding the idea, that the world could be simulated on an IBM XT computer from 1983.

From questioning what we think with to thinking with icebergs, this chapter has elaborated the relations between computational models, prototypes, and the computational imaginary of politics. To be clear, I am not assuming a direct causality; models and prototypes do not determine the computational imaginary of politics today. My point here is not to offer an origin for these ideas but to look genealogically for early models and prototypes that have shaped the computational imaginary of politics. The consequences of this making changed how governments, scientists, politicians, and policymakers imagined governing and governance with computers, as I elaborate in the subsequent chapters.

I SimVoters

3 Political Forecasting and the Scientific Study of Elections

Whereas Romans once read a bull's heart to predict Caesar's fate,[1] Americans turned to computer printouts to predict elections and process the public mood. Election night has become a blockbuster event showcasing the latest technology[2] and promising deeper insights into real-time turns and predictions about the final count. Election night coverage would be hard to imagine now without computer simulations, interactive dashboards, or even holographic hosts. High-tech election night coverage typifies the computational imaginary of politics, but also its beginnings.

Journalists helped reimagine computers' applications from forecasting an atomic blast to an election night blowout.[3] Computers at the end of World War II had few practical civilian applications. For the most part, election campaigns in the early postwar period had no use for computers. Television was the major technological focus. Most guidebooks for winning campaigns before the mid-1960s gave scant attention to any scientific approaches, usually offering only a chapter or two on polling.[4] Election night introduced computers into politics by promising faster data processing. As Jennifer Light notes in her history of computing in politics, "first developed as calculating machines and quickly applied to forecasting an atomic blast, computers soon took on a new identity as modeling machines, helping communities of professionals to analyze complex structures and scenarios to anticipate future events."[5] Mechanical brains became a novelty for political polling and elections. The first digital computer, UNIVAC, predicted the 1952 election, even if CBS decided not to air the UNIVAC's prediction at first. By the next presidential election, all major broadcasters used computers for their election night coverage.[6]

Computer forecasting soon raised worries that maybe voters could become a little too predictable. Frederik Pohl published a satirical short story, "Tunnel Under the World," in 1955 that imagined an American town destroyed in an industrial accident reanimated as machines for a marketing research experiment. Mechanical brains menacing politics became something of a genre afterward—an indication of how fruitful computers could be and their possibilities for page-turning technothrillers.[7] The beginnings of the computational imaginary of politics and voters was not all election night hubris and science fiction. Rather, these examples capture something of a mood that enticed politicians, campaigns, scientists, and even voters to start experimenting with computers in politics.

In what follows, I elaborate the beginnings of a computational imaginary of *domestic* politics. My situation first explores how election night coverage, statistics, and failures in the polling industry set a mood looking for methodological innovations. The mood set up computer simulation as a possible solution. I introduce the theoretical underpinning of early computer simulation, the postwar network of behavioralism, and the desire to predict elections in the first place. From these beginnings in the 1950s, the following chapters explore the splits in the approaches to modeling voters with computers and then follow these models from the lab to the campaign trail.

Bull's Hearts and Mechanical Brains

Journalists helped imagine a political role for computing. Their speculative use of a mechanical brain on election night played along with public interest in computers as a novel solution to all sorts of problems. For decades, newspapers had invested in calculation and manual prediction to call elections, which ultimately led to investing in early computing.[8] These investments were both practical and theatrical. The *New York Herald*, in one of many examples of election night calculation described by historian Ira Chinoy, employed a team of "expert accountants" for its 1890 election night coverage. Chinoy writes,

> Ten were employed, along with 60 "tally clerks," arranged at long tables in a cavernous, block-long room at the Herald building. A detailed drawing of them—formally attired, their heads down in concentration as they worked with pencil and paper—was featured prominently in the *Herald*'s extensive report on its election-night exploits. The accountants are the specialists here. They are described as "lightning calculators." The presence of the experts served multiple purposes, just as computing equipment would later—doing the job at hand while

adding both to the mystique of the election-night process and the prestige of the journalists who organized it.[9]

Newsrooms developed an expertise in rapid calculation for their election night forecasting. Among the most well-known, the *Boston Globe* developed a system now known as key-precinct analysis around the late nineteenth century. The method forecast the election by watching the results in a few key precincts and comparing them to past election trends. Key-precinct analysis was a staple of twentieth-century election forecasting.[10]

Election-night forecasting developed concurrently with public opinion research, polling, and survey research. Pollsters met journalism's demand for election forecasts. Initially pollsters offered a better representation of the American public by developing better social science instruments to measure public opinion. Polling mixed with the emerging social sciences though pollsters, including George Gallup and Elmo Roper, to upset the field. The 1936 presidential election was one year of upset in the industry. In a bit of showmanship, Roper and Gallup challenged the de facto straw polls at the time. The straw polls lost; Roper's and Gallup's superior sampling and methodology won out, correctly showing greater support for the winner, Democrat Franklin D. Roosevelt. Pollsters emphasized the predictive power of their polls, using largely white male voices as oracles for the United States. The industry enjoyed much success predicting elections until 1948, when social scientists failed to predict Democrat Harry S. Truman's win over Republican Thomas E. Dewey.[11]

Truman's victory and polling's defeat led to another crisis in the industry.[12] A key concern was the predictive power of polls, as "the industry failed to pick the winner."[13] As one political scientists recalled, "Pollsters became the butt of an avalanche of criticism, ridicule, and hostility . . . laughs were mingled with sneers at 'so-called social scientists with their IBM equipment and their naive efforts to ape the natural scientists.'"[14] The IBM machines were still tabulation machines, not digital computers, but they were already a subject of ridicule. The Social Science Research Council (SSRC), an advocate for scientific public opinion research, convened an emergency committee to investigate what happened. Eight days after the election, the SSRC struck a committee that released a preliminary report on December 27, 1948. A late swing to Truman hadn't helped pollsters, and the SSRC questioned how well polls could predict elections. The report called for better methods and advancing research on "political behavior"—what would become the behavioral mood discussed above—outlining a trajectory toward a new generation of digital computing for more scientific forecasting.

The 1948 fiasco bolstered systemic approaches to predicting elections over measures of public opinion. Most famous were the predictions of Louis Bean. An immigrant from Russian Lithuania, Bean had been part of the New Deal US government, first at the Department of Agriculture and then at the Board of Economic Warfare, the Bureau of the Budget, and back to Agriculture. Bean relied on economic modeling and by 1940 had begun to popularize his methods in pamphlets. Encouraged by Paul Lazarsfeld, Bean published in 1948, before the election, his book *How to Predict an Election*, which offered a "new method of political-science investigation" that avoided "personalities and organized political effort as factors in elections," instead dealing with "facts and figures."[15] Bean applied his economic training by using statistics to calculate trends in state and national voting. Bean used these methods to read what he called "the political tides." These tides, Bean wrote, "are like the unsubstantiated sea serpent that appears periodically along the Atlantic coast. They are discussed every year by popular political analysts and commentators, but without much factual demonstration."[16]

These tides were long-term trends. The New Deal was one such tide. At the end of the book, Bean forecast a Democratic victory that year. As much as Bean tried to reduce politics to long-term statistical trends, he also left much to judgement. He began his book with an epigraph from Shakespeare's *Hamlet*: "Though this be madness, yet there is method in't." That madness could be reduced to a formula that, Bean claimed, could predict a US state's election results. Bean cautioned that "In spite of the fact that several statistical analyses which proved useful in appraising and anticipating the results of presidential and congressional elections are presented here, the reader is warned against expecting this book to give him a precise and fixed method of predicting elections. The main objective has been to present basic facts so organized that they may serve as a foundation or springboard for the application of one's judgment."[17] Bean went on to argue that forecasting was an art that required judgement to determine what matters and what does not in any election. Automation was not on Bean's horizon, even as the possibility of automation and thinking machines occupied scholars at the Macy Conferences on Cybernetics and Norbert Wiener published his book on cybernetics that same year. Though Bean privately treated his predictions cautiously, his publisher advertised, "Oh Mr. Gallup!

Oh Mr. Roper! Obviously, you don't know Bean's HOW TO PREDICT Elections."[18] The ploy worked, and Bean became famous for predicting the election that everyone else had missed, at least for a couple elections.

Neither Bean nor Wiener decided to use computers to predict politics; that decision happened in the newsroom. Looking for a new spectacle to enliven live television coverage of election night, CBS contracted Remington Rand and its UNIVAC computer to forecast the 1952 election results. UNIVAC was the first popular digital computer, brought into service for the US census a year prior. Predicting elections, which Remington Rand thought would be simple, proved to be difficult, but the company did build a computer program to forecast election results using historical data and incoming poll results. The program worked, predicting early in the night an unexpected blowout victory for Republican candidate Dwight Eisenhower over Democrat Adlai Stevenson. Polling had predicted a close race, and so, as the story goes, Remington Rand refused to pass on the prediction and set about to rework the program to make a safe prediction later in the night. To viewers, the UNIVAC appeared as a novelty (and a prop, as the real UNIVAC was too big to move to the studio). If the election night failed to broadcast the power of computing, UNIVAC's legacy was kept alive by "a combination of after-the-fact efforts to keep the story alive and the inherent appeal of a certain version of election night events that supported a strong wow factor—machine outsmarts human."[19] By the next election, all the television networks relied on digital computers for election forecasting, just as social scientists began to play with the same machines for their own predictions. Computers' spectacular role in election night coverage built excitement for the use of computer simulation in politics.

From One Card to Another

The first computer simulation of the American electorate ran in 1957. William "Wild Bill" McPhee had started to develop the first computer simulation of US elections.[20] McPhee's program seemed a logical next step after UNIVAC. McPhee described the simulation as a "miniature electorate" put "in motion."[21] The simulation ran on punch cards and an IBM 650 machine, the first mass-produced computer. It wasn't much by today's standards, but McPhee's *Campaign Simulator* promised to give researchers—and political campaigns—a new way to model the American voter. His claims are at once uncontroversial and radical—uncontroversial because computers already interpreted survey results and forecasted trends by this time; radical because McPhee's modeled voters were conflicted, multidimensional variables built on newly digitized survey records. Perhaps most surprising is that McPhee's work had already been applied practically by the time he published details about the simulator in 1961.

McPhee's program used computers to simulate interactions between voters, unlike arithmetic models of elections where the computer functioned like a "fast calculator."[22] The program first encoded voters as two strings of ten digits that stored voters' party preferences, ages, social relations, and past actions as well as reprogrammable variables that could simulate racial and interest groups that a simulated campaign might appeal to. The computer simulation started when "the model takes from the input hopper an injection of 'political stimuli' for the period since the last election."[23] Next, as figure 3.1 shows in the flowchart, modeled voters "discussed" their attitudes. Modeled voters agreed or disagreed, and through repeated interactions or the "learning process," gradually changed states until election day when the virtual voters were counted.[24] McPhee's prototype promised to be a "working instrument" where researchers could input issues into the hopper then watch the reactions.[25]

McPhee's research emerged out of one of the founding institutes of American political communication, Columbia University's Bureau for Applied Research. Though less well-known today, William McPhee was a wonder to his colleagues. McPhee so impressed Paul Lazarsfeld that he recruited McPhee—a World War II veteran and public opinion researcher—in 1951 for a doctorate at Columbia University even though McPhee had no undergraduate degree. There, he worked closely on the bureau's seminal election studies, becoming third author of the 1954 book *Voting*, which developed a theory of interpersonal effects McPhee employed in the simulation.[26] Already toying with early computers in processing the book's data, McPhee began further experimentation with computing in 1957. If voters could be represented as data and formulas, could data and formulas be set in motion in a simulation? His program began as an experiment to see if patterns could be found amid this mass of modeled voters. These experiments led to the first simulations of the American electorate: public opinion on demand.[27]

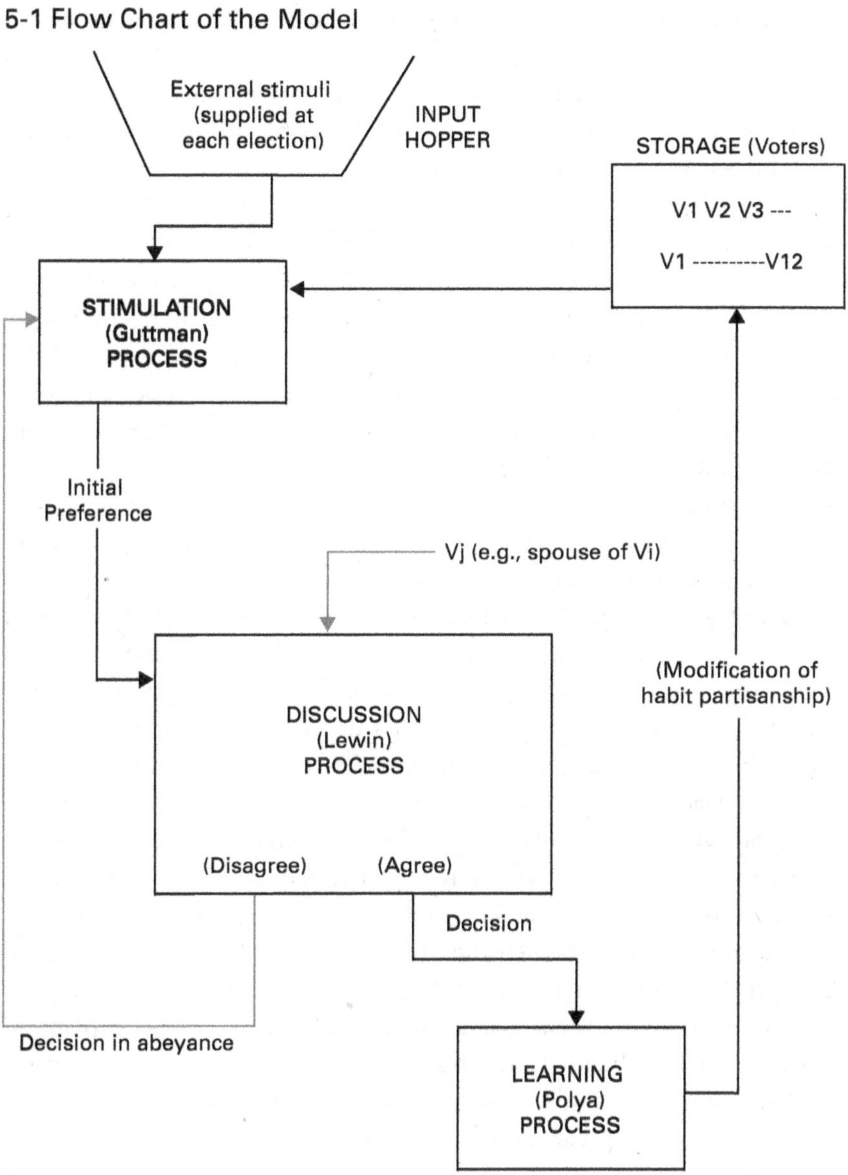

Figure 3.1
Flow chart for McPhee and Smith's program. *Source*: Redrawn from McPhee and Smith, "A Model for Analyzing Voting Systems," 129.

McPhee first began working on his automated American voter with his Columbia colleague and friend, and an important figure in this book, James Coleman. They proposed to study "a class of topics usually called 'mass phenomena' in social psychology, 'collective behavior' in sociology, and often problems of 'the mass society' in humanistic writings" with computers.[28] Comparing the study of natural society to the physical sciences, McPhee and Coleman devised the term "mass dynamics" to "refer to similar problems arising when free-acting individual units form mass social patterns."[29] Theorizing mass behavior was nothing new, nor were attempts at analyzing the behaviors of crowds, publics, or masses. McPhee and Coleman claimed another route to innovation. Systems, in short, produced regularized behaviors traditionally considered impossible to calculate, but new machines were making the prospect increasingly possible. The computer was a means to identify these mass dynamics. McPhee and Coleman demonstrated their approach by outlining a means to model political party identification, demonstrating how mass dynamics might show how voting preferences change. They ended on an optimistic note, suggesting that "there is a glimpse of hope . . . for eventually developing analytical and calculating schemes which will permit a more precise examination of the formidable chains of reasoning involved in such 'dynamic' problems of masses."[30] McPhee continued to explore how computers could study mass dynamics, leading to his first voter simulation.

McPhee's research agenda worked its way through the major US funders of social science research, who were also invested in advancing the methodological rigor.[31] With Coleman, McPhee translated mass dynamics into a grant submission to the Behavioral Sciences Division of the Ford Foundation in 1957. McPhee further learned about the potential for computer simulation through a Social Science Research Council–RAND Corporation Workshop in 1958.[32] Finally, the Watson Scientific Computing Laboratory, a joint venture between Columbia University and IBM, helped McPhee with programming and access to the machine to run the experiments.

The research was intended to study *mass* effects. McPhee's Campaign Simulator was the prototype for him to work out his model of mass dynamics in politics. McPhee, writing later with his collaborator and programmer Robert Smith, described moving from microscopic studies of individual behavior to "some 'macroscopic' picture of how, when it is all put together, the aggregate system works."[33] McPhee and his supporting team produced a working prototype of the Wisconsin presidential primary by 1958;[34] it was one of the first uses of dynamic simulations in politics.[35] McPhee promised that the program was a "completely observable system" that he and his contemporaries believed could help campaigns better forecast voter behavior.[36] James Coleman would later write of innovations like McPhee's Campaign Simulator, "We have no longer forced upon us the sharp separation between different parts of a social system—the separation between different individuals who were interviewed separately and who once were kept separate by the gulf that separates one IBM card from another."[37]

McPhee's macroscopic approach was a computational model of voters, a deeply personal one. Writing to James Coleman, likely around 1958, McPhee stressed the nonmathematical nature of his models: "I make a lot of other assumptions in the voting model too, each of which I think is a lodestar. . . . This is not because I am bright, but because of this: If you know some field of behavior well, and set out to describe it in a model, you tend to hit on assumptions which have much wider empirical usefulness."[38] The math was not as important as that it worked.

How McPhee's Campaign Simulator came to be used in politics, and even was believable *to be used in politics*, is the work of another important person in this book: Ithiel de Sola Pool, a political scientist and defense intellectual. McPhee became enrolled along with Pool in a plan by Democratic supporter and later business partner Edward Greenfield in putting the "macroscope" to practical use.[39] The brief commercialization of McPhee's macroscope put him into contact with a dense, closed world of researchers searching for ways to better understand US and international politics with more advanced science and scientific instruments like early computers. The effort marked an important turn in politics: the beginning of a decades-long effort to bring the same scientism that was in behavioralism and elsewhere in the social sciences to political campaigns and elections. No one better reveals this highly networked world than Ithiel de Sola Pool.

The Highly Connected Ithiel de Sola Pool

When Clotworthy wrote that in "behavioral science 'laboratories' . . . the faintest of beginnings have been made in the application of physical science techniques to the study of societies," he could have been writing about Ithiel de Sola Pool. This book could have been a biography of Pool, and McPhee's interactions with him are just one of many encounters I discovered in researching this world. He sometimes seemed like the red string tying the conspiracy together. Pool's life and work blur the lines between international and domestic politics, between technology and power, and between strategic and humane uses of computing. He will appear throughout the following pages, and his professional journey offers a good introduction to the book's situation discussed in the introduction, which found McPhee's simulation legible, novel, and fundable.

What I want to do here is use Pool to draw together the early applications of computing in politics, which McPhee found himself immersed in for a time. So, my account of Pool is primarily institutional, but a few biographic details establish his path into the heart of American Cold War research.[40] Pool trained at the University of Chicago—a hub of scientism in the American social sciences.[41] The preeminent political scientist Harold Lasswell supervised him. He became deeply enmeshed in Cold War American research in 1953 when he established himself as a professor of political science at the Massachusetts Institute of Technology (MIT), where he taught until his death in 1984. Beginning in 1959, Pool started a consultancy firm, the Simulmatics Corporation, which should be well known in the field thanks to historian Jill Lepore's acclaimed chronicle of its rise and fall.[42] During his career, he met most of the characters in this book. Of course, these connections were less about intrigue and more the product of a white male–dominated world that fostered an aspiration for computers to solve the political turmoil of the twentieth century.

Pool's legacy remains deeply contested.[43] I mostly focus on his career until 1970 when a break occurred. Labeled a war criminal by campus activists and associated with the moral quagmire of the Vietnam War, Pool pivoted from applied research to communication policy. His career then presents two sides, which is another way his life mirrors the larger concerns of this book. Lepore eloquently notes the Janus-like nature of Pool's life in her history of Simulmatics. At once, Pool is seen as the ultimate cold warrior, maybe a grifter for lucrative defense contracts. Daniel Ellsberg, famed leaker of the Pentagon Papers, described Pool "as the most corrupt social scientist I had ever met, without question."[44] Lee McGuigan, writing about Pool's forays into advertising at the Simulmatics Corporation, found reporting "glamorized Pool's status as a jet-setting consultant—one day doing high-tech demonstrations for major advertisers and their agencies, another day advising the US Navy on classified matters of ordnance."[45] Yet, Pool is just as well remembered as an inspiration to the MIT Media Lab, and his vision of technologies of freedom is closely associated with early hype about the internet. The two Pools are assuredly not separate at all, a friction that drives me in writing this history.

Pool's career advanced alongside other defense intellectuals who offered expertise as another front in the Cold War. By the 1960s, scientists had been humbled and positioned as instruments of the military industrial complete.[46] The Red Scare had humbled the independence of scientists like Robert Oppenheimer. Instead, defense intellectuals vied to be part of what historian Chandra Mukerji describes as "an elite reserve labor force," a postwar situation where government patronage cultivated experts that might be useful for the American government.[47]

Computers gave social scientists a new tool to vie for patronage.[48] Nobel Prize–winning American experimental physicist Luis Alvarez suggested to the Pentagon in 1961 that "World War III . . . might well have to be considered the social scientists' war."[49] Figures like Pool's supervisor Harold Lasswell cultivated a *political science* like hard sciences as part of the Cold War. Lasswell even compared his aspirations for political science to the atomic sciences in his 1956 remarks as president of the American Political Science Association.[50] Thanks to Lasswell, Pool had already been part of the US war effort—one of many seminal figures in communication studies to assist in the development of propaganda and psychological warfare during World War II.[51] These connections brought Pool in contact with leaders in the American social sciences and the study of politics, including Paul Lazarsfeld and Hans Speier. Speier was a highly influential defense intellectual who ran the Social Science Division at the leading Cold War think tank, the RAND Corporation. He too cultivated Pool to become director of the International Communications Program at MIT's Center for International Studies. Like Pool, these researchers worked closely with branches of the US military, the State Department, a network of Cold War research academics, and elite social scientists.[52]

Pool was part of what prominent political scientist Robert Dahl called a "behavioral mood."[53] Critics referred to the mood as the new political science.[54] Emerging out of psychological studies of the war, behavioralism sought to study populations through data and data analysis.[55] Dahl described behavioralism as a mood.[56] He argued, "One can say with considerable confidence what it is not, but it is difficult to say what it is."[57] It was easier perhaps to attribute behavioralism to a faith in scientism—a preference for scientific knowledge above all others—that ran through the twentieth-century American social sciences. Historian Dorothy Ross attributes the prominence of scientism to the leadership of Charles Merriam. According to Ross, Merriam's program of research "proposed a science defined by 'method,' orientated to 'control' and sustained by organized professional structures to promote research."[58] Merriam's program made its way into the new political science through his disciple Harold Lasswell, who became "the heir of Merriam's technological imagination."[59] The new political science manifested Lasswell's vision for the field and created the possibilities for computing as a political epistemology.[60]

Behavioralism, controversial in the field itself, had allies in major funders, especially the Ford Foundation and the Social Science Research Council. These were a few of the funders supporting Pool's academic research and, quite relatedly, his corporate consultancy at the Simulmatics Corporation, which started as a collaboration with McPhee. Until the Mansfield Amendments of 1969 and 1973, which limited defense spending in the United States, much funding for behavioral research came from military and defense agencies, most notably the Advanced Project Research Agency (now DARPA).[61] That funding was controversial, provoking debates in the field over behavioralism and the field's involvement in the Vietnam War.[62] Those concerns caught up to Pool, but for the better part of twenty years, his research matched a demand for scientific expertise in politics, both internal and abroad. These efforts became targets of criticism, especially for the field's relationship to the Vietnam War—another wrong of the new political science.[63]

Domestic and international politics shared this mood.[64] Factions in both fields aimed to turn their findings into something more practicable, legible to policymakers through behavioral methods.[65] Behavioralists criticized the status quo as atheoretical or at least in need of more rigorous methods to calculate the balance of power. Implicitly or explicitly, these behavioral scholars continued Harold Lasswell's and, earlier still, Charles Merriam's projects in the social sciences that were the beginnings of what now might be called the policy sciences.[66] David Easton, for instance, wrote a long 1950 review of Lasswell's project that claimed the goal was "to convert political science to a policy science, a discipline contributing to the solution of social problems" in service of a renewed postwar commitment to democracy.[67] Worried about the future of democracy after the war, threatened by the possibility of nuclear war, and driven to find peace in the world system, simulators, even Ithiel de Sola Pool, hoped to advance a "humane" politics against the hawks and purported realists focused on war and its perpetual planning.[68]

The new political science was above all a turn toward new methods, which for Pool meant an embrace of computing. Dahl left the definition to another political scientist, David Truman, who defined political behavioralism as "a point of view which aims at stating all phenomena of government in terms of the observed and observable behavior of men."[69] The definition foreshadows today's interest in big data and machine learning—along with McPhee and Coleman's interest in mass dynamics. Pool's research involved both an investment in better means of quantification and data analysis. After the war, Pool pushed for more scientific methods to study politics and propaganda. From 1948 to 1953, he worked on a team that manually coded sixty-five years of editorials, some 20,000 articles, for keywords.[70] Understandably, Pool became a public advocate for computers to handle and interpret these data.[71] To foreshadow some of the methodological innovations connected to Pool, he built an early political survey database, simulated voters (with McPhee) and then later assisted with the design of computerized world leaders, and funded a major early project in computational social science. Like most of his colleagues, his methodological applications were highly political—more so than the theory behind them—working amid the Civil Rights Movement and the Vietnam War.

International relations was a key site for the new political science, another opportunity for Lasswell's policy sciences.[72] To behavioralists, the backward field relied too much on humanistic and historical accounts. Even classics such as Hans Morgenthau's 1948 *Politics Among Nations* relied on diplomatic history. Another simulator discussed later Oliver Benson's first book, in 1939, was a diplomatic history that appraised the origins of World War I. David Easton's 1953 book *The Political System* and Karl Deutsch's 1963 *The Nerves of Government* broke with the diplomatic, realist approaches in political science.[73] Easton and Deustch overtly challenged traditional approaches. Morgenthau acknowledged that systems thinking threatened to undermine his realist work even as he granted Easton tenure.[74]

The new emphasis on world politics as a complex system in need of modeling recalculated one of the field's main concepts: the balance of power. An age-old term in international politics, "balance of power" emphasized how balanced relations and the prevention of superpowers led to global stability. This is an artifact from an earlier edition I didn't catch. The leading treatment at the time was Morgenthau's 1948 *Politics Among Nations*, which remains the foundation of the realpolitik school. Morgenthau defined the balance of power as follows: "The aspiration for power on the part of several nations, each trying either to maintain or to overthrow the status quo, leads of necessity to a constellation which is called the balance of power and to policies which aim at preserving it."[75] Pool then was part of a new political science working with SimVoters here and SimWorlds in the book's next part.

I want to pause before returning to McPhee to draw one last connection between Pool and a moment in Cold War research around gaming. Gaming, as historian Jennifer Light reminds us, must be taken seriously.[76] Gaming was an active part of the war effort. Nuclear war was the first war that could not be practiced or learned in the field. War was one of many reasons for the embrace of gaming in politics. It had both a history in World War II in attempts to model enemies as well as a much longer pedigree from wargaming.[77] Game theory was also associated with the radical innovations in math and economics then put into practice in public policy.[78] These innovations also spread globally through institutions such as the International Institute of Applied Systems Analysis.[79] Games, as seen in the seminal work of Sharon Ghamari-Tabrizi, quietly became vital to government intelligence while remaining a guarded secret, lest the public believe that bureaucrats and generals spent their days in idle play.[80]

Gaming was a remarkable place of experimentation across both quantitative and qualitative research, between economics and political science. Games were played in war rooms and classrooms. Playing games and thinking about games as explanations of society helped close a gap between how a computer program and a human mind worked (as I discuss later in chapter 5). Pool himself actively participated in the experimental Cold War games developed at the RAND Corporation and then continued at MIT through the work of Lincoln Bloomfield and the Political-Military Exercise. Pool was friends with another important figure in this book's second part, Harold Guetzkow, who turned to computer simulation after playing with human simulations of world affairs. Pool also befriended and served on the doctoral committee of Clark Abt, who popularized the term "serious games" while consulting on games for the defense industry. Finally, Pool worked with McPhee's friend and influential sociologist James S. Coleman at Simulmatics, where they promised to sell games building on Coleman's own embrace of gaming as a new method.[81] Coleman even created a game to teach congressional politics. The procedural, rule-based design of games was an early kind of programming that eased, as I argue, a move to thinking about reality like a computer. The conceptual shift is not so large if the world has already been presented as a rule-based system that could be observed and tinkered with. Gaming, then, demonstrates how the new political science's interest in methods extended beyond statistics and computational social science into simulation, artificial intelligence, and human-machine interaction that extended well beyond game theory itself.[82]

If I have strayed too much into the international, let me be clear that these innovations applied as much to domestic as international politics. Pool exemplifies how the new political science desired to put these advances into practice at home and abroad. In brief, New York businessman Edward Greenfield assembled a team with Pool, McPhee, and others initially advising Democratic campaigns, advertisers, and eventually the US government under the name the Simulmatics Corporation. The firm's links to academia ran deep, with Paul Lazarsfeld and Harold Lasswell serving on its advisory council. Lasswell claimed, "This is the A-bomb of the social sciences. The breakthrough here is comparable to what happened at Stagg Field."[83] Simulmatics' grand rhetoric promised to apply computer simulation to the most pressing problems in the United States: unrest due to racial injustice at home and pacification of villagers in Vietnam.[84] That Simulmatics profited only by managing domestic and international conflicts speaks volumes about the systems that legitimated early computing and behavioral social sciences as more efficient means of population control and social engineering. Even so, the company went bankrupt in 1969.[85]

Modeled American Voters

The next chapters offer both a history and lessons to be drawn from the beginnings of the computational imaginary of politics. Rather than thinking of one way to model voters with computers, chapter 4 looks at three approaches that emerged. McPhee's models became one of three voter models developed from the early 1960s to the mid-1980s, all antecedents to today's data-driven campaigning. The subsequent chapter explores how the computational imaginary imbricated with practical politics. Building on Ranjodh Singh Dhaliwal's concept of addressability, I focus on three moments where models worked their way into prototypes and eventually campaigning practices, resulting in growing correspondence between how models assumed politics should work and how consulting professional expected campaigns to run.[86] Though this occurred decades ago, these different models and prototypes remain influential in describing political simulation today—a link I discuss in relation to recent innovations in online advertising and data-driven campaigning.

4 The Modeled American Voter

A little more than a decade after William McPhee's Campaign Simulator, approaches to voter behavior and simulation diverged. By 1972, political scientist William Shaffer could distinguish three interconnected approaches to voter behavior: sociological, sociopsychological, and psychological. These three "levels of analysis" can be understood as representing macro, meso, and micro views of the electorate.[1] His levels of analysis had implications for the simulation of voter behavior, and each led to a distinctive design. Should a simulation mimic the behaviors of voters as individuals or groups? Maybe both? Without focusing too much on his terms, I use them to introduce how computational thinking diverged and how computer models encoded different political agencies, or how computer models simplified human behavior differently. Political agencies could include whether voters made rational or instinctual decisions. Even whether agency was not personal at all but was instead a mass dynamic. "Political agencies" is a broad concept for thinking about how political agency was modeled but also about how the resulting simulations had a broader impact on campaigns and elections. This history helps reveal the computational imaginary of politics as enduringly conflicted.

I identify three distinct kinds of voter models: cybernetic citizens, rational agents, and data chimeras (summarized in table 4.1).[2] These models encapsulate the theoretical divisions over the rationality or irrationality of voters and the question of whether voter behavior reflected individual or collective beliefs.

The *cybernetic citizens* model imagines voters as cybernetic machines. Cybernetic citizens worked between the system and the individual; the model's voters function like homeostats trying to achieve balance amid

Table 4.1
Voter models

Model	Inputs	Question	Level of analysis	Actors	Prototypes
Cybernetic citizens	Surveys, opinions on voter behavior, election results	What issues might shift voter preferences?	Individuals with overlapping collective identities	William McPhee, Ithiel de Sola Pool	Campaign Simulator, Simulmatics
Rational agents	Theories of expected utility, surveys, election results	Will voters cast a ballot?	Individual decision-making	Anthony Downs, William Riker, James Coleman, William Schaffer	Voter calculus theory, Schaffer's Voter simulation, *Democracy* game
Data chimeras	Census data, ZIP codes, surveys	Where are your supporters?	Aggregated behavior	Eshref Shevky, Marilyn Williams, Wendell Bell, Richard Barabba, Jonathan Robbin	Precinct Index Priority System, Claritas's PRIZM

chaos. I find close parallels to this approach in media historian Orit Halpern's account of the changing models of cognition and reasoning associated with cybernetics.[3] The most salient example of cybernetic citizens being put into application is the Simulmatics Corporation's "people-machine." Although it was one of the earliest voter simulations, cybernetic citizens ultimately lost ground to the next model.

The *rational agents* model imagines the psychology of voters as a calculus of expected utility. Voter cognition was considered analogous to computing, processing inputs and outputting votes for one party or another. This voter model built on the rise of economic approaches to politics and the popularity of game theory, which provided the philosophical underpinnings of American neoliberalism.[4] In contrast to the active cybernetic voter, the modeled rational voter was static and predictable, defined by stable calculations. Rational agents focused on the individual level, and societies could be modeled through the interactions between individual agents playing competitive games.

The chimera is a mythic creature, a hybrid of lion, goat, and snake. The *data chimera* model is another amalgam, composed of economic, social, and urban factors. This third approach shares conclusions with the "stable voter" concept.[5] Data chimeras relied on advances in computational social science developed from survey research. The model was predicated on a sociological analysis that sought to capture the deeper structures that grouped, predicted, and described Americans. Voters were conceived of as holding a stable set of preferences, unchanging enough to be worth identifying. More precise than the established identities of race and class, data chimeras offered new portraits of US residents, at least the ones that their government tracked and recorded.[6]

Despite their sharp differences, all three models relied on computers to better predict and manage voters. These three models introduce how political agency was articulated in the early computational imaginary. These three models framed computers as useful for political and voter management. Whether they would help craft better campaign messages, predict rational voter behavior, or find more persuadable subsets of the American electorate, these models positioned computers to run more efficient, scientific campaigns, and in turn, they set American politics on a path to viewing computing as a means of political innovation.

The Beginnings of Cybernetic Citizens, Rational Agents, and Data Chimeras

All three models drew on major works in political science. The cybernetic citizens model takes its closest inspiration from *Voting: A Study of Opinion Formation in a Presidential Campaign* by Bernard R. Berelson, Paul F. Lazarsfeld, and William N. McPhee. The book was a sequel of sorts to Lazarsfeld, Berelson, and Hazel Gaudet's seminal *The People's Choice: How the Voter Makes Up His Mind in a Presidential Campaign*, published in 1944 and known for introducing the indirect effects model of persuasion, wherein opinion leaders guide their trusting friends to make decisions about elections. Writing about the books' legacies, political scientist Larry M. Bartels notes, "Lazarsfeld's panel studies were carefully designed to measure changes in individual vote intentions over the course of a presidential campaign. . . . Their careful measurement of media content turned out to be of little use in accounting for voters' choices, most of which seemed to be based upon strong 'brand loyalties' rooted in religion and social class and reinforced by face-to-face interactions with like-minded acquaintances."[7] Both books qualified the autonomy of individuals and drove a turn toward larger social systems and shared issues as explanations for how voters worked out their collective attachments when voting, a phenomenon they called cross-pressure. Subsequent work based on the cybernetics citizens model built on the idea of cross-pressure, predictively simulating the ways people attempted to resolve these tensions while seeking internal stability. Bartels's mention of brand loyalty is no accident. Voting was part of what Todd Gitlin famously called the "dominant paradigm" in media sociology, which conflated citizenship with consumption as if voting resembled buying soap.[8] Though critical of this approach, Gitlin implicitly demonstrates its central assumption: The conflation of citizen and consumer frames voting as a matter of choice rather than habit. The result was a theory that presumed an active voter even if that activity was much like shopping.

Rational agents built on *An Economic Theory of Democracy* by Anthony Downs, one of the first books to introduce economic theory to political science. The book was adapted from Downs's doctoral dissertation in economics, completed at Stanford University under the supervision of Nobel Prize–winning economist Kenneth Arrow. Downs described voters as rational agents whose big choice was whether to go to the trouble of voting at all. Parties, also acting rationally, adhered to the center to maximize votes. After Downs, economists and political scientists alike began to restate voting as a rational strategy. Voting became a calculus, quite literally, as subsequent work in the field argued over the best formulas to predict voting in elections.[9]

The data chimeras concept stems from an older tradition, best known as social area analysis. The approach began in the 1920s in urban sociology and political science at the University of Chicago. There, Robert Park drew on ecological theories to study cities. In a history of the method, Brindley and Raine explain, "The very rapid growth of the city of Chicago, as it absorbed successive waves of European immigrants in the early part of this century, gave rise to a number of distinctive and relatively discrete neighborhoods" that Park and others "described on various criteria, including their population structure and mobility, ethnic composition, housing characteristics and employment."[10] These accounts, "compared with modern statistical techniques," were "impressionistic" but nonetheless primed an interest in techniques to classify and sort urban populations.[11] Comparable work happened later in Chicago's political science department, where Harold Gosnell produced some of the first studies of voting behavior. Gosnell published *Getting Out the Vote: An Experiment in the Stimulation of Voting* in 1927 and *Machine Politics* in 1937.[12] Like Park, Gosnell studied Chicago's ward politics, exhibiting journalistic flair in his profiles of ward bosses and precinct captains, but he also included maps of the city's ethnicities and vote distributions that foreshadow how aggregated data might stand in for individuals. While distinct, Park and Gosnell shared an interest in collective behavior, notably the use of data about *groups of people* to provide accounts of individual behavior, animating data about wards as if the wards had unitary identities.[13]

The most recent book likely had the most enduring impact on political science. *The American Voter* was the first major output of the still ongoing National Election Studies project at the Institute for Social Research at the University of Michigan.[14] Written by political scientists Angus Campbell, Philip Converse, Warren Miller, and Donald E. Stokes, the book popularized the Michigan Model of voting, which emphasizes the centrality of party loyalty to voter decisions. Related to Berelson, Lazarsfeld, and McPhee's book, *The American Voter* put elections and voter behavior on the sidelines in favor of the deeper, though still dynamic, effects of partisan political socialization. Larry M. Bartels explains, "*The American Voter* portrayed an electorate whose orientations toward politics were strongly influenced by partisan loyalties developed early in life, whose votes in specific elections reflected the overlaying of short-term forces . . . upon these long-term influences, and whose familiarity with and attachment to abstract ideologies and policy agendas was remarkably limited."[15] Bartels, coauthor of a devastating critique of modern elections in *Democracy for Realists*, argues that the Michigan Model counters the myth of the active voter found in the preceding books. The Michigan Model acts as both a check on the need for computer simulation and a justification for better data science. While its conclusions suggested that voter decision-making was not so complex as to require advanced computer simulation, *The American Voter* nonetheless conversed with computational approaches, especially data chimeras.

The Brief, Tragic Life of Cybernetic Citizens

Cybernetic citizens encoded an active model of politics where voters respond to stimuli, change course, and swing elections. Voters were emotional, conflicted, and loyal to broader social forces like parties, religions, and regional cultures. In contrast to the Michigan Model, Simulmatics' simulated voters were unfixed and capable of being persuaded.[16] Cybernetic citizens, then, perceived voting as akin to shopping, not unlike a shopper moving down a grocery aisle reacting to different products. Put differently, cybernetic citizens functioned something like cyberneticist W. Ross Ashby's homeostat, a simple machine that monitored its surroundings and used that feedback to adapt and correct its course. McPhee's Campaign Simulator, mentioned in the previous chapter, is an early example of a cybernetic citizens–based simulation. The work of the Simulmatics Corporation is another.

Simulmatics enlisted computer simulation to express a relationship between marketing and politics, and their approach blurred the line between voter and consumer. Their business did too. Simulmatics tried to sell its methods to businesses and parties alike. Early business proposals offered to analyze and optimize advertising expenditure.[17]

Simulmatics had its only practical contact with domestic politics in the 1960 presidential election. In early 1959, Simulmatics gained the support of the Democratic National Committee to prepare a report using their methods. The firm delivered its first report just before the Democratic National

Convention in the summer of 1960. The report studied the opinions of Black voters in northern cities, a halting step toward acknowledging the Civil Rights Movement, which had inspired many of Simulmatics' founders. After the convention, Simulmatics convinced the Kennedy campaign to commission three further reports.[18] These reports focused "on the image of Kennedy, the image of Nixon, and foreign policy as a campaign issue" and were the first to use their simulation methods to predict voter behavior.[19]

Data came from survey research. In 1947, pollster Elmo Roper donated his data to Williams College, creating one of the first repositories of social science data. By 1957, the collection had become the Roper Public Opinion Research Center. Ithiel de Sola Pool and others arranged access to the center's surveys under an agreement that their opponents in the Republican Party were granted the same access. The data were not computer readable so Simulmatics spent the summer of 1959 integrating the code books and punch cards from sixty-five surveys conducted between 1952 and 1960.[20] Throughout 1959, Pool solicited data from other centers, including corresponding with Angus Campbell, director of the University of Michigan's Survey Research Center. Simulmatics, however, apparently never used any other data source than the Roper Center's. (Perhaps because it was unnecessary? Campbell replied to Pool that he had "considerable doubt . . . what the effect of adding a few drops of Old Grandad to a gallon of Four Roses will be but our few thousand cards are available to you.")[21]

Translating the survey data to punch cards was an "arduous task" that resulted in what might have been the first political database, which Simulmatics called a "matrix." By the end of the project, they had processed over 130,000 punch cards of individual survey responses that they summarized as 480 voter types.

The 480 types were "defined by socio-economic characteristics." Pool and Abelson explained, "A single voter type might be 'Eastern, metropolitan, lower-income, white, Catholic, female Democrats.' Another might be, 'Border state, rural, upper-income, white, Protestant, male Independents.'" In effect, each voter type was a composite of region, race, gender, and political disposition. Notably, voter types did not include education, age, or specific location. Geographically, voter types were assigned one of four abstract regions. The matrix masked the arduous interpretive work that created it. Voter types only approximated the survey results, since as Pool, Abelson, and Popkin wrote, "it will be noted that we did not use all possible

Table 4.2
Structure of the Simulmatics 1960 model of the American electorate

In each of 4 regions:	7 SES and city size levels	By sex, religion, ethnicity: Protestant males			Protestant females			Catholic males			Catholic females			Jews			Negroes			
South	1. A urban	R	D	I	R	D	I	R	D	I	R	D	I	R	D	I	R	D	I	
	2. A+B town	R	D	I	R	D	I	R	D	I	R	D	I							
East	3. A+B rural	R	D	I	R	D	I	R	D	I	R	D	I							
	4. B urban	R	D	I	R	D	I	R	D	I	R	D	I	R	D	I	R	D	I	
Midwest	5. C urban	R	D	I	R	D	I	R	D	I	R	D	I							
	6. C town	R	D	I	R	D	I	R	D	I	R	D	I							
West	7. C rural	R	D	I	R	D	I	R	D	I	R	D	I							
4X																	96 cells			= 384 cells

In 1 region:	1+2+3 combined	R	D	I	R	D	I	R	D	I	R	D	I	R	D	I	R	D	I	
Border	4+5+6+7 combined	R	D	I	R	D	I	R	D	I	R	D	I	R	D	I	R	D	I	
1 X																	36 cells			= 36 cells

		Rep.	Dem.	Ind.	
Add, in all	1. Protestants without SES rating in non-labor-force families	R	D	I	
5 regions	2. Catholics without SES rating in non-labor-force families	R	D	I	
	3. Persons of no religion	R	D	I	
	4. Persons of other religion	R	D	I	
5X			12	cells	= 60 cells
					480 cells

Structure of the Simulmatics 1960 model of the American electorate reproduced from the original diagram.

Key: R, Republican; D, Democratic; I, means Independent; A, professional, executive, and managerial occupations; B, white-collar occupations; C, blue-collar occupations; SES an acronym forsocioeconomic-status. "Urban" refers to metropolitan areas exceeding 100,000 in population; "town" refers to communities of between 5,000 and 100,000; "rural" refers to places under 5,000.

combinations of all variables, which would have given us some 3,600 voter types, many of which would have been infinitely small."[22]

Each voter type had "opinions" on what Simulmatics called "issue clusters." Issue cluster was "private jargon" that referred to internal interpretations of multiple survey responses about opinions on political matters. For each intersection of voter type and issue cluster, the data bank recorded their occurrence in the population and their attitude. The team manually reviewed survey questions, adding them to a list of issue clusters. Issues included "defend Europe," "neo-fascist," "civil rights," "fear of war," and "concern with rising prices" to name a few.[23]

The simulation worked by running this matrix (or what is called a database today) on a rather old IBM 704 computer.[24] The database consisted of two tapes connected by a program modeled on McPhee's theories.[25] The program used the theory of cross-pressure to simulate voter behavior. Among the many findings in *Voting*, Lazarsfeld, Berelson, and McPhee concluded that people with "cross-pressured opinions" held "opinions or views supporting simultaneously different sides" and could change their vote.[26] Simulmatics emphasized the influence of cross-pressure and noted "a human tendency to maintain a subjective consistency in orientation to the world."[27] Voters face many decisions that might cause inconsistencies, and a desire to maintain consistency might cause a voter to switch party support, usually late in the campaign. In other words, the elusive swing voter could be found and modeled by looking for voters with contradictory opinions and forecasting whether the cross-pressure might cause a change in behavior. Pool, Abelson, and Popkin also cited balance theory from psychology to elaborate the logic of cross-pressure as driven by an internal need for consistency. The result was a program that could simulate "at the beginning of the campaign how voter opinion would divide at the end of the campaign, state-by-state, under various campaign strategies."[28] How, in other words, would certain voters react to a campaign emphasizing particular issues over others?

That sounds mechanical, but the inner workings of the project were human after all. Pool and others mixed their assumptions with McPhee's earlier assumptions. Before the simulation, Simulmatics made numerous interpretations to create a workable database of voter behavior. To study the effects of religion, Simulmatics grouped its "set of 480 voter-types into 9 possible cross-pressure subsets arising from a 3×3 classification on religion and party," reproduced in table 4.3.[29] Cross-pressure here specifically refers to tensions between party and religion.

For each subset, Simulmatics predicted behavior with special attention to those cells marked X: Democratic Protestants and Republican Catholics. Some simulations were simple. Protestant Republicans, for example, "would vote exactly as they did the last time."[30] For most other groups, Simulmatics developed a unique equation to estimate turnout that required a guess about both probable behavior and what data could be an effective proxy for anti-Catholicism, given the lack of a direct question in its sample of surveys. Their interpretations had significant implications for the political importance of White Catholics and Protestants. For Independents and "Negroes," the team "estimated the turnout for these groups to be poorer than par, since Independents never turn out well and Negros [*sic*] are extensively disenfranchised."[31] Simulmatics was not wrong to turn a popular assumption into a working theory—the Voting Rights Act was not passed until 1965—but it is notable which futures these ostensible civil rights advocates did and did not simulate.

Pool and others' assumptions about voter behavior recall McPhee's comments to James S. Coleman implying that McPhee's simulation relied more on guessing and limited personal knowledge than mathematical models. Unconcealed guesswork was sometimes lauded, though. As a review in the *Annals of the American Political Science Association* noted, Pool, Abelson, and Popkin's description of the project "strip[ped] the Great God Computer of many of the obfuscations with which others too often clothed it. They make explicit what many of us long have suspected: that the machine can do only what the human intellect tells it to do with humanly provided materials."[32]

Simulmatics used the results of their simulations in their three reports for the Kennedy campaign. Focusing on religion, the first of the reports discussed perceptions of Kennedy as a Catholic.[33] But the reports seem to have

Table 4.3
Cross-pressure patterns

	Republicans	Democrats	Independents
Protestants	(1)	X (2)	(2)
Catholics	X (4)	(3)	(3)
Other	(4)	(5)	(5)

had negligible impact. Pool and Abelson, reflecting on the campaign, noted that "while campaign strategy, except on a few points, conformed rather closely to the advice in the more than one hundred pages of the three reports, we know full well that this was by no means because of the reports. Others besides ourselves had similar ideas. Yet, if the reports strengthened right decisions on a few critical items, we would consider the investment justified."[34]

If Simulmatics had any immediate effect on politics, it was salting the earth for future political simulations. News of Kennedy consulting a computer sparked fears of political manipulation. Simulmatics did not help the situation. Its larger-than-life accounts of its influence and its claims to have built a "People-Machine" quickly became a liability for Kennedy. His campaign distanced itself from the firm. The reaction proved costly; despite their best efforts, Simulmatics never worked for another campaign again.[35]

Nor did the firm inspire anyone else. Subsequent presidential campaigns ignored the methodological innovations of Simulmatics. Discussion of computing is scant in the 1964 Democratic Campaign Manual for the next presidential election. The manual drew on the recommendations of Lawrence F. O'Brien, who directed Kennedy's 1960 campaign and was a major figure in the development of the political campaign consulting industry.[36] After an inspiring quote from Lyndon B. Johnson, O'Brien's foreword assures readers that "every program and procedure outlined in this manual has been tried and has proved successful." The manual offers advice on everything from how to pick a campaign office to the use of sound trucks, but it makes no mention of computers. Polling is briefly discussed, directing readers to consult the DNC for recommended firms. No mention is made of polling analysis. Looking at the recommendations to use paper cards to track voter data, the manual seems to predate Simulmatics.[37] The manual does provide templates and forms, an antecedent to computer-assisted mailings that personalize generic messages.[38] But the omissions are more significant, as the manual and O'Brien himself trained a new generation of campaign professionals.[39]

Republicans too dismissed the potential, at least in the near term, of computer simulations of electorates. A 1966 report, discussed more in the next chapter, noted that computer simulation had been "used for Democratic Presidential nominees," providing some evidence that professionals on the other side had paid attention to Simulmatics. But the report concluded that "very few people understand this new concept, and any organization or candidate interested in simulation should approach it with great caution."[40] Instead, the report focused on the application of computers to direct mail.

Simulation appeared to be too costly for campaigns immediately after Simulmatics. Writing in the first popular magazine about computing, *Computers and Automation*, in 1962, Peter Kugel wrote that computers were "sideshow curiosities on television news programs."[41] The wide-ranging article even discussed computer models of the electorate without mentioning Simulmatics. Even ten years later, a book-length review of computers in elections by Robert L. Chartrand offers Simulmatics as the only example in his chapter on political simulation, in sharp contrast to its other detailed accounts.[42]

Ithiel de Sola Pool, for his part, did not abandon computer simulation entirely but turned to simulating world leaders (as I discuss in the next chapters). He may have tried to stay in domestic politics even as his interests turned international. Jill Lepore presents compelling evidence that Pool offered Simulmatics' services to Richard Nixon's 1968 presidential campaign by submitting a proposal under the name Simultron.[43] There is no evidence that the campaign took him up or even considered the proposal seriously. Nixon's handwritten note on the proposal, at least what I can read of it, appears to say that the company would provide "info[rmation] that any decent campaign organization should have at its fingertips," suggesting that by 1968 Simulmatics had become mundane.[44] Lepore nicely summarizes the context: "Nixon didn't need the Simultron Project. Between the rise of the Simulmatics Corporation and its fall, American political campaigns had come to be led by computer-run data analysis."[45] These new analyses were guided by other voter models. Simulation, for example, eventually made a reappearance in the form of Decision Making Information, Inc., led by pollster Richard Wirthlin and marketer Vincent Barabba, as we'll see in the following section on data chimeras.[46]

Most political scientists ignored Simulmatics and McPhee.[47] Some found Simulmatics too flashy and McPhee too confusing. One review of McPhee's 1963 book *Formal Theories of Mass Behavior*—which included a chapter on the Campaign Simulator—complained, "The author's slipshod, chatty style is more appropriate for a pitchman's approach to a collection of mathematics amateurs than for a scholarly attempt to demonstrate the merits of a new scientific approach."[48] Clearly, McPhee and Simulmatics did not advance their cause beyond their friends in behavioral sciences and computing. Reviews of Pool, Abelson, and Popkin's book (aptly named *Candidates,*

Issues and Strategies) were mixed as well.[49] Part of the weak reception might have come from Simulmatics' hypothetical active voter. Just as Simulmatics ran its first experiment, *The American Voter* put forward a persuasive argument that voters were not as dynamic as they appeared. Political science turned pessimistic about voter agency. What was the good of an expensive, dynamic simulation if voters were predictable and habitual? Voters and issues continued to be a major theme in the literature,[50] but as one reviewer put it, "the closer the behavioralists came to the micro-foundations of electoral behavior, the more successful they were in explaining the macro-level outcomes of elections."[51]

In contrast to Simulmatics' marginal immediate political impact, the nascent behavioral sciences praised them. The company's Kennedy work became a story repeated in the annals of simulation and modeling in the social sciences. A 1965 special issue of *American Behavioral Scientist* celebrated the work of Simulmatics as the "benchmark in the theory and instrumentation of the social sciences."[52] The editorial was written by Alfred de Grazia, an early editor of the journal and later employee of Simulmatics in its disastrous Vietnam research.[53] Articles included Simulmatics' studies of business systems, communications, and international relations as well as some updates on its methods for the next election.[54] Harold Lasswell wrote the issue's introduction, "The Shape of the Future." In no uncertain terms, he explained that the power, and danger, of Simulmatics' methods was when "new advances in technique make it possible to give the leaders of rival governments, political parties and pressure groups improved advice for managing their campaigns to influence public judgment of candidates, issues and organization." Perhaps in response to critics, Lasswell maintained that "officers of the Simulmatics Corporation are acting responsibly."[55] What is missing from this glimpse of the future is any foresight that Simulmatics would be bankrupt four years later and punch cards would be burned in opposition to this political technology.

Simulmatics's 1960 simulation became one of a few computer simulations of politics developed within the nascent behavioral sciences. Over the next decade, researchers working across national and international politics produced one-off simulations of voters as well as how congresspeople would vote.[56] In 1964, Pool, Abelson, and Popkin reran its code to predict that year's presidential election with modified issue clusters and more attention to geography. Their results had a median error of 3.4 percent, which they felt was acceptable given how much had changed from the last election. MIT's Project MAC supported the research this time, and the simulation ran on its new IBM 7094 machine. The 1964 simulation was their last. Like most of the computer simulations from this time and field, it was never replicated. Over a decade later, an article in *Operations Research* detailed an attempt to apply the technique to a 1970 campaign, a project that noted that "valuable as recent empirical research has been for increasing our understanding of how and why people arrive at their decision on election day, it has yielded little in the way of practical policy-related information for the candidate in the midst of a campaign." The main exception noted in the footnote was the Simulmatics Corporation.[57]

Simulmatics did find an ally in Karl Deutsch. Deutsch was a major figure in political science and popularized its links to cybernetics in his 1963 book, *The Nerves of Government*. In a review of major advances in the social sciences, Deutsch and his coauthors mentioned Ithiel de Sola Pool and Robert Abelson and their work on "computer simulation of social and political systems" in a list of major advances in the social sciences.[58] That Deutsch saw the project as significant even after its bankruptcy and numerous public failures demonstrates determination. Deutsch tried to work with Pool on the ill-fated Project Cambridge that aimed to merge the behavioral sciences with international relations. Deutsch's attitude to Simulmatics reveals conceptual parallels with their voter simulations that led to the GLOBUS project discussed in the second half of the book.

Cybernetic citizens can be understood as part of a broader integration of cybernetics and neural network theory in political science led by Karl Deutsch. Notably, social psychologists developed the theory of cognitive dissonance soon after Lazarsfeld, Berelson, and McPhee published *Voting* and its theory of cross-pressure. Orit Halpern notes that the approach "emerged as one dominant model for human behavior" by 1957. Cognitive dissonance, Halpern writes, "proposed that individuals reconciled seemingly incommensurable possibilities."[59] Similarly, voters modeled by cybernetic citizens attempted to reconcile their cross-pressured opinions. The overall consequences of this cybernetic turn, Halpern continues, was to treat humans as rationalizing, with minds like circuits that "could be discretized, modeled, rebuilt, reenacted."[60]

Even if Simulmatics ended in obscurity, the company's simulations exemplify an enduring voter model that emphasizes agency and the possibility of persuasion—a prototype of elections that computers helped to animate and make believable. Simulmatics, in short, used computers to recover an active voter. That Simulmatics ultimately inspired so few imitators might have been due to the model's hyperactivity. Cybernetic citizens were more active voters than actual voters proved to be. World modeler Morton Gorden described this problem best. He noticed a similar effect during the design of TEMPER, a world simulation contemporary to Simulmatics discussed more in the next part. He reflected that TEMPER's dynamic simulations were the result of "fail[ing] to take into account the rate of change as it occurred over time."[61] In TEMPER, nations quickly escalated toward conflict. In the Simulmatics' people-machine, voters changed their opinions faster than what researchers were finding in the field.

Cybernetic citizens could be *hyperreal*, to borrow a term from theorist Jean Baudrillard, who made simulation famous (at least enough to be read in the Matrix movies). Hyperreal describes how a simulation can have more agency, more activity than its referent system. The hyperreal is when the simulation exceeds, even replaces, reality. Baudrillard writes, "The real is produced from miniaturized cells, matrices, and memory banks, models of control—and it can be reproduced an indefinite number of times from these. It is no longer anything but operational. . . . It is a hyperreal, produced from a radiating synthesis of combinatory models in a hyperspace without atmosphere."[62] The term aptly describes the different politics at work in these cybernetic citizen models. Cybernetic citizens risked being out of step with the field of glacial voter agency, more like a consumer deciding on soap than a voter raised to support the Democrats or Republicans.

Rational Agents

Where William McPhee and Simulmatics modeled *active* voters, Anthony Downs's *An Economic Theory of Democracy* formulated *rational* ones. Amid attempts to reconsider economic rationality, Downs offered a compelling theory of voters faced with information costs and an internal logic for calculating the best decisions.[63] In his book, Downs demonstrated that the actions of voters, parties, and governments could all be explained as strategies of self-interested agents maximizing utility and lowering costs. As Downs wrote, "all rational decision makers in our model—including political parties, interest groups, and governments—exhibit the same qualities."[64] Making good on this claim, the book offered up influential explanations about why parties' positions stay centrist and when voters would bother to vote. Political parties, governments, and nations all could be modeled as rational agents, and this equivalency was both theoretical and methodological. Mathematical formulas for maximizing utility could predict the behavior of humans and institutions alike. And under this holistic framework, experts could work simultaneously on national and international affairs.

Downs was not alone in using rational choice to model voters and institutions. His book was part of a concerted effort to explain the actions of humans, institutions, and superpowers through economic theory. Defense intelligence analysts and peace scholars alike interpreted the threat and prevention of global thermonuclear war through similar economic-minded, rational strategies. Nobel Prize–winning economist Thomas Schelling had begun writing about game theory in the global arms race the same year *An Economic Theory of Democracy* was published. Indeed, Downs's work is best understood as a hybrid of "Cold War rationality," economics, and politics. Cold War rationality aspired to

> be formal, and therefore largely independent of personality or context. It frequently took the form of algorithms—rigid rules that determine unique situations—which were moreover supposed to provide optimal solutions to given problems, or delineate most effective means towards certain goals (taken, in this instance, for granted). Second, complex tasks and episodes were analyzed into simple, sequential steps; the peculiarities of context, whether historical or cultural, gave way to across-the-board generalizations; analysis took precedence over synthesis. And finally, at least ideally advocates hoped that the rules could be applied mechanically: computers might reason better than human minds.[65]

Cold War rationality took on many forms, one of which, was rational agents. The US defense intelligence community legitimated this version of Cold War rationality, especially at the RAND Corporation and in exchanges between defense experts and academia. The Office of Naval Research sponsored Downs's research, a fact that Downs made no secret of. His research and its followers marked a specific continuation of Cold War rationality into politics and political computing.

Downs's modeling of the voter as a rational agent furthered the breakdown of the boundary between voters and computers. Well before the popularization of the computer, the Downsian voter *was* a computer. Voters were information processors, following the turn within economic theory toward

John von Neumann's computational thought.[66] Downs wrote, "Each voter develops his own standard out of his experiences with other governments. By *computing* their performance ratings, he creates a measuring rod with which he can discover whether the incumbents have been doing a good, bad, or indifferent job of governing."[67] Elsewhere, Downs argued that voters read multiple newspapers, compared their quality and relevance of information, and then adjusted their intake to lessen the cost of information acquisition. Downs did not program his model with a computer, even as McPhee was doing just that a year or two later. Compared to McPhee's lodestars, Downsian voter models rendered human behavior as an algorithm.

In academia, Downs's work supported political applications of economics, or the use of statistics on economic data, and what became known as public choice theory.[68] Founded as the Committee on Non-Market Decision Making in 1963, the Public Choice Society applied economic methods to the study of political problems. The scholarly network included economists like Mancur Olson, influential right-wing economist James Buchanan, and commons scholar Elinor Ostrom. The influence of its members is hard to overstate. Olson's 1965 book *The Logic of Collective Action* continues to influence theories of political action. Members did not just come from economics departments. James S. Coleman, mentioned earlier, worked in sociology. William Riker, who developed positive political theory, advanced Downsian theory as a trained political scientist and was president of the society in 1966.[69]

William Riker had a major influence on the adoption of rational theory in political science. Leading the Rochester school, he influenced scholars working on voter modeling and, later, world simulators and games. Riker started publishing political science research that drew on economics methodologies around the same time as Downs. His 1962 book *The Theory of Political Coalitions* countered the voter maximization theory developed by Downs (as well as Duncan Black) that held that parties tried to win the most votes. Instead, Riker outlined a strategy whereby parties did only enough to win the minimum number of voters to be elected using Morgenstein and von Neumann's game theory.

If Downs offered an initial theory of voter calculus, Riker and his student Peter Ordeshook refined it. The *American Political Science Review* published their paper "A Theory of Voter Calculus" in 1967; it remains the journal's fourteenth most-cited paper of all time.[70] The article began by criticizing

Downs and others who attempted to rationalize voting only to conclude that voting was irrational. Downs's model usually found that there was not enough individual benefit to justify the cost of voting. To rectify this paradox, Riker and Ordeshook first presented the Downsian voter calculus thusly:

$R = (BP) - C,$

where

R: Reward of voting, whether it was reasonable to vote;

B: Benefit to voter if their preferred candidate wins;

P: Probability that a vote affects the outcome of the election; and

C: The cost to vote for the individual.

In most cases the calculated reward "is typically negative, even when the citizen votes, which is of course irrational."[71] The problem, Riker and Ordeshook consider in a footnote, is that Downs relied on a narrow theory of rationality that overlooked non-goal-oriented benefits (e.g., nonpolitical benefits to voting). Instead, Riker and Ordeshook described rationality broadly (and rather like an algorithm) as "the ability to order preferences and to choose the more preferred action over the less preferred."[72] This broader definition of rationality allowed them to include a number of "positive satisfactions" independent of the effect of voting on the election. Adding satisfaction as variable D, Riker and Ordeshook restated the voter calculus as:

$R = PB - C + D$

The equation works for most binary-choice elections. Notably, the United States's two-party system allows for a mathematical simplification of voter choice between two options that enables a relatively simple calculus of voting (multiple-choice systems proved much more complicated). To test their model, Riker and Ordeshook interpreted Survey Research Center data from the 1952, 1956, and 1960 presidential elections and classified voters' sense of civic duty as three values for D (high, medium, and low). Results found that high D values led to higher voter turnout. This validation prefigures modern data science.[73]

For Riker and other simulation scholars, rational agents were the successor to the behavioralist project. In the conclusion to Riker and Ordeshook's voter calculus paper, they position themselves as the next step in behavioralist research, moving from inductive hypothesis-testing (stage 1) to "systematic theory" (stage 2). In other words, reason offered a theory to understand the data and dynamic models originating from survey research. This belief was found elsewhere as well. In 1963, Simulmatics employee and pollster Robert Abelson and *Voting* coauthor Bernard Berelson wrote a new computer simulation for community politics (e.g., should a community fluoridate its water?) using small-group theory, supported by Simulmatics and the US Public Health Service. By simulating who talks to whom, the experiment sought to describe changes in attitudes to a designated issue. The authors emphasized that their simulation offered something different from past Simulmatics work. The cybernetic citizens model provided what Abelson and Berelson called a "prognostic simulation" to anticipate the future, whereas their community referendum simulation was a "process simulation" that explained as much as it predicted.

James S. Coleman noted a similar break in a 1965 piece, "The Use of Electronic Computers in the Study of Social Organization." There, he discussed both McPhee's work and the necessity to use economic accounts of behavior to better simulate individuals as a next step. At the end of the article, Coleman made a call to rethink the "fundamental acting unit in society" and, in so doing, modeled a different theory of political agency. Individual choice matters more, and that choice could be explained as rational decision-making. He wrote, "This acting unit is a purposive entity, carrying out his actions with regard to some sort of economy of action based on his past experience. Yet the analytical approaches we employ in examining behavior ordinarily do not regard the individual as purposive, goal-directed, the subject of action. Instead, they regard him as an object, whose behavior is governed by particular parameters (parameters that may be calculated from his past behavior). He is 'passive,' moved about as a mechanical object governed by these parameters."[74] Coleman, to paraphrase, found that voters, when only described as a data output, lacked purposefulness. This model puts an enormous pressure on generating lots of data while never considering the purpose of the individual or their reasons. In contrast, Coleman considered the next step to be modeling the individual with economic theory. Not only does the turn to rational agents "escape from the enormous appetite for data that a model for a complex system has," but it means the computer "takes on the point of view of each actor in turn, and acts from this point of view."[75] Economic voter theory offered a better explanation of the individual, an improvement in the simulation and an easier step toward the use of computers in social theory (the subject of Coleman's article).

Making intelligence artificial, then, preceded artificial intelligence or, as Coleman writes, "by such substitution, and comparison of the computer-actor with the real person, it becomes possible to test and refine the model of purposive action which generates action."[76] In all these examples, the move from behavioralism to rational agents reformatted the voter as easier to explain and easier to program.

While Downs and others worked out voter behavior models without computers, their formulas inspired computer prototypes that encoded these models as variables. A good example of the product of this research is a later computer simulation built by William Shaffer. Well after the numerous simulation attempts discussed in the previous section, Shaffer blended Downsian rational voters with dynamic computer simulation. His 1972 book *Computer Simulations of Voting Behavior* is more notable for its commentary on voter modeling than its reception.[77] Former Simulmatics employee Samuel Popkin discouraged readers in a review for the *American Political Science Review*. "This is not an easy book to review," Popkin began, "for seldom has an attack on such an important problem been so mangled and confused as in this volume."[78] His criticism helps explain the book's marginality.

With the help of Ronald Weber, Shaffer built a working simulation of voter behavior using rational choice theory, seen in figure 4.1. Shaffer and Weber translated voter calculus to a flowchart later written in FORTRAN IV. To test validity, Shaffer and Weber surveyed voters about a mayoral race in West Lafayette, Indiana, outside Purdue University where they worked. Over the summer of 1971, Shaffer and Weber first interviewed voters to collect variables to run their predictions and then reinterviewed the same participants after the election. The study allowed Shaffer and Weber to test their program's predictions against results. They constructed six models of voter behavior. Notably, more complex models fared slightly worse than a simple model based on party identification. Shaffer's original computer model predicted individual results 61 percent of the time, whereas the best-performing model only considered party identification and was accurate 63 percent of the time. Shaffer and Weber concluded that "the residents of West Lafayette had very little 'rational' basis for decision, except their standing loyalty and the preferences expressed by primary group members."[79]

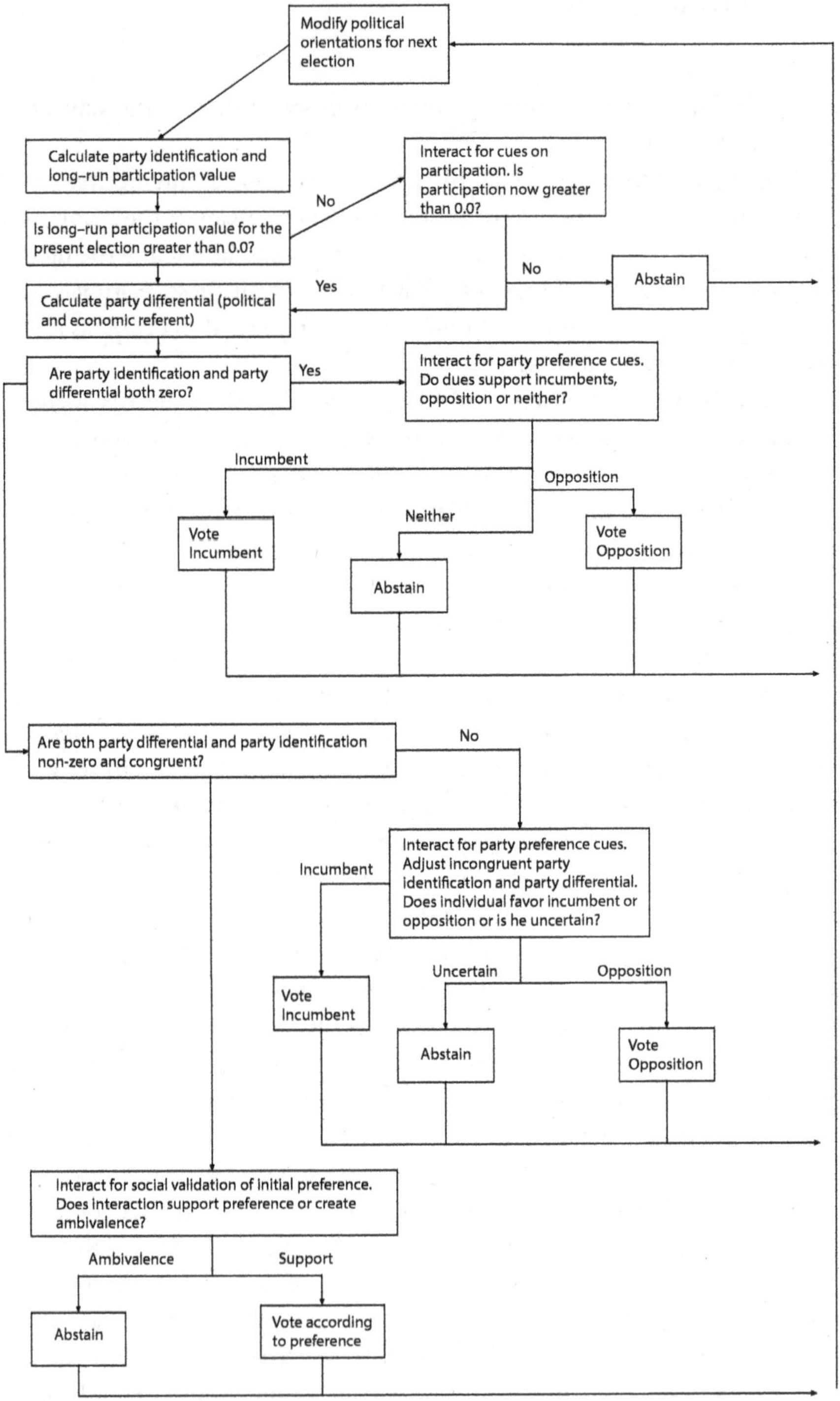

Figure 4.1
Programming flow chart for a rational agents voter simulation reproduced from the original diagram.

Despite the weak results, Shaffer and Weber remained hopeful that future elections might give new opportunities to test the feasibility of voter simulation, which they did.[80]

Crucially, the voter encoded into rational agents stood apart from the social conflicts of its time and even the concerns of its contemporaries. The Simulmatics Corporation's experiments actively considered race, albeit rudimentarily. Rational agents, by contrast, largely relied on the observations of white male Americans about rational behavior, eventually restated mathematically. Rational agents turned to an individualized political calculus at the heights of mass antiwar and civil rights movements. Foundational texts like Downs's book largely ignored race and gender. The closest Downs comes to considering gender is in a short analogy framing beauty contests as a logical problem of inferring average opinion, an analogy attributed to John Maynard Keynes.[81] Riker and Ordeshook, by contrast, acknowledged race not as a shared experience but as another input for individual calculations:

> Consider an election without a secret ballot (as still occurs in one state) in which a Negro farm laborer votes for a candidate opposed by his white employer. The amount of reprisal the laborer can expect is presumably related to the amount of rancor the employer feels. And this will doubtless be greatest if the employer's favored candidate loses by a narrow margin. Hence it will probably not much hurt the laborer to vote for a candidate who loses or who wins by a wide margin; but it may hurt him considerably to vote for a candidate who just barely wins.[82]

They treated the reasonable expectation of racial violence as merely a normal decision input to be weighed along with any other piece of political information. Reason's presumed universality, then, acts as a novel cover for many authors to neglect their historically, culturally, and politically situated perspectives on voting. The computer, as Katherine Hayles notes, metaphorically offered an idealized space free of material constraints to consider idealized political subjects.[83] The fractious politics of 1960s America seem remote when considering the operational life of rational agents. The final approach was far more grounded in social contexts.

Person to Person: Data Chimeras and Direct Voter Contact

Meanwhile, in California, a third voter model developed largely outside these formal academic and big science circles: *data chimeras*. Data chimeras didn't simulate voters or calculate reason. Instead, the model found altogether new voters hidden in the data, unlocked by computers. By using novel statistical techniques and census data, data chimeras could help build other people-machines. This third voter model delegated interpretive work to computers to find emergent groupings for political targeting.

The notion of data chimeras has many origins, but one of the earliest examples can be traced to the Datamatics Corporation (founded in California in the mid-1960s) when the company's cofounder, Vincent Barabba, "realized that campaigns could be significantly improved if people better understood the geographic areas" involved in elections.[84] The result became an early instance of a data chimera, the Precinct Index Priority System.

Barabba belonged to a group of innovative California-based Republican strategists who helped advise Nixon's 1968 campaign as well as, eventually, Reagan's in 1980. California is the birthplace of the campaign consulting industry. Campaigns Inc., a collaboration between Clem Whitaker and Leone Baxter, started there in 1933. The husband-and-wife team mixed advertising techniques with political campaigning to help defeat Upton Sinclair's 1934 Democratic gubernatorial campaign. Campaigns Inc. most famously helped to defeat Harry S. Truman's plan for national health insurance on behalf of the American Media Association in 1949. The firm stayed active, advising Nixon's 1960 presidential campaign. By this time, Campaigns Inc. was one player within a growing industry of political campaigning—the same industry that Barabba joined in 1966.[85]

Barabba held a bachelor's degree in marketing and a master's in business administration. After earning his MBA, Barabba worked part time on campaigns during California's 1964 Republican presidential primaries. There, helping manage campaigns, "it became pretty clear," to Barabba, "that there was some power in combining the electoral data with the demographic data."[86] He dropped out of a PhD program to focus on political work, beginning by working with Stuart Spencer of Spencer-Roberts & Associates, another early consulting firm. Spencer managed Nelson Rockefeller's 1964 presidential primary campaign.[87] After Rockefeller lost, Spencer-Roberts worked closely on Ronald Reagan's gubernatorial campaign in collaboration with Barabba.[88]

Spencer and Barabba founded Datamatics in 1966. After a few campaigns, Datamatics started to collaborate with famed political consultant Richard Wirthlin. Barabba and Wirthlin, after Spencer moved on, founded

Decision Making Information, Inc., to continue advising Republican campaigns. The company's founding employees made for an interesting mix. As Barabba explained, the company

> was made up of an interesting blend of different skill sets: Vince Breglio was a social psychologist; we referred to him as our "rat runner." [Paul Newman] was a speech major, in essence involved in understanding rhetoric and the development of communication philosophies. [Wirthlin] had been an economist, and my background was in marketing. We were able to attract very bright young people into our group from a variety of disciplines, none of which had anything to do with political science. We probably had more impact on the electoral process than most other political scientists.[89]

Barabba added his statistical skills and knowledge of a subfield of urban sociology known as social area analysis, which he had begun to adapt to political campaigns.

Social area analysis already had a strong statistical component by the time Barabba encountered it. First published in 1949 by sociologists Eshref Shevky, Marilyn Williams, and Wendell Bell, the statistically informed approach used multivariate statistics to classify census tracts in Los Angeles.[90] Their bibliography cited methods from Louis Bean as well as research in urban demographics. Where past studies tried to describe the character of different neighborhoods impressionistically, early social area analysis processed 1940 census data to analyze the city's census tracts distinguished by three indexes composed of multiple variables. Shevky and Williams explained, "It is methodologically desirable to think of these variables as constituting a system."[91] Their system was a multidimensional space where variables and axes existed in relation, providing the beginnings of a data chimera where voters could be defined and redefined as statistical properties.[92] Shevky and Williams continued, "[A] system so conceived is plainly a fiction, a conceptual scheme designed to serve as a framework of analysis and description."[93] Their fictional system involved three indexes: Social rank was composed of labor variables, urbanization was concerned with the tract's population variables, and segregation measured the concentration of ethnic groups in a tract.[94] The latter mixed race and ethnicity, adding Black Americans in the mix alongside Chinese, "Mexican-Americans," and "persons born in Russia and Italy."[95]

Shevky and Williams proposed these indexes as theories but validated them with another tool of data chimeras: factor analysis.[96] The approach identified latent variables or "factors" in data that caused variance.[97] Factor analysis resembles Simulmatics's issue clusters, and Pool, versed in factor analysis, acknowledged the similarity. Pool helps explain the difference between Simulmatics's interpretative methods and statistical methods, and in so doing, he defines a key distinction between cybernetic citizens and digital chimeras; discussing Simulmatics, Pool wrote in 1963,

> We could have intercorrelated all questions with all other questions and by factor analysis or other procedure grouped those which intercorrelated highly. For certain purposes that would indeed have been the thing to do. However, for our purposes it seemed essential to define issues in ways close to the substance of current politics. It might be, for example, that a question on school integration would correlate extremely highly with a question on atomic testing. This would prove some interesting things about the structure of political attitudes but it would be hard to use a cluster containing such substantive diverse material in advising a candidate about speech writing. We therefore insisted both on substantive similarity subjectively measured and on correlations as criteria for question equivalence.[98]

Simulmatics manually assigned survey items to its issue clusters, whereas factor analysis automatically identified underlying factors or key issues. Pool worked with a model of what was important politically, making correlations intuitive to political observers. Pool and Simulmatics programmed their own interpretations of human action *into* the cybernetic model—as with the emphasis on cross-pressure. After Shevky and Williams, digital chimeras crossed a threshold, letting statistical computing decide what was politically meaningful. Factor analysis, by virtue of being automated, found unpredictable, uncanny correlations that foreshadowed a belief that computers can detect hidden patterns.

The combination of new statistical techniques and computable forms of data, like the census, illustrates the fundamental characteristics of the third voter model. Data chimeras are models of voters premised on emergent identities found through techniques like factor analysis and, later, clustering and machine learning. Whereas rational agents and cybernetic citizens focused on deploying a behavioral model, be it an equation or a computer program, that simulated voter decision-making, data chimeras largely treated the voter as a product of the data itself. For example, social area analysts assumed that census data about Los Angeles lucidly explained the behavior of its residents.

Researchers using data chimeras debated how best to computationally or otherwise aggregate data, or what was called the study of types. Indexes, clusters, and factors all contributed to a general study of type. Attesting to the interplay between these words, Shevky and Williams defined a type as "a cluster of mutually dependent attributes considered as a whole."[99] Social area analysis marks an important change in the search for types. Shevky and Williams's own search led them to sort Los Angeles's 568 census tracts into eight types. Their first book includes an elaborate color map of these types overlaid over the city—the sort of information Barabba believed would be valuable for Republican campaigns.[100]

Barabba adapted social area analysis in devising another system of types: the Precinct Index Priority System (PIPS). Urban precincts replaced census tracts as the unit of analysis. But bigger changes were involved. Barabba played loose with the underlying factors. As Barabba explained to journalist James Perry, "If Social-Area Analysis describes the kind of people with whom you are dealing, the Precinct Index Priority System (PIPS) tells you how badly you need to deal with them."[101] Political strategy replaced academic judgement in choosing variables; however, true to the model, the system worked by sorting precincts according to how well they fit a campaign's priorities. PIPS, Barabba wrote, "pinpoints the precincts likely to yield the most votes for efforts expended."[102] Through their scores, precincts could be grouped. As historian Gerard DeGroot explains, "PIPS allowed the campaign to target middle-aged white union members who might benefit from Reagan's policies the cohort later known as Reagan Democrats"—one example of these new methods' ability to create new kinds of voters.[103]

In one of his few detailed explanations of PIPS, Barabba describes a 1967 mayoral reelection campaign in South Bend, Indiana.[104] The system aimed to predict safe precincts likely to vote for the Republican candidate again. The ranking included factors such as education, past election returns, and "number of welfare recipients" because "the strategists' opinion [was] that welfare recipients would tend not to vote Republican."[105] Ranking helped the campaign target its resources. "The flexibility of computers" allowed the campaign to adapt its targeting as new survey research identified new likely voters, recalculating the PIPS based on new strategies. He continued to use the system for Reagan's campaign for California governor in 1966 and Nixon's 1968 presidential run.[106] These wins added to the credibility of the data chimera model, but it had its detractors.

Barabba's commercial applications developed seemingly oblivious to scholarly doubts about social area analysis.[107] The leading critique was the *ecology fallacy* attributed to William S. Robinson from his 1950 critique of ecological correlation published in the *American Sociological Review*. Robinson observes that "quantitative sociological studies" where "the statistical object is a group of persons" attempt to describe individual behavior,[108] but he concludes that "ecological correlation is almost certainly not equal to its corresponding individual correlation."[109] This criticism marked a friction between the social area analysis of PIPS against the Michigan Model when applied in politics. Both treated the voter as an enduring data pattern rather than an adaptive homeostat or a rational agent. Both found relative stability in group behavior. But the similarities end there. Social area analyses projected decennial census data into accounts of its residents, while the Michigan Model relied on individual surveys. Michigan Model proponents Campbell, Converse, Miller, and Stokes knew and cited Robinson's critique.[110] In *The American Voter*, they criticized the aggregate approach for having "severe disabilities." They wrote, "Voting choice is an act of individual human beings, and the collective decisions of a state or national electorate are formed from the choices of a great many individual people. Therefore, to unravel the decision fully it is essential that we have information about individual persons."[111] Aggregated census data, in short, could be misleading and could not, therefore, replace individual survey data. Robinson's paper, however, failed to meet its goal of "prevent[ing] the future computation of meaningless correlations"—that became the business of microtargeting.[112]

The friction between individual and aggregated data illustrates both a stability in the data chimeras approach and the tensions in prototyping this model. In this model, the computer is less a stand-in for the voter than a mechanism of machine learning that can better describe voters through its read of the data. In finding new patterns, digital chimeras cast doubt on traditional social identities—like the party identification that was all-important to the Michigan Model—without ultimately disputing the underlying assumption of voter lethargy. People had certain enduring habits, traits, and behaviors that, once found, became predictive. Location mattered more than Coleman's rational agents or Simulmatics's cybernetic citizens. These models offered too much political agency. Campaigns did not really expect to change people's minds, but rather just find like-minded voters better. Yet, the method to operationalize this model raised genuine issues of prediction and validity. Data chimeras—as plural—involved diverse ways to work out how to compute voter patterns.

Data chimeras proved especially useful in contrast to other models. The 1972 Nixon campaign, as one historical marker, considered many but not all the models discussed so far. The campaign ignored voter calculus but considered simulation. A campaign memo dated September 16, 1971 closely read the results of the Simulmatics experiment and its implications for the Catholic vote.[113] The campaign even considered a simulation pitch from a TV executive named Gene Lindstrom, who claimed that Pool had tried to recruit him to Simulmatics. The project does not seem to have gone ahead. The $385,000 proposal in the archives lacks an approval or denial.[114] Simulation, however, was not so novel in 1972. The campaign already used survey forecasts to predict voter share.[115] These simulations fit alongside its use of priority precincts for the 1972 nationwide canvassing.[116] The overall activity shows an uneven but active mix of models and prototypes in a major campaign only a few years after their first use.

Data chimeras became standard practice in Republican and Democratic campaigns. Both adapted PIPS.[117] Priority precincts are frequently discussed in the Reagan and Nixon reelection campaigns in the 1970s, suggesting the technique scaled across the nation. Barabba worked in the business until 1973 when President Nixon appointed him Census Bureau director. Barabba had become skilled in using census data for marketing and political campaigns. In his new position, he encouraged commercial applications of the census, helping to foster what we now call the data-mining industry. There was, of course, a lot of value in that data.

Q1. How Do Computer Models Encode Different Political Agencies?

Ithiel de Sola Pool opened his influential 1983 book *Technologies of Freedom* with a rather bold statement: "Civil liberty functions today in a changing technological context."[118] He meant that different communication technologies—print, broadcasting, and computers—included different imaginaries of political freedom. It is hard to know how much his past experiences factored into that sentence—he does not mention Simulmatics—but his observation does show the evolution of a computational imaginary of politics, one that he could distinguish from other technological forms.

Where Pool saw a general conflict *between* technologies of freedom, I see a nuanced conflict with theories of political agencies expressed in models. This chapter offers one way to consider how the computational imaginary is not coherent but in conflict. There is no one unified computational theory of voters. Voter models encoded conflicting voter behaviors. The most salient example is how cybernetic citizens strengthened a belief in the relation between media and democracy: that media and communications shape voters' opinions. Polling, targeting, and voter analytics proceed from the cybernetic model that considers the voter to be unstable and in flux. The rational agents model, in contrast, requires a much more fixed understanding of voter behavior. Rational agents, though disputed today, introduced political calculus and a sense of the self-interested voter to debates about how to explain voter behavior.[119] Data chimeras fostered an enduring hope in data to reveal hidden patterns in the makeup of voters.

Even as these models have changed over time, and influenced one another, their different abstractions of political agency still matter. The immediate difference concerns the models' subjects, where rational agents concerns the relative importance of individual agency compared to groups or social structures in data chimeras and cybernetic citizens. These variations led to differences in abstraction that had political consequences. Rational agents had little use for context; it only demanded inputs, leading to a strange disconnect from the societal turmoil of the time. At the height of the Civil Rights Movement—when Black activists and their allies put their flesh-and-blood bodies on the line fighting Jim Crow and other forms of violent oppression—rational agents opted for mathematical abstraction. As political theorist S. M. Amadae writes, "Game theory views individuals as abstracted sets of preference rankings free from corporeal embodiment, and it empties the practice of consent of meaning because actors' preferences exist outside of time and thus can be artificially incorporated into public decision-making without the direct participation of citizens."[120] Cybernetic citizens paid more attention to the political context; yet, it relied mostly on its modelers' assumptions to program the behaviors of individuals and their group allegiances as types. Similarly, data chimeras depended on a relatively uniform class of campaign strategists interpreting clusters of census data. All approaches offered simplifications and made assumptions, but rational agents de-situated agency more than the other models.

A second key difference concerned the abstraction of agency in the model overall. Did individual behavior matter? Data chimeras assumed that computational analysis of census data revealed enduring patterns that could describe American behavior for a decade until the next census. Data chimeras' abstraction rested on the stability of the aggregated electorate. By contrast, cybernetic citizens and rational agents offered more dynamic models of individual agency. Cybernetic citizens pegged agency to social classifications that changed—or would have changed if Simulmatics's programmed simulations had extended beyond 1964 with updated code. Writing at the end of their 1964 postscript, Pool, Abelson, and Popkin imagined a new era "where the limitation on data bank operations will no longer be computer capacity but only the imagination of the researcher and the extent to which raw data is available to him."[121] For rational agents, the researcher's imagination comprised a closed world of universal voter calculus. Inputs might change, formulas could improve, but these prototypes maintained an idealized belief in a rational explanation of politics.

A third difference concerned the orientation of the model either toward mining the data for deeper insights or, inversely, extrapolating beyond the data. Data chimeras diverge sharply from the other models in their focus on finding greater meaning in the data, pulling together surveys and other sources to offer deeper knowledge about American consumers and voters. In contrast to this mining, other models entertained more speculative capacities. The logics of rational agents could become the rulebooks for games. James Coleman enjoyed gaming because it allowed him to witness the implications of rational agents in societies; he wrote about "the fascination of the sociologist with social simulation games—the opportunity to learn about social organization by forming a caricature of such organization and then observing this caricature."[122] The unpredictability was novel even as voter calculus and other prototypes of rational agents promised to explain, and predict, individual behaviors. These differences play out in later chapters, especially as rational agents became the basis for new world simulations.

Rational agents have probably the deepest political legacy because of that model's association with neoliberalism. A contentious term,[123] Michel Foucault theorized neoliberalism in his lectures, describing American and German approaches as state-phobic, opposed to the theories of economist

John Maynard Keynes, and committed to the idea of a *homo oeconomicus*, meaning an individual defined by rational conduct.[124] Building on the work of S. M. Amadae, historian Nancy MacLean argues that Public Choice Society founder James Buchanan drew on this human model of rational agents to legitimate a libertarian, neoliberal political agenda in the United States.[125] Buchanan's version of rational conduct (comparable to *homo oeconomicus*) provided the philosophical justification for the movement, reimagining society through the workings of self-interested agents and game theory. Public choice theory, then, was not antistatist, but rather focused on the production of states dedicated to managing self-interested, utility-maximizing individuals.[126]

Amid this history, the computational rational agents found in this chapter stabilized and popularized the deeper philosophical models of human behavior necessary for neoliberalism. As Amadae writes, neoliberalism treated people "as though they were interchangeable with non-human actors" or "strategy profiles derived from expected utility functions standing as programmable algorithms determining choice."[127] Computers provided a medium to express the utility of these new voter models. Rational agents offered a desired explanation—a logic of the deeper processes of behavior—which was found missing in prior computer simulations. Riker and Ordeshook's voter calculus offered a considerably more transparent but less dynamic voter model than cybernetic citizens. In contrast, McPhee's Campaign Simulator and the Simulmatics model were more like homeostats, with voters constantly scanning for information and continually reacting to an unknown electoral landscape. The stability of voter calculus and the application of expected utility functions allowed models to endure from election to election.

Computational modeling changed the political imaginary, letting computational speculation expand theories of democracy and voter agency. Computing held the potential to reimagine politics by creating compelling models that outpaced reality. Models became a hyperreality when simulations that modeled voters acted with more agency than actual voters or data mining resulted in minute clusters based on meaningless statistical differences. Computational modeling even contributed to the political fantasies of neoliberalism and economic democracy when rational agents offered a specific imaginary founded on individualism, reason, and expected utility. Whether, as critics suggested, people actually did reason in the way described in games ultimately mattered less than the affordances of this imaginary space and the possibility to explain and predict behavior through mathematical formulas or by smoothing links between some voter models and consumer behavior.[128]

Putting aside the differences among the three models, to what ends were computers used to imagine politics? H. B. White, a critic of Simulmatics and dean of the New School recalled Lasswell's claim that the firm was the "A-bomb of the social sciences" and pointedly asked, "If Lasswell and Pool really believe that they have an A-bomb, are they willing to leave its powers to advertisers?"[129] The capacity of computational modeling to unlock new political imaginations seems only limited by the demand for better ways to control politics and sell political messages.

5 Addressing American Voters

Figure 5.1
Cartoon above the article "Wooing Voters with a Computer," published in the National Observer, September 11, 1967. *Source*: David Seavey.

"Wooing Voters with a Computer," read the headline of the now-defunct weekly newspaper *The National Observer* where Hunter S. Thompson once wrote. The cover story by journalist James Perry looked at the increasing number of electronic data-processing applications in campaigns. Perry's article mentioned the General Inquirer (a content analysis program often used in international relations), Simulmatics Corporation's "simulator," and a few Republican campaigns experimenting with computers: For a technology that, a decade prior, had been science fiction, Perry could now easily list examples of everyday voters becoming entangled in the magnetic tape of early computers (as the accompanying cartoon illustrated). This chapter explores that entanglement of voters and computers.

From the perspective of those deploying the technology, however, electronic data processing did not so much entangle voters as address them. Computer models could interact with political campaigns thanks to what Ranjodh Singh Dhaliwal terms "addressability"—a term meant to describe how computers connect data to other geographic and physical places. Dhaliwal writes that addressability involves "the practice of giving a locational/spatial index" to data. Addressability here refers to the techniques that campaigns used to link computer models to voters.[1] As Dhaliwal continues, "Addressability appears not as a monolith; it comes in many shapes and forms." And so, the following chapter explores how early prototyping with computers closed various addressability gaps between computer models and everyday campaigning.

I consider three addressability gaps (see table 5.1) through three familiar applications: databases, microtargeting, and computer games. Campaigns used computers to manage data about voters, moving from punch cards to magnetic tape and later to modern databases. Political data, as I discuss, closed an initial addressability gap between voter history and

Table 5.1
Closing addressability gaps

Addressability gap	Applications	Relevant models	Examples
Data to voters	Direct mail, voter contact, electronic data processing	Cybernetic citizens, data chimeras	Winthrop Rockefeller campaign, Name Information Computer System, Aristotle Campaign Manager
Data and models to locations	Geodemographics, direct mail	Data chimeras	PRIZM, REZIDE, ACORN, PINS, PIP
Breakdown between computer behavior and voter behavior	Computer games, training simulations	Rational agents	*Democracy*, *President Elect*, *On the Campaign Trail*

computer records, or what has more recently become a discussion about how campaigns perceive voters with data.[2] These activities blend into microtargeting—that is, campaigns' ability to model voters who could be contacted. Campaigns closed a second addressability gap by managing the difficult dynamic between computers' capabilities to invent voters and the need for the digital electorate to match the actual one.[3] The capacity to make up voters encouraged simulation games—first board games and then computer games. Games taught publics how to play politics. Researchers and campaign professionals designed games as teaching tools, as experiments, and as public literacy campaigns. Games closed a third addressability gap between computer programming and political campaigns as game designers opened the black box of voter behavior to devise a rulebook.

I explore these three applications through brief genealogies that trace the family resemblances between databases, microtargeting, and games beginning in the mid-1960s. I begin with one of the first computer-assisted direct mail political campaigns: the 1964 gubernatorial campaign of Winthrop Rockefeller. Rockefeller's staff claimed that their campaign was the first to use computers to process political data and target mail. Indeed, their efforts became the foundation of the modern computer database industry, with the Rockefeller campaign acting as a critical prototype. Also in 1964, entrepreneur Jonathan Robbin cofounded his first data analysis firm. Robbin's career followed the development of microtargeting in politics, culminating in the Claritas Corporation and its blockbuster geodemographic system PRIZM. His efforts correspond to a larger movement to address voters within the adverting industry.[4] Finally, James S. Coleman, discussed in the previous chapter, turned to games to operationalize his theories of rational choice through the *Democracy* game in 1966.

These prototypes found their way into campaign practice through the pages of *Campaigns and Elections*, a trade magazine established in 1980 that introduced a professionalizing industry to the new personal computer.[5] By 1982, the magazine had a dedicated computer section that featured discussions of programs to manage voter data and games to simulate elections. This coverage drew on the computational imaginary cultivated a decade prior. Publisher Stanley Foster Reed believed in the computer's potential. "Why a special section?" asked Reed in introducing it. "Because we feel that we are seeing today only the bare glimmering of the applications of computers to all phases of political campaigning."[6] Reed's faith and the magazine's coverage shaped these glimmers into the foundation of modern data-driven campaigning. The magazine's archive serves as a rough proxy for the popularization of these three applications.

Addressability introduces a second question to explore the computational imaginary of politics: How do computer systems address political systems? Political systems might be villages, nations, or event worlds; in this chapter, I focus on voters. How did early computer systems address voters? Addressability is a key relationship in the computational imaginary of politics, integral to the lives of models and their relationships to worlds. My history of early campaigns exposes a tension between reality and hyperreality. Virtual space differs from physical space such that computers can describe politics in different ways from the dynamics on the ground. To adopt the words of simulators themselves, the simulated system differs from its referent system. The implication, is that the computational imaginary is marked by a need to coordinate the relationship between its computational and practical dynamics. The characters in this chapter knew the problem better than anyone else. Simulators had to ensure that their models did not become hyperreal and become more active than reality and thus overheat or become disconnected such that the computer simulation had no relation to what it tried to describe. In exploring how campaigns tried to narrow these gaps, I hope to show addressability's consequences and how computer simulation became entangled with the pragmatics of political campaigns.

IBM, Early Databases, and the Rockefeller in Arkansas

Winthrop Rockefeller was oil magnate John D. Rockefeller's grandson.[7] Born in New York City, he moved to Arkansas to launch his professional and political career. His reasons for moving are debated. He was a war veteran with friends in the state but also a sibling to the better-known politician Nelson Rockefeller. Sibling rivalry and his own fraught relations with his father might have made the distance attractive. Perhaps he saw the southern state as a chance to reinvent himself and break out of being cast as another New York Rockefeller. Or maybe Arkansas suited his personality; James Perry described him as "a bit of a maverick" whose "cowboy boots and hat became his trademark."[8]

Rockefeller's gubernatorial campaign began in 1963, a decade after he moved. Arkansas was a Democratic state, an odd fit with Rockefeller's

Republican ties. The Democratic party machine had ensured victories there for twenty-five governors in biannual elections since 1874. When Rockefeller arrived, the incumbent was Francis Cherry. Cherry lost the 1955 primary to Orval Faubus, another Democrat, who remains to this day Arkansas's longest-serving governor. Faubus appointed Rockefeller to lead the Arkansas Industrial Development Corporation, where he courted national firms to relocate to the state. The position gave Rockefeller recognition as a local leader.[9] His philanthropy, business, and ranching coincided with his efforts to build a Republican Party in the state. Creating a two-party state faced long odds. From 1961 to 1964, in-state Republican identification stayed low (11 to 13 percent). Perhaps this was because, second to Democrats (68 to 48 percent), Arkansans identified more as Independents (17 to 35 percent).[10]

Rockefeller's efforts culminated in his first run for governor against Faubus. Rockefeller differed politically from Faubus. Democrat Faubus embraced segregationist politics, whereas Republican Rockefeller warned that such extreme politics scared business away from Southern states.[11] Faubus came to national attention in 1957 for manufacturing the Little Rock Crisis. After *Brown v. Board of Education*, Faubus ordered the National Guard to block nine Black Americans from attending newly desegregated schools in the city. The move prompted President Eisenhower to nationalize the Arkansas National Guard, allowing the students to attend.[12]

Faubus won the 1964 race easily. Rockefeller proved an easy target.[13] The Faubus campaign branded him a "multimillionaire" who "still has to go to New York to get his haircut."[14] Nonetheless, the loss encouraged state Republicans. Faubus won with only a 57 percent majority, a strong lead but less so for a historically Democratic state. Rockefeller would not have to wait long for his next chance. Gubernatorial campaigns happen every two years in Nebraska and Faubus did not run again two years later.

Between the 1964 and 1966 campaigns, Rockefeller turned his wealth toward computing and voter contact. His campaign identified that its voter outreach lagged the Democrats. Campaign manager Marion Burton, who led the campaign's electronic data processing, claimed that Democrats manipulated the voter registry through a poll tax that particularly suppressed Black voters. The Rockefeller camp also struggled with how to identify and contact potential voters. Burton remembers,

> we had index cards about postcard size. We distributed them to all the campaign workers and gave them instructions about [the] kind of information we wanted recorded and named, address, or have they, have they bought a poll tax to vote. Now, there's all the things that you want to know. Are you a member of a party? . . . The canvassing was very successful statewide [but] those cards piled up on three collapsible tables against the wall in the campaign headquarters. Just piled up, they stayed there through the election. What can you do with them? I mean, you couldn't even type a letter. You wouldn't finish typing a letter to enough people to make it worthwhile before the election is over.[15]

After the election, Burton wanted to better compile and use the card-based data, so he started to consider digital computers as a solution.

Burton had heard that other congressmen had experimented with a punch card and typewriter system to expedite voter contact. These efforts, Burton recalls, were a "boiler room operation" with "ten ladies in the basement of that congressional building who spent all day responding to constituents with those typewriters."[16] The process helped duplicate letters but didn't come close to Burton's ambitions. He investigated IBM's offerings, eventually learning that the firm could offer a specially built IBM 1401 machine to mass-produce letters. IBM announced the 1401 in 1959 as an improved system for processing data stored on punch cards. Burton ordered a machine and waited for delivery.

Before the new model arrived, Burton used an IBM 407 accounting machine to start compiling voter data. Arkansas did not have a statewide voter list, so the Rockefeller campaign had to assemble its own. The campaign searched for other ways to create lists of voters—a good example of the list as an enduring cultural technique, following Liam Cole Young, and a technique necessary for the expansion of addressability.[17] This list functioned as an antecedent to a database—data matrix to recall the Simulmatics project—that aligned residence, address, and computer memory.

The Tower Building in Little Rock was the state's tallest when it opened in 1960. In 1966, Rockefeller's campaign rented its fourth floor to install an IBM 1401, set on a raised floor to hide the cables. The machine was up and running by mid-1966.[18] The IBM 1401 connected to an IBM 1402 high-speed card reader, an IBM 1403 line printer, and two IBM disc storage drives that stored four million characters on its twelve magnetic discs. Rockefeller could afford the machine's cost, likely $7,000 a month at the time.[19]

Rockefeller's campaign outdid his Republican peers. The party was still figuring out computers. The 1966 Republican National Committee (RNC) "Report on Data Processing" begins by describing the dawn of the computer age: "Only a very few technical experts wholly understand the computer," it explained. "The great majority of laymen know it mainly as a giant brain with flashing lights and whirring tapes."[20] What did the computer specifically do? Details were scant. The report suggested data processing could lead to a Name Information Computer System (NICS), or what we now call a database, which was a promising opportunity for Republican campaigns that relied on direct mail for fundraising.[21] The report explained that campaigns ran on money and votes, and "people supply both."[22] NICS potentially solved a logistical issue: Campaigns could better manage their supply of voters and money with data processing. The report surveyed both Republican and Democratic efforts. The RNC lacked its own computer or electronic data processing operation, while the Democratic National Committee employed an IBM 1401 machine for direct mail, assisting some eighty representatives. These efforts seem small compared to Rockefeller's 1966 campaign.

Burton set the machine to collect data from canvassing, public records, and phone-banking. The campaign hired a company to convert telephone books into mailing lists. Phones filled in missing data. Perry reports on the campaign's efforts in Pulaski County, where "nine phones were in constant use for three months," resulting in "90 percent of homes in the [county being] surveyed and all the necessary information transcribed on the IBM cards."[23] Campaign managers directed canvassers to collect further voter data, but these records were often incomplete, as many households did not have a phone.[24]

These efforts translated into a system of punch cards fed into the IBM machine's data storage. Burton shared a sample survey sheet during an oral interview, seen in figure 5.2, showing the list of questions and how the campaign digitized answers on punch cards.

Burton recalls that some voters felt obliged to respond, perhaps a sign of how the survey could appear like the census to Arkansans. The effort worked. By the end, the campaign was processing up to 16,000 cards per day and sent 1,000,000 individual items (for 563,527 registered voters) encouraging voters to register.

Rockefeller's strategy resembles modern voter outreach. The campaign used what we might now call a ladder or funnel of engagement to move voters

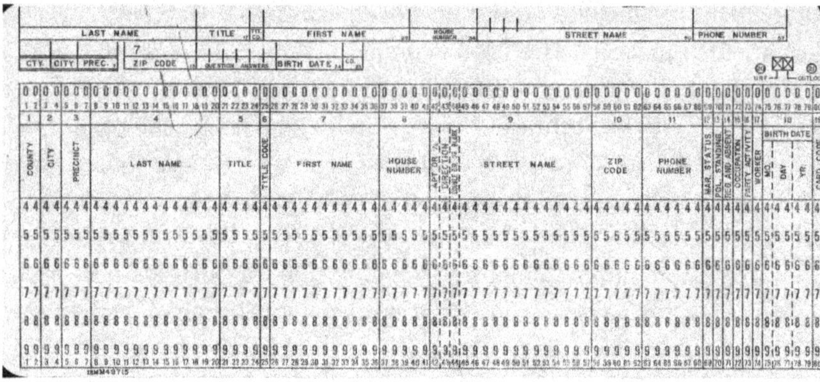

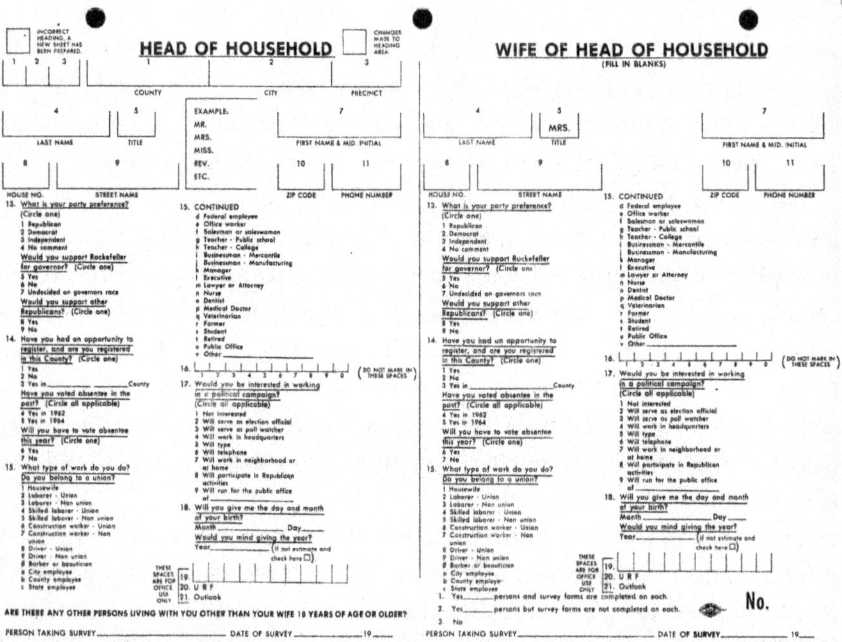

Figure 5.2

Punch cards used by 1966 Rockefeller campaign. *Source*: Center for Arkansas History and Culture.

toward registration. The campaign first contacted the voter with a computer-generated letter signed by Burton, named as "registration chairman." The campaign followed up with a letter signed by Rockefeller and finally made a personalized phone call.[25] Perry reports that these letters appeared to be personal, with Rockefeller's automated signature used strategically.[26]

Rockefeller won in 1966. The IBM machine was remembered as integral to his victory. Burton recounted to Perry, "We couldn't have won without it."[27] National coverage, however, ignored the technical efforts. Indeed, Perry complained about the lack of coverage of Rockefeller's computer usage. *The New York Times* made no mention of the campaign's techniques, instead citing their opponents' evangelical campaign, Rockefeller's reform-minded platform, and the Black vote as the decisive factors. His win was characterized as "a personal rather than party victory."[28]

Rockefeller's party machine kept running until he lost the 1970 election. It is unclear what happened to his voter machine; his team seemed to have moved on. Rockefeller died shortly after in 1973. The campaign's legacy endured in Perry's coverage of the new politics and as part of Democratic and Republican strategy. Rockefeller's campaign offers a glimpse into the work that was happening across the United States to narrow this first addressability gap between voters and data. That effort would grow into the political direct-mail and computer software industries.

What is striking about the Rockefeller campaign's data collection is that addressability was so thoroughly determined by its situation. Digitization was very much the work of a fragile party machine like political communication scholar Daniel Kreiss's more recent observations that technologies "are inextricably intertwined with the broader infrastructures of the parties as well as the expertise the parties have for maintaining them, and they must be institutionalized and cared for over time or they breakdown or disappear."[29]

Not only was addressability very much the work of a party machine—a literal IBM machine—but it was the product of the specific conditions of Rockefeller's well-funded campaign, which included limited ways to collect lists, barriers to contacting voters, and gendered logics of husband and wife when enumerating members of a household. Data collection was not entirely smooth or even. Perry reported that canvassers faced hostility in white precincts that supported segregation. And segregation acted as a rough geographic guide for the campaign to prioritize its data collection efforts. Though the survey did not ask, punch cards included a race variable next to birth year in spot 68. Canvassers did ask about occupation, an indication of the relevance of union politics and professions, in addition to asking directly about candidate support. These conditions determined voters' addressability in the 1966 election. Historic forms of data were human, after all.

Permanent Campaigning Takes Command

The Republican Party was the immediate benefactor of Rockefeller's innovation. The RNC's 1966 report had warned that electronic data processing (EDP) needed to be used judiciously.[30] The committee's next major report, in 1968, concluded, "No one has said that a computer, by itself, will win elections, but many successful political executives have said that EDP is one of the two or three most important tools at their disposal. The time will soon come when it can be said that no major race can be won without [electronic data processing]."[31] The report gives the impression that Rockefeller's campaign was only a few months ahead of other Republican state campaigns. Ohio Congressman Robert Taft Jr., for example, is quoted as saying "The use of Electronic Data Processing gave me a significant advantage over my opponent in the 1966 election."[32] The report quotes similar experiences in Illinois, Louisiana, Washington, and Wisconsin.

By 1968, Rockefeller's experimental processes had become streamlined into best practices for organizational design and campaign practice. The computer was a key instrument to maintain voter lists that, as depicted in figure 5.3, also drove new ways to address voters with greater precision. Direct mail, phone-banking, and canvassing illustrate how computers were integrated into ongoing efforts to simplify contact between campaign and voter. Contact sought to strengthen party loyalty: "The Sustaining Member, having 'bought' the concept of Republicanism with his own money, is the man most likely to discuss Republican politics with his friends, work for the Party and vote the Republican ticket."[33]

Campaigns had to adapt their practices and infrastructures to make the best use of computers. The "most common mistake" is to let "the file become inactive."[34] Parties also had to ensure that they had computer access to maintain these lists. The 1968 RNC report explained, "There are three ways to get a computer. (1) Buy or lease one, (2) rent time from a service bureau or (3) rent time from a business that has extra time to sell."[35] Republican campaigns relied on data services, a practice that eventually went in-house with

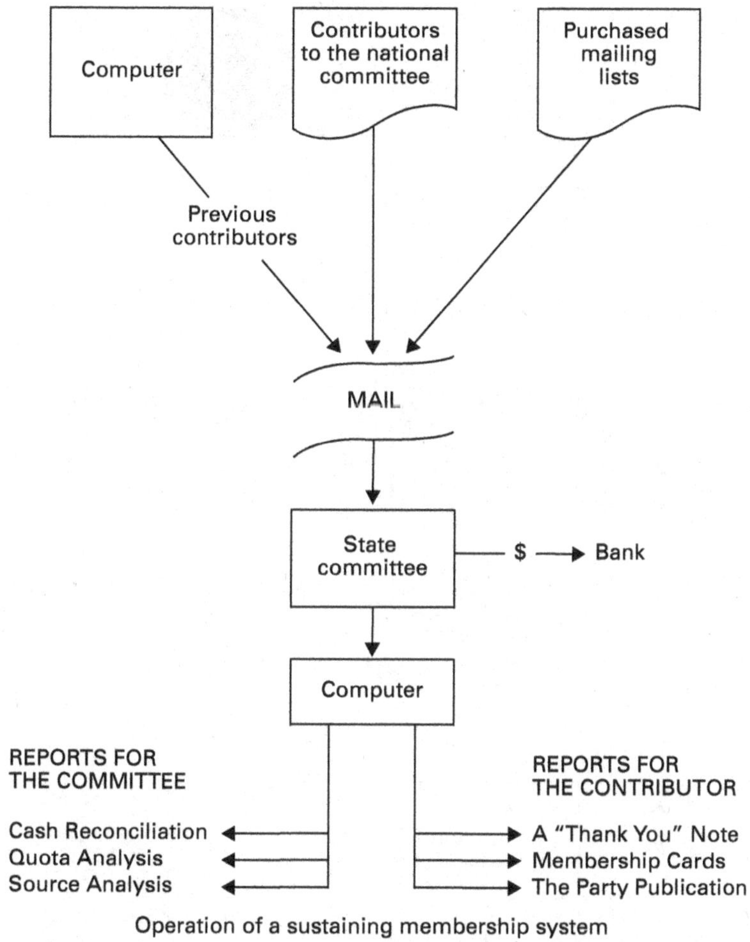

Figure 5.3
Computers integrated into direct mail and voter contact campaigns. *Source*: Redrawn from diagram in "Electronic Data Processing for the Political Executive."

the advent of the microcomputer. These efforts contributed to an expectation of permanent campaigning, at least to fund and maintain party lists.

Democrats embraced computers too, adopting the same best practices as Republicans. A 1972 trade book, *Computers and Political Campaigning*, surveyed both parties' efforts to integrate computers into their campaigns.[36] The book depicts a growing bipartisan consensus, with both parties trying to gain an edge through the production, maintenance, and analysis of voter

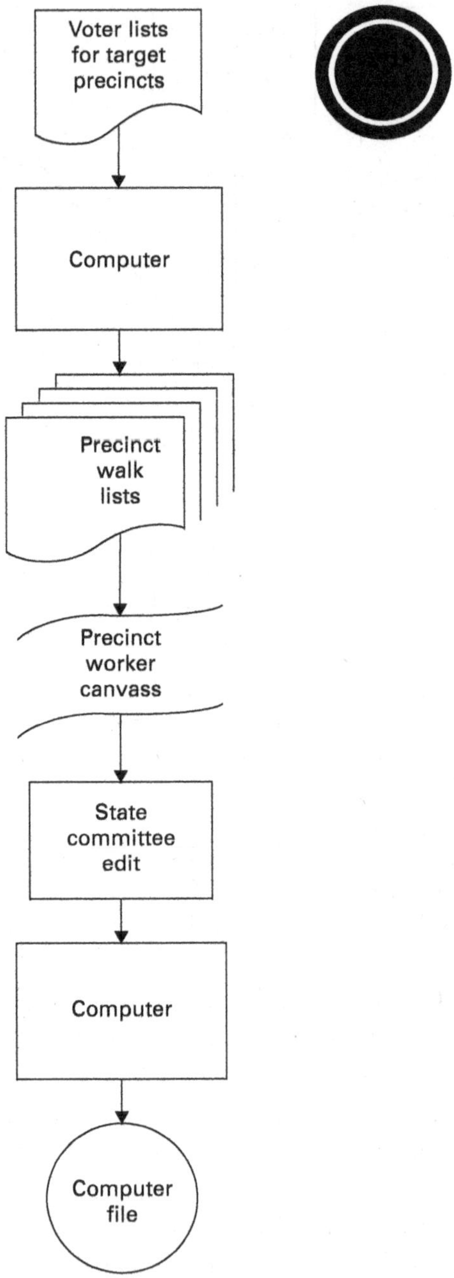

Developing voter lists

Figure 5.3 (*continued*)

files, marking an important moment in the growing standardization and refinement of political data and foreshadowing both parties' investment in better data use.

To condense a long history, computer databases quickly became mundane. Democrats and Republicans might have both invested in electronic data processing by the late 1970s, but Republicans seem to have mastered computer addressability. Ronald Reagan's 1980 presidential campaign was the zenith of this phase of addressability and political data. Reagan's campaign built on his prior gubernatorial campaigns. To recall, Stuart Spencer, Richard Wirthlin, and Vincent Barabba had developed new ways to profile electoral precincts in California, creating data chimeras to describe a region's political identity. Reagan's subsequent campaigns improved the addressability of these chimeras.

Indeed, some of the same people kept working on refining these systems: Spencer managed the presidential campaign and Wirthlin—still running Decision Making Information after Barabba left to run the US Census—ran its polling and data analysis. Wirthlin recruited a third man: Richard Smith Beal, a name that appears later when we discuss international politics.[37]

Wirthlin and Beal developed the Political Information System (PINS), their take on the Name Information Computer System. The system described itself internally as "a Fortran program which outputs to the user's terminal comparative ballot information by state on the major presidential candidates for 1980."[38] Beal explained that PINS sought "to use polling data, not just to satisfy the information needs of the campaign, but to help the campaign decision-makers with their strategic judgements."[39] Review of the code makes the system seems more like an early database to synthesize polling data. A report on PINS from, of all places, the *Propaganda Review*, offers a good summary of how it worked:

> Wirthlin employs about 300 survey operators who call targeted voters around the country. Approximately 1500 people are surveyed every month, day in and day out, during election campaigns and in between elections—unless there is a hot topic to research, in which case they contact about 400 people each day. A typical interview takes about forty minutes and covers a broad range of subjects, from religion to abortion, from Star Wars to the environment. The survey operator asks the questions as they appear on the screen of a computer terminal and then types in the answers.[40]

PINS relied on computer databases to retain a constant intake of voter opinions, an accelerated version of Rockefeller's direct mail. PINS collected polls and enabled simulation of probable election outcomes and some forms of on-demand reporting like Beal had developed for international relations.[41] PINS offered up usable intelligence about the state of the American electorate.[42] PINS was a key prototype for Sidney Blumenthal's concept of permanent campaigning;[43] in 1981, he wrote, "Ronald Reagan is governing America by a new strategic doctrine—the permanent campaign."[44] Reagan's state-of-the-art campaign soon became routine.

By the early 1980s, advertisements and articles for computer-assisted voter data filled the pages of *Campaigns & Elections*.[45] A new class of firms selling software for the personal or microcomputer promised to help campaigns of all sizes manage their voter lists. By 1986, House and Senate campaigns spent an estimated $14 million on computer technology, mostly paid to computer service firms to handle politics data processing.[46] However, a parallel shift in addressability complicates this history. Data were promised to better understand and target voters but also to track their location, a story best told through the Claritas Corporation.

Closing the Second Addressability Gap: Data and Location

The second case regarding addressability concerns direct mail and microtargeting. Once termed the "solid gold mailbox," direct mail offered a way for campaigns to bypass media and target voters directly—hence its association with microtargeting.[47] "Direct mail" is an oversimplification; campaigns did not contact voters directly but in aggregate. To bypass traditional media, direct mailers had to find new methods of aggregating voters. Histories of direct mail are replete with anecdotes about buying a magazine's subscriber list as a proxy for Democrat or Republican voters. Campaigns sought a better way to produce regularities of voter types that corresponded with their location. Could computers classify voters without losing contact?

Campaigns had a compelling motivation to invest in direct mail after the passage of the Federal Election Campaign Act of 1971, which sought to limit campaign spending. Subsequent amendments to the act further restricted the amount of spending in American elections.[48] The law prompted campaigns to focus on direct voter contacts over major donors—creating a market for a new industry of direct mail experts. In the following section, I track one of these firms, the Claritas Corporation, and explore how its PRIZM system minimized this second addressability gap between the statistical clustering of voter as models and the geographic patterns of actual voters.[49]

The Claritas Corporation and Its Electric Cluster-Making Machine

The Claritas Corporation is another source for the data chimera voter model, discussed in the previous chapter, which combined data analysis to find new voter types. Claritas is the most influential example of data chimeras in politics thanks to its collaborations with Democratic political consultant Matthew Reese. The Claritas Corporation relied on the same techniques as other data chimeras. Its PRIZM system built on social area analysis by integrating multivariate statistics with survey, census, and postal data. Importantly, data chimeras did not simulate voters or explain voter reasoning. Instead, chimeras were associated variables, drawn from public data, that firms like Claritas claimed could predict regular behaviors. Claritas closed a second addressability gap concerned with to what degree computationally derived voter types corresponded to voter behavior and location (ZIP codes, to be specific). PRIZM was innovative in classifying voter data to find regularities proximate to behavior and making it possible to contact the voters too.

Claritas's roots can be traced to a psychology lab at New York University. There, doctoral student Jonathan Robbin was beginning to learn the techniques necessary to take advantage of new data sources; his innovations in computational social science eventually became Claritas's PRIZM system. A 1992 profile described Robbin as "a midsize man who dressed in Brooks Brothers casual: khaki pants, blue oxford shirts, loafers, and fine-rimmed tortoiseshell glasses. On a first encounter you might be tempted to call him jolly, but that would miss the mark. Rather, he seems powered by an overheated reactor in danger of spreading statistical shrapnel."[50] That description came over three decades after Robbin had begun studying statistics and computing. By his own account, he worked in many of the hubs of computing research through the 1950s, including Harvard University, Columbia University, and the Rockefeller Foundation.[51] He credits himself with writing some of the first computer software for multivalent factor and cluster analysis on early IBM 650 and 7090 computers. Factor analysis was one of many techniques of data reduction and synthesis that Robbin later used in his political work. At school, he developed cluster analysis programs. K-means analysis, or clustering, calculates the distances between variables and groupings, or "clusters."[52]

Robbin applied these techniques to assist his supervisor Edgar F. Borgatta, an early innovator in the use of computers and statistics in sociology and psychology.[53] Many of Borgatta's papers credit Robbin for his data analysis and assistance with programming the computers.[54] For example, Borgatta used computer methods in research published in a 1959 paper, "Mood, Personality, and Interaction," funded by the US Air Force, assisted by Robbin, and conducted at New York University. The paper addressed concerns in psychology over the relationship between mood and personality by interviewing students. Borgatta used factor analysis to group significant emotions (e.g., tired, sluggish, drowsy, refreshed, and lazy) to assess the utility of prominent personality tests.

When Borgatta left for Seattle, Robbin, feeling disconnected from his less quantitative department, exited academia for the corporate world. He started at the Research Data Processing Corporation in 1961, which was renamed General Analytics Corporation (GAC) in 1964. When the company went public in 1968, the Securities and Exchange Commission described it as applying "computer technology to large scale databases for the solution of a wide range of research, planning and management problems."[55] Robbin left GAC in 1971 to start the Claritas Corporation.

Robbin's entrepreneurialism merged his work in computational social science with his interest in newly available government data.[56] Well before campaigns adopted computers, the federal government faced pressure to better coordinate and share its massive data collections, leading the Census Bureau to begin consulting with external stakeholders in 1955. Over the next decade, a series of three reports called on the government to better coordinate its data, leading to a 1965 proposal for a national data center. Ultimately doomed due to public fears over privacy and state surveillance, the proposed center nonetheless marks an important shift where governments turned to digital media to store the data they gathered, consulted with the private sector and other stakeholders on using that data, and made the data available to marketers and other parties.[57] While the Social Science Research Council's Committee on the Preservation and Use of Economic Data "recommended that the government establish a national data center to preserve data collected by its agencies and make the data available to researchers both within and outside the government,"[58] census directors like Vincent Barabba, appointed in 1973, sought to make census data more useful to businesses and other information consumers.[59]

Census records and ZIP codes were the two major sources of government data. The US Census Bureau had been an early adopter of computing, funding the development of UNIVAC and later using the machine in its census work as early as 1950.[60] By the mid-1960s, the bureau had been running a series of experimental surveys in New Haven in preparation for the decennial 1970 census. In New Haven, a census research group developed two foundational geographic information systems around 1967: Dual Independent Map Encoding (DIME) and its Geographic Base Files (GBF) file format. By 1972, all census products, including the 1970 census, were available on magnetic tape for use in bulk data processing.[61] Innovations at the bureau coincided with the US Postal Service adopting ZIP codes in 1963. A classic, boring infrastructural change, the five-digit Zone Improvement Plan (ZIP) code system changed how politicians and marketers contacted US residents. ZIP codes enabled automated sorting of the mail to keep up with demand, which grew 160 percent from 1940 to 1965. A win for the Postal Service, ZIP codes amounted to a massive subsidy of the advertising industry by providing an open data standard.[62]

Matching addresses, ZIP codes, and census data was a business opportunity.[63] The challenge was to find a way to both analyze and target new clusters of voters while ensuring that these clusters could still be contacted. Robbin called his solution geodemographics, a portmanteau of geography and demographics. He offered this retrospective description of how it worked: "The geodemographer acquires raw data from the census of population and housing and a myriad of other secondary information sources describing small geographic places such as ZIP Code delivery areas or collections of city blocks, for example. These data are heavily preprocessed to render them statistically useful by editing their errors and omissions, projecting and interpolating them in time, space and tabular detail, indexing and standardizing them in comparison to a variety of benchmarks and transforming their measures and scales."[64] Geodemographics was a new way to create data chimeras or, to borrow a phrase from Ian Hacking, "make up" people.[65] As historian Susan Igo writes in a summary of survey research in the 1960s, "after a decade that witnessed the 'discovery' of poverty, major civil rights mobilization, and then Black, Red, Gray, and Gay Power, it would be difficult to speak credibly, either politically or scientifically, of a unitary America."[66] Geodemographics allowed for new ways to describe a growing public acknowledgment of the diverse population. Of course, the money was in marketing, not elections. Even though a changing account of the US population had political consequences, Claritas's first product focused on market segmentation.

Claritas's first product published difficult-to-access census data aggregated by ZIP codes, what Robbin called the "businessman's geography." The firm started by matching census data with ZIP code data, resulting in the REZIDE series published in 1974. A REZIDE reader could look up a ZIP code to find demographic, income, and other census data. Employees at Claritas recall using a mix of newly commercialized academic statistical software packages, including Statistical Analysis System (SAS) and Statistical Package for the Social Sciences (SPSS).[67] Many of these technologies were developed by political scientists to better understand their data and were then adapted into commercial applications, echoing Robbin's career trajectory.[68] Through REZIDE, Claritas started to close the second addressability gap by matching computational data analysis of demographics with business geography. While REZIDE held scant potential to "make up" new Americans, the next iteration of the project tried to find new patterns of Americans scattered across its ZIP codes, unlocking an ability of computer prototypes to produce all sorts of voter models.

Robbin knew that computational techniques could be used in politics to produce new voter models. A year after Claritas's launch, he authored the report "A Guide to the Use of Census Data for Political Campaign Planning and Management."[69] Robbin begins by noting, "information derived from the 1970 census of population housing will play a key role in the planning and management of any intelligent political campaign of the 1970s."[70] In the guide, Robbin details "data linking" between election records and census data, going into detail about comparative units of geographic aggregation, methods with which to estimate voter support with limited records, and weighting of votes by demographic factors. Comparatively, a 1973 how-to book about campaign craft by Edward Schwartzman, who according to the back cover, worked on "over thirty campaigns at virtually every level of political life," does not mention census data when discussing political research.[71] Robbin, by contrast, underlined in his report that "census data by zip code can provide invaluable aids to the more effective use of direct mail."[72]

Robbin's guide aimed to help campaigns target people who voted as well as potential supporters. Though clearly enamored with data, he did not stray far from looking at established patterns of voter behavior. The guide's second part focused on demographic variables that might predict voting behavior, including age, sex, education, ethnic background, mobility of the population, family income, density (urban, suburban, rural), employment level, race, housing, and veteran status. Citing the Michigan Model as a one of its few academic references, Robbin's guide does not consider political issues or offer ways to swing voters; rather, it identifies local demographics assumed to have some behavioral dimension. In other words, this was data-driven decision-making, decades before the term's popularity. It is hard to say how widely read Robbin's report was, as he never mentioned the research in coverage of the firm's later political work with its new system, PRIZM.

PRIZM became the name Claritas used to describe the statistical product of mapping clusters of voters to ZIP codes.[73] Claritas developed its cluster system over two iterations, starting in 1974 with the Claritas Neighborhood Lifestyle Cluster System and then the more streamlined and popular PRIZM system. The methodology for both had roughly three steps. First, Claritas aggregated census data for each US ZIP code. Second, factor analysis reduced the data inventory into thirty-four factors. The three most important factors that caused variations in ZIP code demographics were socioeconomic status, urban density, and ethnicity—not too different from the factors identified in social area analysis. Finally, Claritas put the ZIP codes into forty distinct clusters and sold the data to marketers.[74] *Time* was an early adopter. Claritas clusters helped the magazine identify high-income ZIP codes to which to sell an upscale version of its magazine, *Time Z*.[75] The system became known as PRIZM by the 1980s.

PRIZM was short for Potential Rating Index by Zip Market. CEO Sam Barton and his colleague Robin Page coined the name. Barton decided that the clusters needed further interpretation to scale and be understood by consumers. They hit upon the idea of naming the clusters. Page, with Barton's help, labeled the cluster with colorful monikers such as Single City Blues and Downtown Dixie-Style. These names sounded intuitive, helped customers understand the clusters, and popularized the idea of clusters as a new way to describe Americans. Barton later recalled being amazed to find marketing professors teaching the clusters, evidence of how PRIZM provided a new way to see US populations.[76] That ideal appealed to famed Democratic campaigner Matthew Reese, who popularized PRIZM in American politics as a public spectacle used to promote his firm and the power of microtargeting.

Digital Cherry-Picking: Claritas and Matthew Reese

Robbin started working with Reese in 1978, and they hit it off. By all accounts, theirs was a personal relationship, and other partners at Claritas were disinterested or outright wary of the deal. Reese appealed to Robbin's penchant for showmanship. Robbin offered Reese an exclusive license to use the PRIZM system in politics, a core product of Reese's Targeting Solutions, Inc. The mix worked and Robbin acquired a more public persona, selling geodemographics as a new way to reach voters.[77] Reese once joked that "if you want to pick cherries, go where the cherries are."[78] If sympathetic voters were the cherries, Claritas offered Reese a new way to pick them—geodemographics.[79] Reese's influence popularized the closure of the second addressability gap—the gap between computationally created voters and the actual electorate—as clustering and other computational techniques informed the burgeoning interest in political microtargeting depicted in the pages of *Campaigns & Elections*.

The United Labor Committee of Missouri hired Reese's firm for a November 1978 campaign to defeat a right-to-work bill. His team combined survey research with the PRIZM system to identity sympathetic and persuadable clusters that the campaign later targeted through advertising and direct mail.[80] The results, according to Robbin, led to a "stunning turnaround" and the bill's defeat.[81] To those on the ground, PRIZM was less decisive. Many corporate supporters of the bill did not campaign, while the AFL-CIO actively organized against it.[82] The firm's true impact is lost now, but Reese and Robbin used the win to evangelize their products. In effect, Claritas acted as a political prototype that was sold to subsequent campaigns. By 1980, Claritas was selling to both Republicans and Democrats and helped launch Matthew Reese's consultancy firm.[83]

Reese had called Claritas's PRIZM system "the new magic." Robbin borrowed the phrase as a title in the inaugural issue of *Campaigns & Elections* (figure 5.4). Robbin's article from 1980—as well as reporting by Warren Weaver, Jr., in *The New York Times*—helped popularize geodemographics and Claritas's work in politics.[84] Whether Claritas's geodemographics (or products from one of its competitors, like ACORN) worked as well as advertised was a hot topic in the pages of *Campaigns & Elections*. In its first four years, the magazine published four articles explicitly on geodemographics and helped to introduce the field to direct mail microtargeting.[85]

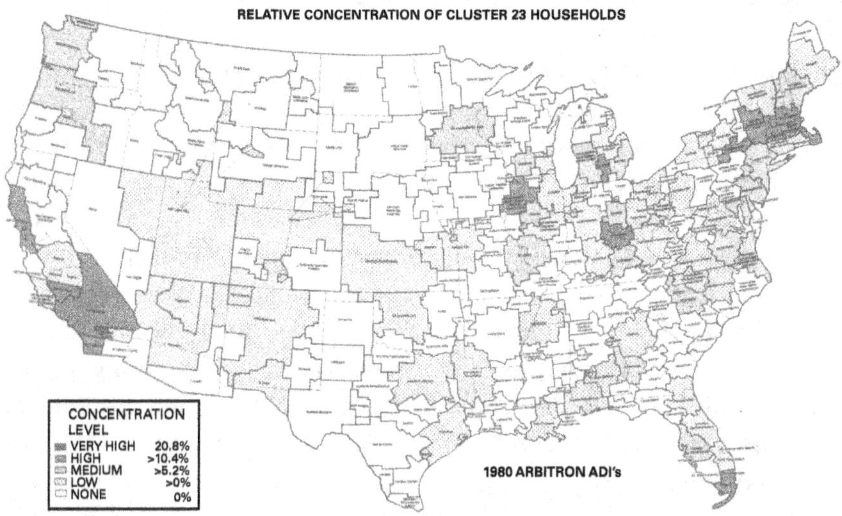

Figure 5.4
Example of Claritas clusters used in Jonathan Robbin's 1980 article for *Campaigns & Elections*. *Source*: *Campaigns & Elections*.

Claritas's influence on US politics waned even as its business grew internationally. Reese and his associates found that PRIZM worked better in business than politics. As Sasha Issenberg writes in his summary of Claritas's political influence, PRIZM's profile had to be rewritten to "invok[e] political behaviors, with terms like *conservative* and *swing voter*, and emphasized that the clusters would nonetheless be useful to campaigns, not necessarily for visualizing types of voters, but for locating them geographically."[86] In the end, few campaigns used the Targeting Systems product, but the electoral legacy of PRIZM matters less than its underlying voter model. Issenberg argued that some professionals believed that the marketing clusters mismatched voter political alignment. Claritas executives also considered politics a side business, especially because of the bad deal between Targeting Systems and Claritas.[87] And there was a deeper divide over perceptions of voters. Issenberg continues, "When pollsters tested the clusters, by looking at how members of different groups answer political questions, they realized that they didn't add much to the basic mix of precinct-based targeting and polling to find demographic splits. The arbitrary lines around ZIP codes had forced Claritas to effectively compromise when it tried to summarize an area's character, defining it only by its dominant lifestyle traits."[88] Claritas's compromise was necessary to ensure that its models could address voters, but this led to a different issue of probability, in which models overgeneralized (or underfit) their regions so that most, but not all, voters fit in a cluster. Political scientist Eitan Hersh came to a similar conclusion decades later. Simple data such as party registration and past donations performed better than the elaborate marketing data promised by microtargeting firms.[89]

Modern marketing depends on clustering. Michael J. Weiss capped off Claritas's growth in the 1980s by writing a book profiling their cluster approach. Released in 1988, the book begins with Weiss recounting his first meeting with Robbin in 1983, who by that time had become the "King of Zip codes." Intrigued by Robbin's "ingenious" methods, Weiss retells the story of America through the PRIZM system, offering deep profiles of the clusters along with journalistic interviews.[90] Seemingly baiting his earlier critics, Robbin claimed in the book, "Tell me someone's zip code, and I can predict what they eat, drink, drive—even think."[91] Weiss's eventual trilogy of books on clusters all proved to be best sellers, key to clusters becoming a mundane marketing tool.[92]

Derivatives of PRIZM remain in use. By the end of the 1980s, Claritas was even bigger, still offering the PRIZM system as well as a new data bank service. Robbin and Barton were gone; the company had been bought and sold and become part of a much more established geodemographics industry, within which Claritas had at least three major competitors.[93] As one major review of marketing innovations noted, "Most of the new technology was used during the 1960s and 1970s on an experimental, piecemeal basis. In the 1980s further advances in technology and the sharing of information allowed companies to begin to implement more sophisticated and integrated programs."[94] Even if Claritas eventually became a small part of the overall market, a company bought and sold, its innovation became central to modern marketing.

Claritas's PRIZM system encapsulates the second problem of addressability. The firm's ability to produce clusters exceeded its ability to match them to voters. Even numbers have limits. Clusters required careful work. Inside the company, the clusters themselves were hardly as neat as publicly presented. As Sam Barton explains about working on the 1980 census, "We found that how [Robbin] said it [worked], which is nice and beautiful with one shot, did not work that way. There is [*sic*] just shades of difference across the space. You need some sort of overlay algorithm to define what the cutoff points are, at that point you're working with the individual input variables." Like Simulmatics, Claritas's employees and programmers had to adjust the data to produce sharper definition between clusters.[95] They also had to be careful to limit the number of clusters produced. Technically, one could exceed forty clusters; there was no computational limit to the number of clusters beyond computer time and processing power. As David Miller, who worked extensively on the 1980 census for Claritas, explained, "You can't have [too many clusters] because you can never measure them accurately. Now if you had a million customers you *could* certainly put them into 500 segments and be happy, but most people don't have a database that is that robust, so you're always sampling. I can't justify going to more segments . . . because you can't measure anything worthwhile."[96] In short, multitudinous small clusters had too few people in them to be useful. As a result, the firm had to judiciously manage its clusters against the allure of ever-narrower targets. You cannot market to no one. The cluster endures as a key example of the limits of a data chimera and the challenges of closing the second addressability gap. The firm had to balance its ability to make any number of clusters with the need to ensure that campaigns could contact the voters. The resulting product offered a balance between precision and aggregation.

The Games of Politics: Closing the Gap between Programming and Behavior

The final addressability gap required a link between voter behavior and computational behavior. Games helped make this link. Through games, voters became understood as artificial intelligences you might find in a gap. The gap never closed entirely, and computational models never promised to completely describe complex human behavior, but computer logics became good enough to mimic voters. Campaigns came to rely on computational explanations of voter behavior as plausible through games.

Thinking of politics as a game wasn't a great leap. Politics is sometimes called "the great game." From pugilistic play-by-play coverage of debates to discussions of chess-like campaign strategies, games are a powerful metaphor for politics. The metaphor goes back a long time. *Baltimore Sun* reporter Frank Kent had a daily column, "The Great Game of Politics," from

1923 to 1942.[97] The W. S. Reed Toy Company published *The Game of Politics, or The Race For the Presidency* in 1887.[98] Games inspired Oswald Bates Lord to invent his *Game of Politics*, eventually published by Parker Brothers in 1935.[99] In it, players race around a map of the United States picking up votes. The metaphor of games changed how people thought about politics. Sociologist Erving Goffman described games as "world-building activities."[100] But games became more than mere metaphors in the political sphere: By the mid-1960s, games had become popular tools in the US military and intelligence communities.[101] Just as federal defense funding subsidized political games, the Department of Housing and Urban Development funded municipal games.[102] Games were popular, too, as historian Jennifer S. Light notes on parallel efforts in urban design: "Easy to use and fun to play, urban simulation games exploded in popularity in the second half of the 1960s."[103] Games functioned as both model and prototype, teaching theories of how politics worked.

Games contributed to the growing popularity of computational models of voter behavior. Early political simulation games functioned as prototypes for rational choice modeling. High school students and defense intellectuals alike played games to simulate situations as varied as racial conflict and urban planning. Some of these "serious games"—to borrow a phrase coined by defense contractor and game designer Clark Abt—put rational choice theories in play.[104] These games, Light writes, were "not a 'first draft' toward computing simulation. Instead, they were scientific instruments on equal ground with other [simulations]."[105]

Games were largely computational prototypes of the rational agent model. Gaming, as discussed earlier, was closely related to computing. As with the previous two cases, political gaming found its way into *Campaigns & Elections*, which even published its own game. I begin this history with a discussion of how members of the Simulmatics group and influential sociologist James S. Coleman turned to games to begin to explore political behavior.

Democracy, Where Voters Play Themselves

James S. Coleman was a major figure in postwar sociology. He is best known for a 1966 coauthored report, commonly called the "Coleman Report," about US education outcomes. At the same time, Coleman was one of the first scholars to focus on games, a line of his research that has received less recognition compared to his other work.[106] Coleman attempted to sell his expertise in games to colleagues at the Simulmatics Corporation alongside his friend William McPhee. An early brochure for the company advertised its collaboration with Coleman's Academic Game Associates.

Coleman's games had a curious relationship to game theory. Game theory modeled the behavior of people as rational players of games. As discussed in the last chapter, Anthony Downs's seminal 1957 book *An Economy Theory of Democracy* considered humans to act like computers, a parallel that came to be more plausible as computers entered professional life. Downs's work, in short, applied game theory to politics. Coleman picked up the thread and used games to teach game theory. A game was, for Coleman, "a kind of caricature of social life. It is a magnification of some aspect of social interaction, excluding all else, tearing this aspect of social interaction from its social context and giving it a special context of its own."[107] Making games provided Coleman a chance to test his theories in the real world and to observe his caricatures in play. Throughout his career during the 1960s, Coleman advocated for the use of games, as is demonstrated in a 1966 special issue of the *American Behavioral Scientist* for which he wrote "In Defense of Games." The effect was not only to teach players how to behave like rational agents but to create a commensurability between computational play and voter behavior. In my interpretation, his work then represents a particular strand of game theory, certainly inspired by Oskar Morgenstern and John von Neumann, but also distinct in its commitment to individual rational action in everyday settings.[108]

Coleman's interest in game design grew out of his educational work. In 1961, Coleman found himself working as a sociologist in an educational setting, in Baltimore-area high schools near his academic home at Johns Hopkins University.[109] The Carnegie Corporation supported what became known as the Johns Hopkins Games Program, one of the first of its kind. The program studied group dynamics, developed computer-assisted research, and made games. Academic Games Associates grew out of these experiments in 1965.[110] The company partnered with Western Publishing in the mid-1960s to release a series of simulation games including *Consumer*, *Economic System*, *Life Career*, *Generation Gap*, the better-known *Ghetto*, and, most important for this book's purposes, *Democracy: The Workings of the Legislative Process*.

Released in 1966, Coleman's *Democracy* was one of the first games about politics ever published. Most contemporary political games were either trivia games or competitors to *Monopoly* or *Risk*. By contrast, *Democracy* was designed to teach players about the workings of government, making it an early entry in the category of educational games. *Democracy* was really eight games, consisting of four variations on two core simulations of a government legislature and a citizens' action meeting. The game lacked a board or any pieces; its box was no bigger than the legal papers it held. Inside the box were cards and a few rulebooks. The simulation happened through a mix of role-playing and calculation. For the legislative game, six to eleven players or teams were dealt cards that described the make-up of their simulated legislator's constituency. The constituents could be for or against eight national issues, such as "federal aid to education," "medicare for the aged," a "defense appropriation bill," or "civil rights moving faster." Players first had to "compute and fill in" their constituency's preferences. Over the game's nine steps, players moved from learning about their constituency to bargaining for and eventually passing a vote on issues before again calculating how well constituents scored. In the second simulation, the citizens' action meeting, "each player [took] a role of an individual citizen" and play continued in a similar manner as in the legislative simulation. This time, players received cards that defined issues important to them and their home region and then negotiated with other players about how to pass resolutions. A successful strategy in both games involved a calculus of sorts, finding deals that prioritized their issues over all else.

Democracy was available to the public, to the best of my knowledge, but found its greatest audience in educational settings. Earlier versions were played at the 4-H Club's national conference (with over 1,200 attendees), and various versions were played in Baltimore schools.[111] Academic Games Associates attracted press attention and became part of the adoption of games in school curricula.[112] The Simulmatics Corporation, to which Coleman was still affiliated, advertised its specialty in making game simulations and even funded game development internally.

Democracy introduced students to rational choice theory. It should be considered a kind of persuasive game, what Ian Bogost describes as "the art of persuasion through rule-based representations and interactions rather than the spoken word, writing, images, or moving pictures."[113] Though Bogost is describing video games, Coleman was teaching rational agents through rule-based representations and interactions worked out with paper and pencil. *Democracy* prototyped politics in a way not unlike William Shaffer's voter simulations discussed earlier. The playfulness of games helped them function as prototypes—inviting players into what game scholars describe as the "magic circle" of play and to imagine what a world would be like if they were rational, deliberate decision-makers. Making individualistic play a distinct thread in the game was intentional on Coleman's part.

Coleman's approach to gaming developed alongside his work on rational theory, and he cited his work on gaming as a motivation to further and explore purposive theories of society. Just as Coleman was writing about computers being able to simulate humans as rational agents, he was also making games where humans played themselves as rational agents. As he later wrote, "It is hardly conceivable, then, that the theoretical framework implied by a social simulation game be anything other than a purposive behavior theory." The emphasis on rational agents was especially palpable for the game's players, where "each legislator is assumed to be motivated solely to stay in office; and it is assumed that the sole factor affecting his tenure is his success in passing those bills of most interest to his constituents."[114] Players, as discussed above, were given a sheet of paper enumerating their constituents' desires, or what might be called their goals or motivations. Coleman's pretend legislator was essentially another computer, looking at the positions of its peers to find enough votes to win reelection (by getting a positive score).

Negotiation was principally an act of calculation because the players had close to perfect information about themselves and looked to other players to further their agendas. Even though the game encouraged lying and bargaining for role-play, a certain Cold War rationality haunted the game, in which there seemed always to be an optimal move based on a role's clear goals. Moreover, the issues themselves mattered little, and players had no incentive or any provisions in the game itself to deliberate or discuss the merits of civil rights or Medicare. Instead, voters and their preferences became strategic resources to be traded between players, amid the threat of betrayal, like in the Prisoner's Dilemma.[115] As one later commentator wrote of Coleman's work, "Simulation games provide particularly good illustrations of implications and predictions of rational choice theory because players are assigned motivations and can be expected to try to make choices that are consistent with their assigned motivations."[116]

Coleman designed games to build worlds inspired by or aspiring to be rational agents, but the results were mixed. Students did learn through the games, but the exact educational impacts were unclear.[117] One study found that playing the game did not have a measurable effect on students' interest in politics.[118] Prominent sociologist and fellow game designer William Gamson argued that the game's model implicitly taught a faith in the "invisible hand of the voting marketplace" but did not explain the underlying political significance of the model well.[119] The game did not work well either. Some political issues were out of date and others strangely irrelevant. The game design let civil rights or defense become only a matter of the player's reelection odds. Reflecting on play tests, Gamson found "it difficult to gain the degree of involvement necessary to make the game go . . . [the game] struck [students] as high schoolish and not very chic, and they frequently played carelessly and quite poorly."[120] The ambiguity of the results was part of the fun for Coleman, as he relished "the opportunity to learn about social organization by forming a caricature of such organization and then observing this caricature."[121]

Coleman did not invent political games, but he put them forward as prototypes of rational agents to explain, as *Democracy*'s subtitle claims, "the workings of the legislative process." The consequences were threefold. First, Coleman popularized games as educational and explanatory tools beyond the inner echelons of the academic-military-industrial complex. Second, games became another kind of programmed simulation, which further blurred offline and online worlds. Third, Coleman emphasized a particular rational agent model of gaming. Far beyond game theory's use of tic-tac-toe or chicken, Coleman created complex, multiuser games where players functioned as rational agents, all while imagining political worlds filled with other rational agents. By suggesting that games could simulate politics using rational agent models, Coleman started to link rules and voters—an addressability that only strengthened as more games promised to simulate political campaigns and legislatures.

Coleman's game was part of a moment of experimentation where political scientists turned to games to explain how politics worked.[122] *New Alexandria* was one such game. Designed by Donald Jansiewicz to teach politics to university students, *New Alexandria* cited Coleman and Abt's *Serious Games* as inspiration. Political scientist William Coplin, who I discuss extensively later, praised the game, calling it "one of the clearest presentations of simulation material I have ever seen."[123] Play emphasized decision-making, bargaining, and coalition-building as students played key roles such as New

Alexandria state legislator or newspaper editor. *New Alexandria*, although now largely forgotten, illustrates the wider impact of Coleman and contemporaries like Abt in popularizing the game as a teaching tool.[124]

Games broke down the distinction between voter behavior and what could be programmed into an early personal computer. Games were part of an early industry of educational computing software that sold simulations for use in the classroom. National Collegiate Software, part of this wave, was a self-described clearinghouse of liberal arts software started in 1989. Modest in its success—in its first three years the firm sold just 9,064 units, including 660 political science units—its 1990 catalog listed a computer-based version of Harold Guetzkow's ARPA-funded international simulation, the Inter-Nation Simulation, along with the game *Presidential Campaign!* These examples, even if of limited success, demonstrate the common idea that games, and later computer games, could teach how politics worked and, in so doing, encouraged voters to think like computer programs.

Games also affected campaign craft. Though barely remembered, *On the Campaign Trail*, published by *Campaigns & Elections*, was perhaps the first serious election simulation aimed not at students or gamers but at campaign professionals. Dr. Murray Fishel served on the magazine's editorial board and had run national campaign schools for years at Kent State University. Along with David Gopoian and J. Michael Stacey, Fishel created *On the Campaign Trail* in 1987. The simulation pulled together different voter models to create a simulation with which to train campaign managers—or that was the hope. After one event when Fishel ran a simulation that was realistic enough, the magazine's staff decided to publish the game.

On the Campaign Trail simulated a senate race in the fictional state of Tarragon. Real data were behind the fake state. Fishel chose the name Tarragon to avoid overt political associations. The name was abstract, but its population was based on 1984 election survey data from the University of Michigan's Center for Political Studies. In the game, counties consisted of aggregates of like-minded voters, a result of clustering this survey data. County names implied their dispositions. The manual explains: "Each county in Tarragon is composed, then, of different types of voters. Tweed County in the northwest corner of the state is heavily Democratic, tends to be blue collar, and has a large black population. Coors County and Schlafly County tend to be overwhelmingly Republican and conservative. Gantry County and Humbard County are located in Tarragon's 'Bible Belt.' Zapata

County, comprised largely of McAllen, Tex., CPS respondents, has a large Hispanic population."[125] The counties' names might have been less colorful than some of the labels used by the Claritas Corporation, but they functioned similarly as a form of clustering.

Two teams competed against each other to identify and mobilize Tarragon's voters. Turns focused as much on collecting data as moving the candidate through their campaign. Players could commission surveys and poll the model electorate, the results of which helped players select media buys, arrange candidate appearances, and target direct mail. Limited time and money required players to strategize. One run in an upper-year political science class lasted six weeks and required a meeting room next to the computer lab for teams to talk through their strategies.[126] As much as these strategies might have tried to change the minds of virtual voters, the simulation left little to persuasion. Voters were programmed as rational agents set in their ways, not cybernetic citizens.

On the Campaign Trail programmed its voters to be rational, or as rational as theory allowed. The manual cites Anthony Downs's economic democratic theory as one of its two key influences and describes a series of calculations the voter makes to eventually decide whether to vote. The manual stresses that voter "attitudes on specific issues will not change across the span of the simulation. The key to winning the election, then, is not to change the minds of voters about their positions on specific issues, but rather to appeal to voters' values and issue predispositions with greater success than the opposing candidate."[127] Seeming to validate claims that voters are static and unpersuadable, the simulation, instead, tested players on whether their performance scored highly enough to warrant a vote.[128] The manual explained that "voters generally vote for the candidates they like the most. Voters add up their likes and dislikes for all the candidates and vote for the one with the highest net approval rating."[129] Winning the game was a matter of computation: Did the player's efforts add up enough to earn a voter's approval, and did enough voters add up to a victory?

These details might seem mundane, but the matter-of-fact presentation and simple explanations show that the simulation did not consider itself to be making controversial claims about voter behavior. If anything, the voter was assumed to be a rational agent, and the manual merely justified the simulation's sources. Nor did the game's reception call into question its central assumption of simulating a state; one review characterized it as "an authentic political experience."[130] Another praised *On the Campaign Trail* as "the most sophisticated campaign simulation I have seen."[131] These reviews, all positive, matched *Campaign & Elections* enthusiastic support of the game. Advertisements appeared frequently in its issues, and Ron Faucheux praised the game in the manual's foreword. For a time, *On the Campaign Trail* was seen as the best simulation around, and it remains unmatched in bringing together academics and professionals.

Q2. How Do Computer Simulations Address Voters?

Databases, microtargeting, and games all tried to narrow addressability gaps. All these efforts refined the careful ways that computer simulations had to address external realities. Having articulated the ways that addressability gaps informed the development of early computing in campaigns and how models of American voters found practical application, I conclude by showing how these early facets of the computational imaginary of politics continues to face similar challenges ensuring the link between real and simulated voters.

Addressability is a defining advantage in the modern computational imaginary. Ensuring that a simulation matches its reality might seem intuitive, but as we have seen, the reflexivity between the two means that addressability is a matter of calibration. Effect calibration can be a political advantage. We can trace this advantage by briefly reviewing Republican efforts in election redistricting. Beginning in the 1980s, a series of court victories allowed Republicans to justify their partisan redistricting methods as well as their investment in new computer technologies. A coalition arose, at least outwardly, between advocates for Black voters and Republicans that redrew the political map. New districts were designed to assemble Black and other minority voter majorities, ensuring victories for their representatives, but at the cost of allowing outlying districts to become safe Republican seats. Managing these efforts became a key service offered by Republican consulting firms.

This uneasy tradeoff ended in the 2010s when Republicans refined manipulation of the redistricting process to ensure stable majorities for the GOP without conceding significant ground to the Democrats. The party's REDMAP program "packed" clusters of Democratic voters into a few districts and "cracked" the rest into others by combining census data, voter records, and other demographic information and by using the popular mapping tool Maptitude. By dispersing Democratic voters into districts with more stable Republican voters, the REDMAP program, as the name unsubtly reveals, sought to turn the electoral map fully red, often deliberately working to suppress Black voters' influence.[132] Republican control of redistricting is a key element of political insider David Pepper's indictment of state-level democracy as "laboratories of autocracy."[133] Pepper's account of the undermining of democratic norms in Ohio is a reminder of how addressability is key to modern political success. Addressability demands voter data to be imaginative yet locative. REDMAP could create more and more elaborate stable seats for Republican thanks to its Maptitude tool that matched state geography, but the imaginative function of redistricting only worked because the system could ensure that its computational imagination was calibrated to eventual voter behavior.

Online advertising today makes a similar promise to ensure new types of voters that remain addressable. The microtargeting that Claritas popularized has had a second life in online political advertising. Facebook owner Meta's advertising division, for example, emphasizes its ability to reach certain voters based on location, demographics, and interests as well as behaviors deduced through purchase and device usage data. Facebook, in other words, aggregates enough data to compose new geo-behavioral-demographics, a hallmark of online advertising.[134] That these composites are seen to offer truer insight into voters—compared to more enduring classifications such as race, class, gender, or party—is reminiscent of the enthusiasm for Claritas's PRIZM and its promise to paint a new picture of America. Computers, in my opinion, do not simulate voters; they compose them with enough detail and data to be predictive without requiring a deeper explanation. But proponents of data chimeras believe that computers compose voters with enough detail to predict behavior.

That the effectiveness of online advertising is almost certainly overstated further justifies the continued relevance of addressability. Tim Hwang points out that online microtargeting systems remain popular because the dashboards and metrics look good; he writes, "It makes for great theatre."[135] That the results do not work hardly seems to matter, as simulation offers enough verisimilitude to appear like interacting with reality. Not unlike critics of Simulmatics or Claritas, contemporary critiques of online advertising suggest that the data are inaccurate, targeting is ineffective, and ads lead to no real behavioral change.[136] The promise, however, that online advertising can reach and even persuade the right people has had powerful and enduring effects on contemporary elections.[137] Their legitimacy relies on this computational imaginary and the promise of cybernetic citizens and data chimeras corresponding with actual voters.

Addressability has empowered Meta to provide compelling new accounts of voters that also mask significant biases. As Kelley Cotter, Mel Medeiros, Chankyung Pak, and Kjerstin Thorson write, "We must continue to unpack the complicated politics that underlie the significance of 'right' in Facebook's promise to help advertisers 'reach the right people.'"[138] Meta's targeting lacks categories "addressing interests of POC, women, [and] LGBTQ+ people," but these political identities seem to matter less than Meta's expansive capacity of making up new groups that correspond to commercial markets.[139] Computer simulation has a power to create new biases through the production of new plausible groups in lieu of others, a kind of data-driven nonknowledge. But what has been the reach of these new abilities to make up people?

Claritas's geodemographics proved formative to debates about microtargeting. With its higher profile, the Claritas Corporation became the go-to target for a critical press worried about microtargeting's threats to personal privacy and individual liberty. Writing for *ComputerWorld*, Marguerite Zientara covered a panel on political technology where the Claritas system was identified as a risk to democracy because campaigns might exclude or ignore voters deemed unpersuadable. In 1983, investigative journalist David Burnham warned about the problem with Claritas: "Common to all systematic targeting programs, is that they tend to encourage individual candidates or special interest groups . . . to systematically exclude voters who live in areas where the polls have determined there are a relatively large proportion of people who will not go to the polls. From the point of view of the individual candidate or group with a limited budget, of course, the process of concentrating all propaganda efforts on those who are favorably disposed or persuadable makes eminent sense."[140] Claritas, in short, shaped worries that data-driven campaigning might undermine politics by allowing politicians to exclude, ignore, or as Burnham writes elsewhere, cater the message to the audiences. Similarly, foundational surveillance studies scholar Oscar Gandy Jr. cited Claritas when characterizing his concept of the panoptic sort—that is, the collection of personal information for the purpose of discrimination and categorization.[141]

These early worries about microtargeting have cast a long shadow, letting addressability be seen as a risk to individual privacy. Reflecting on this decades later, Gandy noted that "much of the scholarly work on privacy and surveillance has been focused on risks faced by individuals" while there remains a need to develop "strategies for pursuing social and legally protected status for these [algorithmically identified] groups."[142] Indeed, Cotter, Medeiros, Pak, and Thorson warn that today's algorithmic classification has a flattening effect: "when issues and identities are collapsed into a broad higher-level category, or when multiple intersecting dimensions of issues or identities are reduced to a single dimension."[143] Claritas's cluster systems functioned identically, taking an intersectional identity and distilling it into one category. Even if Robbin and the firm sold detailed profiles of each voter, the function of clusters in targeting tended to lead to a binary decision to address or not address certain voters. The legacy of these issues remains the framing of privacy as an individual concern—a matter of being tricked or exposed—rather than extending this critique to see data chimeras as a collective harm and potential means of algorithmic discrimination.

As a close to the book's first part, we can easily find examples of these early efforts to simulate voters in the technologies and rhetoric of modern campaigning. Blue State Digital (BSD), a leading digital political strategy firm, asked in a 2018 blog, "What Can AI Teach Brands About Customer-Centric Marketing?" The question was not just rhetorical; Blue State Digital had the answer. In the post, Blue State announced a partnership with AI startup Tanjo, explaining that "AI is all around us, creating breakthrough innovations for companies and consumers alike." "Alike" is an apt way to describe the benefits of the technology. Tanjo uses AI, or what it calls Tanjo's Automated Persona (TAP), to behave *like* humans. Whereas message-testing usually requires real people, Tanjo creates audiences on demand. The TAPs, Blue State Digital continues, simulate "humans' distinct personalities and unique interests" to "predict how they'll react to content." Blue State Digital explains that the personas are "based on data. This data can include solely what is publicly available, such as economic purchase data, electoral rolls, and market segmentations, or it can also include an organization's own anonymized customer data, housed within their own technical environment."[144]

When last I checked, for only $750, anyone could buy their own "simulated customers." The service is the result of the work of the "world's foremost economists and behavioral scientists to augment the persona models created by our machine learning system from streams of data exhaust." Their sales pitch ends, curiously, with a quote attributed to Italian author Italo Calvino: "Electronic brains, even if they are still far from producing . . . the human brain, are nonetheless capable of providing us with a convincing theoretical model for the most complex processes of our memory, our mental associations, our imaginations."[145]

TAPs by this measure are not just cheaper, but more truthful. Blue State continues, "*There is a marked difference between what people say and what they do*. Therefore, persona models created from strong historical data can actually be superior in their predictions to models based on questionnaires." Blue State is implicitly claiming that behavioral data, rather than opinion or commentary, offer a truer predictor of voter response to messaging. Pushing back against "dystopian" arguments about AI, Blue State ends on a hopeful note: "Rather than being a dehumanising force, AI lets organizations get closer to their audiences." These promises seem quaint compared to more recent agentic AIs and campaign chatbots.

This chapter offers historical context to these "breakthrough innovations." The efforts to model voter agencies and close addressability gaps are a prehistory to Tanjo's Automated Persona. If customers are reduced to data, and behave like computers, then why not use a simple substitution of a computer for a voter? TAPs, however, are not pure abstraction but rather an example of the promise of voter addressability, such that they can be simulated to correspond with targetable, actual voters. Cybernetic citizens, rational agents, and data chimeras became theories of voters worked out through databases, microtargeting, and games. TAPs are the opposite of the "hyperreal," or a simulation without a referent; rather, they reflect the careful work done to ensure that computational abstractions could be practical still.

Computer simulations, however, were developed to solve international political problems as well as domestic ones. Keeping national and international efforts in parallel is important to understand the scope and scale of this book's models, prototypes, and imaginaries. Applications and funders clearly differed at the international level. Political parties do not worry about foreign voters. Now the State Department and the intelligence agencies got involved, and winning involved nuclear war, not an election. The stakes, during the Cold War, could not have been higher. SimVoters turned into SimWorlds. The next part of the book explores how the computational imaginary of politics encompassed worlds as well as voters.

II SimWorlds

6 Make-Believe on Mathematical Principles

"Make-believe on mathematical principles" was one definition of simulation offered by the editors of *Harper's* magazine in Thomas B. Morgan's 1961 profile of the Simulmatics Corporation.[1] A favorable piece (a bias that required the magazine to disclose Morgan's relationship with the firm in a later issue), the article's prognostications about simulation's potential for politics addressed international politics as much as domestic. These machines or, broadly, simulations sought to convert world politics into computer programs to analyze war, international relations, and especially, the risk of nuclear conflict. These programs were intended to fill a perceived need for better intelligence across US government services and the armed forces. Computer simulation promised a chance to test new theories of world politics, setting into motion claims about Soviet aggression or national stability.

Just as campaign strategists built computer simulations of voters, their contemporaries built simulations of worlds. Morgan's profile of Simulmatics featured Harold Lasswell, who equated the machine with the future of open societies. Lasswell, to recap, served on the advisory board of Simulmatics and helped cultivate the behavioral mood in political science. His interest in computing extended beyond Simulmatics' electoral successes to world politics. In 1960, Lasswell published an article on *decision seminars* that looked to computers and simulations as means to advance the policy sciences.[2] Like Lasswell, Simulmatics' Ithiel de Sola Pool also sought to use computer simulation in world affairs. Both were part of a movement to model world politics with computer prototypes, as was Oliver Benson, a political scientist at the University of Oklahoma. Benson, though not a self-described member of the new political science, cited Lasswell's new work on decision seminars.[3]

Benson introduced his own experiment in simulating world politics using the *Harper's* definition, citing it in his remarks at a 1962 political science conference.[4] He hoped a little "make-believe" could help the field of international relations. What Benson proposed was a simple diplomatic game—a computer game, or at least what we would now call a computer game. Making a computer game built on the long history of political simulation and war-gaming. Analog simulations prefigured digital ones, a small jump from programming with pen and paper to punch cards.[5]

Benson first proposed the game in 1958, the same year American physicist William Higinbotham programmed a precursor to *Pong* to play on his institute's oscilloscope and one year after McPhee's Campaign Simulator. Benson's game might then be the first of what could be called "serious games" for the computer. As he wrote in his initial description of the project, "Much talk has occurred in recent years by international relations students about the possible application to their field of large modern computers, but little actual work has been done to explore such possibilities."[6] Benson explained that his game was "a pattern for testing general subjective statements about the international behavior of states."[7] He had encoded his diplomatic wisdom onto punch cards that fed into an IBM machine, a process Benson admitted was "stylized and somewhat arbitrary."[8]

Benson had previously written about foreign policy, not computer systems. A diplomacy scholar might seem like an odd reader for a profile of Simulmatics, but by 1958 Benson was one of many scholars influenced by and indebted to the RAND Corporation's research and sponsorship. Since its start in 1948, the RAND Corporation had invested in new ways to model politics with games and simulations in both its mathematical and social science divisions. The RAND Corporation popularized mathematical games for politics as well as new forms of expert prediction like its DELPHI method.[9] The desire to "scientifically" predict world politics predates even these efforts, including back to the work of weather forecaster turned war forecaster Lewis Fry Richardson. By 1935, Richardson had begun developing influential formulas to predict the likelihood of war.[10] Many in the field followed Richardson, both in his scientific attempts and his pacifism.

For those accustomed to modern computers, playing Benson's game requires some imagination. He played the game on the same IBM 650 model as William McPhee's Campaign Simulator, interacting with the machine's printer and punch card reader. When running, the game printed out a prompt: "SPECIFY ACTOR, THEN SPECIFY TARGET." Behind the printout, the game calculated a system of relations between the United States, the United Kingdom, the USSR, West Germany, France, Italy, India, China, and Japan—the major powers according to Benson. Each country differed. The United Kingdom, the United States, and the USSR had access to nuclear weapons, giving them a much higher power index than the other six. Each country could be in an alliance that the game used to calculate the state of the world—balance of power, loose bipolar, or tight bipolar—which changed when the player loaded a new card. Players could pit these powers against each other by acting on "tension areas," which consisted of nine other nations: "Korea, Guatemala, Egypt, Lebanon, Hungary, Vietnam, Taiwan, Cuba, and the Congo."[11] Some of these places reflected recent conflicts, such as the Korean War, which ended in 1953, and the Second Arab–Israeli War, or the Tripartite Aggression, which took place in 1956.

Even though he thought the game offered "limited conclusions," Benson proved to have some power of prediction.[12] The United States invaded Cuba in 1961, and the Vietnam War escalated with a ground invasion in 1965. Players could simulate these events. For example, players could calculate the effect of US mobilization movements in Vietnam by entering the card "0000000001 0000000700 0000000006 STOCH COMP."[13] The command printed out "USA MOBZN VIETN" to validate the input, and then the program looped, recalculating the world state. Players could vary the aggressiveness of their commands from "Diplomatic Protest," abbreviated as KICKS, to all-out war, abbreviated as the grim HBOMB. Benson found that the game tended toward a more polarized world, while others remarked that the game tended to overheat into nuclear war.[14]

Playing the world as a game might have seemed a novelty to Benson's students, and even to Benson himself. He never treated it as more than an experiment, turning more to computational methods than serious simulations in his subsequent work, and he worried that students did not take the game seriously. They preferred to compete rather than simulate, he noted in a comment, foreshadowing how human lives become just another variable in world simulations.[15]

Others continued where he did not. His game represents the curious beginnings of computer simulation's introduction into world politics. Benson's Simple Diplomatic Game might have been the first model world on a computer, but its version of make-believe became ever so real for international relations. Computer simulation, first, emerged as part of a wider discussion about how to simulate world politics. Gaming and computer simulation acted as a trading zone for different disciplines, fields, and theoretical approaches.[16] Games came from economics, political science, the military, and even the American counterculture.[17] One way or another, these efforts connected with Benson's colleague Harold Guetzkow, a political scientist at Northwestern University. Guetzkow's own experiences in the trading zone, so to speak, offer a chance to understand the wider context of Benson's game and the different efforts to prototype world politics at the time.

Inside the Fortress of Technologies: Key Terms for the Computational Trading Zone

The headquarters of IBM Research was only three years old when the company gathered leading experts in computing for its Scientific Computing Symposium on Simulation Models and Gaming. Described by its architect, Eero Saarinen, as a "fortress of technology," the building's late modernist exterior matched the research inside.[18] Behind a smooth thousand-foot curved-glass facade, over three days in December 1964, researchers explored everything from the possibilities of computer simulation for business to new theories of the mind. Participants tried to reflect the complexity of the world in computer models. Experts from across industry, academia, and the defense sector joined to discuss the use of computer models in solving social and economic problems. The conference played host to a mix of approaches to thinking with or around games and simulation. Participants included systems thinkers, such as Jay Forrester and Herbert Simon, as well as cocreator of game theory Oskar Morgenstern and economist and gaming advocate Martin Shubik. Hailing from well beyond the social sciences, participants also included corporate executives and system engineers. Beyond corporate America, attendees came from the RAND Corporation, the US Naval Research Laboratory, defense contractor Raytheon, various Air Force bases, and the Pentagon's War Games Support Division. Topics varied too. Presentations showed off attempts to model the mind, organizations, the business lifecycle, and the transportation system through computers or through schematized play. World affairs was just one of the problems to be tackled.[19]

Harold Guetzkow was an odd person to find in this mix. A conscientious objector during World War II, Guetzkow eventually made peace with the military-industrial-academic complex. He perceived computer modeling as a way to avoid nuclear war. His presence at the symposium speaks to his influence as an early advocate of simulation in international relations and his role in trading between that field and the patrons of early computer research. Guetzkow acknowledged the support of the Department of Defense, the Air Force Office of Scientific Research, the Naval Ordnance Test Station, the Carnegie Corporation, and the Advanced Projects Research Agency in his paper published in the symposium's proceedings.

Guetzkow made an odd representative for political science too because he was a psychologist by training. The move from his home field to political science was a "rocky" one, he noted in a biographical essay. "Even such friends as Ithiel Pool were unable to help me relocate in an international relations program," Guetzkow admitted.[20] But like his other friend, Herbert Simon, Guetzkow did successfully change fields, and by 1957 he held a position in political science at Northwestern University, where he did his most important work. Though now a recognized political scientist, Guetzkow's writing as well as reflections from his peers indicate his muted engagement with political theory. Throughout his career, he came across as more methodologist than theorist, thereby advancing a behavioralist approach in international relations.[21] His apolitical application of computing to politics, or perhaps his emphasis on objective methods over political theory, set the field on a particular path in computer simulation.

Guetzkow had ambitions for the field. He explained that his research tried to innovate in the "backwards field" of international relations.[22] As he put it, "paradoxically, the central reason for using simulation in International Relations is this lack of development in politics as scholarly discipline."[23] His comments reflect the behavioral mood that had set in the field, echoing Robert Dahl's description of the field of political science.[24] Scholars like David Easton, Anatol Rapport, Morton Kaplan, Charles McClelland, and Karl Deutsch—to name the most relevant scholars to come—had settled into turning the study of world politics into a more scientific endeavor. Easton, in his definitive 1954 book *The Political System*, critiqued a turn toward explaining politics as culture or tradition; he wrote, "There is a manifest tendency to turn away from reason to emotion and tradition. In the social sciences this has been associated with the tendency to deny the fruitfulness of searching for universally valid general knowledge."[25] He believed that any system could be researched; his successors thought it could be modeled.

At the symposium, Guetzkow offered a necessary summary of the types of simulations that had developed alongside and after Benson. Guetzkow distinguished three approaches to what I call prototyping: all-human *exercises*, all-machine *simulations*, and human-machine (or "man-machine" in his terms) *games*.[26] Whereas previous chapters considered the models that led to computer prototypes, my reading of Guetzkow emphasizes the different formats for prototyping made possible with or adjacent to computers.[27] Combining his examples with my own, table 6.1 lists key games created in the US social sciences prior to the symposium and illustrates their diverse applications at the symposium and beyond. As I discuss, games at the time could refer to student classroom activities, computer programs like Benson's Simple Diplomatic Game, or experiments in mixing the two. Gaming also included planning at the highest levels for the Vietnam War.

All his life afterward, Harold Guetzkow sought to unite "islands of theory" in international relations and integrate different approaches into a generalized system.[28] His observation demonstrates the great differences, even conflict, in computer simulation. Global modeling developed in isolated silos drawing variously from game theory, cybernetics, system dynamics, decision theory, realist international relations, and early data science. Guetzkow never got his wish, but his work helps to show how the models became divided.

Exercises: Humans and Role-Play

Exercises referred to simulations involving only humans. The name likely referenced the RAND Corporation's penchant for the word. Exercises were one of RAND's "soft" approaches to modeling, prediction, and war strategy along with the forecasting experiments later known as DELPHI.[29] Exercises were developed at the Social Science Division of the RAND Corporation under the leadership of Hans Spier and set against the more mathematical games created elsewhere at RAND.[30] As historian Sharon Ghamari-Tabrizi argues, "Disgruntled with the simple fabrications of the mathematics games, Herbert Goldhamer of the Social Science Division suggested that a war game should instead reproduce the ferment and disorder of history."[31] Goldhamer himself notes highly formalized, quantitative war games were "abandoned when it became clear that the simplification imposed in order to permit quantification made the game of doubtful value for the assessment of political strategies and tactics in the real world."[32] Instead, exercises

Table 6.1
Games, simulations, and exercises

Name	Started	Application	Kind	Developer
Model UN	1927	Politics	Exercise	
Political-Military Exercise/ Cold War Game	1955	Politics	Exercise	RAND Corporation, MIT
Monopologs	1955	Management	Exercise	RAND Corporation
Inter-nation Simulation	1956	Politics	Game	Northwestern University
Executive Decision-Making Program	1956	Management	Game	American Management Association
UCLA Executive Decision Game	~1957	Business	Game	UCLA
Top Management Decision Game	1957	Business	Unknown	University of Washington
Management Decision-making Laboratory	~1958	Business	Game	IBM
Carnegie Tech Management Game	~1958	Business	Game	Carnegie Institute of Technology
Dynamo / System Dynamics	~1958	Business	Simulation	MIT
A Base Logistics Management Game (Baselogs)	1958	Management	Exercise	RAND Corporation
Simple Diplomatic Game	1958	Politics	Simulation	University of Oklahoma
A Game of Missile Logistics (Misslogs)	1959	Management	Exercise	RAND Corporation
Technological, Economic, Military and Political Evaluation Routine (TEMPER)	1960	Politics	Simulation	Joint War Games Agency/Raytheon Corporation
SIGMA Games	~1962	War	Exercise	Joint War Games Agency
The Free Enterprise Game	~1964	Education/ economics	Game	Board of Cooperative Educational Services, New York
The Sumerian Game	1964	Education/ economics	Game	Board of Cooperative Educational Services, New York
The Sierra Leone Game	1964	Education/ economics	Game	Board of Cooperative Educational Services, New York

encouraged open-mindedness, creative solutions, and speculation. Work on these exercises began in the mid-1950s. Proponents argued that exercises encouraged open-ended play, while critics disliked the lack of control.

RAND's method had spread well beyond the corporation by the time of Guetzkow's presentation at IBM. RAND's "political exercises" inspired Guetzkow and others. Subsequent exercises building on RAND's exercises with MIT's Center for International Studies led Lincoln Bloomfield to develop the Political-Military Exercise.[33] The approach partially built on the traditions of war-gaming. At the time of Guetzkow's presentation, many of the war gaming efforts were coordinated by the Joint War Games Control Group created by the Joint Chiefs of Staff in 1961, later known as the Joint War Games Agency (JWGA). By 1962, the group was running game exercises and advising Kennedy's Vietnam strategy.[34]

Exercises also had many nonmilitary applications. Indeed, not all games at RAND were focused on nuclear war. MONOPLOGS simulated the Air Force Supply System, an application of gaming that mirrored developments in American management science.[35] Several management exercises, though not mentioned by Guetzkow, had been developed postwar as well. By 1962, US business schools used a total of twenty-nine exercise-like activities.[36] The 1959 book *Dynamic Management Decision Games, Including Seven Noncomputer Games* includes just that: games to teach management of inventory, personnel, retail, production, sales, scheduling, operations, and negotiations.[37] Exercises were also influential in US defense strategy at the time of Guetzkow's presentation. Curiously, Guetzkow did not mention the Model UN tradition in his overview of exercises, even though it dates to 1927 and the League of Nations.[38] The Model League of Nations, subsequently the Model UN, held annual conferences and maintained a presence on American campuses. Guetzkow himself later regretted not engaging more with the format, but he claimed to have sponsored the club at Northwestern.[39] The omission is minor but raises the question of whether the UN was considered insufficiently realpolitik to be simulated, outside Americans' interpretation of world negotiations, or too much a game played by high school and university students to those anxious about playing games in the first place.

Games: Human-Machine Hybrids

Exercises led to a second kind of prototype described by Guetzkow: games. In his nomenclature, games combined humans and machines. Computers aided play, allowed for faster run times, and simplified in-game calculations. Though Guetzkow did not mention it, adding computers to exercises began in business simulations at US management schools. The American Management Association integrated computers into its 1957 management simulation.[40] US business schools, by 1962, were running at least three hybrid computer-human exercises, or games.[41]

Guetzkow's discussion of his experiences with games mostly detailed his own research and its integration of computers, which he had done in his own game, the Inter-Nation Simulation (INS). (Why he called it or kept calling it a simulation is a little unclear, as INS was a game in Guetzkow's terminology.) INS started out as an exercise meant to test theories of international relations. Teams acted as fictional nations (the tables in figure 6.1), a deliberate choice to encourage players to set aside their expectations of the world order. Each team submitted their moves to a calculation table where human computers processed decisions and calculated status updates.[42]

Subsequent versions replaced the calculation table with a computer. INS became "a mix of computer programs in group surrogates, intermeshed to

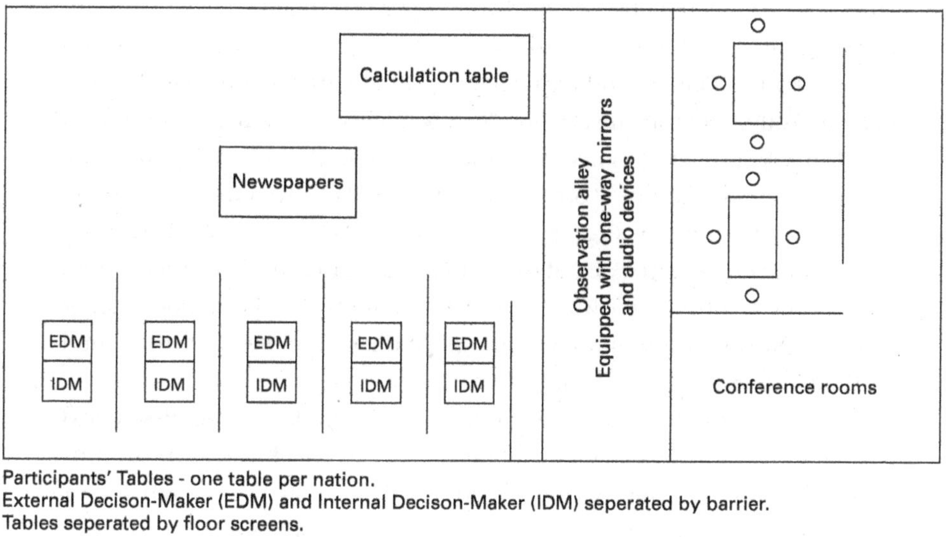

Figure 6.1
A floorplan for the Inter-Nation Simulation that includes a calculation table later replaced with a computer. Source: Redrawn from Guetzkow, "A use of simulation in the study of inter-nation relations," 187.

generate a representation of the international system of world affairs. The humans make decisions about political, economic, and military matters, which then are executed through computer programs and by virtue of the organizational responses of their human counterparts in other nations and in the international agencies."[43] Guetzkow noted that many of the exercises used the same IBM 650 computer as Benson. The machine tracked thirty variables with forty parameters. Computers helped track the state of nations, including the important *probability of officeholding*. The resulting game allowed for "free-play" and behaved "somewhat as a self-organizing system."[44]

Simulations: Early Computer Games

If computers could represent subsystems of games, why not have computers simulate the whole affair—humans and all? Guetzkow's final term, *all-computer simulation*, referred to simulations of world politics run entirely with a computer. Benson's game marked the first time a political scientist turned to all-computer simulation, but the approach was well known in the natural sciences, where computer simulations tested systems with uncertain or random parameters. Named after a game of chance, the Monte Carlo method calculated probable outcomes by taking advantage of the speed of computing to calculate and recalculate states as variables changed like perpetually rolling dice at the casino. The US nuclear weapons program relied on Monte Carlo simulations, with the first computer, ENIAC, performing some of the calculations.[45] Since then, the RAND Corporation had turned to computer simulations using Monte Carlo methods and other quantitative approaches as discussed above. RAND also attempted to model world politics on a computer with its Cold War games, the kind Spier reacted against. Outside international relations, William McPhee and the Simulmatics Corporation also fit into this category.

Guetzkow notably mentioned an important simulation, discussed next, the Technological, Economic, Military and Political Evaluation Routine. The Raytheon Corporation developed TEMPER (as it was called) for the Joint War Games Agency. Likely the first advanced all-computer model of international relations after Benson, its designers, Clark C. Abt, James C. Hodder, and Morton Gorden, started work on the project in 1960. (Abt would go on to found Abt Associates, consult on Project CAMELOT, and develop a genre of counterinsurgency, or COIN, games before purportedly disavowing war games and moving into educational applications of what he called "serious games.") That TEMPER was just one of the prototypes gives a good sense of the state of all-computer simulation: it was just one of three approaches to simulation politics and by no means the preferred way. TEMPER, at least publicly, was nothing more than an experiment, offering a chance to consider how to build a computer simulation but not itself usable.

If Benson offered an introduction to the idea of simulating worlds, then Guetzkow discussed the various simulations happening concurrently. Exercises, games, and simulations are all forms of prototyping world politics wired up some way or another. Outside this fortress of technology where Guetzkow spoke after Jay Forrester, academics like Benson, Abt, and James Coleman were also playing with games and simulations. The enigmatic Buckminster Fuller was designing his *World Game*. His early designs for the game included a computer as something of a game board and data visualization.

Guetzkow did not prefer games, exercises, or simulations. All were valid forms of prototyping world politics—at least at first. The first chapter in this part attends to the debates over prototyping that led to the legitimation of all-computer simulation over the other two approaches. A few years after his talk, Guetzkow had abandoned games for all-computer simulations like many of his peers. Part of the reason for this shift can be found in the curious history of the TEMPER project. TEMPER, even at the time of Guetzkow's writing, was just one way to simulate politics, but its funding—and indeed its promise to be a usable simulation of world politics—illustrates the motivations that steered the community, its eventual turn toward computer simulation, and some of the murkiness of Cold War research.

TEMPER, Philosopher-Kings, and the Ideal of a God's Eye View of the World

Boston University professor and one-time Simulmatics consultant Walter Clemens began the firm's rather critical review of TEMPER with a warning: "So it may be with the aspirant philosopher-king who inquires wonderingly into a computer simulation of global cold war conflict. Gazing for the first time at the impressive descriptions of its models and subroutines, he may well believe that God's finger has finally traced its patterns and revelations for social science. Alas, after studying the TEMPER simulation more closely, he may conclude that it too has been designed by committee."[46]

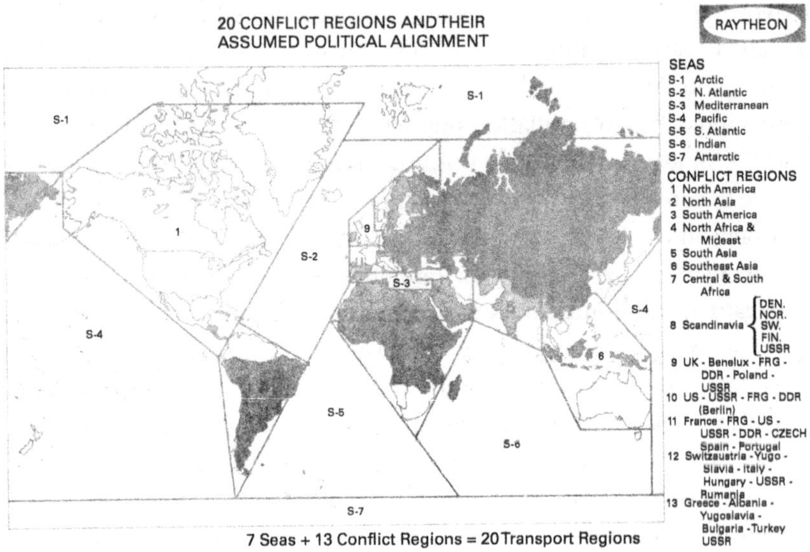

Figure 6.2
Raytheon diagram of the world abstracted for TEMPER. *Source*: Defense Technical Information Center.

While Clemens did not find the hand of God, it is telling that he went looking for it in a computer simulation. TEMPER helped imagine a tool where an expert, a philosopher-king, could interact with a model world displayed before them like a view from nowhere with the most advanced computer technology. The user would trust this computer simulation because its underlying model had been tested and shown to be valid, and its predictions had been shown to be based on the best available data collected from across the globe.

TEMPER did none of this. TEMPER never worked, well at least. Clemens was not wrong. The Joint War Games Agency, in its final evaluation of TEMPER, warned that "there is no expectation that TEMPER will be developed into a practical tool either for analyzing international problems per se or providing insights into crisis management. The TEMPER model, as now constituted, can best be used as a reference to assist in future development through examination of its deficiencies."[47] What I find novel about TEMPER is that it foreshadows the expectations that shaped subsequent efforts in political simulations in world politics. Its shortcomings, in fact, helped to define that possibility. TEMPER inspired so much paperwork, which speaks to its influence as a computer prototype and of computer prototyping as a preferred way of working since it could build on its failures and fine-tune models better than exercises or games could. Here, the aspirational quality of the prototype is clear. TEMPER did not work, but perhaps its successor would?

The Joint War Games Agency supported the developed of TEMPER from 1961 to 1965. The Raytheon Company, oversaw its development, and Abt worked as the lead alongside fourteen other contributors.[48] TEMPER had at least two versions, Mark I and Mark II. The latter rebalanced TEMPER from bipolar to multipolar after France became a nuclear power.[49] The project published seven volumes containing its data, methods, and code.[50] Peers knew about TEMPER, but it is unclear how widely available it was.[51] A 1971 publication noted that "little of the voluminous detail of the TEMPER simulation has appeared in the open literature."[52] Most of what appeared publicly were reviews of the project commissioned by the Joint War Games Agency in 1966. The agency commissioned two reports about the game: one overseen by the Simulmatics Corporation, involving Clemens, and another by the Mathematica Corporation, involving game theorist Oskar Morgenstern and game designer Martin Shubik.[53] Work on TEMPER stopped after that with warnings much like Clemens's above. After development ended, Abt kept working on simulations through his new company, Abt Associates.[54]

TEMPER set in motion a model of world politics as a complex system where individual nations behaved like cybernetic homeostats (see in Figure 6.2) similar to the cybernetic citizens mentioned in the last part. Abt believed that TEMPER's development was a progression "from a theory of international conflict to a computer program exercising that theory."[55] TEMPER demonstrates how prototypes could work out theory. The Simulmatics report on TEMPER—where Ithiel de Sola Pool had the final word—compared TEMPER to the *Kitty Hawk*, the Wright brothers' first working airplane prototype. Like the *Kitty Hawk*, TEMPER "barely flies."[56] The report argues that TEMPER "required courage to pioneer in something as 'far-out' as a computer simulation of international relations process."[57] That pioneering spirit was widespread in international relations. TEMPER was just one of many experiments in prototyping and model-testing.

The world in TEMPER was a database of 117 nations merged into 39 blocks to save computer resources. Canada and the United States composed one of TEMPER's amalgams, or nation-groups. How the world began in TEMPER depended on its "data base" that quantified relations. Each nation-group had key characteristics that included gross national product, public attitudes toward the use of military force, and alignment to the United States and the USSR. TEMPER did not model individual nations but, rather, a system of relations that equated nations to each other. As the author of the project's theoretical assumptions explained, "The fundamental theoretical assumption about world conflict on which the TEMPER Model is based in that the over-all nature of the current world conflict and the national strategies designed for dealing with it are best described in the comprehensive terms of global military, political, and economic interactions. In terms of an engineering analogy, over-all aircraft or communication system design is best accomplished by the systems approach, that considers all the major elements and their interactions, rather than the components approach that refines details in isolation from context."[58]

The theoretical assumptions emphasized that TEMPER offered a holistic approach; yet, as its cocreator Morton Gorden elaborated, "these nation groups are provided with a resource base and goals describing their preferred values. The goal seeking process operates like a homeostat, seeking to achieve a balance among goals and constraints, in the context of other nation groups which may be competing or cooperating for the same ends."[59] Elsewhere, Gorden emphasized that the model did not always behave rationally.[60] The end result was that TEMPER offered a way to express world politics much like Simulmatics' people-machine and other cybernetic citizens models.

TEMPER's code offered a scrutable world view. Nation-groups *acted* through subroutines. In his review, Clemens suggested that TEMPER's governments "behave much as anticipated by Thomas Hobbes or Hans Morgenthau."[61] As the name TEMPER suggested, these subroutines considered the military, economic, and psychological relationships between nations that might change over the course of the simulation as blocs became more threatened or economic conditions weakened. The whole program, shown in figure 6.3, depicts TEMPER's loop from the start in the top-left corner to the sequences of the psychological, economic, war, and decision-maker submodels that looped as the simulation advanced a week at a time. Following Fortran diagram standards, each box represents a particular subroutine, each diamond represents a decision, and the arrows represent the sequences of the program.

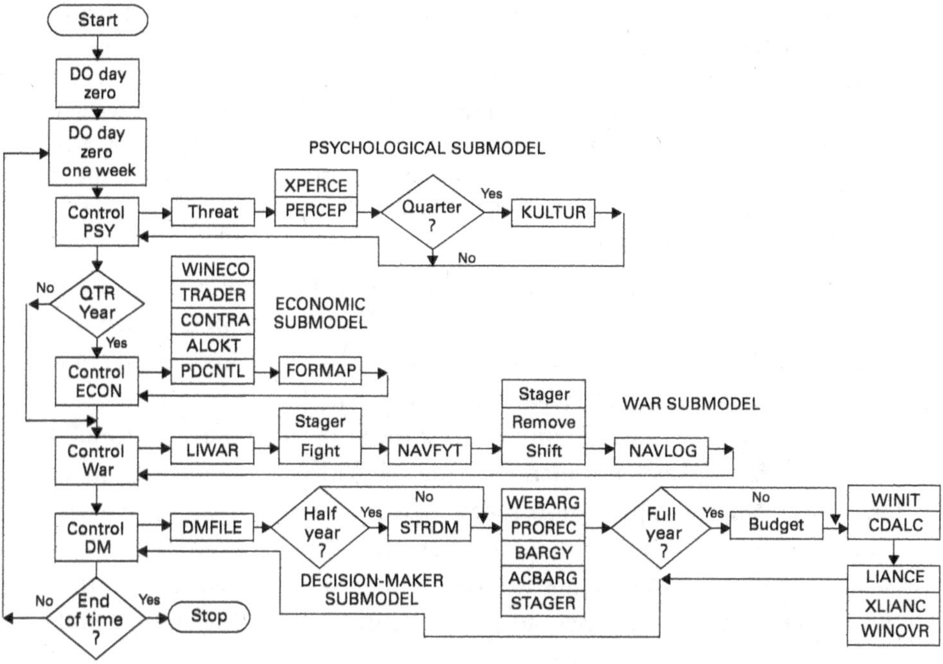

Figure 6.3
TEMPER's programming diagram and subroutines. *Source*: Redrawn from TEMPER Volume 1, Orientation Manual.

These subroutines abstracted theories of state behavior into working formulas. The KULTUR subroutine captured the "feelings" of nation-groups defined by "cultural-ideological factors called *motives*" that included tax rates, spending habits, and propensity to use force.[62] Changes in these feelings altered the balance of power, just as it had in Benson's game.

If these subroutines captured feelings, critics thought they were too mushy. Clemens complained that "a series of debatable policy biases underlie these aspects of the TEMPER model, illustrating how great the intrusion may be of human sentiment into a supposedly scientific and objective simulation of the world."[63] Better data and more defensible assumptions were some of Clemens's recommendations. He became part of a lively discussion about TEMPER's shortcomings that shaped the ideal gaze for computer simulation. He warned,

> The philosopher-king who turned to TEMPER in the hope of finding divine revelations about the nature of world politics would be disappointed. Of course,

> he would have expected a computer simulation of cold war conflict to be difficult. Perhaps some simplifications would be needed for the sake of the computer and for other reasons. Problems would arise regarding the choice of priorities, the models, and the dynamics. The reality of TEMPER fulfills and exceeds these expectations. It seems as if perhaps not a committee but a computer became deranged and decided to put forward some of the least defensible simplifications about the nature of international relations and it did so in such uniqak [*sic*] language designed to hinder rather than facilitate comprehension.[64]

Clemens's frustrations about TEMPER, however, illustrate a desire for a comprehensible world, one equivalent to a computer. TEMPER failed not in principle but in execution. His criticisms, far from stopping research into computer simulation, led to its eventual supremacy.

Calls for a better TEMPER converged on the term "man-machine simulation" as a way forward. The man-machine simulation was something more akin to a computer application today. Less a computer assisting players, than a program that a user could interact with. TEMPER promised to be a working tool for military elites to evaluate their decisions and the world's future. TEMPER allowed users to *play* with theory, inviting the possibility that the tool could be used to predict as well as teach. The simulation advanced, week by week, to project ten years into the future. At first, users waited, usually thirty to forty minutes, for the run to complete. By 1964, Abt's team had begun to allow for more on-line interactions, so the user could pause to adjust some of its parameters and alter the course of the run. They hoped these connections could be carried out through new computer networks.[65] One presentation mentioned a possible collaboration with the computing company BBN, one of the key firms involved in the production of the Arpanet.[66]

TEMPER promised to offer a better view of world politics—or rather its funders expected one. Abt warned against this. In a 1964 presentation to a high-level committee, discussed in the next chapter, Abt warned that TEMPER "will not predict the future. It will not tell you the optimum strategy." Yet, he was corrected. A colonel explained to Abt: "At the risk of over simplification, let me tell you what our real goal is for TEMPER: We would like to use it as a scientific device, to determine the most relevant factors with which high-level advisors should concern themselves during a period of international tension."[67] TEMPER would never meet the colonel's demands, but it would help him make those demands more clear.

Virtual Worlds: From Make-Believe to Made-Believe

The next chapter picks up from this moment of uncertainty, why world modeling moved from these hybrid formats of humans and computers to all-computer simulations. The short answer is a matter of addressability, how a simulation could be a valid proxy of the world. Computer simulation closed an addressability gap between virtual and real worlds. First, measuring computer outputs against world affairs required some *commensurability*. After arguing about how to integrate data into modeling, researchers came to accept that computer simulations were the best way to leverage growing data banks about world affairs. Research focused on how to compare empirical data to the outputs of simulations, or what today might be called synthetic data. Second, researchers found humans to be a little too unreliable and unintelligible for their simulations. In a drive to enhance modeling's *utility*, research removed the human element, thereby shifting the format to all-digital settings. The final reason was *validity*, or how well a simulation corresponded to the world. World models "generat[ed] and extend[ed] global data networks."[68] Simulations legitimated vast networks of political sensing and digital encoding. Being valid also meant being replicable, and computers offered a more reliable instrument for controlled experiments than inconsistent humans.

Chapter 7 concludes by arguing that computer simulations of the world differed from exercises or games by affording, to borrow from Donna Haraway, a view "seeing everything from nowhere."[69] In doing so, computer simulation addressed its God's-eye view of the world toward an emerging project of what Fernando Elichirigoity describes as planetary management, particularly for use by the US government services and armed forces.[70] Richard Ashley, in a review of world modeling at its nadir, described world modelers as attempting to construct a "world-encompassing Panoptic gaze."[71] Prototyping maintained the possibility of seeing the world from an objective outside but also allowed debates to emerge over how the computer simulation could present the world.

Computer simulation subsequently fragmented along similar lines as modeling in electoral politics. Cybernetic theory, game theory agents, and data chimeras evoked theories of worlds recalling the cybernetic citizens, rational agents, and data chimeras from earlier. Chapter 8 reviews the split between rational choice and cybernetics approaches to world politics (in part because there is a better literature on more data-driven analysis of world politics).[72] I focus on the evolution of Harold Guetzkow's Inter-Nation Simulation from his exercises to the all-computer simulation GLOBUS, which was a high-water mark, now receded, of cybernetic approaches to world politics. World modeling turned away, as GLOBUS developed, from complex systems toward rational agents and multiagent modeling with the success of Bruce Bueno de Mesquita's 1981 book *The War Trap*. In these virtual worlds, rational choice and complex systems marked two competing political models of world politics.

As the venture capitalists take generative AI into reality, and we live in the shadow of climate and viral modeling, these two chapters offer one route into understanding how the world became virtual. Where these chapters attend to the tensions and differences found in this history, the conclusion discusses the overall implications. The ensuing computational imaginary allowed the world to be both *imagined* computationally and *imaginable* as computational—computers could predict the future because the world behaved like a computer. Through this history, I show how imaginations of virtual worlds came to be seen as conventional and why experiments at the Defense Advanced Research Projects Agency using AI to predict world futures build on the decades of world modeling found here. Part II offers a second journey into the computational imaginary of politics happening on a world scale—and how make-believe on mathematical principles became all too real for us today.

7 The World on a Wire

At the absolute nexus of US military power, two prominent world modelers—Clark C. Abt and Harold Guetzkow—reflected on the field's future. Both men spoke in October 1964 before INAGROSS, the Inter-Agency Group on Strategic Studies. Three years old at the time, INAGROSS was part of the Joint War Games Agency,[1] which was run by the senior leaders of the Joint Chiefs of Staff who advised the Department of Defense and the president. INAGOSS members sought Abt's and Guetzkow's opinions about how to "advance the state-of-the-art in Political-Military Simulations and gaming techniques."[2] What was the best way forward? TEMPER? How could these experiments become more useful to US operations abroad?

Questions focused on critical measures of advancement. Validity, or how a model matched reality, animated much of the discussion after Abt's and Guetzkow's presentations. The debate was only partially about the right model, or how best to abstract reality into something usable for their planning. The military specifically wanted to know whether exercises, games, or simulations would best test the validity of their underlying models. What way of making a simulation—or prototyping—would decide the best models? The first question to Abt asked about validity: "One of the problems with simulation has always been validity of this sort of thing. It strikes me, maybe you have an ideal way of testing this and maybe you're planning to when you get it running, by trying to run one of the war games that has been run manually in the Agency and see how the results compare."[3] How might a simulation compare to a game, the question implied? Could one prototype better guide decisions than the other? Asking how to compare simulations, games, and exercises implied a debate about the best way to model the world. These debates, less about the models than about how to test them, animated the next decade of applied research in world politics and international relations.

Both Abt and Guetzkow opined with ambivalence about computer simulation's future. They did not discount its potential—a long way from Benson's attitude toward his Simple Diplomatic Game—but neither did they anticipate that computer simulation was the only way forward. Both answered questions from the military attendees without any techno-chauvinism about computers.[4] Abt admitted that "nobody really knows what is the best mix of manual and computer interactions in war gaming. Furthermore, there may not be one answer."[5] Guetzkow explained his research group's goal of comparing different approaches to world modeling, saying, "Because in the long run it may be that decision-makers will want to use simulations as one tool—among others—in the development of their policy."[6] Though undecided about the best way forward, Abt and Guetzkow knew the stakes. Abt noted Guetzkow's work was important "to improve the art more rapidly" but "not only in inter-nation simulation but in combat operations simulation and even in engineering design simulation."[7] Simulation's buffer from reality was always as thin as the punch cards it ran on.

Their ambivalence did not dissuade these modelers from using computers. Abt's worked at the Raytheon Corporation on the first major computer simulation for world politics, the Technological, Economic, Military and Political Evaluation Routine (TEMPER), whereas Guetzkow coordinated the newly ARPA-funded Simulated International Processes Project (SIP) at Northwestern University. Guetzkow's game, the Inter-Nation Simulation (INS), mixed humans and computers. These projects tried to be more useful for predicting politics and managing crises. Often, they failed. Yet, failing, whether in making a game, an exercise, or a computer simulation, had a curious effect on Guetzkow and Abt: It increased their interest in using computers to solve these shortcomings.

Computer simulations became the preferred prototype as experts tried to work out how to build *valid* models. Recalling chapter 4, I understand these efforts to legitimate exercises, games, and simulations as a matter of addressability—the distant ways computer simulations had tangible links to the world—at the international scale. Again, simulators encountered frictions when trying to connect their digital worlds to real ones, but I focus more on the efforts within the community to decide what made a valid computer simulation.

Three frictions appear most often: validity, or the need to ensure that simulated results matched real world outcomes; commensurability to ensure that simulated data used real-world data; and utility, or rather, a need for simulations to be practical. These frictions led modelers like Abt and Guetzkow to favor computer simulations over exercises and games. To be clear, computing did not completely solve the gaps, but instead, modelers, upon reflection, considered computer simulation the best way to lessen the three frictions when trying to build simulations to address global systems. As a result, computers shifted from being *a way* to prototype a model to being *the preferred way* to prototype models. Modelers still disagreed about other matters. There was no consensus about international relations—just a common way to prototype.

Guetzkow and Abt did not decide that computer simulation should be the preferred prototype, nor did they endorse computer simulation alone; rather, they helped to normalize computer simulation in international relations. That field was caught up in the fallout from the blockbuster *The Limits to Growth.* Political science proved to be just one of many fields conflicted about its attraction to computer simulation. Indeed, the scholars in this account might be seen as marginal figures, but, I argue, their debates and scholarship explain how world politics came to be seen as comparable to a computer system. Abt's and Guetzkow's efforts offer an alternate way to interpret the popularization of world modeling, often attributed to the launch of the Club of Rome's 1972 report. On the contrary, world modeling had already largely embraced computer simulation by then. Peers of Abt and Guetzkow could criticize only the report's epistemology and methods, not the plausibility of modeling the world as a computer system; that had already been decided.[8]

The turn to computer simulation had consequences, which helps me to explain how computer simulations addressed world political systems in specific and important ways. Where computer simulations at the national stage tried to probe deeper into the minds of American voters, at the international stage computer simulations looked to greater abstractions for a global view. Computer simulation allowed for what Donna Haraway calls a "god's trick of seeing everything" or what Richard Ashley called "the eye of power" in his seminal retrospective of the modeling boom.[9] Computer simulations could observe and interact with the international system *as if* produced from a view from nowhere.[10] Haraway is aware of this history, noting "world systems" as the counterpoint to "local knowledges." All these efforts led to thinking about world politics as a tool, as one researcher put it, for the "philosopher-king," to recall the last chapter's discussion of TEMPER.[11] Computer simulations came to be accepted to present a God's-eye view that addressed the world, orienting players in command of the globe. These simulations remain the most dominant legacy of the turn to computers to model world politics.

The Key Question: Validity and the Move to Computers for Theory-Testing

Harold Guetzkow dedicated most of his 1964 INAGOSS talk to problems of validity. Validity referred to how well a model (or operating model in the language of the time) matched reality—also called a referent system or observable universe. Hopes that world models could inform, even predict, politics made validity "*the* key question" for Guetzkow as he wrote later,[12] and for Abt too. At the INAGOSS meeting, Abt asked, "How valid are the models now in existence—and how might their reasonableness and credibility be increased?"[13] Validity called into question whether further investment in INS or TEMPER was the right way forward for the field. Validity, in effect, defined the future of all efforts in world modeling.[14]

Validity was both a long-standing desire and contested ground for world modelers trying to outdo each other.[15] Validity was a wedge at the RAND Corporation between mathematical modeling and more humanistic exercises. Mathematicians at RAND touted the predictive capabilities of their models. Social scientists rejected their confidence and turned to more lifelike exercises to study how actual humans would make decisions.[16] These debates foreshadowed and informed the conflicts between games, exercises, and simulations.

Outside RAND, validity also mattered for the emerging field of future studies. Games, exercises, and simulations shared a common promise to make the world more predictable. An international community had started to explore methods to study the future with a focus on making those predictions valid and actionable.[17]

Validity was a friction point where realists and traditionalists as well as defense industry hawks and peace activist doves conflicted.[18] Guetzkow, reflecting on his motivations in a late-career interview, stated that he wanted "to help create a more peaceful world."[19] He was not alone in viewing better analysis of international relations as a way to encourage world peace. Peace and conflict studies developed alongside quantitative political science.[20] As David J. Singer, another peace scholar and key figure in quantitative international relations, said in a late-career interview, his early work was "an effort, really, to meet the hawks, as far as I could go, on their assumptions, most of which I thought were preposterous. But I was wanting to grant them that and still try to demonstrate that the arguments they made were dangerous and unfounded."[21] His comments reflect a broader effort to turn social science rigor against the logic of mutually assured destruction by promising not only to explain the Cold War but to predict its evolution.

If validity was the goal, how could it be measured? How could competing models be compared? Guetzkow's INAGOSS presentation detailed how he intended to compare different operating models' validity, offering a way to systematically deal with these questions. To do so, Guetzkow's project funded extensive testing of games, exercises, and simulations. INS tests involved several different scenarios, including the outbreak of World War I and the Vietnam War.[22] One of the most ambitious studies, led by Guetzkow's doctoral student Richard Brody, aimed to prove, or claimed to prove, that the Inter-Nation Simulation results did not "merely [gain] knowledge about the behavior of high school students in a defined laboratory situation" but were generalizable methods to study nuclear proliferation.[23] Brody and Guetzkow stressed that INS could test theory. As Brody wrote in the conclusion of the nuclear proliferation study, "a cycle of THEORY-BUILDING, EXPERIMENTATION, PREDICTION, OBSERVATION, THEORY-BUILDING . . . until the model is fine-tuned."[24]

The escalating Vietnam War loomed over validity-testing efforts. Another of Guetzkow's students, Paul Smoker, who later became a noted peace scholar, adapted INS to study the Vietnam "situation." In a rare collaboration with peace institutes in Canada and the United Kingdom, Smoker found that the modified tool did not work well as a policy-testing instrument but was more effective as a training tool for policymakers. His peer, Stuart Bremer, remarked that "participants reported severe feelings of frustration due to their inability to control the unfolding situation."[25] That frustration prompted some self-reflection about the relationship between the model and the world it abstracted. Smoker and his coauthor noted, "[the] Vietnam simulation, for example, during the first four development runs massive nuclear war broke out once, limited nuclear war (the destruction of North Vietnam) once, Russian and Chinese intervention in South Vietnam with troops once, and an uneasy truce under a Buddhist pro-Vietnam neutralist government in South Vietnam once. Are we to concludes from this that the simulation is unreliable, or are we to conclude that each of these events is equally as likely? More generally one would expect considerable between-run variance when highly probabilistic events are involved."[26] Half the outcomes led to nuclear war. Was that a validity issue or a reflection of a world at the brink? Smoker, like his peer Stuart Bremer, later developed a successor to INS: the International Process Simulation (IPS), an all-computer simulation used in peace research.[27]

Validity research begat more validity research. Just after he presented at the IBM Symposium, Guetzkow organized the Conference on Problems of Validation in Simulation in February 1965, supported by ARPA and the Joint War Games Agency.[28] At the conference, one of Guetzkow's students, Charles F. Hermann, presented an early version of what became a seminal paper elaborating validity as a concept, defining it as "how well one system replicates properties of some other system."[29] Hermann's paper complicated both the *why* and *what* aspects of validity. He acknowledged that a game's validity depended on what it aimed to do and that simulations had a pedagogical function, so measuring required considering the simulation's instructional purpose. (He was writing just as James S. Coleman was also making hybrid educational-theory games).

After making the distinction between predicting and teaching simulations, Hermann summarized the literature to identify five types of validity:

1. *Internal validity, or a simulation's replicability*, referred to a simulation that could be run multiple times and produce consistent results had strong internal validity.
2. *Face validity*, which is a wonderfully obtuse scientific term referring to how "real" a simulation looked to its players. In other words, did the simulation correspond to the cultural expectations of world politics?
3. *Variable-parameter validity* referred to the correspondence between quantitative data and simulation variables. Returning to prior discussion of the influence of factor analysis, Hermann's noted the work of another important modeler. Richard Chadwick who "factor [analyzed] core variables in the *Inter-Nation Simulation* and separately factor analyzed

quantifiable real world indices" to compare whether the INS's in-game parameters matched important factors in reality.[30]

4. *Event validity* concerned whether a simulation matched its event. Hermann gave the example of Simulmatics here, stating that the degree to which its people-machine matched election results was a good test of event validity.
5. *Hypothesis validity* resembled event and variable-parameter validity in that it compared statistical results to simulation results, but instead of "individual units," it looked at "connections between two or more units" to test how a simulation's stated hypothesis compared to a similar hypothesis in the observable universe.[31]

Evaluating simulation validity under these tests became a major theme in Guetzkow's Simulated International Processes project, and the teams' efforts helped turn its members toward computer simulation.

Computer simulations happened to be easier to control and test for Hermann's five validities, an implicit conclusion found in the largest validation study of its time. Conducted by Hayward Alker Jr. and Ronald Brunner and funded by Guetzkow, the study was a centerpiece of validation research. From 1965 to 1966, Alker Jr. and Brunner set up a complex comparison between Guetzkow's hybrid human-machine game INS, Abt's all-computer simulation TEMPER, and the all-human Political-Military Exercise, or PME (a continuation of RAND's social science exercises). The study compared how all three reacted to the DETEX II scenario. Set in 1967, the scenario began after "a nuclear explosion had occurred near the Soviets' clandestine test site."[32]

The study aimed to compare the specific models, but it had direct implications on the best way to prototype world models, with Alker Jr. and Brunner becoming embroiled in the validity debates. They acknowledged that how models related to their referent systems involved "theoretical assumptions."[33] Validity might not be that important in certain settings, as they explained:

> If the theories embedded in these simulations are to an appreciable extent a function of their different uses, it is only fair to argue that the validity of such simulations also depends on their uses. A good example of this viewpoint would be the claim by a DETEX II participant that the run was not designed to predict the most likely outcome of such a crisis situation, but rather to explore decision-makers' responses when put in an exceptionally difficult yet plausible situation. . . . An

INS researcher, on the other hand, could similarly argue that experience in thinking about long-range changes in international relations is far more valuable than the validity of any one particular hypothetical exercise. TEMPER designers could similarly argue that greater awareness of the relevant factors in conflict situations would be an important validation of the simulation model.[34]

Alker Jr. and Brunner suggested that all three project had merits if evaluated by different applications, but when validity mattered, which was the case for "political scientists with an interest both in teaching and policy matters," then the field required more "highly developed classifications of inputs, actors, and actions than from our backward understanding of decision rules and interactive sequence."[35]

Computer simulations offered a better way to build systematic knowledge about international relations, even if TEMPER had "debatable relationships" itself.[36] Consider Alker Jr. and Brunner's flow charts used to compare INS, TEMPER, and PME (figures 7.1–7.3). The flow charts mapped

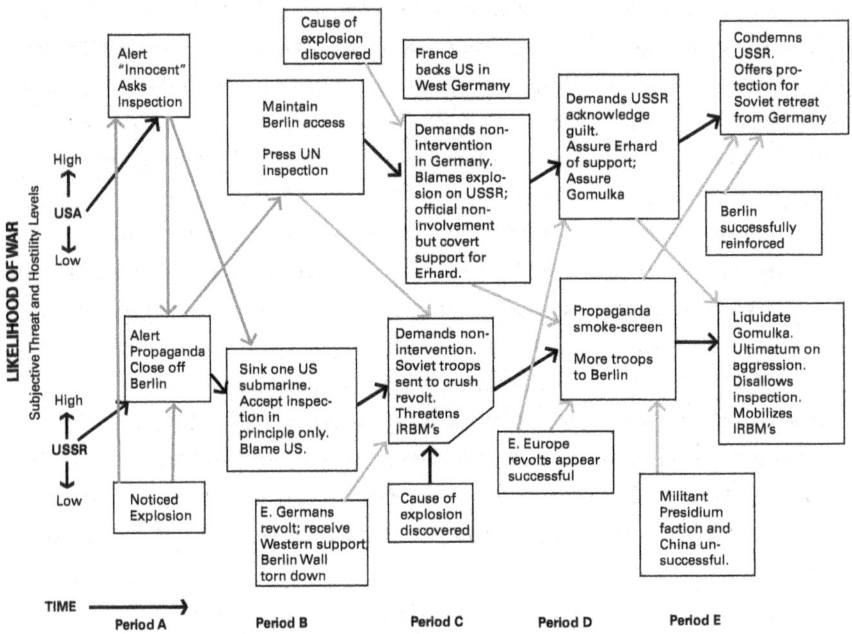

Figure 7.1
Timeline of events using PME during DETEX II simulation reproduced from the original diagram. *Source*: Redrawn from Alker and Brunner, "Simulating International Conflict," 91.

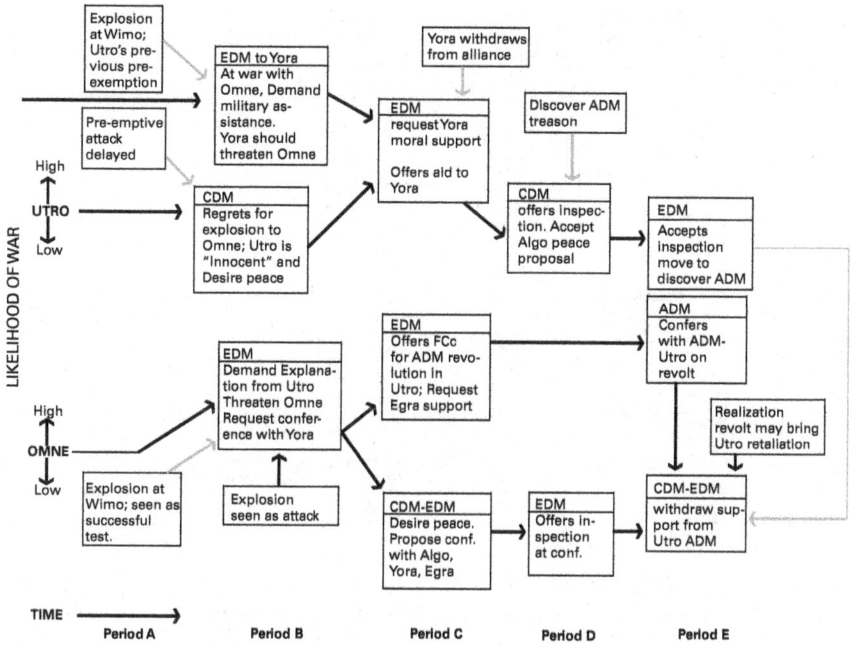

Figure 7.2

Timeline of events using INS during DETEX II simulation reproduced from the original diagram. *Source*: Redrawn from Alker and Brunner, "Simulating International Conflict," 92.

the likelihood of war over the run time, mapping how different events changed this variable.

The diagrams show the growing interest in controlling elements in a test run. Alker Jr. and Brunner implied, in their conclusion, that evaluating a model's validity required more test runs, indicating a need for more efficient ways of performing tests. Computer simulation proved a better way to keep this cycle running, as it allowed for tighter control of the different relations than was possible in exercises that lacked formal relationships or in games that still included the uncertainty of human decision-making.

Even the diagrams used to compare the models (Figures 7.1, 7.2, and 7.3) looked like computer programs, even though only TEMPER was a computer simulation. The charts—and the modelers' desire to increase validity—had the effect of treating games and exercises like computer simulations. The diagrams abstracted away the messiness of exercises, letting computer

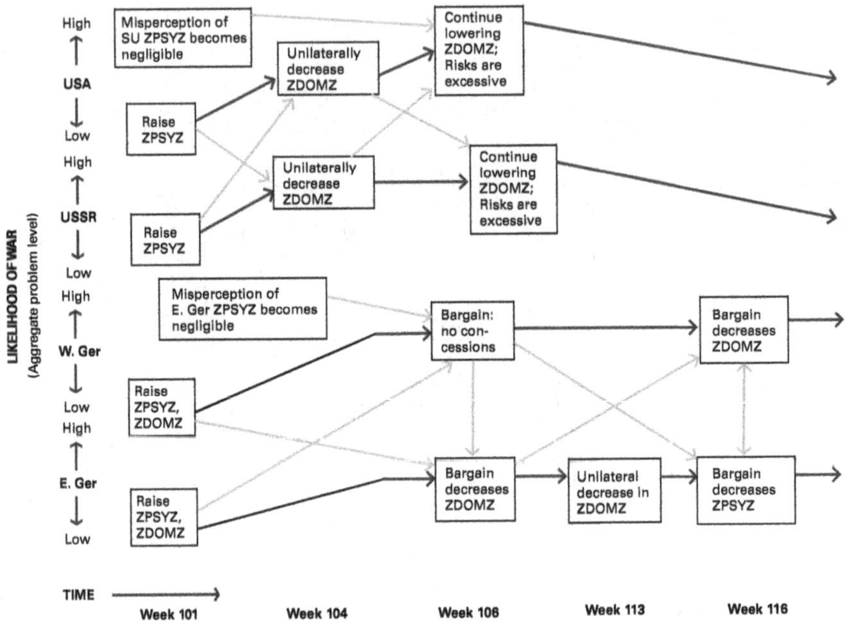

Figure 7.3
Timeline of events using TEMPER during DETEX II simulation reproduced from the original diagram. *Source*: Redrawn from Alker and Brunner, "Simulating International Conflict," 93.

simulations become an ideal type. Computer simulations, to be clear, did not resolve the problem of predictive capacity—there were still debates about what the results mean. Rather, computer simulations streamlined the complexity of research *trying* to be predictive, promising to make the goal more measurable and achievable.

The differences between prototypes became even more pronounced when considering Hermann's expanded definition of validity. Computer simulation had better internal validity and variable-parameter validity than games or exercises. I am extrapolating here, because Alker Jr. and Brunner stated that their comparative study supported comments that were "impressionistic ones" at the level of "face validity" at best.[37] Computer simulation as a form of prototyping offered, at the very least, better internal validity than other forms of prototyping: exercises and models. The outcomes did not change with the same inputs.

Computer simulations achieved better validity by removing an inconsistent component, human participants. Humans created too much instability. A high school student might just do something different, but that could lead to different results altogether.[38] Humans were just too much of a black box for researchers looking to fix their prototypes and prove their models.

An anecdote from Alker Jr. and Brunner's study illustrates the challenge of variable-parameter validity, or knowing how simulation variables compared to the real world. After an INS where participants acted as the fictional nations of Omne and Utro, one Utro participant correctly surmised the intended similarities between his nation and the United States. But an Omne participant immediately responded, "What do you mean you were the United States? We were the United States!"[39] Clearly, what the designers thought were the correct variables in the simulation differed from how they played out. Paul Smoker, reflecting on his Vietnam studies, made a similar point: "It is not an easy matter to locate the necessary number of people with the required psycho-political attitudes and the necessary time and interest to participate in a simulation."[40] Another reminder that these machine worlds were never as virtual as might have been hoped.

By putting primacy on validity, modelers desired a God's-eye view. Either to better advise or, more often, prevent war, this kind of modeling sought predictive validity and emphasized the operating model's relationship to the referent system as the most important consideration for their prototypes. Addressing validity necessitated a schematization that advanced a computer-oriented view over games and exercises. Validity, especially in its complexity, involved a second friction: whether operating models and referent systems could be commensurate, another facet of Hermann's variable-parameter validity.

The Less Dispensable Element, Political Data

What was the point of simulation when there were not enough data about the referent system in the first place? This was the thrust of David Singer's argument in a 1965 commentary for the journal *Behavior Science*, one he later described as a critique of Guetzkow. Peace researcher Singer was a political scientist and early advocate for better political data. His commentary explored "the conversion of facts and information into a form suitable for scientific purposes," or data-making, as the title put it.[41] He had two forms of data-making in mind: content analysis, which generated data from the real world, and simulation, which generated what we now call synthetic data. Singer preferred content analysis. Data generated from the real world, Singer thought, were "the least dispensable element in the circular process of theory-building."[42] That critique became a central theme in the field as simulators sought to better integrate data from what Singer called the "natural world" to increase variable-parameter validity. More data required more computers, a loop that reinforced the preference for computer simulation.

Creating political data became a massive undertaking in Cold War political science. In contemporary critical data studies, these efforts are called datafication: "the transformation of human life into data through processes of quantification, and the generation of different kinds of value from data."[43] The concept helps interpret all the work happening across the United States to build sets of international data about politics. Declarations of war, trade flows, and news articles all became pieces of data in what became known as databases, a process of datafication. Datafication involved the metrics to both measure world populations and create political indicators. Researchers applied these new data to computer simulations to evaluate their validity.[44] By using the term "datafication" over "data collection," I mean to emphasize that the encoding of human life into quantitative data is not an objective process but rather a politically contested one, in which competing claims over the value of data are realized in competing models and prototypes.

Datafication was more global in *focus* than in *practice*. Writing on the important history of climate and weather science, Paul Edwards distinguishes between *making global data* and *making data global*. Making global data involved "collecting planetary data in standard forms, through interconnected networks, to build data images of global weather and general circulation"; this is complementary to "making data global: building complete, coherent, and consistent global data sets from incomplete, inconsistent, and heterogeneous data sources."[45] Many of the data projects I have encountered in the early days of quantitative international relations concerned making global data—that is, collecting data about world politics and making that data useful to research, but not creating global collaborations. Much of the work involved developing American interpretations of world events—global data collected domestically.

Political datafication efforts date back to the beginnings of behavioralism with Charles E. Merriam and, later, his student Harold Lasswell.[46] As historian Joy Rohde notes, a desire for data to better manage society was pervasive across academia and the US government, but it was especially pronounced in quantitative international relations.[47] In international relations, Karl Deutsch and Charles E. McClelland—both early advocates of systems thinking—encouraged and collected international data expressly for model-building and model-testing. Writing in 1956, Deutsch noted, "There is beginning in political science, as there has been in the field of economics, a gradual shift from the sole reliance on qualitative or literary representation, with its potential richness and sensitivity, to its supplementation by quantitative models with their relatively greater poverty and rigidity, but also their possibilities of greater precision and penetrating power. Where such quantitative models are attempted, however, they raise the question of operational definitions and techniques of measurement for the variables they employ."[48] Though Deutsch did not aim to replace qualitative approaches, his efforts, like those of his peers David Easton and Ithiel de Sola Pool, focused on the maturation of these quantitative representations.

Political data were a point of contention in the field. Deutsch, for example, understood that calls for better quantitative data placed behavioralist and systems approaches at odds with historical, humanistic approaches to the field. For as much as Deutsch desired "to go beyond political intuition and historical narratives," he also acknowledged a need for balance.[49] As he wrote in 1960, "We need to combine the insight of the literary and historical traditions of political scholarship as well as the quantitative skills of analysis and verification, if our understanding of international politics is to become less inadequate than it has been in the past."[50] Similar arguments justified the humanistic outcomes of exercises and games.

Prioritizing data in international relations led to several different academic projects to create data banks or databases. Data work happened across the United States from Hawaii to Massachusetts, in academia and at the Pentagon. Bruce M. Russett, Karl Deutsch, Hayward R. Alker, and Harold Lasswell collaborated through the World Data Analysis Program at Yale University to produce the first World Handbook of Political and Social Indicators Series with data for 141 countries from 1961 to 1963.[51]

The Correlates of War project "generated the data for the bulk of the hypothesis tests in IR for decades."[52] Started by David J. Singer around

1963 at the University of Michigan, the project merged systems analysis, computational social science, and political behavioralism. Singer's writings before the start of the project call for more behavioral research in world politics. He claimed in 1961 that only Karl Deutsch and Harold Guetzkow had done any "serious, affirmative discussion" of behavioral social science in international relations.[53] Like Guetzkow, Singer sought to turn the social sciences against Cold War truisms, objectively testing peaceful strategies and, in doing so, contributing to the development of peace and conflict studies.[54] A systems approach informed Singer's quantitative analysis of the "structure of the system or on the relationships among its components."[55] Singer relied on League of Nations and UN data for one of his first outputs from the project, a study of political alliances and their relation to the sum total of war globally.[56] Correlates of War, like many other projects, promised researchers reliable, legitimated data sets to model and test their theories of world politics, even though their indicators and how they collected were was deeply political. Data often interpreted secondary sources—news reports—so researchers operated far from their objects of study. We can debate the bias in the data, but the bigger effect of datafication was to use measures of international politics that mimic computational systems.

The most influential projects leveraged novel data techniques that advanced deeper and sometimes controversial political perspectives. Rudolph J. Rummel's Dimensionality of Nations (DON) project developed out of Harold Guetzkow's application of the behavior sciences to international relations. Guetzkow tasked Rummel, his PhD student until 1963, to collect data for the Inter-Nation Simulation. Data encoded interactions between two nations—or dyadic relations—along with national characteristics. Rummel aimed to uncover which national characteristics affected international behavior.[57] Dimensionality referred to Rummel's early adoption of factor analysis (along with his colleague Dr. Richard Chadwick), which produced "a continuum—a dimension—along which nations can be distributed."[58] Factors—not unlike data chimeric work—aimed to express the deeper logics in international relations. A major data set, the DON was maintained by Rummel throughout his career at the University of Hawai'i. Even though he was technically sophisticated, Rummel was controversial for his concerns about murder by government (or democide) and his libertarian sympathies.[59] Whether or not Rummel's views impacted the data is debated, but certainly the DON illustrates that datafication implied political theory.[60]

Datafication was a massive, distributed undertaking. Event data best capture this scale. Events, broadly speaking, meant units of action pulled from news reports—usually from *The New York Times* to give a sense of just where the data was coming from—into indexed, regularized variables. Event data was a field in and of itself with rival standards for coding. A leader in quantitative international relations, Charles E. McClelland joined these efforts in 1967 when ARPA funded the World Event/Interaction System (WEIS) project to provide regular analysis of world events suitable for computer analysis.[61] Other event data projects included the Conflict and Peace Data Bank (COPDAB) at the University of Michigan, which by 1979 had amassed about five hundred thousand entries.[62]

The complexity of the data helped legitimate the use of computers to counteract warnings of information overload. As Joy Rohde notes about WEIS, "The implications for McClelland's vision of international relations were potentially devastating. With the international system composed of thousands of daily interactions between approximately 160 nations, investigators needed to monitor 25,440 two-nation relationships to unearth its underlying patterns. As one of McClelland's protégés explained, tracking and analyzing this volume of data was 'literally impossible for human beings.' Computers, however, offered a solution."[63] Event data offered an early use for machine intelligences. The data relied on newspapers, usually Western sources like *The New York Times*. Articles contained information about world events, but the reporting had to be encoded to be useful. Here, computers were enlisted to ease the process and enhance the results. The first computer-assisted content analysis tool was the General Inquirer, which relied on a syntax for coders to tag content to assist in computerized analysis. Developed in 1963, the General Inquirer was not an attempt at automated content analysis—that would have to wait—but, by 1964, it did allow users to code dictionaries of words that informed a program that scanned and tagged articles. The General Inquirer was one of a few attempts to code and analyze event data with computers. Another program, Tag Tally, counted the results to give macroscopic descriptions of large corpuses of texts.[64]

Data necessitated computer systems and networked resources. To give a sense of the output, by 1971, the ARPA-funded International Data Center at the University of Michigan housed twenty-four different data sets. (Warren E. Miller, coauthor of *The American Voter* and cocreator of American National Election Studies, served as co–principal investigator of the center.)

The center was not ARPA's only initiative in this area. In 1968, it gave funds to the former director of its Information Processing Techniques Office, J. C. R. Licklider, and Ithiel de Sola Pool to start Project Cambridge, another data center founded on a promise to develop new data management and analysis programs for governments to harness the power of behavioral research. The General Inquirer, for example, was part of its system.[65] Both Project Cambridge at MIT and the International Data Center developed computer systems to access these data. Political data were an early use case for time-sharing systems and the Arpanet. Students at Michigan could call up data using its OSIRIS system. Researchers like Richard Chadwick at the University of Hawai'i could call up data through the early ARPANET.[66]

Political data, though independent from computer simulation, was well suited to its adoption. They shared the same medium. Computer simulations integrated data into their runs. Guetzkow turned to data to improve INS's variable-parameter validity, either by using it to develop better inputs or by testing outputs. He cites the Yale Data Program, Dimensionality of Nations, and Correlates of War as data sources. Data evaluate outputs against real-world events. Indeed, the runs of INS on World War I data also experimented with data-informing and data-evaluating simulations. Guetzkow's students started political data projects too, with Richard Brody working at the Institute of Political Studies at Stanford University to develop a way to measure conflict and Charles Hermann collecting events data through the Comparative Research on the Events of Nations (CREON) Project, which ran from 1959 to 1968.[67] As Guetzkow moved away from INS to all-computer simulation, it became easier to use these data. Indeed, the simulation, data, and analysis all began to share the same digital format.[68]

The friction between quantitative international relations and world modelers led to a reflexive datafication of the world. Whereas international relations analysts struggled to enumerate complex politics into data banks of world indicators, modelers, conversely, tried to find meaning in the results of the synthetic data generated from simulation. The two sides debated the utility of each form of data but shared a sense that the world could be commensurate with data. The emergence of commensurability advanced the promise of addressability: If the world was data, then the world could be better seen through data. Not only was the world data, but the simulation allowed that world of data to be usable and interactive.

The Limited Utility of the American High School Student

Running a game like Guetzkow's Inter-Nation Simulation was a lot of work. When Richard Brody ran a summer-long simulation, he needed 18 research assistants, 6 staff and faculty at the Program of Graduate Research and Training in International Relations at Northwestern University, and 357 high school students. The summer of 1960, in Brody's words, was "a long, hot summer."[69] The effort was needed to ensure that the simulation was valid, to close an addressability gap between a simulation's responsiveness and results and its practical use. How could so much effort ever be practical? Or able to offer up timely advice? Just that year, the influential computer scientist J. C. R Licklider published his now-famous call for "man-computer symbiosis," where computers and humans would augment each other.[70] Otherwise, Licklider warned,

> Imagine trying, for example, to direct a battle with the aid of a computer on such a schedule as this. You formulate your problem today. Tomorrow you spend with a programmer. Next week the computer devotes 5 minutes to assembling your program and 47 seconds to calculating the answer to your problem. You get a sheet of paper 20 feet long, full of numbers that, instead of providing a final solution, only suggest a tactic that should be explored by simulation. Obviously, the battle would be over before the second step in its planning was begun.[71]

If Licklider was worried about simulation's results taking weeks, how must have Brody felt taking months? So, the problem arose: Could there be an easier way to run a simulation that would be accepted as valid? Though expensive for their time, computers required far less complicated administration.

The jump to computer simulation from human exercises proved minor. Simulation research always included an element of "artificial" intelligence, usually students pretending to be world leaders or computer programs acting on behalf of industrial nations. The high costs of running a game prompted a reflection about whether humans or machines were the best subjects to test a model. Did a computer or a human more successfully close the gap between operating model and referent system? Utility, or at least a desire for utility, encouraged replacing human intelligence with machine intelligence.

Cold War social science saw human intelligence as being interchangeable with machine intelligence. During World War II, operations research, game theory, and cybernetics were applied to predicting an enemy's movements—leading to a growing addressability of machine behavior to human behavior.

I find the same in political campaigns, but it is found earlier still by Peter Galison, who traces the beginnings of this addressability matter between humans and machines to Norbert Wiener. Wiener's experiments in anti-aircraft targeting provoked speculation that the mind could be duplicated through circuits, smoothing the way for an eventual conflation of humans and machines in later neural network theory and in these discussions of computer simulation.[72]

Computer simulation drew on these traditions. Rulemaking for exercises or computer simulations involved a kind of system design. Game theory encouraged the comparison of humans and machines, as both could play games with similar rational strategies. Similarly, in cybernetics, humans and machines could both be said to be homeostats. World simulations, then, regarded the distinctions between humans and computers with disinterest; they were less important than the relevance of the operating model. These facts remained true well after the war. Recall that CIA analyst Orrin Clotsworthy wondered if electronic memory could mimic Mao Zedong. That computers found utility specifically in predicting enemy behavior offers a reminder of the contested status of the human in the postwar period as well as of continuing investment in computing as an instrument of war and domination.

Modelers believed that both humans and computer programs had similar agencies. To Guetzkow's student Charles Hermann, an operating model was "capable of producing events that an observer could not readily derive from the initial conditions of the simulation."[73] The simulation produced "emergence" and "unforeseen events." Hermann's description encouraged thinking of humans and machines as comparable agents; both humans and computers exhibited emergent behaviors. Whereas other fields in the social sciences were slower to collapse the difference between humans and machines, the switch was important to the advancement of world modeling.[74] Moving to computers created spaces for the imagination of what we now might call artificial intelligence.

Work on building a political artificial intelligence started in 1965. Ithiel de Sola Pool and recent economics graduate Alan Kessler made a working prototype where computer programs played out the events leading to World War I. Pool and Kessler's CRISISCOM project simulated the behavior of national leaders.[75] Funded by the US Navy, their motivations reflected the postwar reconsideration of human intelligence as akin to machine intelligence. Specifically, they said CRISISCOM "represent[s] the ways in which psychological mechanisms enter into their processing of the information they receive. It is designed to simulate the process whereby two different decision makers acquire in their own minds quite different pictures of the world in which they are interacting. A flow of messages representing the real world comes to the decision makers. They selectively attend to different messages in this flow leaving each decision maker with a quite different image of the world from that of the other."[76] Such a cybernetic view of human decision-making was markedly different than the rational agents but still left little distinction between human and computer processes. Pool and Kessler's understanding of decision-making drew on "sociopsychological hypotheses" that stated that an actor had a certain limited "attention space" and needed to evaluate what signal to add to this space, an act of cognitive filtering. CRISISCOM's only publicly documented run simulated two players, the Tsar and the Kaiser. Though Pool and Kessler provide scant description of the specific design of the Tsar and the Kaiser, the simulation tracked how these players' "image of the world" changed over the seven days leading up to World War I by sending each other public and private messages collected from newspapers at the time. Each player's algorithm interpreted these messages to change a running attention matrix, shown in figure 7.4.

The two modeled "men" ended up ignoring unrest in Ireland and trouble on the Panama Canal; "By the end of the seven days [the Kaiser] and [the Tsar] are not looking at the same world although reality impinges itself on each. Three events, Russia's mobilization, Germany's mobilization, and the secret treaties, are in the attention space of both men. But two events, the collapse of Europe's stock markets and Germany's military precautions, are also in the attention of the Kaiser, while two other events, Serbia's Balkan allies and the Russian press, are in the attention of the Tsar."[77] CRISISCOM further systematized human intelligence to make it simple enough for a machine to carry out. The goal, eventually, was for CRISISCOM to "provide inputs for teams that cannot be staffed with humans and to represent aspects of the environment that are not played out by the human players."[78] There is little evidence that CRISISCOM achieved these goals or that its methods were adopted (although its design foreshadows interest in the agent-based modeling discussed in the next chapter). Nonetheless, CRISISCOM let modelers open the player's inner black box, much like Coleman's political games.

Early artificial intelligence promised to replace human players. Humans were too difficult to use. Specifically, there was a concern about whether

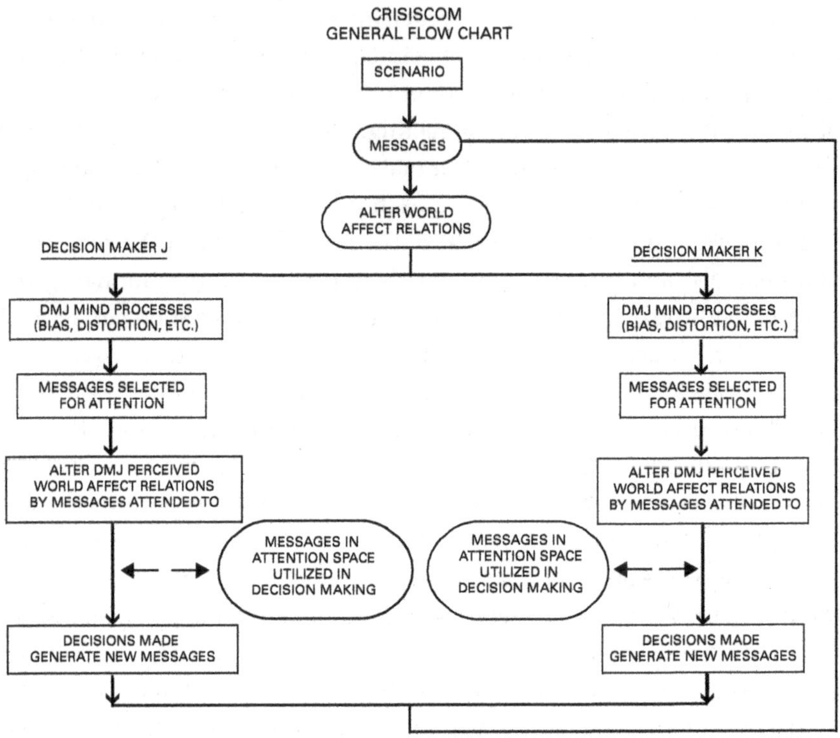

Figure 7.4

The "sketchy" flowchart of the CRISISCOM Project reproduction from the original diagram. *Source*: Redrawn from Pool and Kessler, "The Kaiser, the Tsar, and the Computer," 34.

humans, generally high school students, could role-play world leaders effectively. The problem was not only for validity-testing, as discussed in Alker Jr. and Brunner's study, but with the humans themselves. As Charles Hermann put it bluntly, "How can American participants represent the cultural values of other societies?"[79] How well could one culture understand another? Players often treated the simulation as a game. In 2009, an alumnus of the 1969 Upper Arlington High School class remembered INS fondly as a "political role-playing game" that, in their first run, prevented the outbreak of World War I. The "game" proved so successful that they ran it a second time (its newsletter is shown in figure 7.5). This run did not go as well; they wrote, "Unfortunately, this second world had nuclear weapons and did not survive to the scheduled end time. I guess maybe we

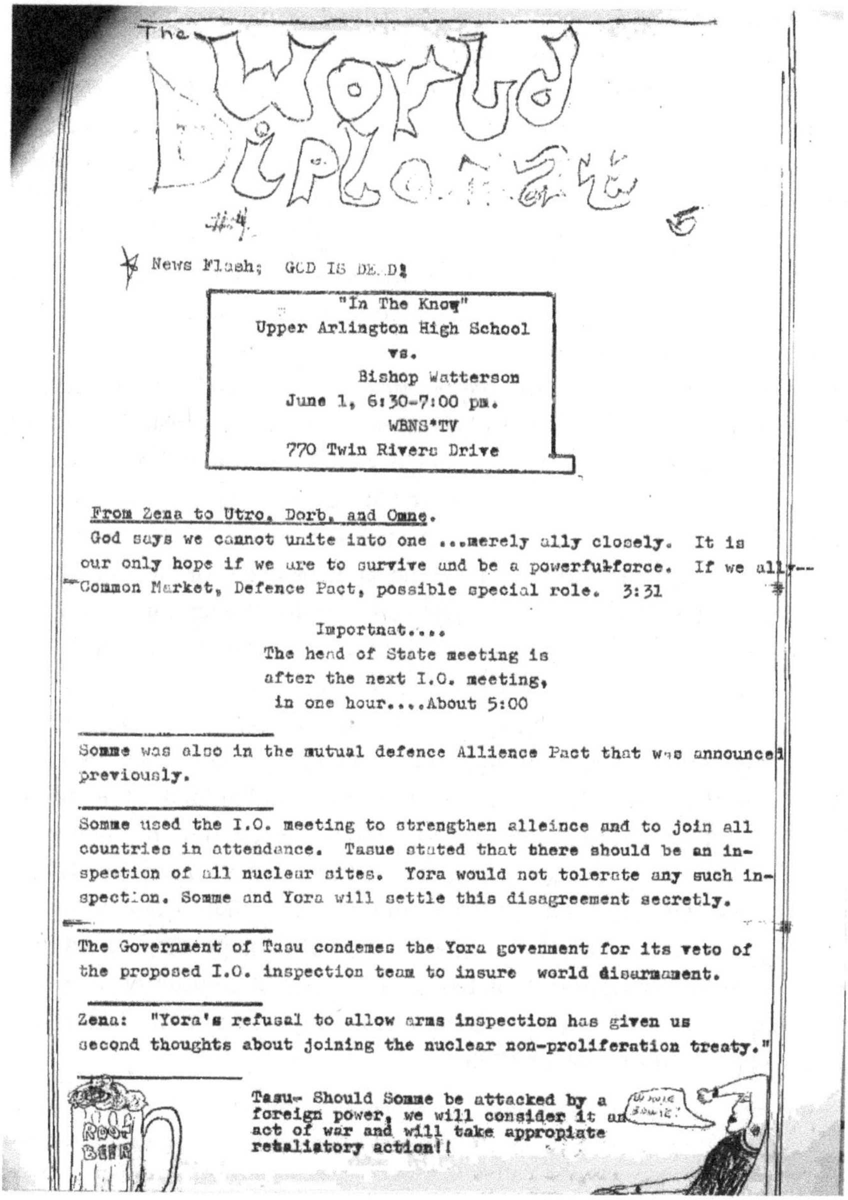

The World Diplomat

#4

News Flash; GOD IS DEAD!

"In The Know"
Upper Arlington High School
vs.
Bishop Watterson
June 1, 6:30-7:00 pm.
WBNS*TV
770 Twin Rivers Drive

From Zena to Utro, Dorb, and Omne.
God says we cannot unite into one ...merely ally closely. It is our only hope if we are to survive and be a powerfulforce. If we ally--Common Market, Defence Pact, possible special role. 3:31

Importnat....
The head of State meeting is after the next I.O. meeting, in one hour....About 5:00

Somme was also in the mutual defence Allience Pact that was announced previously.

Somme used the I.O. meeting to strengthen alleince and to join all countries in attendance. Tasue stated that there should be an inspection of all nuclear sites. Yora would not tolerate any such inspection. Somme and Yora will settle this disagreement secretly.

The Government of Tasu condemes the Yora govenment for its veto of the proposed I.O. inspection team to insure world disarmament.

Zena: "Yora's refusal to allow arms inspection has given us second thoughts about joining the nuclear non-proliferation treaty."

Tasu- Should Somme be attacked by a foreign power, we will consider it an act of war and will take appropiate retaliatory action!!

Figure 7.5

Newsletter created by high school students playing the Inter-Nation Simulation. *Source*: Holloway, "The Upper Arlington High School Class of 1969."

weren't the Peace Generation after all."[80] Imagine Richard Brody hearing these comments after his summer described above.

A move from in-person to hybrid to online formats for the testing environment eased the replacement of humans with machines. Guetzkow experimented with running INS on the PLATO system, one of the first interactive, educational computer systems, which was housed at the University of Illinois.[81] Players used PLATO's terminal to play the game.[82] His former student Robert Noël moved to the University of Santa Barbara in 1963, where he experimented further with conducting simulation games on newly established long-distance computer networks in addition to running an experimental space to observe political simulations. With William D. Hyder, Noël established the Polis Laboratory (short for political institutions simulation) in 1969. The lab facilitated games and simulations for over thirty-five institutions across the United States and eventually ran simulations over Arpanet.[83] While notable for being one of the first examples of networked play, Polis also reoriented the game from a room to a lab, interfacing the players through computers—a move like the famous Turing test where, as media theorist Friedrich Kittler notes, "game man and his simulation coalesce."[84] They became one and the same on screen or teletype.[85]

The way machine intelligence acted as a surrogate for human intelligence was deeply political, though not always discussed as such. Whereas the tsars and kaisers of European history required individualized programs, towns and villages in the Global South could be dealt with in the aggregate. Abt Associates developed a series of counterinsurgency games (POLITICA, or COCON-COUNTERCONSPIRACY, and AGILE-COIN). These were war games played as military training and, arguably, for developing military strategy. Abt's prototypes simulated the influence of counterinsurgents or belligerents on government influence and support from the "villagers." One scenario run in 1965 or 1966

> was set in Lucretia, the agricultural province of the hypothetical South American country of Inertia. The population of this particularly underdeveloped region had been divided between the native Inertian majority and the Asian Sarakhanese sugar worker minority and attempts at integration had been discouraged by the Suballa military dictatorship. During the POLITICA play, the Sarakhanese workers, inspired and assisted by the local FLN under Jimenez, overthrew the provincial military government. Although the native peasants were initially neutral, Jimenez was able to form a coalition with them and the Sarakhanese and maintain control of the province. The central government was virtually powerless in

> this province when the game ended, but Cervantes, then chief of state, had firm control of the middle and lower classes in the rest of the country.[86]

The nations simulated were real, but the named had been changed. The CIA assisted a coup in Guatemala in 1954. The United States supported the Bay of Pigs strike against Cuba in 1961. Normally, players played all teams in the simulation. Abt Associates also built a computer simulation of the game to enable an all-machine run where machines could *play* as the government, villages, or insurgents. In these all-machine simulations, governments skirmished with belligerents and spread propaganda to win hearts and minds. What's notable is that these simulations focused on the imagined lives of "America's backyard" and that the logics of these players could be so easily translated to a computer.

Simulations desired their models to be useful enough to accept exchanging humans with subroutines, algorithms, and code. The result appeared to be something superior. Indifference to the choice of human or machine in the operating model freed world modeling to experiment more with abstracted views. All these processes could be better analyzed too. Computer code promised to open the black box of decision-making—better explicability, if I may. Coded versions of governments and leaders could be better analyzed than their human counterparts. In tandem with validity and commensurability, utility positioned the computer as the preferred prototype that was easier to manage and quicker to get results.

The Modeling Boom: Computer Simulations Grow in Popularity

Quantitative political scientists, peace activists, and even the war-gaming establishment might have believed in computer simulations, but they did not popularize them. Despite spending years questioning, testing, and validating computer simulations, the modelers who legitimated computer simulation—Guetzkow and Abt—found themselves on the sidelines of what happened next.[87] Political scientists were outmaneuvered, and their approach was replaced by Jay Forrester's system dynamics. Out of the twenty-four computer simulations created between 1970 and 1979, only five included political scientists on their teams (see table 7.1).[88] Politics became merely one subsystem of these world models, often an unnecessary one. But even if it was marginalized in what became known as the "modeling boom," the political science community had already integrated

Table 7.1
Known computer simulations beginning in 1970

Name	Start date	Type	Project location	Country	Discipline
World 2 / 3	1970	Simulation	MIT	USA	Systems dynamics
Latin American World Model (Bariloche Model)	1970	Simulation		International	Mathematics
World Integrated Model (WIM)	1972	Simulation	Case Western Reserve University	USA	Mathematics, economics
ILO Basic Needs Model	1972	Unknown	International Labor Organization	International	
Nations-in-Conflict	1972	Simulation	MIT	USA	Political science, history, economics
MOIRA	1972/1980	Simulation	Free University, Amsterdam	Netherlands	Economics, ecology
Systems Analysis Research Unit (SARUM)	1973	Simulation	UK Department of the Environment	United Kingdom	Systems analysis
United Nations World Model or UN Global Input/Output Model	1973	Simulation	New York University, Brandeis University	USA	Economics
IIASA Energy Model	1973	Unknown	IIASA	International	
Future of Global Interdependence (FUGI)	1974	Simulation	University of Tokyo, Soka University	Japan	Economics
World Bank Model for Global Interdependence (SIMLINK)	1974	Simulation	World Bank	International	
Simulation of Political, Economic and Strategic Interactions (SIMPEST / SIMSWISS)	~1974	Simulation	University of Geneva	Switzerland	History, political science, mathematics
World Politics Simulation	1975	Simulation			History, political science, artificial intelligence
Dynamico	1975	Unknown	UN Department of International Economic and Social Affairs	International	

Name	Start date	Type	Project location	Country	Discipline
IIASA Food and Agricultural Program	1976	Simulation	IIASA	International	
Systems for Modelling Global Development Processes (SIM/GDP)	1977	Unknown			
AIM	1977	Unknown	UN Institute for Training and Research	International	
Australian Resources and Environmental Model (AREAM)	1978	Simulation	Department of Home Affairs and Environment	Australia	Political science
ZENCAP-D	1978	Unknown	Technical University, Zurich	Switzerland	Economics
INTERLINK	1978	Unknown	OECD	International	
Rastogi Model	1979	Unknown	Indian Institute of Technology	India	
International Futures (IFs)	1979	Simulation	University of Denver	USA	Political science
Generating Long-Term Options by Using Simulation (GLOBUS)	1980	Simulation	WZB	Germany	Political science
Indian Basic Needs Model	1980	Unknown	Systems Research Institute	India	
Global 2000	1980	Simulation	Council of Environmental Quality and Department of State	USA	
Global Models and the Policy Process (G-MAPP)	1981	Simulation	East-West Center	USA	
FORECASTS	1982	Unknown	Prospective Decision Models	USA	
World Model Project	1983	Simulation	University of Groningen	Netherlands	
Regional World III / IV	Late 1970s	Unknown	Social Modelling Project, Aid Association for Lutherans	USA	
Bradford Six-Sector Model	Late 1970s	Unknown	University of Bradford	United Kingdom	
Model of the World Economy	Mid-1970s	Unknown	Siberian Academy of Sciences	USSR	

politics into abstracted political modeling. The next section summarizes the consequences of the modeling boom and highlights the crystallization of computer modeling as the God's-eye vantage point for politicians and policymakers.

Much has been written about the still-active Club of Rome,[89] but, to summarize, the group was started in 1968 to address the "predicament of mankind." As historian Matthias Schmelzer noted, the initial club was an "elite group of engineers, scientists, and businessmen, all male and all from the global North" with close connections to the Organization for Economic Cooperation and Development (OECD).[90] In formulating a response, the group eventually turned to a computer simulation developed by Jay Forrester, then at MIT's Sloan School of Management. Forrester's "system dynamics" had previously been applied to corporate, urban, and industrial policies. System dynamics was more akin to control and system engineering than the systems theory happening in political science. The lower cost and high self-confidence of Forrester's proposed model won the support of the Volkswagen Foundation, which funded *The Limits to Growth* report published in 1972.[91] Notably, the Club of Rome had deadlocked over an earlier proposal written by another founding member, Hasan Özbekhan. Özbekhan's report built on the DELPHI method, which he learned when he worked as a forecaster for RAND and its offshoot, the System Development Corporation. Özbekhan's report had a much more strongly normative focus than Forrester's world system, which, historian Jenny Andersson writes, "evacuated the complex issue of human values from the analysis."[92] The final model, *WORLD3*, did not include politics in its system.

If the model and analysis avoided politics, the club's executive did not. The Canadian government, for instance, was an early supporter, inviting the club to an event at the prestigious Montebello resort that prompted the team to turn *The Limits to Growth* report into a book to reach a more public audience.[93] The club sent 6,700 copies of the accessible report to numerous heads of state, US politicians, and journalists; club members also promoted the book in interviews and press appearances.

The reception among established world modelers was cold. The report never received a review or much formal discussion in the academic literature. Even before the report, Forrester's 1971 book *World Dynamics* was reviewed in *Science* by Martin Shubik, a developer of political exercises and MIT professor. He deemed *World Dynamics* "blatant and insensitive advocacy for unsubstantiated model building on a very large scale," even larger than Forrester's past work.[94] Most bluntly, American economist and Cowles Commission member William Nordhaus described the report "as measurement without data. The model contains 43 variables connected by 22 non-linear (and several linear) relationships. Not a single relationship or variable is drawn from actual data or empirical studies."[95] Nordhaus's criticism exemplified the problem of hyperreality of simulation and known concerns about commensurability. Nordhaus was not alone. Another rebuttal of the report, published as *Models of Doom*,[96] along with discussions in the emerging global systems community, led to a second Club of Rome report based on a new model, the *World Integrated Model* (WIM).[97] But far from dismissing the approach, these criticisms only propelled further discussion.

Not all models aimed to predict, and some still included politics. An early presentation of *WORLD3* in Rio de Janeiro prompted the Fundación Bariloche of Argentina to develop the Latin American World Model, better known as the Bariloche Model. Supported by the Argentinian Fundación Bariloche and, later, the Canadian government, the model rejected the eschewed *WORLD3*'s Malthusian fatalism.[98] As its colead Amilcar Herrera explained at the Second IISAS Symposium on Global Modelling in 1974, the model "starts from the assumption that at least for the foreseeable future, the main obstacles to the harmonious development of mankind are not physical; rather they are social and political in nature and depend on the present distribution of power both at an international and national level."[99] Developed principally between 1972 and 1974, the Latin American World Model sought to set and meet development targets, in effect offering a way to steer sustainable development.

Herrera's remarks foreshadow media theorist Sun-Ha Hong's criticism of technology futurism as conservative, a "kind of fiction through which power relations are tested and entrenched."[100] The Bariloche Model responded to *The Limits to Growth*'s static perspective that extrapolated the world as-is; instead, the Bariloche Model sought to model what could be. Of course, the model was often criticized for being too socialist in its orientation, but coverage of the modeling boom distinguished the Bariloche Model's interventionist approach from the doomsaying of the Club of Rome models.[101]

Even if their methods faced widespread criticism,[102] the club's executive believed that the first report popularized the utility of modeling within the policy community, in effect repositioning modelers from testing to predicting.[103] Political interest in *The Limits to Growth* was expected, but its uptake by the public less so. Its critics, rightly, attacked the neo-Malthusian bent of the final report,[104] but even Özbekhan's early, more normative report had put population at the top of its list of concerns, ranking above poverty (second) and inequity (eighth). That a small group of technocratic elites, whose network started at an OECD conference at the Rockefeller family villa in Italy, advocated for population control made them an easy target. Another systems thinker, Buckminster Fuller, did not hold back in noting that "the Club of Rome's *Limits to Growth* pronouncement represented the last attempt on the part of organized capitalists' selfishness to justify to the world public why their wealth would be unable to do anything about the third world."[105] Nonetheless, *The Limits to Growth* was a bestseller and something of a capstone. As one of the founders of peace research Johan Galtung noted, "many have been saying [there were limits to growth] for a long time; and when this book has been given particularly much attention it is not only because of excellent public relations for the book, but also because it is riding on a wave created by others."[106] That wave—consisting of environmentalism,[107] futurism,[108] and, as seen earlier, interest in computers and systems—propelled the Club of Rome and dramatically altered the context of political world simulations, again situating computer modeling as a new, powerful means to understand the Earth.

Computers delivered on the potential for prediction but not via the prototypes envisioned by Guetzkow or other peace researchers. Though oriented toward the use of models in politics, the makers of world simulations were uneasy about their reception. Harold Guetzkow later remarked, "the decade of the 1970s . . . has been a tremendous time for those of us concerned with global modelling in international affairs. Thanks in part to the initiatives of the Club of Rome, world modelling has become an integral part of the intellectual scene throughout the world. It is regretted that our work in Simulated International Processes provided no catalyst for these activities."[109] This self-reflection emphasized political science and peace research's relegation to the margins but also acknowledged that Guetzkow's aspirations for computer simulation were as ambitious as *The Limits to Growth*'s success.

After the modeling boom, Abt and Guetzkow found themselves in an odd place. Having urged on the turn to computers, these political world simulators faced a new consensus that the computer could model the world, while their reservations and concerns were taken merely as encouragement for more, better models. If world simulators were on the outside looking in, that was a view they had chosen. By treating the human as an unnecessary variable and cutting the flesh from the simulation, so to speak, prototypes like TEMPER and Bremer's SIPER (see below) contributed to an overall stabilization of computer simulation with its God's-eye views of Earth.

Harold Guetzkow largely abandoned work on the Inter-Nation Simulation by the mid-1960s. He attempted to market INS as a teaching tool. Instead, Guetzkow's Simulated International Processes turned toward all-computer simulations. These proved cheaper and easier to use when modeling theory and capable of better integrating new quantitative data. At least three world simulations developed out of Guetzkow's game, including Paul Smoker's previously discussed all-computer International Processes Simulation (IPS), completed by 1968. Smoker described the model's theoretical orientation as building on the work of Karl Deutsch and Talcott Parsons.[110] The next year, a promising doctoral student from Michigan State University, Stuart Bremer, arrived at Guetzkow's project and proceeded to write another all-computer version of INS, the Simulated International ProcessER (SIPER). Bremer's project, one he credits to Guetzkow's mentorship, would become one of the only lasting major political world simulations.[111] All these changes happened with the support and interest of the Joint War Games Agency and ARPA, Guetzkow's funders. The US government, in its many forms, maintained an active interest in supporting these computer prototypes. Bremer, finally, went on to develop a third model, GLOBUS, discussed in depth next.

Guetzkow's career path shifted from developing models to working directly in international relations, first with a senior internship at the US Department of State from 1969 to 1970 and then at the UN Secretariat until 1971. These gigs did not expand his reach but hinted at some of the politics behind his modeling efforts. Guetzkow admitted that he had little influence at the UN because he was "unable to establish a non-Central Intelligence Agency (CIA) status," making it "impossible to have conversations with delegates and members of the bureaucracy." Moreover, he continued, "the ever-present and obvious interest of Russian State Security Committee (KGB) agents in my work in simulation, being funded by the US military, undermined my credibility as an American scholar."[112] Guetzkow's admission is oddly naive considering he was a major recipient of ARPA funding. Why would his international peers not approach him with suspicion, especially as his efforts benefitted from feedback and support from the US military?

The end of the modeling boom was something of a "monkey's paw" scenario for world simulators. Abt, curiously, abandoned simulation altogether. By 1970, Clarke had published his popular book *Serious Games*. According to one of Abt's collaborators, Daniel del Solar, Abt Associates largely abandoned world modeling after learning about its applications. Del Solar claimed that Abt's counterinsurgency game POLITICA was used to help plan the US-assisted coup against democratically elected Chilean President Salvador Allende.[113] Though del Solar's allegation has never been substantiated, the claim is a good reminder that these models and prototypes had an ambiguous relationship to power even when devised by self-described peace scholars. Maybe POLITICA was not used to plan the coup, but the rumors speak to the models' proximity to power.

Q3. How Do Computer Simulations Address Worlds?

Efforts to build simulations of the world led to computer simulations that could be accepted as presentations of the globe that addressed the world as a system. The effect was to legitimate a way of addressing the world, what Haraway calls a "god's eye view," a system of vision that sees the world from nowhere, providing an omnipotent gaze of total vision and control. Haraway writes, "The eyes have been used to signify a perverse capacity—honed to perfection in the history of science tied to militarism, capitalism, colonialism, and male supremacy—to distance the knowing subject from everybody and everything in the interests of unfettered power. . . . Vision in this technological feast becomes unregulated gluttony; all perspective gives way to infinitely mobile vision, which no longer seems just mythically about the god trick of seeing everything from nowhere, but to have put the myth into ordinary practice."[114] Sure, 1960s-era computer printouts might seem dull compared to Haraway's description of "scanning electron microscopes, computer-aided tomography scanners, color enhancement techniques, [and] satellite surveillance systems," but nonetheless the computer became a specific prototype that could offer new presentations of the world at a scale distinct from a mere human observer.

The desirability of a God's-eye view became a secondary effect of closing three major addressability gaps. Validity proved to be a gap, requiring a view wherein the outcomes of the computer matched world models and world events. Growing amounts of International Data—considered to be useful for world modelers—blurred the boundary between worlds and data, driving generations of research into integrating political data in modeling. Validity and commensurability involved an interaction between models and their prototypes. Utility, finally, problematized the human in the simulation. Humans were too unreliable and irrational. Dealing with computer agents rather than humans made prototyping more manageable. Computer programming provided more direct access to the operating model and data than humans. Utility legitimated a world view where systems or subsystems, human or actors, were both programs and programmable. The outcome was a view of the world focused on prediction rather than speculation or ideation, seeking to replicate the world as it was. In doing so, both the world and its simulation became more computational.

The God's-eye view remains compelling today. The United Nations in 2023 hired the firm CulturePulse to simulate Israel and the Palestine Territories after the Hamas terror attacks and the subsequent AI-assisted war in Gaza. CulturePulse offered the UN a chance to better understand the conflict thanks to artificial intelligence and a computer simulation. Writing in *Wired* magazine, journalist David Gilbert explains that the project, "will initially model the socio-ecological aspects of the Israeli-Palestinian region that are relevant to the conflict."[115] The hope is that the computer simulation might offer some guidance to a situation with no apparent solution—a faith that draws deeply on the possibility of a God's-eye view of politics embedded in the computational imaginary of politics. Indeed, CulturePulse's marketing draws on all the promises of computer simulation found in this chapter.

CulturePulse's website highlights its research as evidence of its validity. Gilbert reports that CulturePulse's cofounders "claim their model predicts outcomes with clinical accuracy of over 95 percent confidence to real-world outcomes."[116] The firm prefers the term digital twin to describe its computer simulation. Where digital twins often refer to smart cities or replicating traffic systems, CulturePulse claims to make digital twins for entire societies. One paper created a digital twin of Northern Ireland that "uncovered critical drivers of conflict and cooperation" after the 1998 Belfast Agreement.[117] Similar to Guetzkow's studies above, the study tried to prove the methods of digital twins as a valid way to explain politics.

CulturePulse, at least what has been reported, makes a powerful claim about the commensurability of its models. Its tool, ARES, "creates psychologically realistic digital twins of any target group so you can test new strategies without risk and analyze global news streams so you can quickly turn insight into action predicting likely outcomes."[118] Simulated digital agents psychologically react to global event data inputted through data from world event projects.[119] A profile in *Wired* claims that CulturePulse has created digital down to the individual.[120] Its website advertises the ability to make "psychologically realistic digital twins."[121] The promise is not unlike TANJO's simulated voters; indeed, what is striking is the convergence of world and voter scales, a sort of hyper-resolution of infinite detail.

CulturePulse's marketing trades on offering up a God's-eye view of politics to its clients. Their digital twins are meant to act "as virtual laboratories in which policymakers can explore and discover the conditions under which—and the mechanisms by which—individual and social variables change in the artificial society."[122] Dr. Justin Lane, one of the cofounders, explained to *Wired* magazine, "We know that you can't solve a problem this complex with a single AI system. That's not ever going to be feasible in my opinion. . . . What is feasible is using an intelligent AI system . . . to explore the potential solutions that are there."[123] Hopefully, this chapter teaches a lesson in questioning these claims.

Appeals to the God's-eye view are what Catherine D'Ignazio and Lauren Klein, building on Haraway, call an "impossible standpoint." In their feminist critique of data analytics, D'Ignazio and Klein describe this impossible standpoint as a claim to see the world at untold scale.[124] The God's-eye view promises addressability as well as scale. Creating a God's-eye-view—no matter the cause—most often legitimated a politics of addressability. Few computer simulations, no matter how abstract, could escape the dominance of funding from the US government and military, the lack of regional expertise in favor of system knowledge, and the narrow ranks of elite male academics that set the relation between computational and political systems.[125] Villages and even entire nations could become a single variable or agent, in contrast to the need for detailed profiles of US voters happening at the same time. Black media philosophy, as introduced to me by Armond Towns, offers a critique of the nature of the taken-for-granted feasibility of the God's-eye view where white, Western academics presume to reformat the world on a disk. As Towns elaborates, "Rather than to forget the human, the goal of a Black media philosophy is to ask the question: If a specific human is largely overrepresented as white, male, heterosexual, cis-gender, and middle classed, what media have led to the creation of his current status?"[126] The same might be said for who decides what is valid, what peoples can be abstracted. Only in Pool's CrisisCom, did the individual mind of a non-American opponent become the object of programming, but even then, the God's-eye trick presumed that US social scientists could easily abstract the minds of foreign opponents.

The consequences of computer simulations' influences—especially in the form described here—have shaped the world's presentation, often with disastrous consequences. As Lucy Suchman argues, "the aspiration to closure itself is the source of the continued destructiveness of US interventions and the associated regeneration of enmity."[127] Early computer simulations did not cause war or create peace and instead should act as a warning to those today seeking to solve the next war with a computer simulation. The powerfulness of the God's-eye view might be a hyperreality, projecting the world as something that can be solved like a game to be won. Political agencies, instead, are much humbler than presented by the simulation. Such warnings seem to go unheeded.

8 Worlding Models

As politicians, analysts, and scientists reduced international relations to clusters of information in their models, a question arose: How should the virtual nations behave? Like rats in a digital maze scurrying to find some hidden order? Like card sharks trying to play their hands without being eaten by their peers? Like cool computers in a game of thermonuclear war? If there was agreement about the promise of computer simulation, there was little consensus on how these computer simulations should understand the world, much less on how they should be used. Growing interest in environmentalism, international communication, and the possibility of globalization encouraged viewing modeling as a proxy to global thinking.[1] But this view led to greater division, and computer simulations diverged. This chapter investigates how different computer simulations present different agencies to the user. Results matter to how computer simulation presented world agency—how the world worked—and how that interface became a tool for users to interact with the real world.

I return to my three models of politics—cybernetic citizens, rational agents, and data chimeras—to explore these different agencies. I begin by reintroducing a familiar character, Harold Guetzkow, and then focus on two projects that represent major *political* computer simulations respectively for cybernetic citizens and rational agents. I also briefly note how political event data and mathematical modeling created the field of crisis forecasting and early warning systems as an example of the data chimera model's legacies. Drawing on the work of historian Joy Rohde, I delineate how data-chimeric approaches drove investment in event modeling.[2] All three models help explicate the conflict over agency in political simulations. How the computational imaginaries include conflicts over world agency as well as addressability. GLOBUS offered a world of limited agency and speculation that consequently reduced its uptake in research and policy sectors, whereas FACTIONS presented a strategic outlook that became a guiding influence on the US intelligence communities. Through comparing the two, I aim to foreground a sense of the politics of the world, and of computer simulation itself, posed in this chapter's critical questions. Should computer simulations present the challenges of interacting in a complex, multistakeholder world? Or should computer simulation just help its users win, in which case world agency becomes just a matter of self-interest? In the chapter conclusion, an example of the *Hidden Agenda* computer game illustrates how simulations play with their presentations of agency, offering a counterpoint to the two main examples here.

After the Modeling Boom: Cybernetic Citizens, Rational Agents, and Data Chimeras Globalized

Divergence was natural given the modeling boom. As discussed in the previous chapter, 1967 to 1972 was a remarkable period of institution-building in the modeling and future studies communities, leading to a wider embrace of computer modeling.[3] Modeling, forecasting, and future studies developed in the United States, in the USSR, and internationally in parallel to the political simulations discussed earlier. The United States led efforts to establish an international organization, called, in 1968, the International Center for the Study of Problems Common to Advanced Industrialized Societies and eventually named the International Institute for Applied Systems Analysis (IIASA) when it opened in 1972. As noted in Elgė Rindzevičiūtė's fantastic history of the IIASA, the institute brought together an international community dedicated to objective systems analysis of policy matters.[4] The IIASA held its first conference on global modeling in 1974, and subsequent symposiums hosted international debates about the future of modeling. That same period saw the launch of at least four academic journals on the subject: *Futures* (1968), *Technological Forecasting* (1969), *Simulation and Gaming* (1970), and *Policy Sciences* (1970). And, as a final note, Buckminster Fuller published his book *An Operating Manual for Spaceship Earth* in 1969, popularizing planning and systems analysis as a tool for the emerging problem of "planetary management." These journals, along with the IIASA, became the settings for debates about what computer simulation should do. Merely classifying the differences among models constituted a literature unto itself with numerous projects comparing approaches.[5]

Self-reflection became a theme in the modeling community, as seen in the symposiums held by the Institute for Applied Systems Analysis and in the academic literature.[6] A special 1982 issue of the journal *Futures* brought together most of the key figures in the Club of Rome to consider their impact as well as the limited political uptake of the club's vision. The reflections are curious for focusing on modeling's humanistic side—lamenting the field's inability to foster long-term world thinking—while also restating the importance of computer simulations' God's-eye view (though now more tempered).[7] *The Limits to Growth* coauthor Dennis Meadows nicely captures these views by paraphrasing some "profound contributions" made at a then-recent modeling conference.[8] Meadows quotes US government advisor Gerald Barney: "Every government already operates with a global model. Most such models are, like that of the USA, fractionated, with different parts in different agencies."[9] Barney's comments reflected the difficulty of his own work for the US government but also the impact of the boom on governments' self-awareness. The business of government became just another model. Seeing like a state became just another God's-eye view.

The boom led to computer simulations escaping their military contexts as well. In 1968, a group of RAND researchers founded the Institute for the Future (IFTF) with the support of the Ford Foundation and other private sources. The IFTF sought to commercialize the RAND Corporation's DELPHI expert forecasting system. (DELPHI forecasting is a precursor to today's superforecasters.) Repositioning DELPHI as a policy and business forecaster was part of a broader trend at RAND to move away from war and toward social policy. IFTF's launch promised, among other things, "computer programmes that represent complex relations among relevant factors, simulation facilities to allow participation in forward-looking activities by groups of interested officials, and services to client organizations in the form of access to data banks."[10] The result was a wider consideration of computer simulation as a policy tool, or what political scientist Karl Deutsch called a steering model.

The modeling boom fueled interest and investment from governments. The Club of Rome's success prompted governments across the globe to invest in their own world models. Japan, the United Kingdom, and Australia all developed models inspired by the system-dynamics approach.[11]

Again, the computer offered a scientific, objective means for forecasting that fit with the self-presentation of researchers in the policy sciences, but also, in the context of the Cold War, helped advance US expertise in forecasting against the Soviets.[12] In this context, the models of new computer simulations restated the cybernetic citizens, rational agents, and data chimeras models to describe world agencies.

Data Chimeras and Crisis Modeling

Could simulations predict crises? The first split involved a move toward computer simulation for crisis forecasting. Guetzkow's students Charles and Margaret Hermann shifted the predictive capacity of the Inter-Nation Simulation from simulating the historical (e.g., predicting World War I) to anticipating the future.[13] Predictive models, connected as they were to the international relations data projects discussed in the previous chapter, foreshadowed data analytics, advances in computational social science, and eventually, forms of machine learning.

Charles McClelland, a leader in event data and systems thinking, had perhaps the greatest influence in turning data collection into forecasting tools. As described in the previous chapter, McClelland's World Event/Interaction System (WEIS) converted *New York Times* articles into numerical codes that could be recorded on punch cards. The database became an important source of political data and started a field, still active today, dedicated to collecting and coding event data.[14] Subsequent work with the WEIS database at DARPA led to new systems of crisis forecasting, an application McClelland approved, though he was no longer involved in the process.[15] One such system, the Integrated Crisis Early Warning System (ICEWS), sounded a lot like existing defense tools like the Ballistic Missile Early Warning System. Indeed, it hoped to predict crises just like the military predicted a missile's arc.

The ICEWS and its contemporaries illustrated a data chimeric approach to world modeling. Such an approach—illustrated in figure 8.1—asks whether events or other global data include patterns that could anticipate conflicts.

The ICEWS's designers, Stephen J. Andriole and Robert A. Young, wrote that they sought to "avoid the extreme of undirected data collection as well as excessively abstract exercises in the construction of theories and 'pretheories.' Central to our research is the conviction that there must be

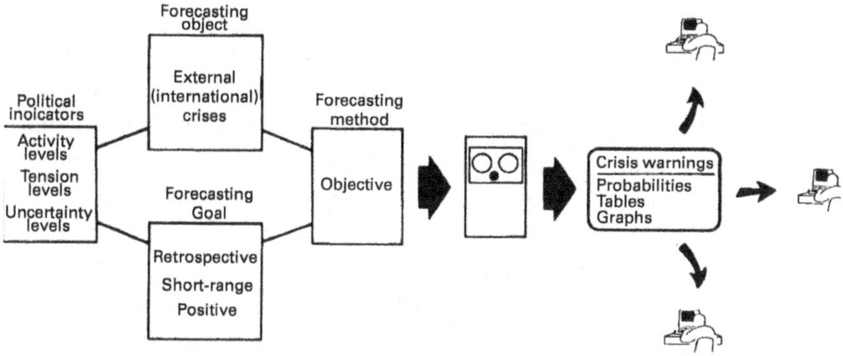

Figure 8.1
The Integrated Crisis Early Warning System. From Stephen J. Andriole and Robert A. Young. 1977. "Toward the Development of an Integrated Crisis Warning System," *International Studies Quarterly*, 21 (1): 107, https://doi.org/10.2307/2600149. Reproduced by permission of Oxford University Press on behalf of the International Studies Association.

a dynamic dialogue between data collection and theory building."[16] Their conviction led to the proposed "integrated system . . . designed for the purpose of eventually placing the capability to forecast crises of all types (internal, external; military, political, economic; of more or less importance to U.S.) into the hands of those most in need of such a system."[17]

Crisis forecasting's links to data chimeras were not purely theoretical. Reagan's presidential campaign manager worked closely with Richard Smith Beal. Beal graduated from the University of Southern California with a degree in international relations under the supervision of Charles McClelland. Funded by ARPA, Beal's dissertation research focused on predicting international crises.[18] His subsequent research initially sought to use event data to offer "Systems-Cybernetic Analysis" of international relations and eventually became a book.[19] He later focused more on how data analysis could act like a dashboard for political action, resembling the work of his data chimera peers more than his references to cybernetics suggest. How exactly Beal came to work on Reagan's 1980 campaign is unclear, but after the election he served in the White House. There, his research for the Office of Planning and Evaluation blurred domestic and international politics, using computers and computer-assisted analysis to offer at-a-glance insights into world states and voter states. Beal's work ended abruptly with his death in 1984 at the age of 38.[20]

Cybernetic Citizens and GLOBUS

A second approach drew more inspiration from integrated cybernetic systems. The most significant of these projects was GLOBUS, developed by two of Harold Guetzkow's peers, Stuart Bremer and Karl Deutsch. GLOBUS aimed to make a simulation built on cybernetics, political theory, and systems theory to provide long-term advice and predictions decades into the future. GLOBUS stands in for a few different attempts to build a working system where cybernetic homeostats could play in a complex representation of the world system. Where ICEWS designers Andriole and Young avoided abstract theory, GLOBUS's 940-page companion book included complex explanations of its economic and political subsystems.

Rational Agents and the Political Intelligence Industry

A final approach focused on the decision-making function of models, trying to strip away complexity to focus on how models informed decision-makers and, recursively, how they might also model decision-makers. This too was a split from the Inter-Nation Simulation, as William Coplin who at first replicated Guetzkow's work, turned toward simulating and enhancing decision-making to become part of a strategic intelligence industry for world politics and through his later work in political intelligence. The work of his competitors, Abramo Fimo, Kenneth Organski, Jacek Kugler, and Bruce Bueno de Mesquita, inspired the CIA's FACTIONS tool. Their efforts represented an application of rational agent models to world politics and, in some projects, a move toward agent-based modeling to simulate the emergent behavior of global systems. The focus on decision-making involved and emphasized reasoning and self-interest. Whereas Deutsch sought to find a better common future, another school wanted to help decision-makers and, in so doing, conceived of the entire world as individuals seeking to maximize utility.

These methodological splits stand in for deeper conceptual and political divisions. There was a consensus to build simulations that helped with decision-making; however, who and what those decision-makers were offers a glimpse into obscured strategic motivations. Data-driven approaches and utility maximization logics usually led to models for short-term, strategic decision-making. The examples that I discuss often involved tools employed to advance US interests to win on the global stage, but not always.

GLOBUS: The Last Stand of Cybernetic World Modeling

Cybernetics' last stand started with a phone call. Karl Deutsch, one of the key figures in political systems thinking, was at home in Cambridge. An émigré from what is now the Czech Republic, Deutsch had been a professor at Harvard University since 1967. He was a founding figure in postwar international relations, helping to establish a systems approach.[21] Now it was 1974, and someone was calling from Europe.[22] The West German Federal Ministry of Research and Technology offered Deutsch the opportunity to lead a project at its relatively new Berlin Social Science Center (Wissenschaftszentrum, or WZB for short). In the twilight of his career, the prospect appealed to Deutsch.

The position offered Deutsch a chance to put his cybernetic approach to politics into practice. He popularized cybernetics in political science. Deutsch had actively worked on international political data, was interested in better use of cybernetics in government (what he later described as steering models), and participated in modeling after the boom.[23] His major book, published in 1965, *Nerves of Government* marked a key shift in the theory of governance as it advanced cybernetics over game theoretical approaches.[24] Deutsch's theories of the cybernetic state were seen as too abstract—perhaps too associated with the Vietnam War—to be considered feasible.[25] Times were different now. Deutsch acknowledged that after the Club of Rome's success, his approach seemed more feasible.[26] There was, according to Deutsch, "a climate of opinion in which public support for world modeling efforts became possible."[27] With GLOBUS, Deutsch could finally build his nerves of government. Three years of discussion later, Deutsch started as codirector of the WZB's Institute for Comparative Social Research.

From Cybernetics to Steering Models

In the lead-up to joining the WZB, Deutsch started framing his approach for world modeling as a system of cybernetic steering. He held a 1976 conference and published a 1977 book that were both aptly titled *The Problems of World Modelling*. In the book, he distinguished between two agencies for world modeling; drift models and steering models were Deutsch's way to describe the major design paradigms. Drift models showed how the present course of the world would play out if left to drift into the future. Steering models sought to foresee the implications and evaluate the feasibility of setting targets to meet policy and development goals.[28]

Drift modeling referred to most applications of system dynamics, econometrics, and input-output analysis of world models. Drift models, to Deutsch, posited that "if mankind moves mostly with its existing momentum, then chances are outcomes will be of a certain type."[29] The Club of Rome's WORLD3 was a drift model that warned of impending crisis—hence the title *The Limits to Growth*, projecting the status quo into the future.

Deutsch sought to build his own computer simulation to be less deterministic than either WORLD3 or even the Bariloche model with its focus on an optimal outcome. In doing so, he joined a growing turn toward steering models. Deutsch equated steering models with his cybernetic approach to international relations—cybernetics being, etymologically, a play on the concept of steering. Computer simulation in his view could enhance "the steering capabilities not only of the nation state, but of the international organizations and of the world society and the political world system."[30] He continued, "Modelling activities could critically increase the lead of mankind's foresight" to prevent steering failures or "oversteering."[31] Implicitly, Deutsch proposed that simulation have a specific function: intervening. His vision was for an "all-computer, nation-based, political world model from empirical data"—that is, what became GLOBUS.[32] He started the project through his leadership at the WZB. The project drew together an all-star collection of world modelers, assembled for what would become one last job. The team shared a systems approach to modeling, hoping to create a working equivalent of a world system.[33]

Team GLOBUS

Before Deutsch had formally joined the WZB, he recruited Stuart Bremer, who started during the summer of 1976. Guetzkow had introduced Bremer to Deutsch. Bremer would stay on with the project until its end, roughly 1988. As mentioned earlier, Bremer was brilliant. He had come from the University of Michigan to work with Guetzkow for his doctoral research in the of fall 1968.[34] There, Bremer, by himself, programmed what Guetzkow considered the crowning achievement of his Simulated International Processes project: the Simulated International ProcessesER (SIPER), an all-computer simulation inspired by the Inter-Nation Simulation.[35] Guetzkow's celebration of SIPER shows just how much computer simulation had won the day as the preferred way to model world affairs.

Bremer's subsequent work built on all-computer simulations. His doctoral thesis, based on SIPER, won the American Political Science Association's annual award for best dissertation in 1972; Bremer published it as a book in 1977. In the book, he thanked David Singer and placed SIPER alongside TEMPER, Benson's Simple Diplomatic Game, and other attempts to develop an all-computer version of INS. SIPER functioned similarly to TEMPER; it had smaller modules (e.g., trade, aid, and conflict) that ran in sequence to simulate an international system that resembled a referent system with a "low level of economic development and growth, coupled with a high level of conflict and arms competition."[36] Bremer hoped SIPER would inspire new models and advance Guetzkow's hope to unify the "islands of theory."[37] Deutsch offered Bremer a chance to fulfil that desire.

Bremer started with a team of two that grew to twenty-five at its peak.[38] Two had direct experience with system dynamics models popularized by the Club of Rome: Barry Hughes and Peter Brecke. Hughes a stellar reputation with building running models. Still active in modeling today, he joined the GLOBUS team after working on the Club of Rome's second model, the World Integrated Model. MIT professor Hayward Alker—a contemporary of Guetzkow, prominent modeler, and neighbor of Ithiel de Sola Pool—supported the project, seeing GLOBUS as a major step in the evolution of the field.[39] Alker encouraged his student Peter Brecke to join the team. Brecke brought practical programming skills that he had acquired in pursuit of global modeling, an interest inspired by the psychohistory in Isaac Asimov's *Foundation* novels. His doctoral dissertation used the influential system dynamics programming language DYNAMO.[40]

GLOBUS attempted to be a holistic cybernetic world model. Bremer gave special attention to Deutsch's theories in the introduction to the 1987 GLOBUS book, one of the project's major outputs. He explained, "The central theoretical element of GLOBUS has been given many names but here I refer to it as the cybernetic conception of behavior."[41] In this conception, nations behaved like cybernetic homeostats, adjusting their actions based on their interactions with the virtual world (not unlike voters in domestic modeling efforts). Bremer quoted Deutsch's own example of steering: "to the statesman, guiding a difficult program to success may thus resemble the art of driving an automobile over an icy road: his problem is to anticipate the skids quickly enough so that he can still control them by small corrections at the steering wheel, where slowness of the action or oversteering would provide worse skids and might wreck the car."[42] Deutsch clearly hoped for GLOBUS to function as a steering model, helping world leaders steer the world. Bremer took the steering example in another direction, he explained, "Carrying the metaphor one step further one could portray the GLOBLUS world as a large ice lot in which 25 automobiles (nations) are all steered by front seat and backseat drivers (governments) seeking independent destinations with virtually no traffic rules to regulate their behavior."[43] Deutsch imagined GLOBUS providing a benign God's-eye view, whereas Bremer, deep in the code, saw agency in the machine. There was no God's-eye view available to the cybernetic agents or, ultimately, to GLOBUS's human users; there was only a front-seat view of an icy parking lot.

Building GLOBUS

The core team worked on GLOBUS in its various stages from Bremer's arrival in 1976 to the project's release of MicroGLOBUS in 1988. GLOBUS stands for Generating Long Term Options by Using Simulation. The name illustrates some of the motivation behind conceiving the project as a steering model. The project's development was anything but smooth. GLOBUS went through at least three phases: first, a review phase; second, a few different attempts to build a world model; and finally, an endeavor to democratize access to computer simulations through a PC version, MicroGLOBUS.

Work on GLOBUS began with the team reviewing and critiquing other world models. Bremer's SIPER model inspired group reflection on the purposes of modeling and how SIPER compared to its competitors. The team reviewed all the major simulations, including many of the models discussed in the previous chapter.[44] They likely had access to these model's source codes, which enabled them to study both the underlying models and the working prototypes. The team published a series of reports and a major book.[45] The book, *Weltmodellstudien* (World Modeling Studies), was released only in German in 1980, even though Bremer continued to publish findings in English as well.[46] Altogether, these efforts gave the GLOBUS team a heightened sense of self-consciousness about their work.

The team considered GLOBUS the world's first serious *political* simulation. That was arguably true when they started, but GLOBUS strongly resembled TEMPER, so perhaps it's best to think of GLOBUS as a pioneer in less militaristic political simulation. Amid growing coordination of modeling by the International Institute for Applied Systems Analysis, GLOBUS stood out for its strong conceptual focus on politics and a team populated by political scientists.[47] As Bremer explained in one of his research reports, "The world models developed so far are essentially economic models, occasionally linked to demographic models. This is neither an unfair statement nor a staggering conclusion, but we feel that all of these models are incapable of incorporating other (perhaps more important) problems than those for which they were originally designed. In our view, it is quite possible to construct a model that brings the 'political dimension' into global modeling."[48] The political orientation of the project made the team an outlier in the world modeling community. Most system dynamics models included modules for demographic or environmental trends, but none focused on political systems. GLOBUS team member Barry Hughes had direct experience with the latter. World Integrated Model (WIM)—the model Hughes worked on—modeled five strata of what it called the world system and grouped the world into ten regions, effectively abstracting national politics. The abstraction was only partially the result of limited modeling capacity. World systems had a strong normative preference for a one-world or global vision, which necessitated huge abstractions that ignored nations states and broke down world agency to the interactions between large regions. For GLOBUS, politics—international and domestic—was core to the project. Deutsch insisted that GLOBUS simulate nation states.[49] Hughes, in an interview, suggested that WIM's concerns reflected its times by focusing on shortages of food and energy, while the later GLOBUS reflected growing concerns about the Cold War.[50]

This historical context helps to explain the project's evolution as it moved from design to development. By late 1982, work had turned to building the GLOBUS simulation in opposition to other approaches. Bremer and his team stressed that GLOBUS was not an econometrics model or a symbolic model or an optimization model. Unlike rational agents, the model's nation-states behaved according to cybernetic theory and were influenced by Herbert Simon's thinking on bounded rationality.[51] GLOBUS did not provide a deductive mathematical model or a symbolic model, and it did not follow any logic, such as a Downsian utility maximization, that could be expressed as a neat mathematical formulation. Bremer claimed, "The

GLOBUS model has no general solution."[52] This claim was a direct retort to the Bariloche model that set goals (or optimization targets) and used the simulation to advise how to meet them.

GLOBUS's development always exceeded the computer resources at hand. GLOBUS initially ran on a "hopeless overloaded machine." The team measured response time "in hours rather than seconds."[53] As GLOBUS developed, its complexity and size outstripped the capacity of existing modeling software. By 1984, the team was working on its modeling package using a Cray-1M supercomputer with the latest version of FORTRAN (FORTRAN 77).[54] These advances gave the team the required resources to code the complex simulation, but the difficulty of the coding itself was a limitation. Hughes recalls "spending nights in the conference room that reeked of smoke from all the Berlin smokers." These long hours were often spent waiting, "because you would submit a run to the central computer and it might take an hour or two before you got results back and found out you misspelled something in the line of code."[55] Developers worked on microterminals connected to supercomputers.[56] Simulations could take up to six hours to finish, so programmers developed a twenty-four-hour cycle: working at home or at the office, sleeping, waking up at home to see the results, and then debugging.

The whole project was complex. Mistakes were hard to find. Brecke distilled the experience into one vignette. Days before GLOBUS's 1985 world debut—when the team would present their work to their peers, including Guetzkow, David Singer, Dina Zinnes, and Hayward Alker—the team assembled to review the results.[57] As Brecke recalls, "[The team was] sitting in the room going through a slide show of the model's results to see where we were. We were watching the first few images coming up and we were ready to crack out the champagne. . . . And then as the slides keep coming we realized, 'Oh no, somewhere we screwed up.' . . . The change in mood in the room was something I would never forget."[58] Brecke worked through the night to correct the error so the launch could go ahead as planned. Given how the team was pushing the limits of its hardware and FORTRAN, the effort was remarkable.

The GLOBUS Simulation

GLOBUS, in its final form, was a program to simulate world states from 1970 to 2010.[59] Deutsch would have simulated the entire world had there been enough time and budget, but the team settled on twenty-five representative countries (not unlike TEMPER's thirteen conflict regions).[60] The choice of nations reflected Cold War dynamics and included East Germany and the USSR, while excluding conflict zones like Vietnam and Korea. The team drew data from all possible sources, drawing often on McClelland's, Singer's, and others' quantitative political data sets (a reaction to critiques of other political simulations).[61] Using these data sets meant that the team's choice of countries was fixed and hard to reprogram. The nations could interact with each other and a "rest-of-world" entity meant to approximate the international system.

GLOBUS's core was a fixed simulation. The model had over eight hundred variables. These variables defined the world in a run of the simulation. Once set, however, GLOBUS offered little in terms of interaction. Bremer explained, "GLOBUS is essentially deterministic."[62] Users could only manipulate inputs and read the results. The simulated world did allow for some degree of randomness, but GLOBUS's initial inputs had a powerful effect on its course. Once set up, a typical simulation lasted forty years. Each year began at the start of the loop, seen in figure 8.2, and advanced the clock by a year. The loop began by calculating international trade between nations, after which GLOBUS would update the status of its simulated nations in sequence, beginning with the United States and ending with Indonesia. Each national module calculated, sequence by sequence, how its changing population affected the nation's internal economy, government budget, and domestic politics. These modules then updated the nation's foreign relations, and the simulation turned to the next nation in sequence. After updating each of the twenty-five nations, the loop finished by calculating diplomatic and trade relations with the rest-of-world entity before either advancing the simulation or ending if its target was met (figure 8.2).

A nation's submodules were extensive models in and of themselves. The domestic politics module included variables, such as the number of violent events in Western nations (ACVIOL) and elite satisfaction in Eastern nations (ELSAT) and could be adjusted with its own series of parameters.

GLOBUS's outputs were projections of world states in the near-term future based on starting conditions. The team encouraged researchers to use the model to test their own scenarios. The final GLOBUS book included numerous examples of how to use the model, such as gauging the effects of population growth. How would developing nations with predicted

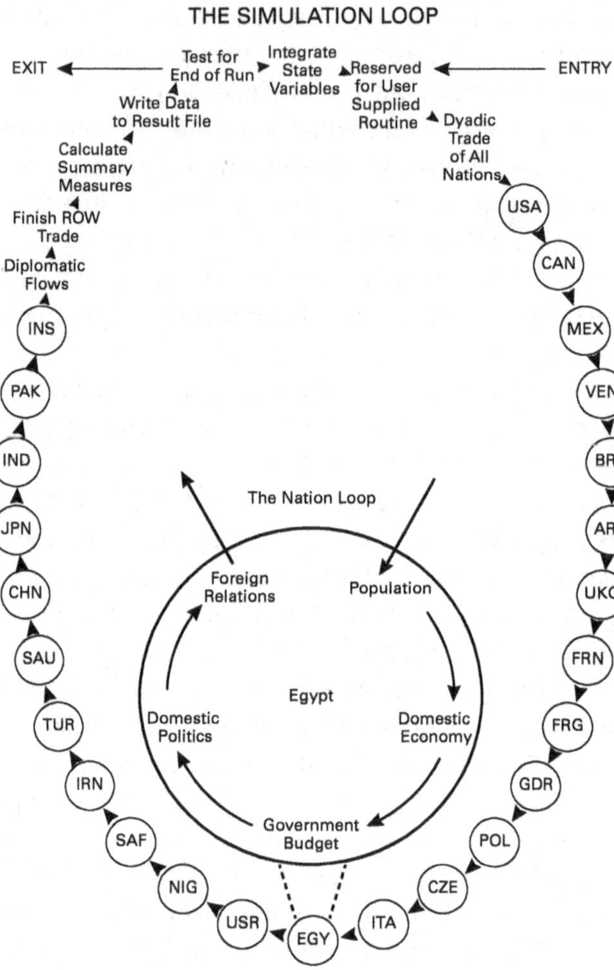

Figure 8.2
The GLOBUS simulation loop reproduced from the original diagram. *Source*: Redrawn from Bremer, "The Globus Model," 787.

high population growth fare? Poorly. Higher population growth led to increased scarcity of resources.[63] Another predictive use case, called "Reagan in machina," considered the long-term implications of Reagan's defense spending. In a subsequent chapter, the team warned that "GLOBUS is not a crystal ball and these results do not tell us what the world will look like either with or without Reagan," but the case found that, if Reagan's hawkish spending continued, US foreign policy would lead to a "dangerous deterioration in superpower relations."[64] Looking back now, the results can be read as artifacts of predicted futures long passed—familiar variables from an unrecognizable world.

The team aimed to present an objective account of the world system. While Bremer stressed that at a "conscious level ideological considerations did not play a major role," he reluctantly suggested that GLOBUS's outlook might be labeled "liberal internationalism."[65] Certainly, that attitude matched Deutsch's plans for steering models. This slight bias does appear in the simulation's variables that tracked cooperative and hostile behavior, letting the world be something more than a game of mutually assured destruction or nuclear utilization target selection.[66] But if the model lacked an optimal world system, the project's written record communicated the constant hope that GLOBUS might reveal a more benign, objective way forward for politics, one founded on the best data and systematic thinking without being prescriptive. The team's openness to building a multipurpose tool is apparent in the model itself. The simulation presented options and variables seemingly as complex and endless as the world it represented.

Twilight GLOBUS

With the model complete, the team made a final effort to share the model with the global community. Thanks to FORTRAN developments and a few advanced IBM computers at the WZB, the team could port its mainframe model to the personal computer. The result was MicroGLOBUS, a working equivalent of GLOBUS that could run on an IBM PC. The simulation came with a thick blue binder with over three hundred pages loaded onto five 5¼-inch floppy disks (figure 8.3),[67] all for sale, according to one review, for $110.[68] MicroGLOBUS was a major advance in turning a prototype into a working tool. Barry Hughes recalled a shared frustration with "user interfaces that consisted of a blinking cursor." Most researchers lacked access to a supercomputer, and time-sharing was costly: a typical forty-year run cost $150 (about $400 in 2024). As these costs added up quickly, the team looked to new microcomputers to address the problem of access.

With a lot of work, but comparatively less than renting a mainframe, a user could install MicroGLOBUS on a PC, run their own simulations, and analyze the results. This development was significant, placing one of the most advanced simulations on the desktops of researchers globally. But the results proved less successful. By 1992, the WZB had records of 104

Figure 8.3
MicroGLOBUS at the WZB Library.

registered users.[69] The tool was easier to use than the mainframe edition but still daunting. The experience of trying to get answers out of the simulation is hard to describe. Even the screenshots shown in figures 4 and 5 could be produced only after hours of study. As one review explained, "MICRO GLOBUS has no utility independent of the theoretical assumptions of the designers and the quality of the data, and these two requirements of research agendas will take years to meet. Political scientists who want to use GLOBUS seriously will have to learn more about economics and differential equations than they commonly know."[70] MicroGLOBUS, even when trying to simplify its user experience, still assumed a lot about its users.

MicroGLOBUS did not really exactly a God's-eye view. Much like Bremer's drivers in the icy parking lot, users never had a complete view of the world. The interface was never unified, and the results never crystallized into a coherent account. Out of its world of data, MicroGLOBUS only offered more data. When a user ran MicroGLOBUS, they merely watched the world move from start to finish based on the initial variables. There was no opportunity for interaction and no interruptions, starting at the screen in figure 8.4. Making

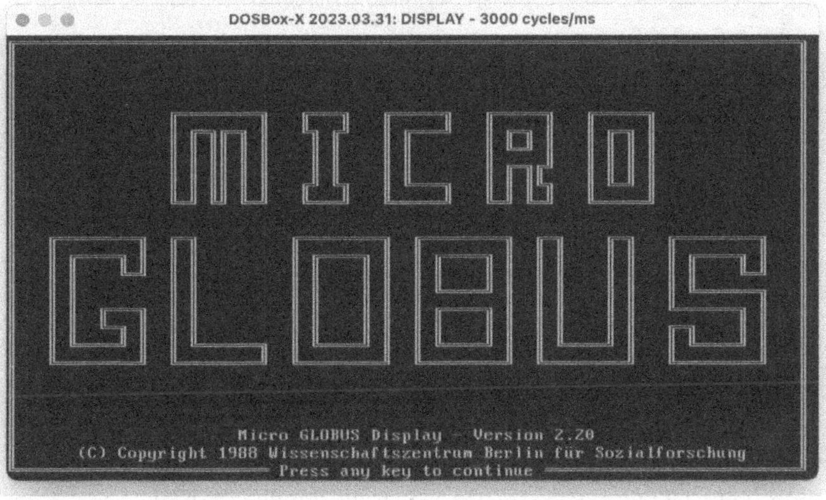

Figure 8.4
The MicroGLOBUS run screen. *Source*: Screenshot from emulation of program in DosBox-X.

matters worse, desktop computers struggled to run the complex model. Users required different programs to run the model and to analyze the results.

When finished, the simulation ended by outputting a result that the user had to explore themselves, as MicroGLOBUS offered no interpretations. For example, the display program produced tables and results of the simulation data as shown in figure 8.5.

Whether these models were accurate is difficult to consider. Many of the variables were specific to GLOBUS and are hard to benchmark with public data today. Other variables were indexed to 1970 dollars, which are difficult to update at scale.

Many of its estimates tended to be conservative. In the model shown in figure 8.6, the simulated population increased but not at the observed rate; the same went for GDP. Given GLOBUS's configurability, its estimates likely could have been adjusted for different, more correct scenarios. As intriguing as it might be to know whether GLOBUS correctly predicted our future, the simulation was never intended to do so. Simulations aimed only to depict possible futures given certain scenarios. The closest the GLOBUS team got to the Club of Rome approach—releasing universal predictions about the world—was to offer illustrations of how the tool could be used to make predictions.

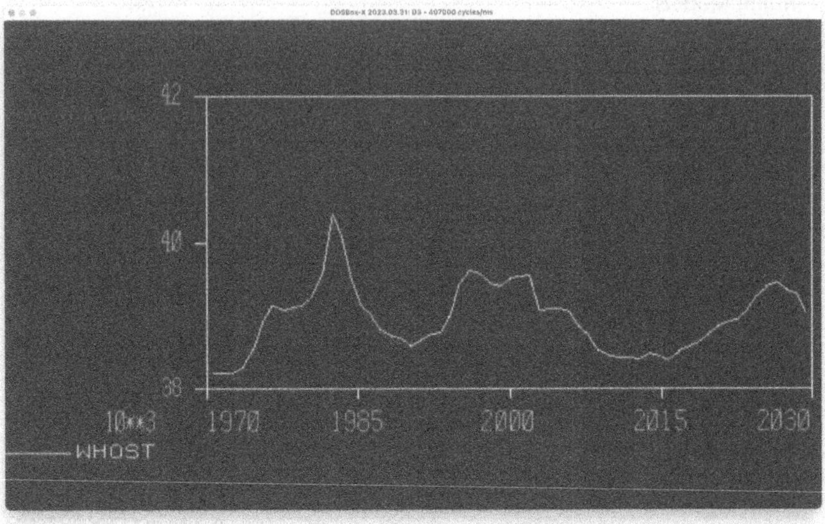

Figure 8.5
Display output for times series of changes in world hostility (WHOST). *Source*: Screenshot from emulation of Display program in DosBox-X.

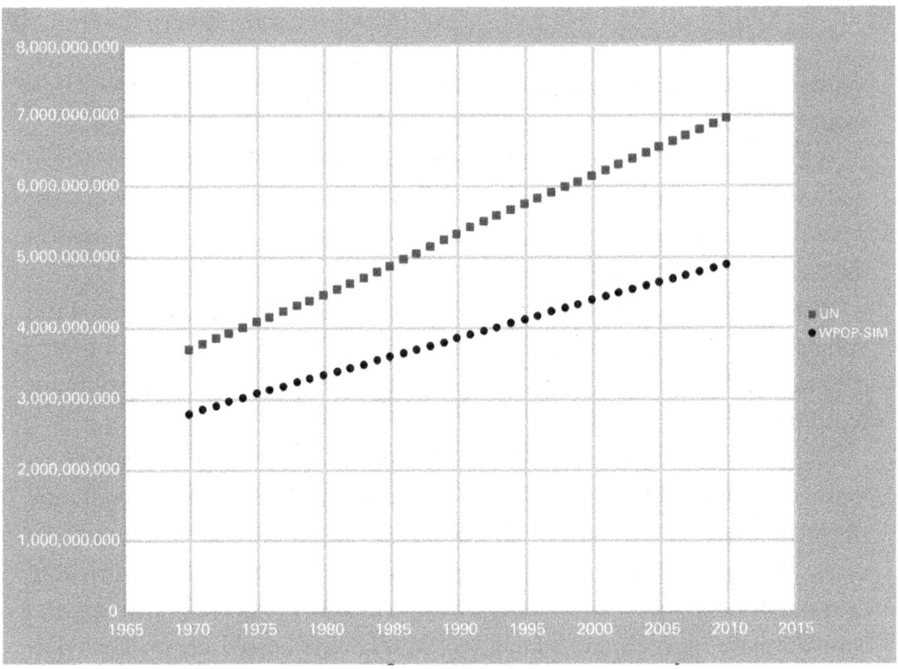

Figure 8.6
Comparison of actual UN records of world population versus GLOBUS simulation. *Source*: Adaptation of the output of GLOBUS display including actual historic figures.

Nor did the team try to turn MicroGLOBUS into a game. The simulation's formidable interface was no accident; its topics were too serious to be trivialized into a game.[71] By contrast, players of the 1985 computer game *Balance of Power* used an interactive world map to simulate how Cold War enemies played the game of nuclear war (figure 8.7).

The game's interface—a God's-eye view of the world map—was easy to use, making it fun to play out somewhat fanciful scenarios like Soviet coups. MicroGLOBUS, conversely, promised a tool to predict and question the real fate of the world.

The team made significant efforts to ensure that the tool could be modified. Well before the popularity of free software, MicroGLOBUS included the ZHOCK routine that allowed users to add ad hoc functions to the model. Copies included the entire FORTRAN source code of the project with an invitation for users to update the data and modify the routines. As the introduction stated, "It is impossible to estimate how many man-years of work have gone into developing the GLOBUS model. It is a fervent hope that, by making the model available in this form, many others may benefit from the deep investment."[72] That hope provides a good epitaph to the GLOBUS project.

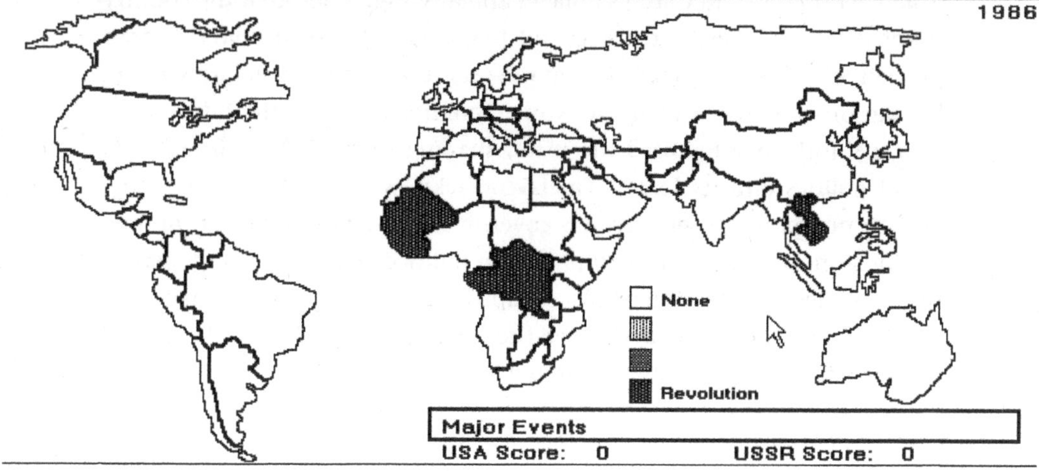

Figure 8.7
Balance of Power. *Source*: Internet Archive.

GLOBUS ended just before the fall of the Berlin Wall. Peter Brecke summed up the feeling that circulated around that time: "We got the darned thing built, time to move on."[73] The team, who by then had faculty jobs, largely disbanded by 1988. Deutsch died in 1992. Before his death in 2002, Bremer took over David Singer's Correlates of War project.[74] Brecke ported MicroGLOBUS to Macintosh and Peter Rindfuß ported it to C++. Continuing work seemed to have become a hobby for most of the team.

The project also came to be isolated from the US government's approach to modeling after Reagan's election. When the project started, the US government supported modeling to coordinate the government's efforts as a system. In 1977, President Jimmy Carter directed the Council on Environmental Quality and the Department of State to study "probable changes in the world's population, natural resources, and environment through the end of the century."[75] The directive led to theoretical physicist Gerald Barney being tasked with producing the *Global 2000 Report,* which synthesized knowledge across federal government departments. The project brought together fourteen federal agencies with a budget of approximately $950,000 and resulted in a thousand-page multivolume report to the president, published in 1980. The report and its findings resembled *The Limits to Growth,* forecasting doom while courting public attention.[76] The report's release coincided with the election of Ronald Reagan, who was eager to distance himself from Carter's policies and any suggestion that the country suffered from malaise. At his second inaugural address, in 1985, Reagan proclaimed, "We believed then and now there are no limits to growth and human progress when men and women are free to follow their dreams."[77] Reagan's influence haunted the team, shaping how GLOBUS interpreted world politics and its legacy. Guetzkow acknowledged the link directly: "When my more conservative US government disallowed further funding of global modeling (with its emphasis on politico-economic components), the West Berlin government picked up the thrust in global modeling."[78] These factors seemed to have muted the reaction to GLOBUS, as the time of giant models had passed in the United States.

The overall academic reaction to GLOBUS seems quiet in retrospect. The simulation received few reviews. The team continued to use GLOBUS in their own work, but the simulation did not inspire much of a following. There were some critical obstacles to its success. It depicted a world that looked dramatically different only a few years after its release. It was stale and outdated. One major scenario that GLOBUS did not account for was the Cold War's end, which would have required dramatic change to its international system variables. That GLOBUS did not predict the end of its own world is a telling parable, a cautionary tale for future modelers. No other major project in political science appeared as its successor. The world had moved on.

GLOBUS had negligible impact in Germany as well. There was some limited press coverage, more than in the United States, but little evidence of uptake by the German government or the international community. Reviewing the German reaction, historian of technology Markus Ramsauer explains, "The tenor of the published results of the GLOBUS simulations can be roughly summarized as follows: overcoming current crises is important, but not as hopeless as WORLD3 has made it out to be."[79] Press attention emphasized GLOBUS's cold, scientific view, which struck critics as antidemocratic. Left-wing critics in Germany accused the model of being too apolitical in its approach to politics.[80]

Research on GLOBUS did continue after the team disbanded. Bremer and Hughes started GLOBUS Associates, Inc., focused on marketing the simulation to members of the US government. Business was slow and the last major contract came from the US Army's Intelligence and Threat Analysis Center. The contract resulted in MicroGLOBUS II, a Windows program with a modest user interface. GLOBUS Associates, Inc., advanced the base year from 1970 to 1990 and increased the number of countries to thirty-three to account for the collapse of the USSR. The program worked largely the same as before, providing predictions of trends based on its default scenario. MicroGLOBUS II was the last update; faced with the impracticality of relying on military contracts to perpetually update the data, the team moved on. That MicroGLOBUS only found buyers who had US interests in mind speaks to the political-economic conditions behind computer simulations.

Cybernetic-system models—like GLOBUS—continue. Barry Hughes, after Bremer's passing, continued to develop computer simulation. Today, he is the only GLOBUS modeler still building models. Hughes developed the long-running global model International Futures. Started in 1980, International Futures developed in parallel to GLOBUS. While Hughes consulted on GLOBUS, International Futures was his main passion. International Futures provided speculative ways to think about the world, framed with "ifs." Still running to this day at the Frederick S. Pardee Center for International Futures at the University of Denver, International Futures provides the UN and the US government assistance with future modeling. Its simulation includes data from 1960 to the present, simulating 186 countries and forecasting up to the year 2100. Like GLOBUS, the code is open source and the project free for anyone to use online.

In the end, the GLOBUS project added nuance to Deutsch's steering model, showing how computer models present forms of agency both in their referent systems and to the user. While, in theory, Deutsch distinguished between steering and drift models, in practice, little difference could be found. Both conform to Sun-Ha Hong's evaluation of technofuturism, where models project a certain conservativism by projecting a future extrapolated from a specific moment.[81] Drift models explicitly predicted the future using a fixed system based on the present. Where the Club of Rome's WORLD3 model was rightly criticized for keeping certain functions stable that should have been dynamic (e.g., technology or political orders), the deeper critique was that system dynamics as an operating model present change without dramatically altering the system itself. Repeated runs of world simulations functioned similarly to other myth-making and speculative designs in which "futures are produced, legitimated, and repeated, in ways that actively foreclose alternatives."[82] Sure, the model produced results, but only through the state of feedback between components on variables not in ways that would alter the starting world order. Something like the collapse of the USSR required reprogramming the entire simulation to account for the new countries. The status might change, but not the system itself. Politics, even if not included explicitly in the model, was embedded in its operating assumptions.[83]

Steering models promised the user an open world to see how change could happen, and this was exactly what GLOBUS promised in its design. Yet GLOBUS also stabilized contemporary future goals in the settings of the initial run, locking in the effects of starting parameters over decades. Moreover, the tool assumed that the user had questions to answer. It encouraged global thinking, but the scale of the model eclipsed the user. The consequence of creating a simulation as complex as the world was having to understand the results. GLOBUS's complexity was daunting, the user interface lacking, and the results meaningful only after hours of interpretation. GLOBUS presented the biggest world possible on a microcomputer, and the experience was overwhelming.

Prince, Policon, and FACTIONS: Optimizing for Power

In contrast to GLOBUS, other tools assumed less of their users, expecting and presenting a self-interested world. Turning world models into rational agents involved competition, not just within the models but between them as well. There was no one coordinated effort, but rather a growing industry, starting in the 1970s, that offered to apply innovations in economics, positive political theory, and game theory to the problems of world politics. Clients included businesses, governments, and even intelligence agencies—all hoping to have a better perspective on their strategies and risks within a globalizing world. As one 1990 *New York Times* article admitted, "Judging by the number of crises in the world lately, profits must be soaring in the political-risk business."[84] The political-risk business was one name for a separate tradition in world modeling that considered the heuristics, calculations, and decision-making of agents and became something of a world system in the same vein as GLOBUS.

The rational agents approach to world modeling differed substantially from cybernetic approaches and was more influential. Instead of modeling a *system*, rational agents modelers focused on the interactions of individual agents, letting these behaviors stand in for a system. Historian Paul Erickson has masterfully outlined the evolution of what I call rational agents from game theory to world modeling. Erickson begins his account of the turn toward agent-based modeling with another story of the advent of computer simulation:

> In the fall of 1973, a war unfolded in an article on the pages of the journal *Nature*. The combatants were animals that had enjoyed only a fleeting existence in a computer program, encoded on punchcards and run on an IBM mainframe at the University of Sussex many months before. "Hawks" pursued a strategy of "total war," fighting tooth and nail against all challengers. Other participants in the conflict adopted more nuanced strategies of "limited war," "retaliating" and "escalating" the conflict if attacked, but generally using "conventional tactics" against the hawks' "dangerous" tactics. When the electronic dust cleared and a body count was performed, the outcome seemed decisive, if counterintuitive: the practitioners of "limited war" had survived as the fittest. The Cold War had been fought in nature, and the hawks had lost.[85]

Hawks cried total war in simulation and in reality. Peace activists such as David Singer and Anatol Rapoport dueled with rival strategists like Herman Kahn and Thomas Schelling over mathematical expressions of nuclear war.[86] But through these debates, a new dynamic emerged, one that, as Erickson describes it, led to a breakdown between systems and actions or agents. Whereas Erickson follows simulation and rational agents into the intersection of game theory and biology, I turn to the ways that theories of agent-based political behavior—principally utility maximization—became a major theme in political science and its commercial applications.[87]

Prince and New Power Generalization

William Coplin started his first faculty position at Wayne State University in Detroit amid general enthusiasm for the new field of simulation. The position became a crash course for Coplin in world modeling, a field he helped to publicize with the 1968 edited collection *Simulation in the Study of Politics*.[88] The collection came out of Coplin's experiences with others in the field, his training at Michigan State in quantitative research, and his interactions with Guetzkow. At Wayne State, he developed his own version of the Inter-Nation Simulation, the World Politics Simulation to train members of the State Department in simulation methods. The World Politics Simulation and its uptake in government and military training, however, proved less significant than Coplin's lessons from game design.

Convinced to develop a computer player for their simulation, Coplin and his colleagues tried to work out a simple formula for decision-making. Coplin realized the resulting logic had applications that extended well beyond the game. He developed the formula into the Prince Political Accounting System. Prince became its own project, but Guetzkow recognized the link, calling Prince "another derivative of the Inter-Nation Simulation."[89]

Prince moved away from simulation as it developed. Intentionally avoiding the complexity of computer simulation, Coplin turned to a simple calculus of consensus. Prince stood for PRobe, INteract, Calculate, Execute—and it did just that. It consisted of simple worksheets that asked decision-makers to evaluate their own and their peers' position, power, and salience (defined as "the importance each actor attaches to the particular issue") relative to key actions or issues.[90] Prince's calculations resembled a Downsian approach to politics. Instead of calculating whether someone would or would not vote, Prince evaluated support and opposition for different issues. Filling out an issue position matrix required the user to estimate an actor's values for each position. The results delivered the probability of an issue finding support or opposition and predicted the effects of possible alliances on political outcomes.[91]

Prince was not a computer simulation, but Coplin and his collaborator developed one: PROBE, which stood for Policy Research, OBservation, and Evaluation.[92] The program, now lost, was not markedly different than Prince's spreadsheet; however, it allowed users to speed up calculations and to compare scenarios. PROBE allowed for more than ten actors to be calculated at a time—more than the sheets—but followed the same formula as Prince.

Prince's simplicity possibly obscured the novelty of its claims. Unlike other simulations, its only referent system was that of decision-making, broadly. The tool itself worked just as well to model classroom politics as it did a world system. Nor did it offer a God's-eye view, per se, but rather a view to win—a tool for strategy and decision-making first. The user even became part of the system because Prince encouraged self-reflection when strategizing outcomes and how one fit within its matrices. There was symmetry between the observers and the actors, unlike in GLOBUS. Such an emphasis on strategy and utility is best seen in Prince's longtime commercial application in political-risk forecasting, an industry it helped create.

Coplin used the Prince system as a basis for a consulting practice in political risk analysis. International Political Surveys offered the service of creating issue position matrices with which to analyze international politics and better understand national actors' support for a regime or other sources of turmoil. The adapted Prince system evaluated the user's orientation, certainty or fixedness, power, and salience in relation to key issues.[93] By the late 1970s, International Political Surveys had been sold to the New York–based forecasting firm Frost & Sullivan, who rebranded the service under the name World Political Risk Forecast Service. By aggregating different experts' Prince surveys, this new service ranked nations by their risks of regime change and reception to international trade. The system found a clientele in US businesses looking to take advantage of their global market power.

Prince achieved success, but its influence is hard to measure. Prince's promotional materials claimed it was used by the CIA to predict strategies at an international radio conference.[94] Other users included the State Department, the US Army Corps of Engineers, police chiefs, social workers, and chief executive officers.[95] In retrospect, International Political Surveys was a key figure in the start of the political-risk forecasting industry.[96] Frost & Sullivan, Inc., had $17.5 million in sales in 1987 and is still active today.[97] Coplin cowrote a trade book, *Power Persuasion*.[98] Yet for all its success, Prince was less influential than another approach to utility maximization in international politics: its direct competitor, Policon.[99]

Policon, Factions, and the Agency

Policon merged two traditions in political science. The first was the Rochester School of Political Science, which was begun by William Riker and focused on rational choice theories known as positive political theory.[100] The second was the more data-focused Michigan approach, which stemmed from a realist approach to international relations called power transition theory. The merger happened in 1981 when A. F. K. Organski, his student Jacek Kugler, and Bruce Bueno de Mesquita founded the Policon Corporation.[101] Organski and Kugler represented the Michigan approach. Together they had just published *The War Ledger* in 1980, which tested power transition theory in the study of international politics.[102] Representing Rochester was Bruce Bueno de Mesquita, who had published *The War Trap* in 1981, a now classic application of expected utility theory to international politics.[103] Together, these approaches joined quantitative political data and rationalistic explanations of behavior—principally, utility maximization. The result was a business-oriented approximation of their research interests, offering straightforward analysis that endured even as their research changed the underlying theories.

Policon started as a consulting firm, offering "political forecasting and risk assessment for government and business."[104] Though records are scarce, the firm had clients in business and government, with the CIA as its best-known client.[105] The agency, and intelligence agencies more broadly, celebrated their association with Policon, one of the "few methods specific to the domain of intelligence analysis" according to one study by the agency's Center for the Study of Intelligence.[106] The CIA used Policon from 1982 until 1986 when it developed a similar tool internally, FACTIONS.[107] "Only a few academics willingly come to the agency to talk with the analysts," explained a report by a training college for US intelligence agencies.[108] The one exception? FACTIONS was "a good example of research and development (R&D) work done in collaboration with members of the academic community."[109] One internal assessment claimed that "forecasts done with traditional methods and with Policon were found to be accurate about 90 percent of the time. Thus, while traditional and Policon-based analyses both scored well in terms of forecast accuracy, Policon offered greater detail and less vagueness. Both traditional approaches and Policon often hit the target, but Policon analyses got the bull's-eye twice as often."[110] These internal assessments capture both the practical application of Policon in US strategy and a more hidden history. The CIA used Policon to predict the outcomes to such scenarios as "What policy is Egypt likely to adopt toward Israel? How open will the political system be in Turkey? What is the Philippines likely to do about US bases? What stand will Pakistan take on the Soviet occupation of Afghanistan?"[111] But outside of brief mentions, few records exist of later uses of Policon, FACTIONS, or the firm's history. The impact of Policon can only be approximated and is likely underappreciated. But what did Policon do differently than the traditional approaches mentioned above?

Policon was a computational method—a spreadsheet before it became a program—that assisted decision-makers in converting a political situation into a quantitative environment. Policon helped decision-makers predict the possible actions of their competitors and advised on business and government strategy. According to public records at least, Policon consisted of three steps, similar to Prince. First, users had to define an issue or controversy between a fixed number of actors. Policon reduced disagreement between agents to a linear scale, placing each actor's preferred choice as a value on that scale. One explanation of this scaling process estimated Italy's probable 1983 government deficit. Analysts broke down the key actors and then positioned them on a scale from a fifty trillion lira deficit to a hundred trillion lira deficit as shown in figure 8.8.

These estimates marked a shift in the underlying game theory from determining rational action to probable action. Distances on the x-axis mattered too; they indicated how far apart actors were on the issue. The first step ended by calculating the strongest actors and how important the issue was to each actor.[112] The next step involved calculating each actor's support for every other actor, expressed by the formula (between actor A and actor B):

$$\text{A's support for B} = (\text{A's resources}) \times (\text{salience of issue to A}) \times (\text{A's utility for B's position})$$

Policon also used estimates to mathematically find a winner, specifically a mathematical Condorcet winner.[113] The winner was the one most other

Actors			
Ministry of Budget	BUD	Christian Democrats	CDM
Socialists	SOC	Communists	COM
Employers' Association	COC	Unions-Socialist	UNS
Unions Communist	UNC	Unions-Christian Democrats	UND
Financial Press	FIN	Political Press	POL
Bank of Italy	BAN	Treasury Ministry	TRE
Pertini	PRE	Spadolini	SPA

Issue Diagram
What size deficit will the Italian Parliament permit?

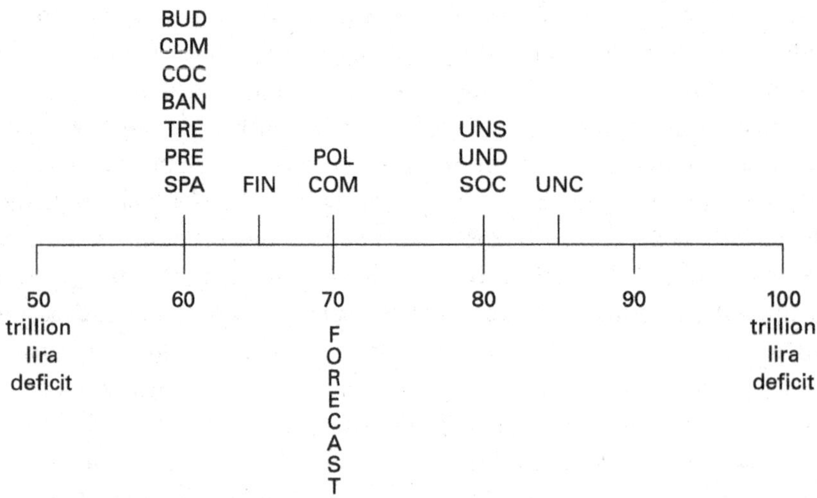

Figure 8.8
Actor's position on the Italian deficit in Policon reproduced from the original diagram. *Source*: Redrawn from "FACTIONS and Policon: New Ways to Analyze Politics," 278.

agents would choose over all other options. Returning to the Italian deficit example, the winner was "which group's position would win if the policy contest came down to a choice between only two alternatives. In other words, is there an actor or set of actors who support the same position that can defeat every other actor or coalition in a pairwise contest?"[114] The winner's position helped predict a probable policy outcome, but Policon offered further predictions about each actor's likely action based on the expected utility of each policy option. Much like a Downsian decision over whether to vote, each actor had to decide whether to do something or not, as shown in figure 8.9.

By calculating both the value to the actor and the likelihood an outcome would happen, Policon calculated a "forecast of the policy to be adopted, patterns of conflict and cooperation among the various groups, and insights into the strengths and vulnerabilities of each of the groups."[115] However, this was merely the public explanation of Policon.

How Policon *actually* worked has been debated—even in the courts. A rift between Policon founders offers rare public discussion of the program's inner workings. In 2006, Policon, now called Decision Insights, sued a new firm, Sentia Group, which was started by ex-employees. Decision Insights claimed that Sentia had copied its code. Much of the case hinged on whether Policon's methods had been disclosed in the public literature or the code contained trade secrets.[116] Bueno de Mesquita, now working for Sentia, acted as an expert witness in the trial, claiming he cowrote the code and that "the method for calculating the value of the discount term that triggers the stopping rule and—crucially—leads to the predicted outcome is proprietary; that is, unpublished. . . . No formula for the actual calculation is stated in . . . [any] publication that addresses the forecasting model on which DII's software is based."[117] Bueno de Mesquita's disclosure leaves vague how Policon

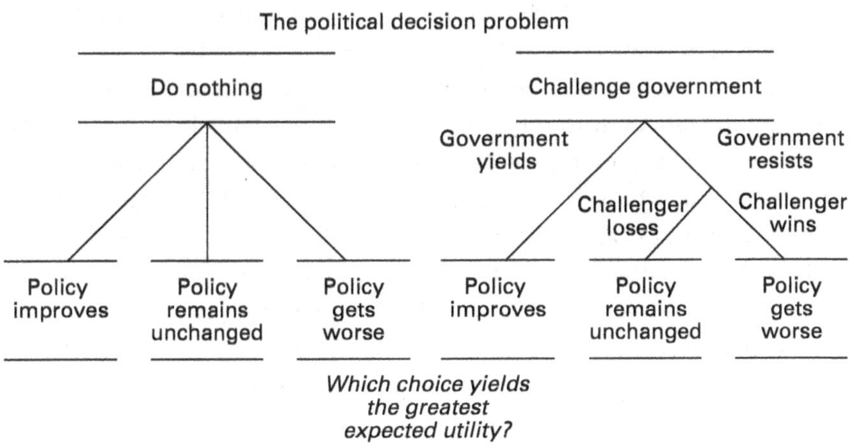

Figure 8.9
An actor's possible actions in Policon. *Source*: Redrawn from "FACTIONS and Policon: New Ways to Analyze Politics," 280.

worked. Discovery for the trial also found that Policon's development had largely stopped after Bueno de Mesquita had programmed it; the program might have changed, but not the underlying code or theory. These technical debates matter less than the overall orientation of the tool.

Policon—like Prince—offered a simple view of world agency whose purpose was to find a winning strategy for the analyst, not an optimal strategy for all the actors. The tool was expressly oriented toward the analyst. Utility calculations were a somewhat self-reflective process, requiring the analyst to decide their preferred outcomes. The tool did not include any calculation for the *best* decision or even the implications of the decisions. Calculations only focused on power, influence, and who could gain the most support. In sharp contrast to GLOBUS's complexity Policon offered a highly abstract representation of the world, reducing systematic factors as well as any sense of agency. The world itself had little internal agency, and there were no subsystems. Policon's designers assumed that its users were trying to maximize their utility just like its internal agents. It is no wonder the system enjoyed wider success than GLOBUS. Policon provided an immediate utility and made good on its promises, providing a way to predict and intervene in its modeled worlds for the benefit of its users.

Policon has successors in addition to FACTIONS. Bueno de Mesquita has had a noted career as a political forecaster, launching several other consulting firms and creating The Predictioneer's Game.[118] Jacek Kulger later collaborated with Mark Abdollahian to create Senturion, which advanced the actor model from expected utility to "rule- and equation-based algorithms" that "model the intuition behind each stakeholder's political calculus by breaking the process into sub-elements that can be modeled."[119] Senturion is still in use today; it is one of the products offered by Abdollahian and the ACERTAS firm, whose client list ranges from the RAND Corporation and the Department of Defense to CNN and the BBC.

Policon's successors fit within a turn toward agent-based modeling.[120] Policon was a simple agent-based model that sought to predict events based on interactions between agents that were programmed to maximize utility. Better data and more complex algorithms—as in Senturion—led to multiagent systems (an advancement that recalls economic historian Phil Mirowski's assertion that economics became a cyborg science through the embrace of John von Neumann's automata theory).[121]

Prince and Policon exemplify a distinct branch of the computer simulation meant to steer political strategy. Policon illustrated a steering model geared toward confrontation or, at least, assisting its users in winning in their own utility maximization. Implicitly, GLOBUS envisaged a simulation that emphasized cybernetic interconnection. Other system dynamics models outright called for global cooperation and governance—the original globalists. None of these approaches tangibly or substantially shifted world models outside the Global North.

Policon's uptake reflected the times. The US government's support for collaborative modeling ended with the Reagan presidency. As Stuart Bremer noted, "Coincidentally, perhaps, the Reagan administration chose to withhold American financial support for IIASA around this time. This may relate directly to the impact of the political climate on global modeling."[122] Instead, from Reagan's reign to the present day, modeling supported by US intelligence agencies has focused on strategic capability.

Agent-based models have flourished, with successors to Policon still in operation today. Researching GLOBUS felt like an archaeological dig, but my study of Prince and Policon was comparatively mundane. These tools are now part of established industries of risk calculation or they have been absorbed into larger, more complex systems. Much like Ray Fair's voter predictions, utility calculations provide a sensible, usable heuristic with which to interpret the world. Even data-driven models continue with extensive advances in event-based coding and analysis.

The split continues between cybernetic and rational agent simulations. Some machines function to advise US strategy, while others attempt to guide more international affairs, such as Hughes's International Futures, now in its eighth version, advising the United Nations' and other international organizations. And yet, these differences may be less significant than they appear. International Futures integrated agent-based systems after Hughes collaborated with former CIA senior economist Evan Hillebrand. Bueno de Mesquita, once part of Policon, has turned to chronicling world history.[123] What is most striking is the convergence of all these models into more elaborate models promising more total accounts.

The Integrated Crisis Early Warning System (ICEWS) is perhaps the best example of a convergence in computer simulation. Run by defense contractor Lockheed Martin, ICEWS is, according to their website, "a comprehensive, integrated, automated, generalizable, and validated system to monitor, assess, and forecast national, sub-national, and internal crises. ICEWS supports decisions on how to allocate resources to mitigate crisis. Using ICEWS, Combatant Commanders (COCOMs) have a powerful capability to anticipate and respond to stability challenges, allocate resources in accordance to the risks they are designed to mitigate, and track and measure in real time the effectiveness of resource allocations toward end-state stability objectives."[124] As convoluted as ICEWS may sound, its sources should be clearly legible by now. Joy Rohde cites ICEWS as a clear successor to McClelland and Beal's work in the Reagan administration.[125] ICEWS relies on event data, including subsequent data created by noted political scientist Phil Schrodt, who is a leader in global event data, and sources like the Correlates of War, which Stuart Bremer worked on. With these inputs, however, the system also turned to agent-based modeling in political forecasting. ICEWS was originally proposed in a 2010 article in *International Studies Review* by a DARPA researcher who cited Policon and Senturion as inspirations. ICEWS integrated agent-based modeling by surveying "Subject Matter Experts (SMEs) to develop highly detailed profiles of archetypical leaders and followers for government and non-governmental groups within each country. PS-I models were created with agents representing population elements of various ethnic/political identities organized geographically and in authority structures designed to mirror the society being studied."[126] ICEWS combines globalized data, extensive modeling, and theories of agent-based systems, all with a promise of utility and predictability.

Q4. How Do Interfaces Present Different Political Agencies?

GLOBUS, Prince, and Policon presented different world and user agencies, as well as distinct relations between world and user agencies. Each simulation had a theory of world agency—whether cybernetic systems or rational agents—that interfaced with a user's agency or how a user could interact with the modeled world. These examples reveal the relationship between world models and theories of change in the computational imaginary of politics. Troublingly, the expansive, complex GLOBUS struggled to present a clear sense of agency, whereas Policon presented a world of strategic interests to be commanded by the goals of its users. Policon helped its users win; GLOBUS tried to understand this place in a larger world system. These different presentations of agency had clear politics, not the least of which was the uptake of rational agents in the intelligence community, in spite of GLOBUS Bremer and Hughes's best efforts. But as much as GLOBUS or Policon might seem at odds, both still attempted God's-eye views to command. By way of conclusion, I want to push this analysis further, but looking at how another computer simulation offered a quite different presentation of the world and user agency.

Based on his own experiences with US interference in Nicaragua, game designer Jim Gasperini tried to build a game that changed the perspective of its players. Best known for designing *Sim City 3000*, Gasperini cocreated the 1988 computer game *Hidden Agenda* to teach players about the experience of running a small country that gets pulled into the Cold War. *Hidden Agenda* became the game equivalent of Bruce Cockburn's song "If I Had a Rocket Launcher," an underdog of video game history.

Gasperini had written *Choose Your Own Adventure*-like books before more moving to early computer text adventures. His books had a loosely educational purpose, using the trope of time travel to teach history. After one project was cancelled in the 1980s, Gasperini visited his brother, a journalist, in Nicaragua. While there, Gasperini witnessed the US involvement in the region, the latest chapter of a history he felt was overlooked in the United States. He recalled visiting a village and noticing a burnt-out bus; a local explained that the bus had been destroyed by US-backed paramilitaries known as the Contras. With the Sandinista-Contra civil war in mind, he returned inspired to make an educational game about the region.[127]

Hidden Agenda differed from other political games. Gasperini knew about other political simulation games, like *Balance of Power*, but felt they played more like spreadsheets that didn't let players explore the worlds they claimed to represent. His game was less a formal simulation and more a world of relations and issues that drew on his readings from across Latin America. The goal was to map out a world that captured Gasperini's experiences in Nicaragua as well as the general state of Latin American politics. The setting was the fictional country of Chimerica, a play on the Chimera and a nod to Gasperini's synthesizing. Writing about the game later, he stressed that he wanted to counter the status quo politics of games often set on the precipice or in the aftermath of nuclear war. Gasperini quotes Chilean writer Ariel Dorfman on other games' hidden politics: "Every window that industrial works of fiction opens looks out not onto another reality, but into a mirror that always reflects the same thing—the reader's own familiar surroundings."[128] *Hidden Agenda* tried to change that perspective.

The game starts by putting the player in front of the press. Newly appointed by a military junta, the player fields questions from a journalist about their political agenda. Did the player favor a market economy or the fair distribution of wealth? The game does not disclose what these answers mean for the game's outcome. After the questioning, the player finds themselves behind a desk, able to make calls, read reports, and later, appoint advisors (figure 8.10). Gasperini recalls, "You are leader of a country. How to go about making decisions? Well, a lot of it is meetings."[129] Gameplay echoes this sentiment. The player tries to stay in power for up to three years by meeting with representatives from unions, militias, and foreign embassies. Being stuck behind a desk acted as a metaphor for the player's limited agency in the global balance of power. Gasperini did not want the game's underlying model to be entirely under player control. The various factions that a player meets have their own agencies. Gasperini distinguished this kind of play from American works of fiction about the region. He wrote,

> With rare exceptions Central America and its people become background, a wild place given over to what appears to be an irrational Latino propensity for

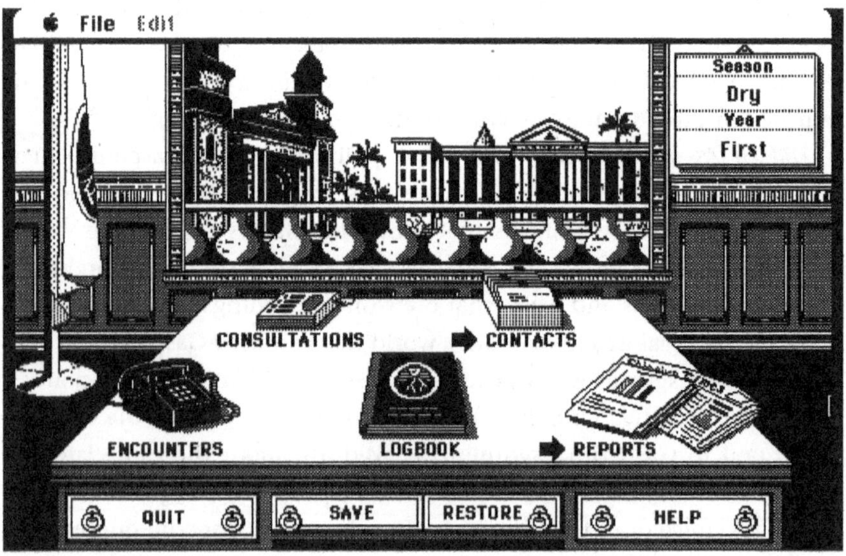

Figure 8.10
The home screen in *Hidden Agenda*. *Source*: the author.

violence. The real story focuses on the more civilized liberal gringos who steam upriver and confront the heart of darkness. The horror!

In [*Hidden Agenda*], we use the unique strengths of the interactive medium to approach the subject differently. In this case that means subordinating the particular story of the central character to the larger dramatic conflicts of a highly polarized political system. Problems of audience identification are swept aside. You are yourself the protagonist, and therefore must begin to think like an actor, not like an audience.[130]

The result makes the game something of an experiment for the player, with lots of ways to fail. Playing the game can feel like guesswork. A player might promise to increase education funding, only to later be faced with a budget shortfall. The game tracks spending and social indicators, so the player's decisions add up. Bad choices—too much opposition to the United States or too close an alignment with the USSR—could force the player to resign or lose power in a coup. As Gasperini described it, the game was like a zipper, in that the player's choices pulled in one direction or the other: toward the game's proxies for the Contras or the Sandinistas. Every move had a tradeoff; every move pulled the zipper.[131]

Hidden Agenda, at least, *tried* to show the potential for detail and specificity in a game even though Gasperini was an outsider to the region and was telling a regional history for American audiences. Perhaps that is what makes the game so interesting. Gasperini did not try to recreate the world as a model or engage in holistic system-building. He could only see how the game played out by compiling its code and then play testing the new game world. There was no formal model underneath, and this bespoke approach might have been its undoing.

The game's specificity contributed to its marginalization. Beyond its publisher Springboard Software's failed move into desktop publishing, Gasperini and his codevelopers had built a game that was not easy to repurpose. Gasperini had planned to release *Hidden Agenda* as part of a series; he had three other games organized conceptually and had started work on a sequel. The next game was to be set in Eastern Europe and required a lengthy development time—a timeline that world history would foreclose, as the collapse of the Berlin Wall in 1989 effectively ended development. The proposed sequel represented a world that no longer existed. Gasperini had a long career outside games, returning to the industry only briefly to lead *Sim City 3000*'s development (while Will Wright worked on what became *The Sims*). Gasperini added advisors to *Sim City*'s interface, echoing

Hidden Agenda, and introduced garbage as a game element, another way the world could be snuck into an idealized system.[132]

Hidden Agenda was not altogether forgotten. The game managed to reach a documentary filmmaker working at PBS's *Frontline*, Suzanne Seggerman, who was "not very interested in video games." A gift of *Hidden Agenda* changed her mind: "I played it nonstop for the next ten hours."[133] The experience transformed her practice, and in 2004 she cofounded Games for Change. Still active today, the organization and its annual event celebrates video games with a social purpose. The organization remains central to academic and professional development and research, offsetting the otherwise largely industrial forces behind game development. Its annual awards have recognized games that teach about the environment, world conflict, health, and emotions. *Hidden Agenda* is now part of its Hall of Fame. Perhaps acknowledging a lack of agency is what became the catalyst for the game's enduring legacy.

Hidden Agenda is an apt conclusion for a chapter questioning interfaces and agencies. I find the simplicity of the desk view helpful in articulating the politics of the God's-eye view, a view that assumed an interface between a world agency and a user agency. Hidden Agenda was novel for its situated view. Cybernetic and rational agent models, by contrast, discussed a utilitarian simulated world that encoded a model of world agency validate enough to offer a new capacity to understand and interact with the real world. GLOBUS, roughly to collaborate, Policon to win. These simulations were different answers to the questions of how interfaces present agencies, questions that linger in the new generation of simulations of AI that make similar promises to enhance their users and render new knowledges. As I have done here, the challenge is to understand the politics in these presentations, and in the next chapter, I push this speculation a little further.

9 Are Other Computer Simulations Possible?

Not everyone hoping to simulate politics believed in a computational approach, least of all Norbert Wiener. As Norbert Wiener became more critical of the military-industrial-academic complex, he turned his criticism to international strategy, games, and simulations—themes discussed earlier. He wrote, "War and business are conflicts resembling games, and as such, they may be so formalized as to constitute games with definite rules. Indeed, I have no reason to suppose that such formalized versions of them are not already being established as models to determine the policies for pressing the Great Push Button and burning the earth clean for a new and less humanly undependable order of things."[1] Wiener worried that games trivialized nuclear war—a very real fear when US nuclear strategy relied on game theory. Weiner also thought that computer simulations could never predict the world if they were bound by the formal rules of their creators, could never be anything other than servants following orders. As with his example of the fabled Golem, Wiener feared that no simulation could ever surpass the hand of its maker as he warned, "Can God play a significant game with his own creature? Can any creator, even a limited one, play a significant game with his own creature?"[2]

Wiener was skeptical, but about the very premise of simulated agency. Could a simulated world ever become autonomous, beyond the imagination of its designers? Furthermore, as he grew to oppose the military-industrial complex, Wiener grew distrustful of attempts to use mathematics to manage societies.[3] His warnings hint at growing criticism of and within the computational imaginary of politics.

I see Norbert Wiener's worries as early criticisms of the emerging computational imaginary. Could imagining politics with computers undermine good political judgement? His worries about simulations' distorted agencies extended into concerns that their presentation of problems did not address their global consequences. What did it mean to treat political negotiations like a mathematical problem to be optimized? Wiener was not alone.[4] Others tried to work reflectively in developing world models counter to these computational approaches.

In this chapter, I focus on critical responses to early computer simulation that questioned encoded theories of agencies and addressability. I introduce two examples to consider the limits of the computational imaginary of politics. I begin with Buckminster Fuller's *World Game*. The *World Game* had many iterations that over time involved computers less and less. Instead, the *World Game* tried to offer up something of the opposite of a God's-eye view: tiny humans on a massive game map trying to find a way to steer spaceship Earth. The *World Game* illustrates how games and simulations might create new perspectives and player agencies. Less well known, the World Order Models Project (WOMP) was a decades-long attempt to collaborate on the design of new world systems. Unlike the attempts described above to define the world *as-is*, WOMP aspired to create new world orders and global systems of governance, shifting expectations about how simulations had to *match* reality. WOMP illustrates the possibilities of modeling as a task of speculation and idealizing; perhaps it's no surprise that it's the lesser known of the two. These examples gesture toward new possibilities within and outside the computational imaginary of politics that animate the last chapters of this book.

Buckminster Fuller's World Games

Buckminster Fuller evangelized *another* kind of systems thinking—becoming a rebel in a closed world. Fuller was, according to a 1966 *New Yorker* profile, an "intellectual outlaw."[5] Certainly, he performed being an outlaw. He was also a US Navy veteran and leaned on his service record as credentials for his self-described systems thinking. His midlife prominence, active engagement with the government, and embrace by the counterculture makes Fuller a difficult figure to situate, at once a critic and a proponent of the US high modernism.[6]

Fuller is often remembered as an advocate of computers' social purpose. Governments, readers of the *Whole Earth Catalog*, and world simulations embraced his writings on computing. Dennis Meadows, who managed the

Limits of Growth report, begins his coauthored 1983 book *The Electronic Oracle* with a quote from Fuller. Meadows's book was sponsored by the Institute for Applied System Analysis, one of many organizations dedicated to the production of simulations for experts and policymakers. The book opens with Fuller prophisizing,

> You may very appropriately want to ask me how we are going to resolve the ever-acceleratingly dangerous impasse of world-opposed politicians and ideological dogmas. I answer it will be resolved by the computer. Man has ever-increasing confidence in the computer; witness his unconcerned landings as air transport passengers . . . in the combined invisibility of fog and night. While no politician or political system can ever afford to yield to their adversaries and opposers, all politicians can and will yield enthusiastically to the computer's safe flight-controlling capabilities in bringing all of humanity in for a happy landing.[7]

Fuller once envisioned his *World Game* as the computational tool for that happy landing. Those dreams inspired modelers, and Fuller, but his efforts grew to reject computer simulation. The *World Game,* then, moved in the opposite direction of other simulations. Where Harold Guetzkow's Inter-Nation Simulation moved from a human-machine game to a simulation, the *World Game* started being described as a computer simulation—though never built—but ended up as an all-human exercise. The *World Game* should be remembered as an attempt to think against computational approaches to politics, albeit an idealistic one still centered on a US audience.

Buckminster Fuller claimed to have started working on the *World Game* as early as 1927, when he applied his experiences with war-gaming in the navy to another worldly project. The game was, in Fuller's words, "an anticipatory design project" where winning meant finding a way for "the world to work rather than one side survive."[8] The project was one of a few of his inventions meant to inspire a shared governance of Spaceship Earth. Years before images of Earth seen from space appeared on magazine covers, Fuller had already popularized a view from space with the Dymaxion world map projection, a popular prototype of world thinking. *Life* published a version of in 1943 for readers to cut out and assemble at home.[9]

Fuller proposed the first coherent *World Game* in a 1964 proposal for the US government's iconic Expo '67 pavilion in Montreal, Canada.[10] The proposal featured his signature geodesic dome and what would have been a working version of the game. Within the dome, visitors would be able to look down from above at a map on the pavilion's ground floor. It was a unique mixture of politics and vision, of open design and data visualization.[11] A computer on the observation floor would allow visitors to interact with the map as computers in the pavilion's basement updated the vast, interactive Dymaxion map in response to commands.[12] The game was less a playable game than an elaborate data visualization. It was never built; the planning committee accepted his proposal of a geodesic dome but rejected the idea of turning the interior into a working version of the *World Game*. The dome still stands in Montreal, now skeletal after a 1976 fire destroyed its skin.

Fuller positioned his *World Game* against his contemporaries as an antiwar game. His Expo '67 proposal opened up the game to the public, such that Jonathan Massey described the map and controller as "a limited yet suggestive form of 'electronically operative democracy' descended from the vocational voting scheme—a kind of United Nations assembly broadened to include not merely the delegates of the world's governments but also thousands of their citizens."[13] The interactive map reflected "the pedagogical mission of his work," as film scholar Janine Marchessault writes about the proposal. Marchessault continues, "As a futurist, Fuller wanted to demonstrate the evolution of humankind, an evolution that he believed was being enabled for better or worse through the capitalist and technological innovations of the military industrial complex."[14] Unlike those computer simulations discussed by the Joint Chiefs of Staff or elsewhere in the closed world of Cold War America, Fuller's proposal attempted to democratize access to the planning functions of computer simulation. Medard Gabel, who helped build a subsequent version, described Fuller as critical of other war games. The *World Game* was designed "not to be another tool for the status quo or the power structure . . . but to give the high school student or the college student equal footing with our friends in the Pentagon and the Kremlin in terms to access to global data . . . that would allow them to create a compelling strategy that would be equal to or better than what friends in the Pentagon were doing to justify another $100 billion dollar expenditure for a new fighter jet or aircraft carrier or other weapons of mass destruction."[15] Fuller used the *World Game* subsequently to demonstrate alternative ways to understand world problems and help participants discuss solutions.

Fuller gradually positioned the *World Game* against more structured approaches to computational thinking. In 1969, Fuller presented to the US Senate Subcommittee on Government Operations about the possibility of creating a new Select Senate Committee on Technology and the Human Environment. As the first witness, Fuller laid out a wild vision of a *World Game* that would be "an organization of computer capability to deal prognosticatingly with world problems." Aware of game theory, Fuller paused to stress how the *World Game* functioned as an alternative. He continued, "In playing the game I propose that we set up a different system of games from that of Dr. John Von Neumann whose 'Theory of Games' was always predicated upon one side losing 100 percent. His game theory is called 'Drop Dead.' In our *World Game* we propose to explore and test by assimilated adoption various schemes of 'How to Make the World Work.' To win the *World Game* everybody must be made physically successful. Everybody must win."[16] Fuller's testimony led, in a small part, to the launch of the Office of Technology Assessment, which advised the US government on technology trends until being de-funded in 1994.[17] For everybody to win, however, his team had to abandon the computer, the very device Fuller used to popularize the game.

In its final form, the *World Game* was sort of a God's-eye view for hippies. Fuller's vision of an anti–war game informed how his team, the World Game Institute, built the next version. This *World Game*—which was successfully built—was a giant board game big enough for players to walk around it. The *World Game* developed into an all-human exercise in 1969 with the first workshop in New York City. The team dropped the computer but kept the large Dymaxion map from the Expo '67 proposal. Fuller thought the map should be the size of an American football field. It ended up being a 70-by-35-foot map that the *World Game* team, not Fuller, assembled, disassembled, and replayed across American colleges and corporations and, later, across Japan about one hundred times per year from 1969 to 1982.[18] The massive Dymaxion map acted as a physical proxy for the dreams contained within the first 1968 *Whole Earth Catalog*—Fred Turner's exemplar of the amalgam of cyberculture and counterculture—whose cover featured one of NASA's images of Earth viewed from space.[19] The map no longer acted as a real-time display as in the Expo proposal nor presented a world that the player could control. The scale meant players felt small on the map, something the opposite of a view from nowhere.

The game itself encouraged a different, emergent kind of play. In contrast to the machinic agency of computer simulations, *World Game* players worked in teams across rounds to solve world problems. Play was unstructured and emergent—probably best considered as proximate to the wider countercultural embrace of gaming, especially the New Games Movement. Writing on the movement, media historian Fred Turner explains than the New Games rebelled against games that served as "intellectual and practical support for a vision of the natural and social worlds as closed systems."[20] Turner continues,

> It was these boxes that the New Gamers hoped to crack open. In their view, the social rules that their parents had played by had helped create a world in which nuclear holocaust was possible. They had helped segregate the adults of the Cold War era from one another, helped cut them off from the whole range of their own emotions, and turned them into mechanical creatures, working the "system" to survive. In building New Games, the young adults of the late 1960s and early 1970s hoped to create a new set of rules and with them, a new way to live. If the games of the Cold War had presumed competition and enmity, New Games would foster cooperation and empathy.[21]

The *World Game* worked best when the outcomes were emotional, not informational, when it had an emotional impact on its players. One of Medard Gabel's clearest memories of the game was when the team discovered around 1971 that there were an estimated fifty-five thousand nuclear weapons on the planet. A nuclear detonation affected the size of a bingo chip at the scale of the game map. They purchased fifty thousand phosphorescent orange bingo chips. At the end of a game in Washington, DC, five facilitators walked out onto the game board, each with ten thousand chips, and began to cover the world in bingo chips while playing a soundtrack and visuals of nuclear explosions. This act of theatre had its effect, leaving the players silent; some cried. What happened next surprised Gabel and the other facilitators. Without being prompted, people came out and started cleaning up the map. The same reaction happened in hundreds of subsequent runs of the game.[22]

The World Game Institute later experimented with personal computers. Fuller's ideas helped inspire this new vision of democratic computer. In the 1990s, the institute published *Global Recall*, an interactive atlas for schools, and recreated the Dymaxion map in Apple HyperCard, shrinking the gym-size board down to the black-and-white screen of an Apple Macintosh. The institute later tried to create an online version, NetWorldGame, but development stalled after a change in ownership of the game assets in 2001.[23] The hope was that an online version would inspire a new type of global thinking in the same way the analog version once did.[24]

Even though Fuller started to describe the game as a computer simulation, it ended up being an exercise designed to help inspire global thinking for those walking its massive game board. Indeed, the *World Game* might just as easily be seen as a God's-eye view for hippies, with the massive Dymaxion map acting as a physical proxy for the dreams contained within the first 1968 *Whole Earth Catalog*—Fred Turner's exemplar of the amalgam of cyberculture and counterculture—whose cover featured one of NASA's images of Earth viewed from space.[25]

The *World Game* did not try to simulate nations so much as provoke global thinking. The difference is subtle but profound. At their most basic, computer simulations of all kinds tried to replace political agencies with machine agencies, letting the computer stand in even as a crude abstraction. The *World Game*, by contrast, offered a limited gaze and player agency. Indeed, the game seemed to have worked best as an experience. The *World Game* attests to the growing desire to step outside a computational imaginary of politics, one site of a growing effort to create alternative world models and futures also seen in the World Order Models Project.[26]

World Order Models Project: Imagining Other Worlds

The World Order Models Project (WOMP) was, to one of its key members, focused on the "the design of *relevant utopias* that could be realized in the 1990's."[27] Utopia was not a word encountered a lot in discussions of politics in computer simulation's trading zone. However, WOMP aimed not to create utopias but to create a "positive model of world order" that "includes *transition* proposals and strategies to bring it into being."[28] As other simulators argued about their validity, WOMP rejected the idea that the goal of modeling was to replicate reality, but rather proposed that the goal was to imagine better ones. Furthermore, the project, as American as it was, tried to include voices usually on the margins of the simulation communities.

The largely academic project united scholars globally who were willing to entertain theories of the international order, proposals for a better one, and plans to make these changes happen. Far from trying to represent the actual world—or referent system—WOMP scholars tried to model entirely new world orders. WOMP's models did not transform the United Nations or upset the global order, but the project exemplifies how modeling could be something other than a simplification of reality.[29]

The World Order Models Project had its roots in the internationalist movement. Often called the world federalism movement, the term refers to a variety of efforts to imagine a new system of global governance.[30] World federalism was an influential idea in postwar America, but it declined after becoming a target of McCarthyism, which considered it a proxy for communism.[31] World federalists included figures like H. G. Wells and Albert Einstein. They were committed to global cooperation or even a one-world government. One key document, the Dublin Declaration, called for a dramatic expansion of the United Nations' systems.[32] The declaration found favor in elite American circles, which helped the movement gain financial backing. Bankers Harry B. Hollins and C. Douglas Dillon founded the Fund for Education Concerning World Peace through World Law in 1961 to promote the movement.[33] The organization, through its World Law Fund, decided to support WOMP. Funded in 1968, WOMP was created by law professor and antiwar activist Saul Mendlovitz.[34]

Saul Mendlovitz started his academic career at Rutgers University in 1956 in its School of Law. Mendlovitz was an activist and advocate for "human global governance."[35] His views put him at odds with other members of the world modeling community. Mendlovitz appeared in the previous chapter as a critic at Karl Deutsch's 1972 conference that led to GLOBUS.

Mendlovitz's friend and colleague Richard Falk, who he met at Harvard, was another key member of the project. Falk had become interested in new forms of international order after his experiences at Yale, including interactions with Harold Lasswell. Though not easy to pin down ideologically, Lasswell studied the possibilities of global governance and a just international order, putting him at odds with realists like Hans Morgenthau.[36] Mendlovitz and Falk shared an interest in global governance and a skepticism of world federalist schemes as "mainly Western oriented" and "a postcolonial effort to perpetuate Western influence."[37] (Indeed, the American United World Federalists was governed for a time by Cord Meyer, who later worked at the Central Intelligence Agency.)[38] Mendlovitz, according to Falk, was something of an entrepreneur, able to find support for his ideas and research.

Falk was a self-described "public intellectual," then and now one of the greatest global advocates for human rights and critics of its abuses.[39] To give some context, famed whistleblower Daniel Ellsberg collected two sets of secret documents: the famous Pentagon Papers and a second trove of documents related to US nuclear strategy. He never released this second set—at least at the time—but shared it with fellow critics of US foreign policy Howard Zinn, Noam Chomsky, and the lesser-known but just as influential Richard Falk.[40] Falk was a critic of the Vietnam War, a law professor at Princeton, and a member of the long-forgotten WOMP. That a friend of Ellsberg would participate in WOMP speaks to the project's unorthodoxy.

WOMP—Mendlovitz started it, Falk participated—aimed to advance Mendlovitz's desire for global cooperation through new methods for modeling world orders.[41] More a literacy ideal than a working model, WOMP notably tried to build an international team of experts to discuss and debate world models that were in sharp contrast to the kinds of computer simulations discussed in the last chapter. Harold Lasswell clearly acknowledged the differences. He wrote, "The significance of WOMP is what needs to be considered—and that is the modelling process itself. It is reliance on modelling that carries significance for science, scholarship, and policy. World order modelling indicates that something new is taking shape in the use of the mind as an instrument of collective purpose. Not that modelling exemplifies perpetual motion; rather, it is a mode of perpetual, focused participation that strives to draw upon and further improve collective ways of thinking, feeling, and acting."[42] The eventual project drew on an international pool of scholars and critics of US foreign policy whose inspirations ranged from critical theory to world systems and science fiction.

WOMP began around 1966, when Falk and Mendlovitz coedited a book, *The Strategy of World Order*. The book, published by the World Law Fund with an introduction by Lasswell, sought "to build toward an integrated approach to the study of world order," which in effect comprised an extended discussion of global institutions to avoid nuclear war.[43] Subsequent funding enabled the team to grow and to continue conversations about new world models. Members of the WOMP team first gathered in New Delhi in February 1968 (just after the Tet Offensive began in Vietnam) at the Center for the Study of Developing Countries. Members representing "West Germany, Latin America, Japan, India, and North America" gathered to offer a progressive vision for world politics. Participants at these meetings debated world orders, and WOMP held at least nine global meetings before publishing results in a book series edited by Mendlovitz and titled *Preferred World for the 1990s*. By then, the organization had grown to include representation from the USSR as well as African, Chinese, Middle Eastern, and

Scandinavian perspectives. Support for the project grew beyond the World Law Fund to include the Rockefeller Foundation and Carnegie Endowment. Reflecting on these meetings, Mendlovitz explained that their purpose was "to create the basic instructional materials, needed for a worldwide educational movement whose ultimate price would be global reform."[44]

WOMP tried to imagine a desirable *world*. Just as the Club of Rome published its warnings of a future world, WOMP was trying to design a better one, an effort best seen through its book series. Mendlovitz edited the first book, *On the Creation of a Just World Order*, which include contributions from distinguished faculty from across the globe. The project was pluralist, seeking "multi-perspectives rather than a database or ideas generated from one national source."[45] Subsequent books tried to decenter Western experts by publishing noted scholars from Africa and India. Famed international political scientist Ranji Kothari, founder of the Centre for the Study of Developing Societies, published his own 1975 volume that included a call for a decentralized global federation.[46] Prominent international scholar Al'amin Mazuri, an Oxford graduate then at Makerere University in Uganda, wrote *A World Federation of Cultures: An African Perspective*, a 1976 book that included an appendix outlining a global world order designed to provide "an infrastructure . . . for a new and more equitable process of cultural interaction."[47] Falk contributed his own extended volume, *A Study of Future Worlds*, which was entirely dedicated to analyzing world models and offering proposals. Filled with diagrams of world orders and analyses of global power, Falk's book tried to develop a superior world system. Though all its outputs remained largely academic, the project expressly tried to imagine how to turn a reference model into a "preference model."[48]

WOMP tried to widen participation beyond the Global North, and, even if modest in its success, the project stands in marked contrast to parallel American efforts to simulate the globe that largely relied on the same densely networked elites. Where International Political Data tried to make data global—to return to a phrase from Paul Edwards—WOMP created the networks and interconnections to make global data, including voices and positions that would as easily have been abstracted away like villagers in a simulated Vietnam.[49]

There was direct opposition. Falk recalls that the project "tried to be value-neutral and tried to project a vision of the future that came from trend analysis or a data set of some kind, or some kind of scenario-constructed futures."[50] WOMP attracted critics but also advocates like Lasswell, whose existing interest in modeling and policy work made the project appealing.[51] Other world system approaches abstracted "real" political interactions, whereas WOMP allowed these interactions to be imaginative. WOMP could be called early political speculative fiction. Falk even defended the project through a coy reference to science fiction writer Stanislaw Lem's *The Futurological Congress*'s mockery of the nascent futures industry. Falk quoted Lem: "Oh Professor—I felt like shouting—here you sit, and out there the world is coming to an end." To which Falk agreed, "the perils of the world situation are so severe that we need to gather our energies for constructive effort."[52]

The World Order Models Project was and was not a world federalism project. Members of the team never entirely agreed with one another, and the project's outputs varied. A critic called WOMP "a hodge-podge of essays related, higgledy-piggledy, by a collective judgment that the existing world order is rotting away, that it will inevitably be replaced, and that neither the process of transition nor its product are beyond the reach of benign intervention calculated to reduce the trauma of change and the potential human costs of the new international system."[53] But within that criticism lies the core of WOMP's novelty: The group was unafraid to imagine desirable world orders even if they never agreed on the right one. As Richard Falk explains, "The basic idea of the project was to stimulate transnational scholarly inquiry into the requirements of a world peace system, which these leading academicians thought would lead indirectly in the Clark/Sohn direction of global governance. Saul was a smart enough salesman of ideas to know that he could not peddle the Clark/Sohn plan as the pre-agreed solution if he wanted to recruit first-class academic participants from non-Western backgrounds. There had to be an openness, an invitation to dialogue, and the promise of give and take."[54] Over its twenty-year run, WOMP played out the tension between Mendlovitz and other project members over a specific plan for world reform or an early international collaboration.

WOMP did not lead to a better world, and the international order remains much the same as when they started. The project continued until the money ran out, and Mendlovitz moved on to projects with participants more sympathetic to his views. Falk continued his international law work. In 2008, the United Nations Human Rights Council appointed him Special Rapporteur on the situation of human rights in the Palestinian territories occupied since 1967—a position he held for six years. A footnote now, WOMP offers a clear example of modeling not bound by worries of addressability. These visions often included formal diagrams, as in Falk's work, but also normative principles and commentary analysis of the world order. WOMP's legacy hinges, overall, on the possibilities it represented as an effort in thinking of future-oriented modeling. In contrast to Deutsch's steering models that tried to scientifically predict the future or even drift models based on current trends, WOMP demonstrates efforts to build global dialogues to imagine better worlds, goals often missing in computer simulations.

The WOMP project has been largely forgotten, but there are efforts to revive it. Aaron McKeil writes that a WOMP 2.0 might clarify "alternative preferable non-great power-centric global order models possible in the medium to long-term future."[55] Over thirty years after its end, the project thus endures to image another kind of modeling, an exercise in imagining a better world through international collaborations.

The Hairline Fractures of Computational Imaginaries

The *World Game* and WOMP would have failed a simple validity test. Neither presented a world as is. But that raises a question: Should all simulations have to be real? These examples suggest a kind of simulation otherwise defined by imagination and radical speculation.[56]

I suggest that both answer media theorist Wendy Chun's hope for modeling to create habits to "make decisions and coalitions beyond our natural sympathies—and, by doing so, invent new relations and futures."[57] Yet, this possibility leaves computers too instrumental, neglecting computer simulation's own place in history. By way of conclusion, let me extend from these examples to outline a project for speculative political simulations.

Could computers express new politics? There is a radical literature on computers and society that is often dismissed as mere science fiction.[58] Computers have been connected to visions of utopia—of better, pluralist worlds without scarcity. Some are more ambivalent but novel—like the computers in Ursula K. LeGuin's ambiguous utopia *The Dispossessed*. The turn toward utopian possibilities is not naive. Frederic Jameson remarks on utopias: "These seemingly peaceful images are also, in and of themselves, violent ruptures with what is, breaks that destabilize our stereotypes of a future that is the same as our own present, interventions that interrupt the reproduction of the system in habit and in ideological consent and institute that fissure, however minimal and initially little more than a hairline fracture, through which another picture of the future and another system of temporality altogether might emerge.[59]

This book's shadow is the parallel speculative history of computers and politics. Often pursued outside political communication or the history of computing, these practices of imagination are critical. Jameson hopes that "utopology revives long dormant parts of the mind, unused organs of political and historical and social imagination which have virtually atrophied for lack of use, muscles of praxis we have long since ceased exercising, revolutionary gestures we have lost the habit of performing, even subliminally."[60] I might suggest the same could be done for circuits and minds as well. What happens when we build games that allow us to imagine different ideal worlds? Louise Amoore asserts that "we social scientists, and humanities and ethics scholars, must also find ways to engage experimentally in algorithmic fabulation. Let us begin by digging under the narratives of the show and tell algorithms, cracking them open to find the moments of nonclosure, writing them in ways that lever open their ethicopolitical orientations."[61] Doing so, I argue, can help us find new ways of being and thinking in the computational imaginary of politics.

The challenge becomes one of critical making. What are the ways to produce new models and prototypes within the computational imaginary of politics? Mainstream games rarely reflect alternatives. As Jim Gasperini noted when making *Hidden Agenda*, discussed in the last chapter, "No matter how fantastic the fantasy, no matter how simulated the simulation, the outlines of our familiar reality will always be discernible underneath."[62] Yet some games do provoke other ways of seeing and being. Games have created spaces for imagining politics otherwise like the bleak fascism of *Frostpunk* or the hopeful *Half-Earth Socialism*. None of them are so particularly technically complex; they are more examples of procedural rhetoric than radical human-machine relations.[63] We can be more ambitious.

Computer simulation might express addressability on new scales. One of Bruno Latour's last publications, written with climate scientists Timothy Lenton and Sébastien Dutreuil, argues that something like Gaia (i.e., Earth as a "global scale entity" that "exhibited goal-directed behavior—self-regulation of habitable conditions") has been overlooked in climate modeling.[64] Modeling is part of the solution. Much like Chun's call to help us know what is beyond us, Latour and his coauthors write, "One can look at these modelling and theoretical endeavors as descriptions of the abstract properties of Life and of Gaia."[65] Part of the challenge now is to think about ways that computer simulations might grant new perspectives that are neither human nor God's-eye views.

Simulations might also help find new ways to agencies. Louise Amoore's ethicopolitical strategies might offer a program here. Amoore offers three aspects of strategies for an ethicopolitical approach: *apertures*, *opacity*, and the *unattributable*. All three are considerations of relations, partial knowledges, and perspectives. "Aperture," a technical term for an opening that lets light in, concerns the orientation of algorithmic epistemologies and knowledges. A God's-eye view can be read as an aperture and as an ideal aperture. If a God's-eye view negates its partial knowledge—its limitations of never being a complete picture—then what other ways might capture the unfolding multiplicity of politics? Opacity, to Amoore, refers to the possibilities when accepting "not knowing in advance what the relations could be."[66] Opacity enables moments of recognizing the political when the very limits—or errors—facilitate a sense of what might be missing or what cannot be. Amoore explains, "When machine learning algorithms segment a social scene, generating clusters of propensities, for example, to vote for a particular political party, or to respond to targeted social media, or to pose a high risk of recidivism, everything must be attributed, even the outliers understood as distant gradients from the curve of normality. The unattributable remains within the scene, however, exceeding the algorithm's capacity to show and tell, and opening onto a different kind of community and a different mode of being together."[67] The temptation of the God's-eye view is to see the world as complete with a knowable future. Opacity and the unattributable become the positive conditions for new kinds of visions enabled by understanding the consequences of models, their abstractions, and their relations to the world. A reconsideration of the function of modeling is not just epistemic but ontological, or maybe a faith (to borrow a phrase from Latour and others above) in life on Earth—a faith in life on Earth that becomes the animus other than closure, to witness the multiplicity of being together such that models become partial accounts of our many political entanglements, solidarities, and exploitations. More concretely, Amoore encourages "a conception of being together as a society of the unattributable, where what we share in common is precisely our singularities, and where our encounters with others can never be limited to a finite collection of attributes"—a shared agency that might be possible, yet is so far unrealized in the discrete systems of computer simulations.[68]

Where might we begin to shape new presentations of the world in the computational imaginary of politics? In her novel *Orbital*, Samantha Harvey narrates the inner lives of astronauts in a space station. They look down on Earth from the space station, a gaze only possible due to life-supporting systems. Their view of the globe has an effect. Harvey writes, "The earth, from here, is like heaven. It flows with colour. A burst of hopeful colour. When we're on that planet we look up and think heaven is elsewhere, but here is what the astronauts and cosmonauts sometimes think: maybe all of us born to it have already died and are in an afterlife. If we must go to an improbably, hard-to-believe in place when we die, that glassy, distant orb with its beautiful lonely light shows could well be it."[69] How do we create the same wonder on Earth that astronauts in their technological homeostasis see? Perhaps new views offer new wonders. How, to borrow from artist Lonnie Holley, can we be part of that wonder?

10 Let X = X, or the Legacies of a Computational Imaginary of Politics

Politics has become another computational problem, a SimPolitics. This book has traced a genealogy of breakdowns in the United States, when the line between political and computational was scratched away like a lottery ticket. While writing this book, I've compiled a file folder (actually a Zotero folder) full of stories about some recent technology or another promising to revolutionize politics. For decades, political scientists, programmers, pollsters, and spies built models on computers to simulate the behaviors of individual voters and the geopolitical power moves of nation-states, and we are still trying to work out the implications of these efforts. Through their efforts, voters and worlds reflectively have been understood to behave like computers. The challenge remains to disentangle politics from computation, not to return politics to being unmediated or to try to do something like ban political ads on Facebook. The challenge is to reclaim a sense of the political within the computational imaginary. These concerns feel ever more urgent.

We live in a moment of heightened importance for the computational political imaginary. Artificial intelligence now defines our political moment.[1] Politicians and policymakers have turned to AI as *the* catalyst for global political upheaval. Programmers, crypto developers, and computer scientists debate whether AI can be automated through blockchain.[2] Artificial intelligence arrives as if by its very nature it might solve *or* break political problems. Examples appear daily. Neil Sahota, writing in *Forbes*, claims that "by harnessing AI's capabilities, political parties and candidates can analyze vast amounts of data, tailor messages, predict voter behavior, and optimize campaign strategies."[3] AI has been suggested as a solution to the tragedy in Gaza, through a "multi-agent AI model" from a firm called CulturePulse (mentioned in chapter 7). This system developed out of international modeling efforts, experimental methods to be sure, but was funded nonetheless by the United Nations.[4]

That these projects might fail—as they have indeed failed but still a risk worth taking—is a faith that the computational imaginary of politics helps to explain. Even as this history has shown that computers never fully became a digital twin to reality or solved their addressability gap, computers seem primed to solve the intractable problems of politics in the United States. Shortcomings become justifications for the next models, from Ahab's Moby Dick to Obama's Project Narwhal.[5] Lucy Suchman writes that "the radical openness of 'actual reality' poses an enduring problem for the project of AI."[6] The digital sublime part of this imaginary is a faith in the next model, the next prototype.

By identifying an American computational imaginary, we can begin to see its influence. The most obvious example of this imaginary is that digital computers, in short, have been associated with winning—an explanation that seems to happen every four years about the candidates' secret data strategy and digital manipulations. If these claims feel familiar today, then this book's contribution is to offer a better sense of the beginnings of these claims, and a way to distinguish between naive claims of using technologies to *solve* politics and the deeper efforts in modeling and prototyping more generally.

The computational imaginary of politics is an American tradition exported across the world. That might seem obvious with today's AI or large digital platforms, but American efforts to solve political problems with computers were always globalized. US political technology firms, for example, actively sought international markets to sell their services. *Campaigns & Elections* dedicated its May–June 1989 issue to international consulting, depicting global trade like a game of *Risk*.[7] Post-Obama US political consultants found a global appetite for their new political management platforms and data-driven expertise.[8] This occurred even while, domestically, political scientist Eitan Hersh questioned how effective big data was for campaigning.[9] But thinking about exportation alone overlooks a deeper facet of how these models and prototypes were designed to go global—to not only win campaigns at home but to help the United States manage populations the world over.[10]

Computer simulations found active funders in American intelligence agencies, and that uptake has had lasting consequences. Political scientist and director of the Notre Dame International Security Center (NDISC) Michael C. Desch laments the overemphasis on mathematics and models in contemporary American intelligence. Desch scolds "political scientists" who "have committed themselves to particular social science methods not so much because they believe they will illuminate real-world policy problems but because they serve a vested interest in disciplinary autonomy and dovetail with a particular image (mathematized and model-based) of what a 'science' of politics should look like" (an image of politics I have shown to have computational roots, and these roots cast a global shadow).[11]

"We live in the shadow of a number, and that makes it hard to see the future."[12] This quote comes from another influential *New Yorker* article, Bill McKibben's "The End of Nature," which foreshadowed the climate crisis. True, I have struggled with writing a book questioning political modeling at a time when climate modeling seems so important for our very survival.[13] Yet the quote casts another shadow for me.[14] I had never read McKibben's "The End of Nature" or, at least, not until recently. I instead found the quote in Ariel Dorfman's novel *The Suicide Museum*, his memorial of sorts for Chilean President Salvador Allende. The article, mentioned in the book, became something of a double revelation. McKibben's article was published on the anniversary of the US-backed coup in Chile: September 11, 1989. As Allende tried to build a new system of government, US intelligence agencies modeled systems that might have been used to plan his demise.[15] Allende's failed Cybersyn project and the largely forgotten Modelo Mundial Latinoamericano of exiled Argentinian Amílcar Herrera point to other computer simulations.[16] These projects, notably, both ended due to US interference in Chile and Argentina, respectively—a reminder, too, of the computer simulations that never could be built at this time. America's computational imaginary thrived where others did not. Acknowledging the limits of my history helps me return to this book's contributions as a specific study of the computational imaginary of politics in the United States.

The Consequences of SimVoters and SimWorlds

This book studied a period of intense pressure that shaped the computational imaginary of politics in the United States. Both domestically and internationally, computer simulation promised to be a better way to manage politics. Each chapter offered a specific moment in this imaginary's genesis and posed key questions to help study and sketch a more nuanced picture of the computational imaginary.

Q1. How do computer models encode different political agencies?

Q2. How do computer simulations address voters?

Q3. How do computer simulations address worlds?

Q4. How do interfaces present different agencies?

Each of these chapters explored how these concepts help make sense of the computational imaginary of politics. Let's return to the main arguments that I discussed in the introduction.

From Lay Theories to Large Models: Shifts in Technical Expertise

The US research community developed models of world and electoral politics contemporaneously with computing technology, often with the same people using the same methods both domestically and internationally. This shifted political expertise from a human science to a cyborg science. I am not the first to observe a move from situated to scalable political epistemologies. Both nationally and internationally, expertise has become computational. International area studies experts lament the rise of game theoretical scholars, who build models that scale rather than deep histories of regions.[17] Historian Manan Ahmed Asif analyzes how US "area studies" became the basis for data studies. Asif traces how "the history of philological sciences and data sciences co-exist for the American imperial past and present."[18] At a lesser scale, better addressability of American populations encouraged the early social sciences and then data sciences. The computational imaginary has enabled certain experts to deliver political accounts that can act and adapt to the needs of political management and control. My account offers another telling of the beginnings of the cyborg sciences and how national and international political sciences became cyborg.[19]

The computational imaginary matters for the performance of political expertise. An entire political consulting industry depends on it—the hope that computers can help win the next election. The first issues of *Campaigns & Elections*, the industry's trade magazine, were filled with advertisements and articles promising to transform politics with computers. As I opened the pages of *Campaigns & Elections* in sequence, a pattern appeared within issue after issue, ad after ad, article after article. Computer innovation promised to revolutionize politics. These advertisements point to how the computational imaginary became invoked in a sort of confidence game.[20] Computers, obviously, did not always revolutionize politics, but that did not stop consultants and companies from using this computational imaginary to sell their products. How can their claims be treated as plausible or persuasive? Because they participate in the cocreation of a computational imaginary—a refrain that changes and endures. Participants in such an imaginary can be said to know an "inside secret," to borrow a phrase from Goffman: "These are ones whose possession marks an individual as being a member of a group and helps the group feel separate and different from those individuals who are not 'in the know.'"[21] The secret evolves, but the consequence of the coproduction of computing and modern campaigning has been that the terms of political change have been set as technological change.

These hopes come with risks. Scams, frauds, and hype all come to mind, as those versed in the computational imaginary can bank on its secrets to gain legitimacy. Political communication theory attends to confidence per se, but less so to this confidence game. As a quick reminder, the confidence game was a textbook case for Erving Goffman's studies of sociological performance. The con artist knew the rules of the game so well as to appear confident, to trick the mark out of their money. The confidence game explains the persuasive power of Cambridge Analytica, a supposedly important firm that never saw major use in American politics.[22] The firm relied on the expectations outlined above, shaping its marketing around this computational imaginary. In a presentation entitled "Data-driven Behavior Change" the firm bragged, "Our background in behavior change has helped us shape events on the global stage." Through computers and data, Cambridge Analytica claimed to better manage voters and governments globally. Their self-promotion led to widespread public concern about the future of liberal democracies in a digital age; yet Cambridge Analytica did not live up to its sales deck. In short, Cambridge Analytica functioned as something of a con because they understood the discourse of this computational imaginary such that their claims could be taken as plausible even without tangible proof. Cambridge Analytica, however, is just one example—one that shows how hopes quickly turn to fears.

Maybe "con" is too dramatic. The issues are broader. Knowing how to talk about politics through computational metaphors can be perceived as a shortcut to both expertise and dominance. Con or not, a shift in expertise invokes new dynamics in knowledge and power. The confidence game involves technical vernaculars, or what Michael Butterworth calls "political sabermetrics."[23] The trick is not that computational stories are less true but that the computational imaginary is generative, addressability gaps and hyperreal agencies allow for creative possibilities. Scholars and journalists need ways to disentangle the computing from these confidence games. If not, as Jill Lepore makes clear in the case of Simulmatics, supremely out-of-touch people assume they can represent a Vietnamese village or the Civil Rights Movement—thus becoming the modern equivalent of Carol Cohn's missile men in ivory towers, who make broad claims about national and international populations without context or care.[24]

Accepting the limits of a computational imaginary and the risk of the con should enable new accounts of the political. Lucy Suchman, addressing the same history, calls for "different but related sites of situational awareness, in the form of wider public understanding of the modes of ignorance on which US militarism depends. Both investigative journalism and critical scholarship have a crucial role to play here, given the significance of their stories in shaping how relevant publics understand the conditions and effects of operations undertaken in their names."[25] Suchman's point is that new journalism and research projects might enable new kinds of situational awareness. Suchman cites the work done by the Bureau of Investigative Journalism to track drone use in war zones. Another example might be the research agency Forensic Architecture's work on tracking bombings in the occupied Palestinian territories.[26] What worries me is that these forms of situational awareness seem legitimate *only* when computational (more so than the result of people risking their lives on the ground). What are the views lost when only looking at the world like a computer?

Political Updates? Technological Change as Political Change

My second argument in this book is that challenges of management and control framed the research agendas and funding contexts for simulation, the production of computational models, and (in some cases) their working prototypes. This framing legitimated technological change as a key driver of political change.

Political change can become reduced to technological change. The two are deeply linked, no doubt, but it has become a scholarly trope to consider the latest social media platform as the next instrument of political revolution. US-based researchers celebrate and cherish the opportunity of so-called liberation technologies while ignoring the failed revolutions of past technologies, from the telephone to Twitter (or, should I say, X). These efforts point to the persistence of the technological sublime in US-based discussion of technology.[27] I do not dispute the close link between technology and politics, but I worry that technology has become too easy an explanation. The risk is not just bad explanations but a growing ignorance of noncomputational life.

Computer simulation can flatten worlds. Games like *On the Campaign Trail* modeled individual voters, whereas world models like *TEMPER* let regional blocks stand in for millions of people. The issue, then, is not the technological sublime so much as the ignorance that the sublime can legitimate. The detailed knowledge collected about individual American voters coexists in the same imaginary as a nonknowledge about international populations. My questions have shown the gaps between simulations and worlds.

Part of the challenge in the United States, however, has been that the political computational imaginary has become so focused on management and control. Efforts to bring about digital parties in Europe never cross the Atlantic.[28] Early pirate parties tried to create new forms of voting and political participation.[29] Subsequent theories of distributed autonomous organizations have been put into practice as little more than financial management tools for buying NFTs of bored apes, misguided attempts to control the *Dune* franchise, or hopes to automate democratic decision-making entirely.[30]

The computational imaginary of politics, as I have traced its development, limits a more radical computational imaginary of politics. The focus on control and management reduces the possibilities of both computing and politics. Louise Amoore writes of this negation, "Contemporary algorithms are oriented toward limiting the unanticipated actions of humans while generating a whole new world of their own unanticipated and unreasonable actions."[31] The computational imaginary of politics too often lets political debates become statistical horse races. What we lose is the wildness of computing itself. This negation positions computing as if it can only ever be an agent of campaigns and empires. And yet, computer simulations never achieved the instrumental aims funders envisaged for these prototypes. What might happen if we risk thinking past wild computer simulation? This book has, hopefully, brought you to this point, to what Beth Coleman calls an "ontological crossroads."[32] Coleman continues, "The dominant paradigm of predictive AI simulates a command-control system that can be aimed like a weapon—the 'killer robots' of a military postindustrial complex as well as the quotidian application of ubiquitous computing. In such a formulation, these are technologies of oppression that continue to power the extractive practices and constitutional imaginaries of a colonial sublime."[33] I have not offered much in the way of an alternative—maybe ways to view the imaginary from skewed angles or outsides.[34] Yet the ending here still feels so much like a beginning.

What comes next might be a posthuman politics, maybe a liberation of both humans and machines. To counter every "Techno-Optimist Manifesto" written in Silicon Valley, we need to see new cyborgs and cyber-organizations.[35] Beth Coleman looks for inspiration in the maroon, "an iconic figure of black techné . . . who is the escaped (black) person occluded in the swamps and forests of the Americas."[36] The maroon invites a chance to think of AI outside the surround, to consider the possibility of a wild AI. "To think AI in relation to the maroon—the subject adrift from the dominion of command-control—is a coincidence of history and innovation."[37] These efforts to imagine a wild AI match efforts to build Indigenous AI. Jason Edward Lewis, Noelani Arista, Archer Pechawis, and Suzanne Kite, writing together and individually from their unique Indigenous epistemologies, propose "an extended 'circle of relationships' that includes the non-human kin—from network daemons to robot dogs to artificial intelligences (AI) weak and, eventually, strong—that increasingly populate our computational biosphere."[38] They are "not worried about rogue hyper-intelligences going Skynet to destroy humanity" but rather about "anonymous hyper-intelligences working for governments and corporations, implementing far-reaching social, economic, and military strategies based on the same values that have fostered genocide against Indigenous people worldwide and brought us all to the brink of environmental collapse." Lewis, Arista, Pechawis, and Kite continue to "fear the rise of a new class of extremely powerful beings that will make the same mistakes as their creators but with greater consequences and even less public accountability."[39] Here is the crossroads.

Pure Scientific Intelligence?

The computational imaginary of politics is conflicted. Efforts to model politics domestically and internationally diverged into competing models with different assumptions of agency and behavior while converging on the computer (or machines) as the principal format for political prototyping. The convergence flattened the conflicts within the computational imaginary of politics itself like a world on screen. How worries about AI undermining human agency might occlude the possibility of AI providing helpful criticism of human judgment or offering a vision of an artificial intelligence that helps imagine better worlds rather than probable threats.

Computer simulation cannot solve liberal democracy's constitutive anxieties. Democracy has a tenuous relation to anything stable, as discussed by theorist Claude Lefort: "The locus of power is an empty place, it cannot be occupied—it is such that no individual or group can be consubstantial with it—and it cannot be represented."[40] A computational imaginary plays off democracy's empty center, filling its radical promise of openness with a digital Pandora's box that fuels liberal anxieties about the corruption of politics by inauthentic, inhuman participants.[41] The unsettling part is that democracy thwarts efforts at *a resolution*, never allowing for a stable definition of a legitimate democratic subject. The solution cannot be to return to some form of ideal voter or to continue to hope that a computational imaginary of politics can absolutely decode the political.

Hopes and fears over democracy are not all equal. Computer simulations, in the examples above, presumed voters to act dynamically, like the cybernetic homeostat, which encouraged imagining campaigns as able to target and persuade those voters. Addressability also mattered, because if campaigns could reach the right voters, they could change minds. Reagan's computer-assisted State of the Union was purportedly more persuasive due to its datafied relation to its audience. Do these approaches create a hyperreality of democracy where we presume computer cycles run faster than election cycles? Computers have offered other ways to imagine an active voter that is at odds with other models. Do cybernetics models appeal to advertisers and campaigners looking to sell their services over other models?

Focusing just on hope and fear can miss how voter models can fill democracy's empty center. Voter models—data chimeras, rational agents, and cybernetic citizens—all promise to explain, or corrupt, the center of democracy: the voter. That voter, however, can never be defined. The implications of a computational imaginary, then, are two-fold. First, attention must be given to the dominant voter models and their working prototypes acting in this imaginary. Second, what could a politics of reimagining a computational voter be? Can we imagine a cyborg citizen outside the histories thus far presented? How could a computational imaginary inform a radical theory of democracy? These questions linger and require further elaboration of this computational imaginary and its inherent antagonism.

The challenge is not in perfecting *an* accurate model but to acknowledge the politics of every model. Cybernetic citizens promise agency, a boon to ad firms and intelligence agencies alike. Rational agents reduce the world to self-interest, offering clear explanations of societies without sociality. Data chimeras reduce us to our data shadows, ensuring a sense of history but locking in a conservatism as well. There are surely more: more models and more approaches that I missed. I see limits in all these models and approached them with a deep ambivalence—except for rational agents, where I had a harder time overlooking its utility in a politics of control and management and an end to politics itself. This book offers an archaeology of prompts, a chance to see other computational possibilities and imagine new ones.

Because the current computational imaginary will not hold. Wendy Chun reflects on the persistent skepticism around climate change as a matter not only of survival but of depoliticization. The turn toward the risk society and the rise of mass skepticism fuels the desire for technological proof that transcends human fallibility as seen in the TV drama *CSI*, short for Crime Scene Investigation. "Because of *CSI*," Chun writes, "lawyers are finding juries increasingly unwilling to convict based on circumstantial evidence, of deduction rather than forensics."[42] With AI, we might be in a new stage, a blockbuster big data turn: *CSI: The Movie*. Yet *CSI*'s fantasy of techno-truth is something of a pharmakon, for the fallibility of humans only stokes a growing political individualism and neoliberalism that invites further skepticism. The challenge seen here and elsewhere: Computing's neutrality is never enough.

Political modeling raises an even more existential risk; its object is empty, at least in democratic societies. The empty center of democracy prevents an optimal closure or conclusion, and yet, without a fixed reference system, the hyperreality of modeling can overheat in this radical fluidity. Bound in the service of management and control, this hyperreality becomes a concern about disinformation, maintaining the allure of facts, which allow new dimensions for political speculation and hyperreality. Worlds and political models overheat simultaneously. The former translates a warming Earth into a model, while the latter lets the indeterminacy of politics overheat into speculation. The exuberance of modeling has been held in check by the limits of the imaginary itself. How might we follow through on Amoore's call for a "methodology of a critical cloud ethics [that] must also fabulate, must also necessarily invent a people whose concrete particularities are precisely unattributable, never fully enclosed within the attribute and its output."[43]

Defining the computational imaginary—the political model and prototypes—is a call to reimagine as well as critique it. Indeed, Indigenous epistemologies have always held, in their diverse ways, something other than a God's-eye view. Lewis, Arista, Pechawis, and Kite write that these perspectives "do not take abstraction or generalization as a natural good or higher order of intellectual engagement."[44] These approaches are crucial for what has to come.[45] They continue, "Our goal is that we, as a species, figure out how to treat these new non-human kin respectfully and reciprocally—and not as mere tools, or worse, slaves to their creators."[46] The risk, in letting go of a politics of control, is to let loose a flood of possibilities, some dark and some hopeful.[47]

The project of imagining alternative futures has been at the edges of this history. Alternatives that can be found largely outside the US context I have focused on suggest that the computational imaginary of politics is more expansive. What could we imagine, what might be the alternatives? Frederic Jameson suggests that "the positing of alternate futures is not itself a political program nor even a political practice: but it is hard to see how any durable or effective political action could come into being without it."[48] The examples I have given are just a start of a celebration for those living at the edges of the computational imaginary, at what Jorge Luis Borges describes in his short story *On Exactitude in Science* as the "tattered ruins of that map."[49] Perhaps in these ruins we might see what light the cracks let in.

Notes

Chapter 1

1. Dan Rockmore, "How Much of the World Is It Possible to Model?," *The New Yorker*, January 15, 2024, https://www.newyorker.com/culture/annals-of-inquiry/how-much-of-the-world-is-it-possible-to-model.

2. Orrin Clotworthy, "Some Far-out Thoughts on Computers," *Studies in Intelligence*, 1962, 5.

3. Clotworthy, "Some Far-out Thoughts," 6.

4. Clotworthy, 7.

5. Clotworthy.

6. Bernhard Warner, "Revealed: The 1962 CIA Paper That Predicts the Big Deal with Big Data," *Bloomberg.com*, March 14, 2013, https://www.bloomberg.com/news/articles/2013-03-13/revealed-the-1962-cia-paper-that-predicts-the-big-deal-with-big-data.

7. Meredith Broussard, *Artificial Unintelligence: How Computers Misunderstand the World* (Cambridge, MA: MIT Press, 2019).

8. Ruha Benjamin, *Race After Technology: Abolitionist Tools for the New Jim Code* (Medford, MA: Polity, 2019); Jackie Wang, *Carceral Capitalism* (South Pasadena, CA: Semiotext, 2018); Alison B. Powell, *Undoing Optimization: Civic Action in Smart Cities* (New Haven, CT: Yale University Press, 2021).

9. Vincent Mosco, *The Digital Sublime: Myth, Power, and Cyberspace* (Cambridge, MA: MIT Press, 2004); David E. Nye, *American Technological Sublime* (Cambridge, MA: MIT Press, 1994); James W. Carey and John J. Quirk, "The Mythos of the Electronic Revolution," *American Scholar* 39, no. 2 (1970): 219–241.

10. Mosco, *The Digital Sublime*, 24.

11. See the September–October 2018 special issue of the *MIT Technology Review*, "Technology Is Threatening Our Democracy. How Do We Save It?," https://www.technologyreview.com/magazines/the-politics-issue/.

12. Louise Amoore, *Cloud Ethics: Algorithms and the Attributes of Ourselves and Others* (Durham, NC: Duke University Press, 2020), 162.

13. N. Katherine Hayles, "Self-Reflexive Metaphors in Maxwell's Demon and Shannon's Choice: Finding the Passages," in *Literature and Science: Theory & Practice*, ed. Stuart Peterfreund (Boston: Northeastern University Press, 1990), 209–238; N. Katherine Hayles, *How We Became Posthuman: Virtual Bodies in Cybernetics, Literature, and Informatics* (Chicago: University of Chicago Press, 1999).

14. Peter Galison, "Computer Simulations and the Trading Zone," in *From Science to Computational Science*, ed. Gabriele Gramelsberger (Zurich: Diaphanes, 2011), 157, http://medientheorie.com/doc/galison_simulation.pdf.

15. Christopher Kelty, *Two Bits: The Cultural Significance of Free Software* (Durham, NC: Duke University Press, 2008).

16. Gilles Deleuze, "Postscript on the Societies of Control," *October* 59, no. 1 (1992): 6.

17. Daniel Kreiss, *Prototype Politics: Technology-Intense Campaigning and the Data of Democracy*, Oxford Studies in Digital Politics (New York: Oxford University Press, 2016), 4.

18. Jessica Baldwin-Philippi, "Data Campaigning: Between Empirics and Assumptions," *Internet Policy Review* 8, no. 4 (2019): 9, https://doi.org/10.14763/2019.4.1437.

19. Philip N. Howard, *Pax Technica: How the Internet of Things May Set Us Free or Lock Us Up* (New Haven, CT: Yale University Press, 2015).

20. Alma Steingart, *Axiomatics: Mathematical Thought and High Modernism* (Chicago: University of Chicago Press, 2023), chap. 3; Alain Desrosières, *The Politics of Large Numbers: A History of Statistical Reasoning* (Cambridge, MA: Harvard University Press, 2011); Theodore M. Porter, *Trust in Numbers: The Pursuit of Objectivity in Science and Public Life* (Princeton, NJ: Princeton University Press, 1995).

21. Hunter Heyck, *Age of System: Understanding the Development of Modern Social Science* (Baltimore: Johns Hopkins University Press, 2015).

22. Fenwick McKelvey, *Internet Daemons: Digital Communications Possessed*, Electronic Mediations 56 (Minneapolis: University of Minnesota Press, 2018).

23. Anna Lowenhaupt Tsing, "On Nonscalability: The Living World Is Not Amenable to Precision-Nested Scales," *Common Knowledge* 18, no. 3 (2012): 508, https://doi.org/10.1215/0961754X-1630424.

24. James M. Perry, *The New Politics: The Expanding Technology of Political Manipulation* (New York: Clarkson N. Potter, 1968), 138–150.

25. For one excellent recent history, see Bernard Dionysius Geoghegan, *Code: From Information Theory to French Theory*, Sign, Storage, Transmission (Durham, NC: Duke University Press, 2023).

26. Theodore Lowi, "Foreword," in *Disenchanted Realists: Political Science and the American Crisis, 1884–1984*, ed. Raymond Seidelman (Albany: State University of New York Press, 1985), ix.

27. Lowi, "Foreword," ix–x.

28. Critic Shoshana Zuboff taps into this history and the power of this imaginary when describing surveillance capitalism as the "Big Other," drawing on *decades* of speculation about computers and the surveillance state. See Shoshana Zuboff, "Big Other: Surveillance Capitalism and the Prospects of an Information Civilization," *Journal of Information Technology* 30, no. 1 (2015): 75–89, https://doi.org/10.1057/jit.2015.5.

29. CrimethInc Ex-Workers Collective, "CrimethInc: Up Against the Wall, Motherfucker—The Game?: Revisiting a Simulation of the 1968 Occupation of Columbia University," CrimethInc., March 14, 2019, https://crimethinc.com/2019/03/14/up-against-the-wall-motherfucker-the-game-revisiting-a-simulation-of-the-1968-occupation-of-columbia-university.

30. Galison, "Computer Simulations."

31. Eden Medina, *Cybernetic Revolutionaries: Technology and Politics in Allende's Chile* (Cambridge, MA: MIT Press, 2011); Slava Gerovitch, *From Newspeak To Cyberspeak: A History Of Soviet Cybernetics* (Cambridge, MA: MIT Press, 2004); Benjamin Peters, *How Not to Network a Nation: The Uneasy History of the Soviet Internet* (Cambridge, MA: The MIT Press, 2016); Andrew Pickering and Katherine Hayles, *Cybernetics for the 21st Century*, vol. 1, *Epistemological Reconstruction*, ed. Yuk Hui (Kwai Chung, New Territories, Hong Kong: Hanart Press, 2024); Eglė Rindzevičiūtė, *The Power of Systems: How Policy Sciences Opened Up the Cold War World* (Ithaca, NY: Cornell University Press, 2016).

32. Paul N. Edwards, *The Closed World: Computers and the Politics of Discourse in Cold War America* (Cambridge, MA: MIT Press, 1996), 7.

33. Paul N. Edwards, "The World in a Machine: Origins and Impacts of Early Computerized Global Systems Models," in *Systems, Experts, and Computers: The Systems Approach*, ed. Agatha C. Hughes and Thomas P. Hughes (Cambridge, MA: MIT Press, 2000), 221–222; Paul N. Edwards, *A Vast Machine: Computer Models, Climate Data, and the Politics of Global Warming* (Cambridge, MA: MIT Press, 2010).

34. Louise Amoore et al., "A World Model: On the Political Logics of Generative AI," *Political Geography* 113 (2024): 1, https://doi.org/10.1016/j.polgeo.2024.103134.

35. Scott E. Page, *The Model Thinker: What You Need to Know to Make Data Work for You* (New York: Basic Books, 2018).

36. Chantal Mouffe, *On the Political* (New York: Routledge, 2005), 9.

37. Jill Lepore, *If Then: How Simulmatics Corporation Invented the Future* (New York: Liveright, 2020).

38. Charlton D. McIlwain, *Black Software: The Internet and Racial Justice, from the AfroNet to Black Lives Matter* (New York: Oxford University Press, 2020).

39. Daniel Kreiss, *Prototype Politics: Technology-Intense Campaigning and the Data of Democracy*, Oxford Studies in Digital Politics (New York: Oxford University Press, 2016), 4.

40. Jessica Baldwin-Philippi, "The Myths of Data-Driven Campaigning," *Political Communication* 34, no. 4 (2017): 628, https://doi.org/10.1080/10584609.2017.1372999.

41. David Karpf, *Analytic Activism: Digital Listening and the New Political Strategy*, Oxford Studies in Digital Politics (New York: Oxford University Press, 2016).

42. Eitan D. Hersh, *Hacking the Electorate: How Campaigns Perceive Voters* (New York: Cambridge University Press, 2015).

43. Philip N. Howard, *New Media Campaigns and the Managed Citizen* (Cambridge, MA: Cambridge University Press, 2006); Dennis W. Johnson, *Democracy for Hire: A History of American Political Consulting* (New York: Oxford University Press, 2016); Adam Sheingate, *Building a Business of Politics: The Rise of Political Consulting and the Transformation of American Democracy* (New York: Oxford University Press, 2016); Sasha Issenberg, *The Victory Lab: The Secret Science of Winning Campaigns* (New York: Crown, 2012).

44. Philip N. Howard, *New Media Campaigns and the Managed Citizen* (Cambridge, UK: Cambridge University Press, 2006).

45. Johnson, *Democracy for Hire*; Sheingate, *Building a Business of Politics*.

46. Issenberg, *The Victory Lab*.

47. Daniel Bessner, *Democracy in Exile: Hans Speier and the Rise of the Defense Intellectual* (Ithaca, NY: Cornell University Press, 2018).

48. Paul Erickson et al., *How Reason Almost Lost Its Mind: The Strange Career of Cold War Rationality* (University of Chicago Press, 2013), 24.

49. Joy Rohde, "Pax Technologica: Computers, International Affairs, and Human Reason in the Cold War," *Isis* 108, no. 4 (2017): 792–813, https://doi.org/10.1086/695679; Lucy Suchman, "Imaginaries of Omniscience: Automating Intelligence in the US Department of Defense," *Social Studies of Science*, 53, no. 5 (2022): 030631272211049, https://doi.org/10.1177/03063127221104938; Joy Rohde, "The Last Stand of the Psychocultural Cold Warriors: Military Contract Research in Vietnam," *Journal of the History of the Behavioral Sciences* 47, no. 3 (2011): 232–250, https://doi.org/10.1002/jhbs.20509.

50. Key examples include Medina, *Cybernetic Revolutionaries: Technology and Politics in Allende's Chile*, 2011; Gerovitch, *From Newspeak To Cyberspeak*; Benjamin Peters, "Normalizing Soviet Cybernetics," *Information & Culture: A Journal of History* 47, no. 2 (2012): 145–175, https://doi.org/10.1353/lac.2012.0009; Philippe Theophanidis et al., "At the Margins of Cybernetics," *Canadian Journal of Communication* 42, no. 3 (2017): 397–405, https://cjc.utppublishing.com/doi/full/10.22230/cjc.2017v42n3e3304; Gilberto C. Gallopin, "The Latin American World Model (a.k.a. the Bariloche Model): Three Decades Ago," *Futures* 33, no. 1 (2001): 77–89, https://doi.org/10.1016/S0016-3287(00)00055-0; Pickering and Hayles, *Cybernetics for the 21st Century*.

51. Adele E. Clarke et al., *Situational Analysis: Grounded Theory After the Interpretive Turn*, 2nd ed. (Los Angeles: Sage, 2017).

52. Lorraine Daston and Peter Galison, *Objectivity* (New York: Zone Books, 2010), 357.

53. Ranjodh Singh Dhaliwal, "On Addressability, or What Even Is Computation?," *Critical Inquiry* 49, no. 1 (2022): 1–27, https://doi.org/10.1086/721167.

54. Tsing, "On Nonscalability," 505.

55. Tsing, 508.

Chapter 2

1. Marilyn Strathern quoted in Donna J. Haraway, *Staying with the Trouble: Making Kin in the Chthulucene*, Experimental Futures: Technological Lives, Scientific Arts, Anthropological Voices (Durham, NC: Duke University Press, 2016), 12.

2. Sal Restivo, "The Social Construction of Mathematics," in *Sociology, Science, and the End of Philosophy* (London: Palgrave Macmillan, 2017), 253–281, https://doi.org/10.1057/978-1-349-95160-4_7.

3. Nick Bostrom, "Are You Living in a Computer Simulation?," *Philosophical Quarterly* 53, no. 211 (2003): 243–255.

4. Soraya de Chadarevian and Nick Hopwood, *Models: The Third Dimension of Science* (Stanford, CA: Stanford University Press, 2004); Ronald N. Giere, "Is Computer Simulation Changing the Face of Experimentation?," *Philosophical Studies: An International Journal for Philosophy in the Analytic Tradition* 143, no. 1 (2009): 59–62; G. David Garson, "Social Science Computer Simulation: Its History, Design, and Future," *Social Science Computer Review* 12, no. 1 (1994): 55–82, https://doi.org/10.1177/089443939401200104; Scott E. Page, *The Model Thinker: What You Need to Know to Make Data Work for You* (New York: Basic Books, 2018); Michael Weisberg, *Simulation and Similarity: Using Models to Understand the World*, Oxford Studies in Philosophy of Science (New York: Oxford University Press, 2013); Margaret Morrison, *Reconstructing Reality: Models, Mathematics, and Simulations* (Oxford: Oxford

University Press, 2015); Mary S. Morgan and Margaret Morrison, eds., *Models as Mediators: Perspectives on Natural and Social Science*, Ideas in Context (Cambridge: Cambridge University Press, 1999), https://doi.org/10.1017/CBO9780511660108.

5. Page, *The Model Thinker*, 13.

6. Page, 6.

7. Cathy O'Neil, *Weapons of Math Destruction: How Big Data Increases Inequality and Threatens Democracy*, 1st ed. (New York: Crown, 2016).

8. Wendy Hui Kyong Chun, *Discriminating Data: Correlation, Neighborhoods, and the New Politics of Recognition* (Cambridge, MA: MIT Press, 2021), 22.

9. Ruha Benjamin, *Race After Technology: Abolitionist Tools for the New Jim Code* (Medford, MA: Polity, 2019).

10. Neda Atanasoski and Kalindi Vora, *Surrogate Humanity: Race, Robots, and the Politics of Technological Futures*, Perverse Modernities (Durham, NC: Duke University Press, 2019).

11. Stefan Helmreich, *Silicon Second Nature: Culturing Artificial Life in a Digital World, Updated With a New Preface* (Berkeley: University of California Press, 2000); Natasha Myers, *Rendering Life Molecular: Models, Modelers, and Excitable Matter* (Durham, NC: Duke University Press, 2015), https://doi.org/10.1215/9780822375630; Özden-Schilling, T. (2024), "Authors of misfortune: interpretation and expertise in a model disaster." *Journal of the Royal Anthropological Institute*, 30: 75–96. https://doi.org/10.1111/1467-9655.14047; Carol Cohn, "Sex and Death in the Rational World of Defense Intellectuals," *Signs* 12, no. 4 (1987): 687–718.

12. Helmreich, *Silicon Second Nature*, 11–12.

13. Key works to me include S. M. Amadae, *Prisoners of Reason: Game Theory and Neoliberal Political Economy*, reprint ed. (New York: Cambridge University Press, 2016); Joy Rohde, "Pax Technologica: Computers, International Affairs, and Human Reason in the Cold War," *Isis* 108, no. 4 (2017): 792–813, https://doi.org/10.1086/695679; Jamie Cohen-Cole, *The Open Mind: Cold War Politics and the Sciences of Human Nature* (Chicago: University of Chicago Press, 2014); Paul N. Edwards, *The Closed World: Computers and the Politics of Discourse in Cold War America* (Cambridge, MA: MIT Press, 1996); Fernando Elichirigoity, *Planet Management: Limits to Growth, Computer Simulation, and the Emergence of Global Spaces* (Evanston, IL: Northwestern University Press, 1999); Paul Erickson et al., *How Reason Almost Lost Its Mind: The Strange Career of Cold War Rationality* (Chicago: University of Chicago Press, 2013); Peter Galison, "Computer Simulations and the Trading Zone," in *From Science to Computational Science*, ed. Gabriele Gramelsberger (Zurich: Diaphanes, 2011), 118–157, http://medientheorie.com/doc/galison_simulation.pdf; Sharon Ghamari-Tabrizi, "Simulating the Unthinkable: Gaming Future War in the 1950s and 1960s," *Social Studies of Science* 30, no. 2 (2000): 163–223, https://doi.org/10

.1177/030631200030002001; Jennifer S. Light, *From Warfare to Welfare: Defense Intellectuals and Urban Problems in Cold War America* (Baltimore, MD: Johns Hopkins University Press, 2005); Eden Medina, *Cybernetic Revolutionaries: Technology and Politics in Allende's Chile* (Cambridge, MA: MIT Press, 2011); Philip Mirowski, *Machine Dreams: Economics Becomes a Cyborg Science* (Cambridge, UK: Cambridge University Press, 2002); Eglė Rindzevičiūtė, *The Power of Systems: How Policy Sciences Opened Up the Cold War World* (Ithica, NY: Cornell University Press, 2016).

14. Peter Krapp, *Computing Legacies: Digital Cultures of Simulation* (Cambridge, MA: The MIT Press, 2024), 2.

15. N. Katherine Hayles, *How We Became Posthuman: Virtual Bodies in Cybernetics, Literature, and Informatics* (Chicago: University of Chicago Press, 1999), 8.

16. Claus Pias, "On the Epistemology of Computer Simulation," *Zeitschrift für Medien- und Kulturforschung*, 2011, 30, https://doi.org/10.25969/MEDIAREP/18462.

17. Pias, "On the Epistemology," 53.

18. For the best summary of these approaches, see Alexander Monea and Jeremy Packer, "Media Genealogy: Technological and Historical Engagements of Power—Introduction," *International Journal of Communication* 10, no. 0 (2016): 19.

19. Mirowski, *Machine Dreams*, 2002.

20. For some good overviews, see Andrew Pickering, "Cyborg History and the World War II Regime," *Perspectives on Science* 3, no. 1 (1995): 1–48; Jamie Cohen-Cole, "Cybernetics and the Machinery of Rationality," *British Journal for the History of Science* 41, no. 1 (2008): 109–114, https://doi.org/10.1017/S0007087407000015.

21. Alain Desrosières, *The Politics of Large Numbers: A History of Statistical Reasoning* (Cambridge, MA: Harvard University Press, 2011), 12.

22. Claude Lefort, *Democracy and Political Theory*, trans. David Macey (Oxford: Polity, 1988).

23. Charles Taylor, "Modern Social Imaginaries," *Public Culture* 41, no. 1 (2002): 106.

24. Sheila Jasanoff and Sang-Hyun Kim, *Dreamscapes of Modernity: Sociotechnical Imaginaries and the Fabrication of Power* (Chicago: University of Chicago Press, 2015), 20.

25. Stephanie Ricker Schulte, "'The WarGames Scenario': Regulating Teenagers and Teenaged Technology (1980—1984)," *Television & New Media* 9, no. 6 (2008): 502, https://doi.org/10.1177/1527476408323345.

26. Schulte, "'The WarGames Scenario,'" 511.

27. I am thinking here of Foucault's 1977–1978 lectures at the Collège de France between 1977 and 1978 where he offered a detailed study and description of governmentally. Foucault defined it:

> First, by "governmentality" I understand the ensemble formed by institutions, procedures, analyses and reflections, calculations, and tactics that allow the exercise of this very specific, albeit very complex, power that has the population as its target, political economy as its major form of knowledge, and apparatuses of security as its essential technical instrument. Second, by "governmentality" I understand the tendency, the line of force, that for a long time, and throughout the West, has constantly led towards the pre-eminence over all other types of power—sovereignty, discipline, and so on—of the type of power that we can call "government" and which has led to the development of a series of specific governmental apparatuses (appareils) on the one hand, [and, on the other]† to the development of a series of knowledges (savoirs). Finally, by "governmentality" I think we should understand the process, or rather, the result of the process by which the state of justice of the Middle Ages became the administrative state in the fifteenth and sixteenth centuries and was gradually "governmentalized."

See Michel Foucault, *Security, Territory, Population: Lectures at the College de France, 1977–78*, ed. Michel Senellart, trans. Graham Burchell (New York: Palgrave Macmillan, 2007), 144.

28. The subject matter is the British civil service, but the scope and detail of Jon Agar's *Government Machine* offers an incredible account of the changes in government bureaucracy through computing. See Jon Agar, *The Government Machine: A Revolutionary History of the Computer*, History of Computing (Cambridge, MA: MIT Press, 2003).

29. Sandra Braman, *Change of State: Information, Policy, and Power* (Cambridge, MA: MIT Press, 2007), 26.

30. Orit Halpern, *Beautiful Data: A History of Vision and Reason Since 1945*, Experimental Futures (Durham, NC: Duke University Press, 2014); Louise Amoore, "Machine Learning Political Orders," *Review of International Studies*, February 15, 2022, 1–17, https://doi.org/10.1017/S0260210522000031.

31. Hunter Heyck, in his important history of systems thinking, notes that the model "is a word with many meanings, and those meanings have changed notably over the past century and a half." Heyck continues that the model's variations pose "an interesting challenge for the historian: is it preferable to define the term . . . searching for when and how people began to use the term to mean something close to that definition question," or "is it better to inventory all the uses of the term and all the debates about its meanings, locating them in context?"[1] Should the model be a concept found outside or inside a history? Since Heyck does both well, I leave this introduction to focus on my definition of modeling and leave the rest of the book to trace the different variations of modeling in American politics.

32. Erica Thompson, *Escape from Model Land: How Mathematical Models Can Lead Us Astray and What We Can Do About It* (New York: Basic Books, 2022).

33. Harold Guetzkow, "A Use of Simulation in the Study of Inter-Nation Relations," *Behavioral Science* 4, no. 3 (1959): 145, https://doi.org/10.1002/bs.3830040302.

34. Haraway, *Staying with the Trouble*, 63.

35. At least according to WikiQuote. See https://en.wikiquote.org/wiki/Buckminster_Fuller.

36. Page, *The Model Thinker*, 15.

37. H. L. Anderson, "Scientific Uses of the MANIAC," *Journal of Statistical Physics* 43, no. 5 (1986): 731–748, https://doi.org/10.1007/BF02628301.

38. Jenny Andersson, *The Future of the World: Futurology, Futurists, and the Struggle for the Post Cold War Imagination* (Oxford: Oxford University Press, 2018).

39. The model makes something out of analogies and analogs. To make a leap into biology to disentangle these terms, the fruit fly is a model, an analog, and an analogy. The fruit fly (genus *Drosophila*) is a model insect whose biology is a suitable analogy to other biological systems as well as a physical analog for and popular experimental subject. The fly's status is so influential that it is a cliché to say that "X is the drosophila of Y." Chess is often said to be the drosophila of artificial intelligence—a relationship that historian Nathan Ensmenger uses as a case to further elaborate the question of model, analogy, and analog. Chess, like games, functions, as Ensmenger writes,

> just as genetics as a science was reoriented around the theories and methodologies most well-suited to the biology of the drosophila, drosophila as a species was reconfigured as a technology for producing new knowledge about complex physiological or biological systems. And in the same way that genetic scientists transformed the wild and highly variable fruit fly into the standardized organism *Drosophila melanogaster*, physically reconstructing it to conform to the fundamental principles of genetic mapping . . . so too did AI researchers redefine how chess was played, and what it meant to be an "intelligent" chess player. In this respect, the parallels between chess and drosophila are impossible to ignore. The history of AI, and of the cognitive sciences more broadly, is incomprehensible without reference to its primary experimental technology." (Ensmenger 2011, 25)

I leave the debate over whether chess is fairly the drosophila of AI to Ensmenger, but his discussion of chess pulls together model, analogy, and analog enough that some distinctions could be made. Chess is analogous and an analog to thought, a productive abstraction. Chess rules bounded questions of human reasoning just as its board provides a space to test artificial intelligences. Models succeed or fail depending on whether they win chess games. Winning chess tournaments "meant an increasing investment in Type-A strategies built around the minimax algorithm and alpha–beta pruning. No other technique could reliably deliver tournament victories" In chess, the model is bound to its analogy and to its analog and, through them, becomes something unto itself. (Ensmenger, 2011, 25).

40. Joel Isaac, "Tool Shock: Technique and Epistemology in the Postwar Social Sciences," *History of Political Economy* 42, no. Suppl. 1 (2010): 133–164, https://doi.org/10.1215/00182702-2009-075.

41. Weisberg, *Simulation and Similarity*, 7.

42. Weisberg, 15–23.

43. Lucy Suchman et al., "Working Artefacts: Ethnomethods of the Prototype," *British Journal of Sociology* 53, no. 2 (2002): 164, https://doi.org/10.1080/00071310220133287.

44. Suchman et al., "Working Artefacts," 166.

45. Suchman et al., 175.

46. I will take this opportunity to thank Scott DeJong for this early research and for mapping the longer history of political computer games with me.

47. Elinor Carmi, *Media Distortions: Understanding the Power Behind Spam, Noise, and Other Deviant Media* (New York: Peter Lang, 2020), https://library.oapen.org/handle/20.500.12657/42373; Yaron Ezrahi, "Dewey's Critique of Democratic Visual Culture and Its Political Implications," in *Sites of Vision: The Discursive Construction of Sight in the History of Philosophy*, ed. David Kleinberg-Levin (Cambridge, MA: MIT Press, 1999), 315–336.

48. Indeed, computer simulation is just one type of simulation. For an introduction to the philosophy of simulation, see: Weisberg, *Simulation and Similarity*.

49. Hunter Heyck, *Age of System: Understanding the Development of Modern Social Science* (Baltimore: Johns Hopkins University Press, 2015), 191.

50. Daniel Kreiss, *Prototype Politics: Technology-Intense Campaigning and the Data of Democracy*, Oxford Studies in Digital Politics (New York: Oxford University Press, 2016), 16.

51. Fred Turner, "Prototype," in *Digital Keywords: A Vocabulary of Information Society and Culture*, ed. Benjamin Peters, Princeton Studies in Culture and Technology (Princeton, NJ: Princeton University Press, 2016), 262.

52. Fred Turner, "Why Study New Games?," *Games and Culture* 1, no. 1 (2006): 108, https://doi.org/10.1177/1555412005281823.

53. Turner, "Why Study New Games?," 110.

54. Cf. Benjamin K. Sovacool and David J. Hess, "Ordering Theories: Typologies and Conceptual Frameworks for Sociotechnical Change," *Social Studies of Science* 47, no. 5 (2017): 703–750, https://doi.org/10.1177/0306312717709363.

55. Stuart A. Bremer and Karl W. Deutsch, eds., "Foreward," in *The GLOBUS Model: Computer Simulation of Worldwide Political and Economic Developments* (Boulder, CO: Westview Press, 1987), 4, https://public.ebookcentral.proquest.com/choice/publicfullrecord.aspx?p=5893287. Note: I have modified this quote by exchanging "model" with "program" for clarity's sake. Model is a complicated word, and for readers of this book, I think program is a more apt term.

Chapter 3

1. Phil Edwards, "6 Myths About the Ides of March and Killing Caesar," Vox, March 15, 2015, https://www.vox.com/2015/3/15/8214921/ides-of-march-caesar-assassination.

2. Charles R. Acland, *American Blockbuster: Movies, Technology, and Wonder* (Durham, NC: Duke University Press, 2020), https://doi.org/10.1215/9781478012160.

3. For a longer history of computers in the newsroom, see Will Mari, *Newsrooms and the Disruption of the Internet: A Short History of Disruptive Technologies, 1990–2010*, Disruptions (London: Routledge, 2022).

4. Lawrence O'Brien, *The Democratic Campaign Manual* (Washington, DC: Democratic National Committee, 1964); James Ertel, *How to Run for Office* (New York: Sterling, 1960); Quincy Howe and Arthur Schlesinger Jr., eds., *Guide to Politics 1954* (New York: Dial Press, 1954); D. Swing Meyer, *The Winning Candidate: How to Defeat Your Political Opponents* (New York: Heinemann, 1966); Harold Faber and James Reston, *The New York Times Election Handbook 1964* (New York: McGraw-Hill, 1964); Hugh A. Bone, "Campaign Methods of Today," *ANNALS of the American Academy of Political and Social Science* 283, no. 1 (1952): 127–140, https://doi.org/10.1177/000271625228300115; James M. Cannon, *Politics U.S.A.* (New York: Doubleday, 1960).

5. Jennifer S. Light, *From Warfare to Welfare: Defense Intellectuals and Urban Problems in Cold War America* (Baltimore, MD: Johns Hopkins University Press, 2005), 348.

6. Ira Chinoy, "Battle of the Brains: Election-Night Forecasting at the Dawn of the Computer Age," 2010, http://drum.lib.umd.edu/handle/1903/10504.

7. Other works include *The 480* (1964) by Eugene Burdick, discussed in depth by Jill Lepore, *Simulacron-3* (1966) by Daniel F. Galouye, and *Colossus* (1966) by Dennis Feltham Jones, to give some other examples.

8. For some key sources that helped me contextualize these events, see C. W. Anderson, *Apostles of Certainty: Data Journalism and the Politics of Doubt*, Oxford Studies in Digital Politics (New York: Oxford University Press, 2018); Mari, *Newsrooms and the Disruption*.

9. Ira Chinoy, "Battle of the Brains: Election-Night Forecasting at the Dawn of the Computer Age" (dissertation, University of Maryland, 2010), 94–95, http://drum.lib.umd.edu/handle/1903/10504.

10. Chinoy, 90–91.

11. Sarah Elizabeth Igo, *The Averaged American: Surveys, Citizens, and the Making of a Mass Public* (Cambridge, MA: Harvard University Press, 2007), 103–105; 134–139.

12. Chinoy, "Battle of the Brains," 94–95.

13. Peter Odegard, Review of *Review of The Pre-Election Polls of 1948 and The Polls and Public Opinion*, by Frederick Mostelle et al., *The American Political Science Review* 44, no. 2 (1950): 459, https://doi.org/10.2307/1950284.

14. Odegard, Review, 460; reviewer Peter Odegaard does not attribute the quote.

15. Louis H. Bean, *How to Predict Elections* (New York: A.A. Knopf, 1948), vii–viii.

16. Bean, *How to Predict Elections*, 12.

17. Bean, 9.

18. Quoted in Theodore Rosenof, "The Legend of Louis Bean: Political Prophecy and the 1948 Election," *The Historian* 62, no. 1 (1999): 73, https://doi.org/10.1111/j.1540-6563.1999.tb01434.x.

19. Chinoy, "Battle of the Brains," 434.

20. In this introduction I rely on some excellent biographical work on William McPhee. See Peter Simonson, "Writing Figures into the Field: William McPhee and the Parts Played by People in Our Histories of Media Research," in *The History of Media and Communication Research: Contested Memories*, ed. David W. Park and Jefferson Pooley (New York: Peter Lang, 2008), 291–320; Jill Lepore, *If Then: How Simulmatics Corporation Invented the Future* (New York: Liveright, 2020).

21. William N. McPhee, "Note on a Campaign Simulator," *Public Opinion Quarterly* 25, no. 2 (1961): 184, https://doi.org/10.1086/267013.

22. William N. McPhee and Robert B. Smith, "A Model for Analyzing Voting Systems," in *Public Opinion and Congressional Elections*, ed. William N. McPhee and William A. Glaser (Glencoe, IL: Free Press, 1962), 125.

23. McPhee and Smith, "A Model for Analyzing,"128.

24. McPhee and Smith, 128.

25. McPhee and Smith, 154.

26. For a broader context, see Igo, *The Averaged American*.

27. Simonson, "Writing Figures into the Field: William McPhee and the Parts Played by People in Our Histories of Media Research"; Lepore, *If Then*.

28. William N. McPhee and James Coleman, "A Program of Research in 'Mass Dynamics,'" *American Behavioral Scientist* 1, no. 4 (1958): 6, https://doi.org/10.1177/000276425800100403.

29. McPhee and Coleman, "A Program of Research," 7.

30. McPhee and Coleman, 10.

31. Emily Hauptmann, "The Ford Foundation and the Rise of Behavioralism in Political Science," *Journal of the History of the Behavioral Sciences* 48, no. 2 (2012): 154–173, https://doi.org/10.1002/jhbs.21515.

32. Simonson, "Writing Figures into the Field," 297–308.

33. McPhee and Smith, "A Model for Analyzing," 123–124.

34. Simonson, "Writing Figures into the Field," 297–308; McPhee, "Note on a Campaign Simulator."

35. Paul E. Johnson, "Formal Theories of Politics: The Scope of Mathematical Modelling in Political Science," *Mathematical and Computer Modelling* 12, no. 4–5 (1989): 397–404, https://doi.org/10.1016/0895-7177(89)90412-3.

36. McPhee and Smith, "A Model for Analyzing," 130.

37. James S. Coleman, "Analysis of Social Structures and Simulation of Social Processes with Electronic Computers," *Educational and Psychological Measurement* 21, no. 1 (1961): 203, https://doi.org/10.1177/001316446102100121.

38. William McPhee to James Coleman, undated, Folder McPhee, Box 53, James S. Coleman Papers, Special Collections Research Center, University of Chicago, Chicago.

39. Lepore, *If Then*, 80–95.

40. For more details about Pool and his life, I recommend Jennifer S. Light, *From Warfare to Welfare: Defense Intellectuals and Urban Problems in Cold War America* (Baltimore, MD: Johns Hopkins University Press, 2005; Lloyd S Etheredge, ed., *Humane Politics and Methods of Inquiry* (New Brunswick, NJ: Transaction Publishers, 2016); Richard Pearson, "Ithiel de Sola Pool, Communication Theorist, Dies," *Washington Post*, March 13, 1984, https://www.washingtonpost.com/archive/local/1984/03/13/ithiel-de-sola-pool-communication-theorist-dies/1ec2df79-f36a-452b-b0b4-31a55d8d86e6/. I will discuss many of these activities in later parts of the book. I will take this opportunity to recommend again Jill Lepore's *If Then*, which offers the best biography of Pool I have encountered. For my review of the book, see Fenwick McKelvey, "Book Review: If Then: How the Simulmatics Corporation Invented the Future," *International Journal of Press/Politics*, January 16, 2021, https://doi.org/10.1177/1940161221989215.

41. Dorothy Ross, *The Origins of American Social Science* (Cambridge, UK: Cambridge University Press, 1991).

42. Lepore, *If Then*.

43. For a good discussion, see Light, *From Warfare to Welfare*, 182–187.

44. Quoted in Lepore, *If Then*.

45. Lee McGuigan, *Selling the American People: Advertising, Optimization, and the Origins of Adtech*, Distribution Matters (Cambridge, MA: The MIT Press, 2023), 72.

46. Patrick J. McGrath, *Scientists, Business, and the State, 1890–1960* (Chapel Hill, University of North Carolina Press, 2012).

47. Chandra Mukerji, *A Fragile Power: Scientists and the State* (Princeton, NJ: Princeton University Press, 1989), 190.

48. S. M. Amadae, *Prisoners of Reason: Game Theory and Neoliberal Political Economy*, reprint ed. (New York: Cambridge University Press, 2016); Paul Erickson et al., *How Reason Almost Lost Its Mind: The Strange Career of Cold War Rationality* (University of Chicago Press, 2013); Joy Rohde, "Pax Technologica: Computers, International Affairs, and Human Reason in the Cold War," *Isis* 108, no. 4 (2017): 792–813, https://doi.org/10.1086/695679; Mark Solovey, "Cold War Social Science: Specter, Reality, or Useful Concept?," in *Cold War Social Science: Knowledge Production, Liberal Democracy, and Human Nature*, ed. Mark Solovey and Hamilton Cravens (New York: Palgrave Macmillan US, 2012), 1–22, https://doi.org/10.1057/9781137013224_1; Hunter Heyck, "Producing Reason," in *Cold War Social Science: Knowledge Production, Liberal Democracy, and Human Nature*, ed. Mark Solovey and Hamilton Cravens (New York: Palgrave Macmillan US, 2012), 99–116, https://doi.org/10.1057/9781137013224_6; Jamie Cohen-Cole, "Cybernetics and the Machinery of Rationality," *British Journal for the History of Science* 41, no. 1 (2008): 109–114; Carol Cohn, "Sex and Death in the Rational World of Defense Intellectuals," *Signs* 12, no. 4 (1987): 687–718.

49. Quoted in Joy Rohde, *Armed with Expertise: The Militarization of American Social Research During the Cold War* (Ithaca, NY: Cornell University Press, 2013), 10.

50. For Lasswell's speech, see Harold D. Lasswell, "The Political Science of Science: An Inquiry into the Possible Reconciliation of Mastery and Freedom," *American Political Science Review* 50, no. 4 (1956): 961–979. Lasswell's embrace of atomic science differed markedly from Lewis Mumford's, who ten years earlier warned that atomic sciences posed a grave threat to society. See Jenny Andersson, *The Future of the World: Futurology, Futurists, and the Struggle for the Post Cold War Imagination* (Oxford: Oxford University Press, 2018), 34–35.

51. Christopher Simpson, *Science of Coercion: Communication Research and Psychological Warfare, 1945–1960*, reprint ed. (New York: Oxford University Press, 1995).

52. Daniel Bessner, *Democracy in Exile: Hans Speier and the Rise of the Defense Intellectual* (Ithaca, NY: Cornell University Press, 2018), 199–203.

53. Robert A. Dahl, "The Behavioral Approach in Political Science: Epitaph for a Monument to a Successful Protest," *American Political Science Review* 55, no. 4 (1961): 763–772.

54. Howard B. White, "The Processed Voter and the New Political Science," *Social Research* 28, no. 2 (1961): 127–150; John H. Schaar and Sheldon S. Wolin, "Essays on the Scientific Study of Politics: A Critique," *American Political Science Review* 57, no. 1 (1963): 125–150, https://doi.org/10.2307/1952724; Benjamin R. Barber, "The Politics of Political Science:'Value-Free' Theory and the Wolin–Strauss Dust-Up of 1963," *American Political Science Review* 100, no. 4 (2006): 539–545; K. W. Kim, "The Limits of Behavioural Explanation in Politics," *Canadian Journal of Economics and Political Science / Revue Canadienne d'Economique et de Science Politique* 31, no. 3 (1965): 315–327, https://doi.org/10.2307/139732.

55. Joel Isaac, "Tool Shock: Technique and Epistemology in the Postwar Social Sciences," *History of Political Economy* 42, no. Suppl. 1 (2010): 133–164, https://doi.org/10.1215/00182702-2009-075; Mark Solovey, "Project Camelot and the 1960s Epistemological Revolution: Rethinking the Politics-Patronage-Social Science Nexus," *Social Studies of Science* 31, no. 2 (April 2001): 171–206, https://doi.org/10.1177/030631270103100203; Jefferson Pooley, "A 'Not Particularly Felicitous' Phrase: A History of the 'Behavioral Sciences' Label," *SocArXiv* (April 21, 2020), https://doi.org/10.31235/osf.io/uzqdj; Emily Hauptmann, "The Ford Foundation and the Rise of Behavioralism in Political Science," *Journal of the History of the Behavioral Sciences* 48, no. 2 (2012): 154–173, https://doi.org/10.1002/jhbs.21515; David Karpf et al., "The Role of Qualitative Methods in Political Communication Research: Past, Present, and Future," *International Journal of Communication* 9 (2015): 1888–1906; Jefferson Pooley and Mark Solovey, "Marginal to the Revolution: The Curious Relationship Between Economics and the Behavioral Sciences Movement in Mid-Twentieth-Century America," *History of Political Economy* 42, no. Suppl. 1 (2010): 199–233, https://doi.org/10.1215/00182702-2009-077; Brett Gary, "Communication Research, the Rockefeller Foundation, and Mobilization for the War on Words, 1938–1944," *Journal of Communication* 46, no. 3 (1996): 124–148, https://doi.org/10.1111/j.1460-2466.1996.tb01493.x; Hunter Crowther-Heyck, "Patrons of the Revolution: Ideals and Institutions in Postwar Behavioral Science," *Isis* 97, no. 3 (2006): 420–446, https://doi.org/10.1086/508075.

56. Behavioralism here should not be confused with the similarly named political behaviorism. See: Karpf et al., "The Role of Qualitative Methods."

57. Dahl, "The Behavioral Approach," 763.

58. Ross, *The Origins of American Social Science*, 396.

59. Ross, 455.

60. Ross, 457.

61. Joy Rohde, *Armed with Expertise: The Militarization of American Social Research During the Cold War* (Ithaca, NY: Cornell University Press, 2013).

62. Clyde W. Barrow, "The Political and Intellectual Origins of New Political Science," *New Political Science* 39, no. 4 (2017): 437–472, https://doi.org/10.1080/07393148.2017.1378297; Clyde W. Barrow, "The Intellectual Origins of New Political Science," *New Political Science* 30, no. 2 (2008): 215–244, https://doi.org/10.1080/07393140802082598.

63. White, "The Processed Voter"; Barber, "The Politics of Political Science"; Barrow, "The Intellectual Origins."

64. Ido Oren, *Our Enemies and US: America's Rivalries and the Making of Political Science* (Ithaca, NY: Cornell University Press, 2003), chap. 4.

65. For international relations, see Michael C. Desch, *Cult of the Irrelevant: The Waning Influence of Social Science on National Security* (Princeton, NJ: Princeton University Press, 2019), chap. 4, http://muse.jhu.edu/book/62654; For politics, see Karpf et al., "The Role of Qualitative Methods"; Dennis W. Johnson, *Democracy for Hire: A History of American Political Consulting* (New York: Oxford University Press, 2016).

66. James Farr et al., "The Policy Scientist of Democracy: The Discipline of Harold D. Lasswell," *American Political Science Review* 100, no. 4 (2006): 579.

67. David Easton, "Harold Lasswell; Policy Scientist for a Democratic Society," *Journal of Politics* 12, no. 3 (1950): 476, https://doi.org/10.2307/2126297.

68. I use the term "humane" here deliberately, referencing the title of Lloyd Etheredge's collection of the writings of Ithiel de Sola.

69. Quoted in Dahl, "The Behavioral Approach," 767.

70. Etheredge, *Humane Politics and Methods*, 4.

71. Ithiel de Sola Pool, "Automation: New Tool for Decision Makers," *Challenge* 11, no. 6 (1963): 26–27, https://doi.org/10.1080/05775132.1963.11469546.

72. Farr et al., "The Policy Scientist."

73. Karl W. Deutsch, *The Nerves of Government* (New York: Free Press, 1963); David Easton, *The Political Systems* (New York: Alfred A. Knopf, 1953).

74. John G. Gunnell, "The Reconstitution of Political Theory: David Easton, Behavioralism, and the Long Road to System," *Journal of the History of the Behavioral Sciences* 49, no. 2 (2013): 198, https://doi.org/10.1002/jhbs.21593; Desch, *Cult of the Irrelevant*, 82–83.

75. Hans Morgenthau, *Politics Among Nations* (New York: Alfred A. Knopf, 1948), 125, http://archive.org/details/in.ernet.dli.2015.237473.

76. Jennifer S. Light, "Taking Games Seriously," *Technology and Culture* 49, no. 2 (2008): 347–375.

77. Peter Louis Galison, "The Ontology of the Enemy: Norbert Wiener and the Cybernetic Vision," *Critical Inquiry* 21, no. 1 (1994): 228–266; Pat Harrigan and Matthew G. Kirschenbaum, eds., *Zones of Control: Perspectives on Wargaming*, Game Histories (Cambridge, MA: MIT Press, 2016).

78. S. M. Amadae, *Rationalizing Capitalist Democracy: The Cold War Origins of Rational Choice Liberalism*, 1st ed. (Chicago: University of Chicago Press, 2003); Philip Mirowski, *Machine Dreams: Economics Becomes a Cyborg Science* (Cambridge, MA: Cambridge University Press, 2002).

79. Elgė Rindzevičiūtė, *The Power of Systems: How Policy Sciences Opened Up the Cold War World* (Ithaca, NY: Cornell University Press, 2016).

80. Sharon Ghamari-Tabrizi, "Simulating the Unthinkable: Gaming Future War in the 1950s and 1960s," *Social Studies of Science* 30, no. 2 (2000): 163–223, https://doi.org/10.1177/030631200030002001.

81. James S. Coleman, "Introduction: In Defense of Games," *American Behavioral Scientist* 10, no. 2 (1966): 3–4, https://doi.org/10.1177/000276426601000201.

82. Ghamari-Tabrizi, "Simulating the Unthinkable," 2000.

83. Thomas Bruce Morgan, "The People-Machine," *Harper's Magazine*, January 1961, 53.

84. Thomas J. Hrach, "An Incitement to Riot," *Journalism History* 37, no. 3 (2011): 163–171, https://doi.org/10.1080/00947679.2011.12062856; Charlton D. McIlwain, *Black Software: The Internet and Racial Justice, from the AfroNet to Black Lives Matter* (New York: Oxford University Press, 2020).

85. For a complete history, see Lepore, *If Then*, 2020.

86. Dhaliwal, "On Addressability, or What Even Is Computation?," *Critical Inquiry* 49, no. 1 (2022): 1–27, https://doi.org/10.1086/721167.

Chapter 4

1. William R. Shaffer, *Computer Simulations of Voting Behavior*, Studies in Behavioral Political Science (New York: Oxford University Press, 1972).

2. These three approaches will be familiar to historians of the social sciences. These works are foundational to the competing voter models as I discuss in this chapter: *Machine Politics* (1937), *Voting: A Study of Opinion Formation in a Presidential Campaign* (1954), *An Economic Theory of Democracy* (1957), and *The American Voter* (1960). To give an approximation of influence, Google Scholar found 34,431 citations for *An Economic Theory of Democracy*, 12,282 citations for *The American Voter* and 5,819 citations for *Voting: A Study of Opinion Formation in a Presidential Campaign*

on October 29, 2020. To give some context, the top 25 books in 2016 according to Google Scholar had between 81,311 and 37,318 citations. See https://blogs.lse.ac.uk/impactofsocialsciences/2016/05/12/what-are-the-most-cited-publications-in-the-social-sciences-according-to-google-scholar/.

3. Orit Halpern, *Beautiful Data: A History of Vision and Reason Since 1945*, Experimental Futures (Durham, NC: Duke University Press, 2014).

4. Wendy Brown, *Undoing the Demos: Neoliberalism's Stealth Revolution* (New York: Zone Books, 2015); S. M. Amadae, *Rationalizing Capitalist Democracy: The Cold War Origins of Rational Choice Liberalism*, 1st ed. (Chicago: University of Chicago Press, 2003); S. M. Amadae, *Prisoners of Reason: Game Theory and Neoliberal Political Economy*, reprint ed. (New York: Cambridge University Press, 2016).

5. I understand the stable voter from the legacy of the 1960 book *The American Voter*, later called the Michigan Model, which emphasized voter behavior's relative stability.

6. Data profiling was not possible for US residents not well tracked by the state, most notably Indigenous people and members of US oversea territories.

7. Larry M. Bartels, "The Study of Electoral Behavior," in *The Oxford Handbook of American Elections and Political Behavior*, ed. Jan E. Leighley and George C. Edwards III (Oxford: Oxford University Press, 2010), 240.

8. Todd Gitlin, "Media Sociology: The Dominant Paradigm," *Theory and Society* 6, no. 2 (1978): 205–253, https://doi.org/10.1007/BF01681751; Michael Schudson, "The Troubling Equivalence of Citizen and Consumer," *Annals of the American Academy of Political and Social Science* 608 (2006): 193–204.

9. S. M. Amadae and Bruce Bueno de Mesquita, "The Rochester School: The Origins of Positive Political Theory," *Annual Review of Political Science* 2, (1999): 269–295, https://doi.org/10.1146/annurev.polisci.2.1.269; Bernard Grofman, "Anthony Downs (1930—)," in *Readings in Public Choice and Constitutional Political Economy*, ed. Charles K. Rowley and Friedrich G. Schneider (Boston: Springer US, 2008), 91–95, https://doi.org/10.1007/978-0-387-75870-1_6; Robert M. Solow, "How Did Economics Get That Way and What Way Did It Get?," *Daedalus* 126, no. 1 (1997): 39–58; Gary J. Miller, "The Impact of Economics on Contemporary Political Science," *Journal of Economic Literature* 35, no. 3 (1997): 1173–1204.

10. T. S. Brindley and J. W. Raine, "Social Area Analysis and Planning Research," *Urban Studies* 16, no. 3 (1979): 274.

11. Brindley and Raine, "Social Area Analysis," 274.

12. Sue Curry Jansen, "Forgotten Histories: Another Road Not Taken—The Charles Merriam-Walter Lippmann Correspondence," *Communication Theory* 20, no. 2 (2010): 127–146, https://doi.org/10.1111/j.1468-2885.2010.01357.x.

13. Jari Niemelä, *Urban Ecology: Patterns, Processes, and Applications*, ed. Jürgen H. Breuste et al. (Oxford University Press, 2011), https://doi.org/10.1093/acprof:oso/9780199563562.001.0001.

14. Robert Groves and Eleanor Singer, "Survey Methodology," in *A Telescope on Society: Survey Research and Social Science at the University of Michigan and Beyond*, ed. Eleanor Singer et al. (Ann Arbor: Uiversity of Michigan Press, 2004), 21–64.

15. Bartels, "Study of Electoral Behavior," 244.

16. Schudson, "The Troubling Equivalence"; Todd Gitlin, "Media Sociology: The Dominant Paradigm," *Theory and Society* 6, no. 2 (1978): 205–253.

17. Lee McGuigan, "Automating the Audience Commodity: The Unacknowledged Ancestry of Programmatic Advertising," *New Media & Society* 21, no. 11–12 (2019): 2366–2385, https://doi.org/10.1177/1461444819846449.

18. Jill Lepore, *If Then: How Simulmatics Corporation Invented the Future* (New York: Liveright, 2020), 116–121.

19. Fenwick McKelvey, "The Other Cambridge Analytics: Early 'Artificial Intelligence' in American Political Science," in *The Cultural Life of Machine Learning: An Incursion into Critical AI Studies*, ed. Jonathan Roberge and Michael Castelle (London: Palgrave Macmillan, 2021), 117–142, https://doi.org/10.1007/978-3-030-56286-1; Ithiel de Sola Pool and Robert Abelson, "The Simulmatics Project," *Public Opinion Quarterly* 25, no. 2 (1961): 167–183, https://doi.org/10.1086/267012; Ithiel de Sola Pool et al., *Candidates, Issues, and Strategies: A Computer Simulation of the 1960 Presidential Election* (Cambridge, MA: MIT Press, 1964).

20. The number is either 65 or 66. In their book, Pool, Abelson, and Popkin state that they used 65 surveys, but they claim 66 surveys in their 1961 article in *Public Opinion Quarterly*.

21. December 11, 1959 from Campbell to Pool, Simulmatics: Campbell, Angus, Box 96, Ithiel de Sola Pool papers (MC-0440). MIT Libraries, Department of Distinctive Collections.

22. Pool et al., *Candidates, Issues, and Strategies*, 27.

23. Pool et al., 27–31.

24. Pool, Abelson, and Popkin mention the machine in a later simulation of the 1964 presidential election. For more, see Ithiel de Sola Pool et al., "A Postscript on the 1964 Election," *American Behavioral Scientist* 8, no. 9 (1965): 39–44, https://doi.org/10.1177/000276426500800910.

25. Ithiel de Sola Pool, "Use of Available Sample Surveys in Comparative Research," *Social Science Information* 2, no. 2 (1963): 16–35, https://doi.org/10.1177/053901846300200202.

26. Bernard R. Berelson et al., *Voting: A Study of Opinion Formation in a Presidential Campaign* (Chicago: University of Chicago Press, 1954), 19.

27. Pool et al., *Candidates, Issues, and Strategies*, 1964, 9.

28. de Sola Pool, "Use of Available Sample Surveys," 19.

29. Ithiel de Sola Pool et al., *Candidates, Issues, and Strategies*, 46.

30. Pool et al., 47.

31. Pool et al., 54.

32. John H. Kessel, review of *Review of Candidates, Issues and Strategies*, ed. Robert P. Abelson, Samuel Popkin, and Ithiel de Sola Pool, *Midwest Journal of Political Science* 10, no. 4 (1966): 159, https://doi.org/10.2307/2108932.

33. Lepore, *If Then*, 2020, 116–121.

34. Ithiel de Sola Pool and Robert Abelson, "The Simulmatics Project," 173–174.

35. Lepore, *If Then*, 2020, 129–134.

36. Dennis W. Johnson, *Democracy for Hire: A History of American Political Consulting* (New York: Oxford University Press, 2016), 102.

37. Asked to comment about Simulmatics for a review of Eugene Burdick's *The 480*, the manual's author, O'Brien, claimed to have never heard of the company or had found it so unimportant he had forgotten about it. See Sidney Hyman, "If Computers Called the Tune; THE 480. By Eugene Burdick. 313 Pp. New York: McGraw-Hill Book Cam-pany. $5," *New York Times*, June 28, 1964, sec. BR.

38. Lawrence O'Brien, *The Democratic Campaign Manual* (Washington, DC: Democratic National Committee, 1964).

39. Johnson, *Democracy for Hire*, 2016, 102–103.

40. Republican National Committee Committee on Data Processing, *Electronic Data Processing and Politics*. (Washington, DC: Republican National Committee, 1966).

41. Peter Kugel, "Computers and Political Strategy," *Computers and Automation*, XI, no. 5 (1962), 17.

42. Robert Lee Chartrand, *Computers and Political Campaigning* (New York: Spartan Books, 1972).

43. Lepore, *If Then*, 2020, 604, n86.

44. Memo (August 5, 1968) From Nixon to Buchanan Re: Huston discussion of Simulmatics., Folder 8, Box 35, White House Special Files, Contested Materials Collection, Richard Nixon Presidential Library.

45. Lepore, *If Then*, 2020, 402.

46. Warren Weaver Jr., "Computers Counseling the Candidates," *New York Times*, October 30, 1970.

47. See Paul Johnson, "Simulation Modeling in Political Science," *American Behavioral Scientist* 42, no. 10 (1999): 1509–1530.

48. Harrison White, "Review of Formal Theories of Mass Behavior," *American Sociological Review* 29, no. 5 (1964): 771, https://doi.org/10.2307/2091444.

49. Kessel, *Review of Candidates*; David Wallace, "Review of Candidates, Issues, and Strategies: A Computer Simulation of the 1960 and 1964 Presidential Elections. Pp. Xi, 193. Cambridge, Mass.: M.I.T. Press, 1965. $2.45," *Annals of the American Academy of Political and Social Science* 366, no. 1 (1966): 159–160, https://doi.org/10.1177/000271626636600130.

50. Bartels, "Study of Electoral Behavior."

51. George Harris Walker, *A Study on the Simulation and Optimization of a Hypothetical Total Firm* (Ann Arbor, MI: University Microfilms, 1969), 167.

52. Alfred de Grazia, "Social Research with the Computer," *American Behavioral Scientist* 8, no. 9 (1965): 2, https://doi.org/10.1177/000276426500800901.

53. Sharon Weinberger, *The Imagineers of War: The Untold Story of DARPA, the Pentagon Agency That Changed the World* (New York: Vintage, 2017), 174–182.

54. Pool et al., "A Postscript."

55. Harold D. Lasswell, "Introduction: The Shape of the Future," *American Behavioral Scientist* 8, no. 9 (1965): 3, https://doi.org/10.1177/000276426500800902.

56. Michael J. Shapiro, "The House and the Federal Role: A Computer Simulation of Roll-Call Voting," *American Political Science Review* 62, no. 2 (1968): 494–517, https://doi.org/10.2307/1952944; Cleo Cherryholmes and Michael Shapiro, *Representatives and Roll Calls: A Computer Simulation of Voting in the Eighty-Eighth Congress* (Indianapolis, IN: Bobbs-Merrill, 1969); Shapiro, "House and the Federal Role"; Pool et al., "A Postscript," 43; William N. McPhee and Robert B. Smith, "A Model for Analyzing Voting Systems," in *Public Opinion and Congressional Elections*, ed. William N. McPhee and William A. Glaser (Glencoe, IL: Free Press, 1962); James Coleman et al., "Computers and Election Analysis: The New York Times Project," *Public Opinion Quarterly* 28, no. 3 (1964): 418, https://doi.org/10.1086/267264.

57. Joel D. Barkan and James E. Brun 6, *Operations Research* 20, no. 5 (1972): 926.

58. K. W. Deutsch et al., "Conditions Favoring Major Advances in Social Science," *Science* 171, no. 3970 (1971): 454, https://doi.org/10.1126/science.171.3970.450.

59. Halpern, *Beautiful Data*, 168.

60. Halpern, 168–169.

61. Morton Gorden, "Burdens for the Designer of a Computer Simulation of International Relations," in *Computers and the Policy-Making Community: Applications to International Relations*, ed. Davis B. Bobrow and Judah L. Schwartz (Englewood Cliffs, NJ: Prentice-Hall, 1968), 233.

62. Jean Baudrillard, *Simulacra and Simulation* (Cambridge: Semiotext (e), 1983), 2.

63. Bryan D. Jones, "Bounded Rationality," *Annual Review of Political Science* 2, (1999): 297–321, https://doi.org/10.1146/annurev.polisci.2.1.297; Hunter Crowther-Heyck, *Herbert A. Simon: The Bounds of Reason in Modern America* (Baltimore: Johns Hopkins University Press, 2005).

64. Anthony Downs, *An Economic Theory of Democracy* (New York: Harper & Row, 1957), 6.

65. Paul Erickson et al., *How Reason Almost Lost Its Mind: The Strange Career of Cold War Rationality* (University of Chicago Press, 2013), 3.

66. Philip Mirowski, *Machine Dreams: Economics Becomes a Cyborg Science* (Cambridge, UK: Cambridge University Press, 2002).

67. Downs, *An Economic Theory*, 45.

68. Grofman, "Anthony Downs (1930—)."

69. Amadae and Bueno de Mesquita, "The Rochester School"; Jonathan Cohn, "Irrational Exuberance," *The New Republic*, October 25, 1999, https://newrepublic.com/article/78956/political-science-irrational-exuberance; Kellie Maske and Garey Durden, "The Contributions and Impact of Professor William H. Riker," *Public Choice* 117, no. 1 (2003): 191–220, https://doi.org/10.1023/A:1026117828869; Iain McLean, "William H. Riker and the Invention of Heresthetic(s)," *British Journal of Political Science* 32, no. 3 (2002): 535–558, https://doi.org/10.1017/S0007123402000224.

70. According to the journal's Allmetric ranking collected on November 5, 2020.

71. William H. Riker and Peter C. Ordeshook, "A Theory of the Calculus of Voting," *American Political Science Review* 62, no. 1 (1968): 25, https://doi.org/10.2307/1953324.

72. Riker and Ordeshook, "Theory of the Calculus," 27n7.

73. Where Riker and Ordeshook used survey data, AI recommendation systems use a comparable technique called split validation, where a certain number of future actions are hidden from the model to compare its predictions to the actual results.

74. James S. Coleman, "The Use of Electronic Computers in the Study of Social Organization," *European Journal of Sociology / Archives Européennes de Sociologie / Europäisches Archiv Für Soziologie* 6, no. 1 (1965): 101.

75. Coleman, "Use of Electronic Computers," 104.

76. Coleman, 106.

77. Shaffer, *Computer Simulations*.

78. Samuel L. Popkin, "Computer Simulations of Voting Behavior. By William R. Shaffer. (New York: Oxford University Press, 1972. Pp. 164. $7.50, Cloth; $2.95, Paper.)," *American Political Science Review* 68, no. 4 (1974): 1747, https://doi.org/10.2307/1959973.

79. William R. Shaffer and Ronald E. Weber, "Computer Simulation of Voting: A Test of a Revised Model," *Political Methodology* 3, no. 2 (1976): 275.

80. Political scientist Neil Schechter ran a similar experiment in Las Cruces, New Mexico, in 1972, and his work warrants brief mention for its parallels to world modeling. First, Schechter predicted voter behavior with slightly better results. World modelers, at the same time, struggled with the same problems of justifying whether their results meant anything. I discuss the importance of validity to voter simulation in the next part. Second, Schechter suggested reprogramming the model in DYNAMO or GPSS rather than FORTRAN. The former two languages were frequently used in world modeling, suggesting some shared modeling methodologies. See Neil Schechter, "Further Investigations of a Computer Simulation of Voting Behavior," *Political Methodology* 2, no. 4 (1975): 437–454.

81. Downs, *Economic Theory of Democracy*.

82. Riker and Ordeshook, "Theory of the Calculus," 27.

83. N. Katherine Hayles, *How We Became Posthuman: Virtual Bodies in Cybernetics, Literature, and Informatics* (Chicago: University of Chicago Press, 1999).

84. Vincent Barabba, "Oral History," interview by Barbara Milton and David Pemberton, August 7, 1983, https://www2.census.gov/prod2/2003pubs/oh-Barabba.pdf.

85. For a more extensive history, see chapter 5 in Adam Sheingate, *Building a Business of Politics: The Rise of Political Consulting and the Transformation of American Democracy* (New York: Oxford University Press, 2016); Dennis W. Johnson, *Democracy for Hire: A History of American Political Consulting*, 1st ed. (New York: Oxford University Press, 2016), 25–36.

86. Barabba, "Oral History."

87. Gerard J. De Groot, *Selling Ronald Reagan: The Emergence of a President* (London: I.B. Tauris, 2015), 41–44.

88. Barabba, "Oral History."

89. Barabba, 2.

90. Eshref Shevky and Wendell Bell, *Social Area Analysis: Theory, Illustrative Application, and Computational Procedures*, Stanford Sociological Series 1 (Stanford, CA:

Stanford University Press, 1955); Eshref Shevky and Marilyn Williams, *The Social Areas of Los Angeles: Analysis and Typology* (Berkeley: University of California Press, 1949); Georges Sabagh et al., "Eshref Shevky, Anthropology and Sociology: Los Angeles," December 1970, http://texts.cdlib.org/view?docId=hb629006wb;NAAN =13030&doc.view=frames&chunk.id=div00040&toc.depth=1&toc.id=&brand =calisphere.

91. Shevky and Williams, *Social Areas of Los Angeles*, 34.

92. cf. Nick Seaver, *Computing Taste: Algorithms and the Makers of Music Recommendation* (Chicago: University of Chicago Press, 2022), https://press.uchicago.edu/ucp /books/book/chicago/C/bo183892298.html.

93. Shevky and Williams, *Social Areas of Los Angeles*, 34.

94. Shevky and Williams, 35.

95. Shevky and Williams, 35.

96. Shevky and Bell, *Social Area Analysis*, 18.

97. Douglas F. Vincent, "The Orgin and Development of Factor Analysis," *Applied Statistics* 2, no. 2 (1953): 107, https://doi.org/10.2307/2985729.

98. Pool, "Use of Available Sample Surveys," 23.

99. Shevky and Williams, *Social Areas of Los Angeles*, 62.

100. James Perry's profile of Vincent Barabba provides great deal of similar-colored maps—"The whole color spectrum!" Perry quotes Barabba as saying.

101. Quoted in James M. Perry, *The New Politics: The Expanding Technology of Political Manipulation* (New York: Clarkson N. Potter, 1968), 158.

102. Vincent Barabba, "Basic Information Systems—P.I.P.S.," in *The New Style in Election Campaigns*, ed. Robert Agranoff (Boston: Holbrook Press, 1972), 225.

103. De Groot, *Selling Ronald Reagan*.

104. Barabba first used the Precinct Index Priority System in two 1965 Los Angeles city council elections, directly applying Shevky and Williams's study to politics. See De Groot, *Selling Ronald Reagan*, 95–96.

105. Barabba, "Basic Information Systems," 232.

106. De Groot, *Selling Ronald Reagan*, 95–96.

107. Brindley and Raine, "Social Area Analysis," 276.

108. William S. Robinson, "Ecological Correlations and the Behavior of Individuals," *American Sociological Review* 15, no. 3 (1950): 351, https://doi.org/10.2307 /2087176.

109. Robinson, "Ecological Correlations," 357.

110. Angus Campbell et al., *The American Voter* (Chicago: University of Chicago Press, 1960), 14, https://press.uchicago.edu/ucp/books/book/chicago/A/bo24047989.html.

111. Campbell et al., *The American Voter*, 13.

112. Robinson, "Ecological Correlations," 357.

113. Memo (September 16, 1971), From: Roy Morey To: Ed Harper and Ken Cole RE: The Catholic Vote and 1972, Folder 11, Box 19, Contested Materials Collection, Richard Nixon Presidential Library, www.nixonlibrary.gov/sites/default/files/virtuallibrary/documents/contested/contested_box_19/Contested-19-11.pdf.

114. Memo from Flanigan and Magruder to Haldeman RE: Simulation in the 1972 campaign, Folder 4, Box 25, Contested Materials Collection, Richard Nixon Presidential Library, https://www.nixonlibrary.gov/sites/default/files/virtuallibrary/documents/contested/contested_box_25/Contested-25-03.pdf.

115. Report of election simulation based on Gallup poll dated September 20–22, by state, with breakdown of electoral votes (October 6, 1968), Folder 14, Box 36, Contested Materials Collection, Richard Nixon Presidential Library, https://www.nixonlibrary.gov/sites/default/files/virtuallibrary/documents/whsfreturned/WHSF_Box_36/WHSF36-14.pdf.

116. Copy of a memo from Malek to MacGregor RE: the state of the presidential campaign in various states. Figures on budgets, completed workshops, and telephone campaigns attached (September 22, 1972), Folder 1, Box 15, Contested Materials Collection, Richard Nixon Presidential Library, https://www.nixonlibrary.gov/sites/default/files/virtuallibrary/documents/contested/contested_box_15/Contested-15-01.pdf.

117. Sasha Issenberg, *The Victory Lab: The Secret Science of Winning Campaigns* (New York: Crown, 2012), 41–45.

118. Ithiel de Sola Pool, *Technologies of Freedom* (Cambridge, MA: Belknap Press, 1983), 1.

119. For an extended critique of rational choice theory, see Donald Green and Ian Shapiro, *Pathologies of Rational Choice Theory: A Critique of Applications in Political Science* (New Haven, CT: Yale University Press, 1996).

120. Amadae, *Prisoners of Reason*, xxiv.

121. Pool et al., "A Postscript," 44.

122. James S. Coleman, "Introduction: In Defense of Games," *American Behavioral Scientist* 10, no. 2 (1966): 4, https://doi.org/10.1177/000276426601000201.

123. William Davies, "Neoliberalism: A Bibliographic Review," *Theory, Culture & Society* 31, no. 7–8 (2014): 309–317, https://doi.org/10.1177/0263276414546383.

124. Foucault elaborates that "Homo oeconomicus is someone who accepts reality. Rational conduct is any conduct which is sensitive to modifications in the variables of the environment, and which responds to this in a non-random way, in a systematic way, and economics can therefore be defined as the science of the systematic nature of responses to environmental variables." See Michel Foucault, *The Birth of Biopolitics: Lectures at the College de France, 1978–79* (New York: Palgrave Macmillan, 2008), 269.

125. Nancy MacLean, *Democracy in Chains: The Deep History of the Radical Right's Stealth Plan for America* (New York: Viking, 2017); Amadae, *Prisoners of Reason.*

126. Philip Mirowski, "A Brief History of Neoliberalism, David Harvey. Oxford University Press, 2005, VII+247 Pages," *Economics and Philosophy* 24, no. 1 (2008): 111–117; Aeron Davis and Catherine Walsh, "Distinguishing Financialization from Neoliberalism," *Theory, Culture & Society* 34, no. 5–6 (2017): 27–51, https://doi.org/10.1177/0263276417715511; Philip Mirowski, "Postface: Defining Neoliberalism," in *The Road from Mont Pèlerin*, ed. Philip Mirowski and Dieter Plehwe (Harvard: Harvard University Press, 2009), 417–456, https://doi.org/10.4159/9780674054264-013.

127. Amadae, *Prisoners of Reason*, 2016, 223.

128. Schudson, "The Troubling Equivalence."

129. Howard B. White, "Rejoinder for the 'New Political Science' Reexamined: A Symposium," *Social Research* 29, no. 2 (1962): 150.

Chapter 5

1. Ranjodh Singh Dhaliwal, "On Addressability, or What Even Is Computation?," *Critical Inquiry* 49, no. 1 (2022): 4, https://doi.org/10.1086/721167.

2. Eitan D. Hersh, *Hacking the Electorate: How Campaigns Perceive Voters* (New York: Cambridge University Press, 2015); Daniel Kreiss, *Prototype Politics: Technology-Intense Campaigning and the Data of Democracy*, Oxford Studies in Digital Politics (New York: Oxford University Press, 2016); Jessica Baldwin-Philippi, *Using Technology, Building Democracy: Digital Campaigning and the Construction of Citizenship* (Oxford: Oxford University Press, 2015).

3. David Karpf, *Analytic Activism: Digital Listening and the New Political Strategy*, Oxford Studies in Digital Politics (New York: Oxford University Press, 2016); Ian Hacking, "Making Up People," in *Reconstructing Individualism: Autonomy, Individuality, and the Self in Western Thought*, ed. Thomas C. Heller and Christine Brooke-Rose (Stanford, CA: Stanford University Press, 1986), 161–171.

4. Lee McGuigan, *Selling the American People: Advertising, Optimization, and the Origins of Adtech*, Distribution Matters (Cambridge, MA: The MIT Press, 2023), chap. 6.

5. Israel Waismel-Manor, "Spinning Forward: Professionalization Among Campaign Consultants," *Journal of Political Marketing* 10, no. 4 (2011): 350–371, https://doi.org/10.1080/15377857.2011.614556; Adam Sheingate, *Building a Business of Politics: The Rise of Political Consulting and the Transformation of American Democracy* (New York: Oxford University Press, 2016).

6. Stanley Foster Reed, "Campaigns & Computers," *Campaigns & Elections*, Fall 1982, 66.

7. Winthrop Rockefeller's life is well documented. For more, see John L. Ward, *The Arkansas Rockefeller* (Baton Rouge, LO: LSU Press, 1978) ; John A. Kirk, *Winthrop Rockefeller: From New Yorker to Arkansawyer, 1912–1956* (Fayetteville: University of Arkansas Press, 2022), https://muse.jhu.edu/book/98968/; John L. Ward, *Winthrop Rockefeller, Philanthropist: A Life of Change* (Fayetteville: University of Arkansas Press, 2004); Cathy Kunzinger Urwin, *Agenda for Reform: Winthrop Rockefeller as Governor of Arkansas, 1967–71* (Fayetteville: University of Arkansas Press, 1991).

8. James M. Perry, *The New Politics: The Expanding Technology of Political Manipulation* (New York: Clarkson N. Potter, 1968), 141.

9. Ward, *The Arkansas Rockefeller*, 4–5.

10. Ward, 28–29.

11. John A. Kirk, *An Epitaph for Little Rock: A Fiftieth Anniversary Retrospective on the Central High Crisis* (Fayetteville: University of Arkansas Press, 2010), 52, 60; Urwin, *Agenda for Reform*, 11.

12. Ravi K. Perry and D. LaRouth Perry, *The Little Rock Crisis* (New York: Palgrave Macmillan US, 2015), https://doi.org/10.1057/9781137521347.

13. Ward, *The Arkansas Rockefeller*, 28–29.

14. Ward, 40–41.

15. Marion Burton, "Kaye Lundgren interview with Marion Burton," October 25, 2019, https://arstudies.contentdm.oclc.org/digital/collection/p1532coll1/id/16627/rec/1.

16. Burton, "Kaye Lundgren interview."

17. Liam Cole Young, *List Cultures: Knowledge and Poetics from Mesopotamia to BuzzFeed* (Amsterdman: Amsterdam University Press, 2017), https://doi.org/10.2307/j.ctv5jxm7n.

18. Marion Burton claims the machine was installed in May 1966. James Perry reports that the machine was installed on July 1, 1966.

19. Perry, *The New Politics*, 1968, 139–140; IBM Archives, "IBM 1311 Disk Storage Drive," TS200, January 23, 2003, https://web.archive.org/web/20190403052229/www.ibm.com/ibm/history/exhibits/storage/storage_1311.html.

20. Republican National Committee, *Electronic Data Processing for the Political Executive* (Washington, DC: Republican National Committee, 1968), 6.

21. Takahito Moriyama, *Empire of Direct Mail: How Conservative Marketing Persuaded Voters and Transformed the Grassroots* (Lawrence: University Press of Kansas, 2022), 83.

22. Republican National Committee, *Electronic Data Processing*, 8.

23. Perry, *The New Politics*, 143–144.

24. Perry, 143.

25. cf. Rasmus Kleis Nielsen, *Ground Wars: Personalized Communication in Political Campaigns* (Princeton, NJ: Princeton University Press, 2012).

26. Perry, *The New Politics*, 1968, 143–146.

27. Burton quoted in Perry, 145.

28. Terence Smith, "Arkansas Victory Rockefeller's Own," *New York Times*, November 10, 1966.

29. Kreiss, *Prototype Politics*, 4.

30. Republican National Committee, *Electronic Data Processing*, 26.

31. Republican National Committee, ii.

32. Republican National Committee, 24.

33. Republican National Committee, 9.

34. Republican National Committee, 12.

35. Republican National Committee, A.

36. Robert Chartrand wrote the book. Chartrand is notable for being a former US naval intelligence officer, Korean War veteran, and CIA before joining the Library of Congress. His work at the Congressional Research Service at the Library of Congress included numerous reports on computers' impacts on politics and showed a wide-ranging interest in politics and information management.

37. Sidney Blumenthal, "Marketing the President," *New York Times*, September 13, 1981; Richard Pearson, "Richard Beal, Special Aide to Reagan, Dies," *Washington Post*, November 4, 1984, https://www.washingtonpost.com/archive/local/1984/11/04/richard-beal-special-aide-to-reagan-dies/71b0e75d-0cf8-4c20-a63b-8308f9ebb515/; Wolfgang Saxon, "Richard Smith Beal Dies at 38," *New York Times*, November 4, 1984,

sec. Obituaries, https://www.nytimes.com/1984/11/04/obituaries/richard-smith-beal-dies-at-38.html.

38. Political Information System, Computer Code, undated, Box OA 12387, Richard S. Beal Files, Ronald Reagan Presidential Library, Simi Valley, California.

39. Quoted in David S. Broder, "How They Rehearsed the Election," *Washington Post*, November 16, 1980, https://www.washingtonpost.com/archive/opinions/1980/11/16/how-they-rehearsed-the-election/92f4c395-47ed-4c9a-ad14-cd7d83b047f7/.

40. Johan Carlisle, "Marketing Reagan," *Propaganda Review*, 88 1987, 12.

41. While working for Reagan after the election in 1982, Beal installed a comparative information system for world politics, the Early Warning and Monitoring System (EWAMS) Project, in the new National Security Council (NSC)'s White House Situation Room.

42. Wynton C. Hall, "The Invention of 'Quantifiable Safe Rhetoric': Richard Wirthlin and Ronald Reagan's Instrumental Use of Public Opinion Research in Presidential Discourse," *Western Journal of Communication* 66, no. 3 (Summer 2002): 319, https://doi.org/10.1080/10570310209374740.

43. Greg Elmer et al., *The Permanent Campaign: New Media, New Politics*, Digital Formations, vol. 81 (New York: Peter Lang, 2012).

44. Blumenthal, "Marketing the President."

45. cf. Rasmus Kleis Nielsen, "Mundane Internet Tools, Mobilizing Practices, and the Coproduction of Citizenship in Political Campaigns," *New Media & Society* 13, no. 5 (2011): 755–771, https://doi.org/10.1177/1461444810380863; Anthony R. Fellow, "Computers and Politics: Innovation and the Role of Uncertainty in Political Campaign Organizations," *Social Science Computer Review* 10, no. 1 (1992): 29–41, https://doi.org/10.1177/089443939201000102.

46. Bob Davis, "Grand Old Party Tunes Up New Technology to Battle Democrats in Next Year's Elections," *Wall Street Journal*, August 19, 1987.

47. Andrew N. Case, "'The Solid Gold Mailbox': Direct Mail and the Changing Nature of Buying and Selling in the Postwar United States," *History of Retailing and Consumption* 1, no. 1 (2015): 28–46, https://doi.org/10.1080/2373518X.2015.1012863.

48. Maciej Turek and Paweł Laider, eds., "The Federal Election Campaign Act of 1971: 86 Stat. 3 (1972)," in *Basic Documents in Federal Campaign Finance Law* (Kraków, Poland: Jagiellonian University Press, 2015), 34–39, https://www.cambridge.org/core/books/basic-documents-in-federal-compaign-finance-law/federal-election-campaign-act-of-1971-86-stat-3-1972/1EB2DF1CE5B692FD1CEB548AF78717A4.

49. While I focus on Claritas, I have found even more examples of data chimeras and their use in closing this second addessability gap. Q-methodology was another

psychological method to debut in political consulting and survey research . Psychologist Steven Stephenson first published on the methodology in 1935, and its approach came to influence American academics and advertising. According to Denis Kinsey, who introduced q-methodology to the Democratic Decision Research Corporation, the approach offered a "method for the scientific study of subjectivity" that measured "a holistic view from negative to positive whereas survey research measures bits and pieces of an attitude." Participants, well before computers, sat in front of a desk and sorted issues or statements into piles, eventually producing a ranked list of items from least important to most important. The results were unpredictable. Part of the appeal of Q-methodology for Kinsey was its ability to discover different voter types, new composites, from the factor analysis. The legacy of computational psychology's impact on politics, then, is broader than just Claritas: Its history is important to the popularization of data chimeras. Q-methodology could produce clusters comparable to those produced by the Claritas Corporation, though it was given less attention. One example of q-methodology comes from Democrat Edward Farrell "Ed" Feighan's 1986 congressional campaign. One of the campaign's advisors was Dr. Murray Fishel, a key figure in the early political consultancy industry. Fishel was a professor at Kent State University, where he managed one of the earliest programs in political campaigning, the Campaign Management Institute. It started in approximately 1972, ran until the early 1990s, and hosted many of the leading players in the industry at its workshops. Fishel also worked actively on campaigns through his firm, Grassroots Political Campaigns. He served on the first editorial board of *Campaigns & Elections* when the magazine launched and published some of the first articles on microtargeting in its pages. In 1986, Fishel advised Ed Feighan's Democratic campaign. Feighan had won a narrow election in 1984 and sought to ensure that more supporters did not switch sides. To do so, the campaign surveyed voters at malls in the suburbs of Cleveland, looking for weak supporters. Q-sorting established their preferences and opinions. Results identified what it called defecting Democrats and the group's key issues. (Fishel recalls that in another campaign, he developed clusters like "Joe Six-pack" and "Mary the Traditional Democrat"). The campaign discovered that these voters considered aid to Central America a waste. Based on the results, Feighan's campaign ran a television ad campaign opposing foreign aid to Central America, quite successfully.

50. Erik Larson, *The Naked Consumer* (New York: H. Holt, 1992), 38, http://archive.org/details/nakedconsumerhow00lars.

51. The timeline comes from Jonathan Robbin's personal CV online at https://ricercar.com/JRCV-D.html. https://web.archive.org/web/20040606141050/https://ricercar.com/JRCV-D.html.

52. Hans-Hermann Bock, "Clustering Methods: A History of k-Means Algorithms," in *Selected Contributions in Data Analysis and Classification*, ed. Paula Brito et al., Studies in Classification, Data Analysis, and Knowledge Organization (Berlin: Springer, 2007), 161–172, https://doi.org/10.1007/978-3-540-73560-1_15.

53. George W. Bohrnstedt, "Borgatta, Edgar F.," in *SAGE Research Methods Foundations*, ed. Paul Atkinson et al. (London: SAGE, 2020), https://doi.org/10.4135/9781526421036926258.

54. Edgar F. Borgatta and Robert F. Bales, "Interaction of Individuals in Reconstituted Groups," *Sociometry* 16, no. 4 (November 1953): 302, https://doi.org/10.2307/2785935; Edgar F. Borgatta, "Mood, Personality, and Interaction," *Journal of General Psychology* 64, no. 1 (January 1961): 105–137, https://doi.org/10.1080/00221309.1961.9920431; Edgar F. Borgatta, "The Coincidence of Subtests in Four Personality Inventories," *Journal of Social Psychology* 56, no. 2 (April 1962): 227–244, https://doi.org/10.1080/00224545.1962.9919393.

55. Securities and Exchange Commission, "General Analytics Files for Offering and Secondary," *News Digest*, October 3, 1968, 68–194.

56. Sarah Elizabeth Igo, *The Averaged American: Surveys, Citizens, and the Making of a Mass Public* (Cambridge, MA: Harvard University Press, 2007); Colin Koopman, *How We Became Our Data: A Genealogy of the Informational Person* (Chicago: University of Chicago Press, 2019).

57. Rebecca Kraus, "Statistical Déjà Vu: The National Data Center Proposal of 1965 and Its Descendants," *Journal of Privacy and Confidentiality* 5, no. 1 (2013), https://doi.org/10.29012/jpc.v5i1.624.

58. quoted in Kraus, "Statistical Déjà Vu," 6.

59. Barabba, "Oral History."

60. Census History Staff US Census Bureau, "UNIVAC I—History—U.S. Census Bureau," accessed December 1, 2020, https://www.census.gov/history/www/innovations/technology/univac_i.html.

61. Jake Newman, "Data Firms Mining Gold from Census Information," *Washington Post*, June 7, 1982, sec. Business.

62. Jeff Colvin et al., *The Untold Story of the ZIP Code*, (Washington, DC: US Postal Service Office of Inspector General, 2013).

63. Newman, "Data Firms Mining Gold."

64. Jonathan Robbin, "What Is Geodemography?," 2004, https://ricercar.com/gdef.html.

65. Hacking, "Making Up People."

66. Igo, *The Averaged American*, 87.

67. Dave Miller, interview by author, online, 14 January 14, 2021.

68. The Michigan Model did contribute to the adoption of computing for better statistical analysis. The resulting software packages functioned as important, understudied

"inscription devices." How these programs worked, their features and limitations, made choices for how politics could be recorded and analyzed. The University of Michigan's Institute for Social Research (ISR) relied on large-scale computing to calculate sample standard errors and, by 1962, had developed its own statistical software. Later, ISR developed the OSIRIS Statistical Software Package. OSIRIS was a collection of different programs developed by the ISR (its namesake was an Egyptian god said to have been cut to pieces and put back together again stronger than ever). As ISR adopted OSIRIS, it also started using another important statical package, SPSS. SPSS, short for Statistical Package for the Social Sciences, was developed at Stanford University around 1968. Elsewhere, North Carolina State University developed the Statistical Analysis System (SAS) around 1966. Both SPSS and SAS developed into their own companies. These were the uncontroversial packages. Around the same time, MIT researchers working on what became an obscure statistical package called the Constituent System had to smell tear gas as they worked. The ARPA-funded Project Cambridge had become a target of the student antiwar movement, part of a wider rejection of university computing and its links to the war.

69. Robin claimed that the Census Bureau published this report, but I have only been able to review an internal copy. Thanks to Adrian Robbin for the generous help in copying the report for me.

70. Jonathan Robbin, "A Guide to the Use of Census Data for Political Campaign Planning and Management" (Claritas Corporation, 1972), I–1.

71. Edward Schwartzman, *Campaign Craftmanship: A Professional's Guide to Campaigning for Elective Office* (New York: Universe Books, 1973).

72. Robbin, "A Guide to the Use of Census Data for Political Campaign Planning and Management," III–20.

73. For an extended discussion, see Fenwick McKelvey, "When the New Magic Was New: The Claritas Corporation and the Clustering of America," *IEEE Annals of the History of Computing* 44, no. 4 (2022): 44–56, https://doi.org/10.1109/MAHC.2022.3214223.

74. Claritas, by the 1980s, actively self-promoted, leaving many public descriptions of their methods as well as a small critical literature of geodemographics. Claritas was also one of the frequently discussed topics in the first issues of *Campaigns & Elections*, with Robbin including an article in the first issue. The description here is a synthesis of these descriptions.

75. Dave Miller, interview by author, online, January 14, 2021; Sam Barton, interview by author, online, December 5, 2020.

76. Robin Page proposed the name OZMA for Original Zip Market Analog, which was rejected, as Barton recalled, for being too mystical. Sam Barton, interview by author, online, December 5, 2020.

77. Sam Barton, interview by author, online, December 5, 2020.

78. Rudy Maxa, "Can Matt Reese and a System Called Claritas Answer the Prayers of Democrats Everywhere? The Search for Votes Is Never Ending," *Washington Post*, July 22, 1979.

79. Johnson, *Democracy for Hire*, 2016, 103–104.

80. Joseph Mockus, "Geodemographics II: Targeting Your Turnout," *Campaigns & Elections*, 1980.

81. Jonathan Robbin, "Geodemographics: The New Magic," *Campaigns & Elections*, 1980, 32.

82. David Burnham, *The Rise of the Computer State*. (New York: Random House, 1983), 88–96.

83. Johnson, *Democracy for Hire*, 2016, 189–199.

84. Warren Weaver Jr., "A Pinpoint System Is Developed for Finding Voters for an Issue: Supposedly Reversed Opinion Old Method Computerized Other Factors Held Immeasurable," *New York Times*, February 3, 1979; Warren Weaver Jr., "New Polling Technique Offers a Way to Reach Similar Voters Over U.S.: Attitudes in 40 Classifications," *New York Times*, June 24, 1980, sec. Business & Finance.

85. Mark Atlas, "Gambling with Elections: The Problems of Geodemographics," *Campaigns & Elections*, 2, no. 3 (1981), 4–12; Robbin, "Geodemographics: The New Magic," *Campaigns & Elections*, 1, no. 1 (1980), 25–25; Mockus, "Geodemographics II: Targeting Your Turnout," *Campaigns & Elections*, 1, no. 2 (1981), 55–66; Edward J. Schneider, "Geodemographics Refined: An Alternative to Standardized Clustering," *Campaigns & Elections*, 3, no. 4 (1983), 62–73.

86. Issenberg, *The Victory Lab*, 126.

87. Sam Barton, interview by author, online, December 5, 2020.

88. Sasha Issenberg, *The Victory Lab: The Secret Science of Winning Campaigns* (New York: Crown, 2012), 127.

89. Hersh, *Hacking the Electorate*.

90. Michael J. Weiss, *The Clustering of America* (New York: HarperCollins, 1988).

91. Weiss, *The Clustering of America*, 1.

92. Morris B. Holbrook, "Market Clustering Goes Graphic: The Weiss Trilogy and a Proposed Extension," *Psychology & Marketing* 18, no. 1 (2001): 67–85, https://doi.org/10.1002/1520-6793(200101)18:1<67::AID-MAR4>3.0.CO;2-1.

93. Hugh Malcolm Beville, *Audience Ratings: Radio, Television, and Cable* (Hillsdale, NJ: Lawernece Erlbaum Associates, 1988), 138.

94. Lisa A. Petrison et al., "Database Marketing: Past, Present, and Future," *Journal of Direct Marketing* 11, no. 4 (1997): 118, https://doi.org/10.1002/(SICI)1522-7138(199723)11:4<109::AID-DIR12>3.0.CO;2-G.

95. For the 1980 census, Claritas also went down to the census tract level both to improve clustering and to offer better targeting to compete with new competitors like British CACI's ACORN system. Lower computing costs also allowed for greater precision.

96. Dave Miller, interview by author, online, January 14, 2021.

97. Theo Lippman Jr., "First One 'Inside the Beltway' Politics," *Baltimore Sun*, April 16, 1997, https://web.archive.org/web/20210622164118/https://www.baltimoresun.com/news/bs-xpm-1997-04-16-1997106020-story.html

98. For more details, see https://www.senate.gov/art-artifacts/historical-artifacts/other/93_00013.htm.

99. Geoffrey T. Hellman, "Lord's Politics," *The New Yorker*, May 23, 1952, https://www.newyorker.com/magazine/1952/05/31/lords-politics.

100. Quoted in Jennifer S. Light, "Taking Games Seriously," *Technology and Culture* 49, no. 2 (2008): 372.

101. Daniel Bessner, *Democracy in Exile: Hans Speier and the Rise of the Defense Intellectual* (Ithaca, NY: Cornell University Press, 2018); Ghamari-Tabrizi, "Simulating the Unthinkable: Gaming Future War in the 1950s and 1960s," *Social Studies of Science* 30, no. 2 (2000): 163–223, https://doi.org/10.1177/030631200030002001.

102. Light, "Taking Games Seriously," 2008.

103. Light, 355.

104. Clark C. Abt, *Serious Games* (New York: Viking Press, 1970).

105. Light, "Taking Games Seriously," 2008, 373.

106. Peter V. Marsden, "The Sociology of James S. Coleman," *Annual Review of Sociology* 31, (2005): 1–24, https://doi.org/10.1146/annurev.soc.31.041304.122209.

107. James S. Coleman, "Introduction: In Defense of Games," *American Behavioral Scientist* 10, no. 2 (1966): 3, https://doi.org/10.1177/000276426601000201.

108. Paul Starr, "Seductions of Sim," *American Prospect*, no. 17 (1994): 19–29.

109. Sarane S. Boocock, "An Experimental Study of the Learning Effects of Two Games with Simulated Environments," *American Behavioral Scientist* 10, no. 2 (1966): 8–17, https://doi.org/10.1177/000276426601000203.

110. Lloyd Green, "Use of Games in College as a Means of Teaching," *Ottawa Citizen*, July 11, 1966.

111. Boocock, "An Experimental Study"; Sarane S. Boocock and James S. Coleman, "Games with Simulated Environments in Learning," *Sociology of Education* 39, no. 3 (1966): 215, https://doi.org/10.2307/2111969; Samuel A. Livingston, "Effects of a Legislative Simulation Game on the Political Attitudes of Junior High School Students," *Simulation & Gaming* 3, no. 1 (1972): 41–51, https://doi.org/10.1177/104687817200300104.

112. Green, "Use of Games in College."

113. Ian Bogost, *Persuasive Games: The Expressive Power of Videogames* (Cambridge, MA: MIT Press, 2007), IX.

114. James S. Coleman, *Simulation Games and Social Theory* (Baltimore, MD: The Johns Hopkins University, 1968), 14, http://archive.org/details/ERIC_ED017237.

115. Thank you to Scott Dejong, Courtney Blamey, Nick Gertler, Michael Iantorno, Theo LePage-Richer, and Ryan Scheiding for play testing the game on March 15, 2021. My observations are drawn from a close read of the rules and this online play-through. Thank you to Scott for organizing and Ryan for illustrating the betrayal mechanism.

116. Scott L. Feld, "Simulation Games in Theory Development," *Sociological Forum* 12, no. 1 (1997): 105–106, https://doi.org/10.1023/A:1024608707275.

117. Boocock and Coleman, "Games with Simulated Environments."

118. Livingston, "Effects of a Legislative Simulation."

119. William A. Gamson and Russell J. Stambaugh, "Simulation Review Essay: Democracy," *Simulation & Gaming* 5, no. 4 (1974): 436.

120. William A. Gamson and Russell J. Stambaugh, "Simulation Review Essay: Democracy," *Simulation & Gaming* 5, no. 4 (1974): 438.

121. Coleman, "Introduction," 4.

122. Bernard C. Cohen, "Political Gaming in the Classroom," *Journal of Politics* 24, no. 2 (1962): 367–381.

123. Donald R. Jansiewicz, *The New Alexandria Simulation: A Serious Game of State and Local Politics* (San Francisco: Canfield Press, 1973), 40, http://archive.org/details/newalexandriasim00jans.

124. Donald Jansiewicz remembers New Alexandria being short-lived, but he continued to develop another simulation game, the Game of Politics, in 2007.

125. Murray Fishel et al., *On the Campaign Trail* (Washington, DC: Campaigns & Elections, 1987), 69.

126. Nadine S. Koch, "Winning Is Not the Only Thing 'On the Campaign Trail': An Evaluation of a Micro-Computer Campaign Simulation," *PS: Political Science and Politics* 24, no. 4 (1991): 694–698, https://doi.org/10.2307/419407.

127. Fishel et al., *On the Campaign Trail"* 68.

128. Stanley Kelley and Thad W. Mirer, "The Simple Act of Voting," *American Political Science Review* 68, no. 2 (1974): 572–591, https://doi.org/10.2307/1959506.

129. Fishel et al., *On the Campaign Trail*, 69.

130. Jeremy R. T. Lewis, "Software Reviews: Political Science Simulations: A Review Essay," *Social Science Computer Review* 7, no. 3 (1989): 373, https://doi.org/10.1177/089443938900700313.

131. Clyde Wilcox, "Election Simulations: President Elect (1988 Edition), Campaign Promises, and on the Campaign Trail," *Computers and the Humanities* 25, no. 4 (1991): 259.

132. David Daley, "The Secret Files of the Master of Modern Republican Gerrymandering," *The New Yorker*, September 6, 2019, https://www.newyorker.com/news/news-desk/the-secret-files-of-the-master-of-modern-republican-gerrymandering.

133. David Pepper, *Laboratories of Autocracy: A Wake-Up Call from Behind the Lines* (Cincinnati, OH: St. Helena Press, 2021).

134. John Cheney-Lippold, *We Are Data: Algorithms and the Making of Our Digital Selves* (New York: New York University Press, 2017).

135. Tim Hwang, *Subprime Attention Crisis: Advertising and the Time Bomb at the Heart of the Internet*, FSG Originals x Logic (New York: FSG Originals, 2020), 16.

136. Hwang, *Subprime Attention Crisis*; Baldwin-Philippi, "The Myths of Data-Driven Campaigning," *Political Communication* 34, no. 4 (2017): 628, https://doi.org/10.1080/10584609.2017.1372999; Eitan D. Hersh and Brian F. Schaffner, "Targeted Campaign Appeals and the Value of Ambiguity," *Journal of Politics* 75, no. 2 (2013): 520–534, https://doi.org/10.1017/s0022381613000182; Hersh, *Hacking the Electorate*.

137. Daniel Kreiss and Shannon C. Mcgregor, "The 'Arbiters of What Our Voters See': Facebook and Google's Struggle with Policy, Process, and Enforcement Around Political Advertising," *Political Communication* 36, no. 4 (2019): 499–522, https://doi.org/10.1080/10584609.2019.1619639.

138. Kelley Cotter et al., "'Reach the Right People': The Politics of 'Interests' in Facebook's Classification System for Ad Targeting," *Big Data & Society* 8, no. 1 (2021): 14, https://doi.org/10.1177/2053951721996046.

139. Cotter et al., "'Reach the Right People,'" 12.

140. Burnham, *The Rise of the Computer State*, 95–96.

141. Oscar H. Gandy Jr., *The Panoptic Sort: A Political Economy of Personal Information*, 2nd ed. (New York: Oxford University Press, 2021).

142. Gandy, *The Panoptic Sort,* 274.

143. Cotter et al., "'Reach the Right People,'" 9.

144. Samir R. Patel, "What Can AI Teach Brands About Customer-Centric Marketing?," Blue State, May 18, 2018, https://www.bluestate.co/news/ai-customer-marketing/.

145. "TAP," Tanjo, accessed February 23, 2021, https://www.tanjo.net/tap.

Chapter 6

1. Thomas Bruce Morgan, "The People-Machine," *Harper's Magazine,* January 1961, 53.

2. Harold D. Lasswell, "Technique of Decision Seminars," *Midwest Journal of Political Science* 4, no. 3 (1960): 213–236, https://doi.org/10.2307/2108975.

3. Oliver Benson, "A Simple Diplomatic Game," in *International Politics and Foreign Policy: A Reader in Research and Theory,* ed. James N. Rosenau (New York: Free Press, 1961), 504–511.

4. Address to Midwest Conference of Political Scientists, May 12, 1961, Folder 4, Box 4, Oliver Benson Collection (WHC M2597) Western History Collections, University of Oklahoma Libraries.

5. For more on the history of war gaming and precomputational simulation, see T. Allen, "The Evolution of Wargaming: From Chessboard to Marine Doom," *War and Games* 3 (2002): 231; Matthew B. Caffrey, *On Wargaming: How Wargames Have Shaped History and How They May Shape the Future,* Naval War College Newport Papers 43 (Newport, RI: Naval War College Press, 2019); Pat Harrigan and Matthew G. Kirschenbaum, eds., *Zones of Control: Perspectives on Wargaming,* Game Histories (Cambridge, MA: MIT Press, 2016); Philipp Von Hilgers, *War Games: A History of War on Paper* (Cambridge, MA: MIT Press, 2012); Hemda Ben-Yehuda, *All the World's a Stage: The Theater of Political Simulations,* International Studies Intensives (New York: Routledge, 2021).

6. "SIMPLE DIPLOMATIC GAME—Or Putting One and One Together," (August 1958) Folder 3, Box 5, Oliver Benson Collection (WHC M2597) Western History Collections, University of Oklahoma Libraries.

7. Benson, "A Simple Diplomatic Game."

8. "SIMPLE DIPLOMATIC GAME."

9. Christian Dayé, "How to Train Your Oracle: The Delphi Method and Its Turbulent Youth in Operations Research and the Policy Sciences," *Social Studies of Science* 48, no. 6 (2018): 846–868, https://doi.org/10.1177/0306312718798497; Daniel

Bessner, *Democracy in Exile: Hans Speier and the Rise of the Defense Intellectual* (Ithaca, NY: Cornell University Press, 2018).

10. Michael Nicholson, "Lewis Fry Richardson and the Study of the Causes of War," *British Journal of Political Science* 29, no. 3 (1999): 541–563.

11. Benson, "A Simple Diplomatic Game," 505.

12. Benson, 507.

13. The command here is a guess based on Benson's example of US Troop Mobilization in Lebanon. The only number in question is the country code for Vietnam since Benson does not provide it. Vietnam appears sixth in the list and Lebanon fourth. Lebanon has a country code of 4, so I am guessing Vietnam has a country code of 6.

14. Benson, "A Simple Diplomatic Game."

15. Benson, 509.

16. Peter Galison focuses on computer simulation mostly as a trading zone in nuclear physics, see Galison, "Computer Simulations and the Trading Zone," in *From Science to Computational Science*, ed. Gabriele Gramelsberger (Zurich: Diaphanes, 2011), http://medientheorie.com/doc/galison_simulation.pdf.

17. S. M. Amadae, *Rationalizing Capitalist Democracy: The Cold War Origins of Rational Choice Liberalism* (Chicago: University of Chicago Press, 2003); Paul Erickson et al., *How Reason Almost Lost Its Mind: The Strange Career of Cold War Rationality* (University of Chicago Press, 2013); E. Roy Weintraub, *Game Theory and Cold War Rationality: A Review Essay*, SSRN Scholarly Paper (Rochester, NY: Social Science Research Network, 2016), https://papers.ssrn.com/abstract=2737005.

18. Scott G. Knowles and Stuart W. Leslie, "'Industrial Versailles': Eero Saarinen's Corporate Campuses for GM, IBM, and AT&T," *Isis* 92, no. 1 (2001): 14, https://doi.org/10.1086/385038.

19. For more about this moment, see Paul N. Edwards, "The World in a Machine: Origins and Impacts of Early Computerized Global Systems Models," in *Systems, Experts, and Computers: The Systems Approach*, ed. Agatha C. Hughes and Thomas P. Hughes (Cambridge, MA: MIT Press, 2000), 221–254; Quinn Slobodian, "How to See the World Economy: Statistics, Maps, and Schumpeter's Camera in the First Age of Globalization," *Journal of Global History* 10, no. 2 (2015): 307–332, https://doi.org/10.1017/S174002281500008X; Fernando Elichirigoity, *Planet Management: Limits to Growth, Computer Simulation, and the Emergence of Global Spaces* (Evanston, IL: Northwestern University Press, 1999); Joy Rohde, *Armed with Expertise: The Militarization of American Social Research During the Cold War* (Ithaca, NY: Cornell University Press, 2013).

20. Harold Guetzkow, "Recollections About the Inter-Nation Simulation (INS) and Some Derivatives in Global Modeling," *Simulation & Gaming*, August 18, 2016, 459, https://doi.org/10.1177/1046878195264007.

21. Charles McClelland characterized Guetzkow as a behavioralist in the field. See Charles A. McClelland, "The Function of Theory in International Relations," *Journal of Conflict Resolution* 4, no. 3 (1960): 309.

22. By contrast, see other efforts to reform international relations at the time; see Robert Vitalis, *White World Order, Black Power Politics: The Birth of American International Relations*, reprint ed. (Ithaca, NY: Cornell University Press, 2017).

23. Harold Guetzkow, "Simulation in International Relations," in *Proceedings of The IBM Scientific Computing Symposium on Simulation Models and Gaming* (White Plains, NY: IBM Data Processing Division, 1966), 164.

24. Robert A. Dahl, "The Behavioral Approach in Political Science: Epitaph for a Monument to a Successful Protest," *American Political Science Review* 55, no. 4 (1961): 763–772.

25. Easton David, *The Political System* (New York: Alfred A. Knopf, 1953), 35, http://archive.org/details/dli.ernet.507692.

26. Women were undoubtedly part of these games, though less documented. Joy Rhode notes the importance of women assistants working long days for the experts to play iterations of the PME.

27. Guetzkow likely drew up this taxonomy after the conference. A month prior, on October 15, 1964, he presented at the Inter-Agency Group on Strategic Studies of the Joint War Games Agency. The talk, later published with SIP associate director Lloyd Jensen in 1966, includes a discussion of the state of the art organized by manual or automated, simple, or complex. See Harold Guetzkow and Lloyd Jensen, "Research Activities on Simulated International Processes," *Background* 9, no. 4 (February 1, 1966): 261–274, https://doi.org/10.2307/3013650.

28. Michael D. Ward and Daniel Guetzkow, "Harold S. Guetzkow," *PS: Political Science & Politics* 42, no. 2 (2009): 413–414, https://doi.org/10.1017/S104909650922066X.

29. Herbert Goldhamer and Hans Speier, "Some Observations on Political Gaming," *World Politics* 12, no. 1 (1959): 71–83, https://doi.org/10.2307/2009213; Christian Dayé, "'A Fiction of Long Standing': Techniques of Prospection and the Role of Positivism in US Cold War Social Science, 1950–65," *History of the Human Sciences* 29, no. 4–5 (2016): 35–58, https://doi.org/10.1177/0952695116664838; Sharon Ghamari-Tabrizi, "Simulating the Unthinkable: Gaming Future War in the 1950s and 1960s," *Social Studies of Science* 30, no. 2 (2000): 163–223, https://doi.org/10.1177/030631200030002001; Jenny Andersson, *The Future of the World: Futurology, Futurists, and the Struggle for the Post Cold War Imagination* (Oxford: Oxford University Press, 2018), 75–97.

30. Since its start in 1948, the RAND Corporation applied game theory and linear programming to solve military problems and advance Operations Research. Paul Erickson's book offers a detailed history of this research, particularly the close

coordination between RAND staff and John von Neumann. RAND research popularized and adapted Von Neumann and Morgenstern's 1944 *Theory of Games and Economic Behavior*. Research into games, according to Erickson, trailed off at RAND by the late 1950s in favor of other methods, including exercises[1] Though game theory may have lost its theoretical appeal, Kennedy's win and the subsequent appointment of Robert McNamara as Secretary of Defense in 1961 established a new link to RAND's game theory and nuclear war. RAND's mathematical games were central to US nuclear strategy, a war that had no veterans. As former RAND economist Alain Enthoven reportedly said to one general, "I have fought as many wars as you have."[1] The strategic adoption of game theory along with "hawkish" expertise then forms something of a majoritarian position against which exercises and other computational methods could, to borrow a word from today, innovate. For more on games at RAND and its research leadership, see Bessner, *Democracy in Exile*.

31. Ghamari-Tabrizi, "Simulating the Unthinkable," 174.

32. Goldhamer and Speier, "Some Observations," 72–73; Andersson, *The Future of the World*, 82–90.

33. Lincoln P. Bloomfield and Norman J. Padelford, "Teaching Note: Three Experiments in Political Gaming," *American Political Science Review* 53, no. 4 (1959): 1105–1115, https://doi.org/10.2307/1952078.

34. Francis McHugh, "Fundamentals of War Gaming, Third Edition," AD686108 (Newport: The Untited States Naval War College, 1966), 2–40; Moya A. Ball, *Vietnam-on-the-Potomac* (New York: Praeger, 1992), 93.

35. J. R. Renshaw and Annette Heuston, *The Game Monopologs* (Santa Monica, CA: RAND Corporation, 1957), https://www.rand.org/pubs/research_memoranda/RM1917-1.html.

36. Alfred Hartmann Hausrath, *Venture Simulation in War, Business, and Politics* (New York: McGraw-Hill, 1972), 200–201, 322–327.

37. D. G. Malcolm, "Bibliography on the Use of Simulation in Management Analysis," *Operations Research* 8, no. 2 (1960): 169–177, https://doi.org/10.1287/opre.8.2.169; Jay R. Greene and Roger L. Sisson, *Dynamic Management Decision Games, Including Seven Non-Computer Games* (New York: Wiley, 1959).

38. James P. Muldoon Jr., "The Model United Nations Revisited," *Simulation & Gaming*, August 18, 2016, https://doi.org/10.1177/1046878195261003.

39. Guetzkow, "Recollections About the Inter-Nation," 461.

40. Harold Guetzkow, "A Use of Simulation in the Study of Inter-Nation Relations," *Behavioral Science* 4, no. 3 (1959): 145, https://doi.org/10.1002/bs.3830040302.

41. Hausrath, *Venture Simulation in War*, 200.

42. An interesting side note is how Guetzkow's topology blurred the lines between programmer and players, computers, and user. Gaming, first, allowed computers to be a new means of expressing political theory and knowledge. Play was at once a form of rules, programming, and theory. At the symposium, playing games was a way programming a computer, and programming was a way to play with a computer. Guetzkow, for example, notes that one-player games, as opposed to his team games, could occur between the computer and the programmer. Peers of Guetzkow also turned from writing games to simulation programming languages like DYNAMO and SIMULA. Guetzkow's comments suggest that what was programming in a simulation had not stabilized yet.

43. Guetzkow, "Simulation in International Relations," 258.

44. Guetzkow, , "Simulation in International Relations," 252.

45. Stanislaw M. Ulam, "Monte Carlo Calculations in Problems of Mathematical Physics," *Modern Mathematics for the Engineers*, 1961, 261–281; Nicholas Metropolis, "The Beginning of the Monte Carlo Method," *Los Alamos Science* 15, no. 584 (1987): 125–130; Galison, "Computer Simulations and the Trading Zone," 2011.

46. Walter Clemens Jr., "A Propostional Analysis of the International Relations Theory in Temper: A Computer Simulation of Cold War Conflict," in *Simulation in the Study of Politics*, ed. William D. Coplin (Chicago: Markham, 1968), 59.

47. Defense Technical Information Center, *DTIC AD0653606: TEMPER as a Model of International Relations: an Evaluation for the Joint War Games Agency Department of Defense*, 1966, http://archive.org/details/DTIC_AD0653606.

48. *TEMPER Volume 1, Orientation Manual* (Bedford, MA: Raytheon, 1965), https://apps.dtic.mil/sti/citations/AD0470375.

49. Morton Gorden, "Comments on Clemens' Paper," in *Simulation in the Study of Politics*, ed. William D. Coplin (Chicago: Markham, 1968), 102.

50. Only the first two are available online.

51. Richard Brody cited a 1961 Raytheon report about TEMPER in a 1963 journal article. See Richard A. Brody, "Some Systemic Effects of the Spread of Nuclear Weapons Technology: A Study Through Simulation of a Multi-Nuclear Future," *Journal of Conflict Resolution* 7, no. 4 (1963): 673, https://doi.org/10.1177/002200276300700401.

52. Hausrath, *Venture Simulation in War*, 273n9–28.

53. Hausrath, 329.

54. Abt Associates attracted its share of controversy, as I will discuss. Abt worked on the Politica game, which began as part of the controversial Project Camelot. See Mark Solovey, "Project Camelot and the 1960s Epistemological Revolution: Rethinking the Politics-Patronage-Social Science Nexus," *Social Studies of Science* 31, no. 2 (2001):

171–206, https://doi.org/10.1177/0306312701031002003. Later Abt appeared to have a falling out with a colleague over the use of his counterinsurgency games in Chile. Daniel del Solar, "How We Planned a Coup," *Berkeley Bard*, September 14, 1973.

55. "Guetzkow project on simulation of international affairs (includes Joint War Games Agency, Inter-Agency Group on Strategic Studies [INAGROSS])," Ithiel de Sola Pool papers (MC-0440), MIT Libraries, Department of Distinctive Collections. https://archivesspace.mit.edu/repositories/2/archival_objects/226074.

56. Defense Technical Information Center, *DTIC AD0653606*, 3.

57. Defense Technical Information Center, 2.

58. "TEMPER Volume 1, Orientation Manual," 41.

59. Metropolis, "The Beginning," 224.

60. Gorden, "Comments on Clemens' Paper"; Clemens, "A Propostional Analysis."

61. Clemens, 60.

62. "TEMPER. Volume 2. The Theory of the Model" (Bedford, MA: Raytheon, 1965), 25, https://apps.dtic.mil/sti/citations/AD0471458.

63. Clemens, "A Propostional Analysis," 72.

64. Clemens, 94.

65. "Guetzkow project on simulation of international affairs (includes Joint War Games Agency, Inter-Agency Group on Strategic Studies [INAGROSS])," Ithiel de Sola Pool papers (MC-0440), MIT Libraries, Department of Distinctive Collections, https://archivesspace.mit.edu/repositories/2/archival_objects/226074.

66. Fenwick McKelvey, *Internet Daemons: Digital Communications Possessed*, Electronic Mediations 56 (Minneapolis: University of Minnesota Press, 2018).

67. "Guetzkow project on simulation."

68. Edwards, "The World in a Machine," 247.

69. Donna Haraway, "Situated Knowledges: The Science Question in Feminism and the Privilege of Partial Perspective," *Feminist Studies* 14, no. 3 (1988): 581, https://doi.org/10.2307/3178066.

70. Elichirigoity, *Planet Management*.

71. Richard K. Ashley, "The Eye of Power: The Politics of World Modeling," *International Organization* 37, no. 3 (1983): 529–530, https://doi.org/10.1017/S0020818300032768.

72. See Joy Rohde, "Pax Technologica: Computers, International Affairs, and Human Reason in the Cold War," *Isis* 108, no. 4 (2017): 792–813, https://doi.org/10.1086/695679.

Chapter 7

1. Alfred Hartmann Hausrath, *Venture Simulation in War, Business, and Politics* (New York: McGraw-Hill, 1972), 273n9–29.

2. "Guetzkow project on simulation of international affairs (includes Joint War Games Agency, Inter-Agency Group on Strategic Studies [INAGROSS])," Ithiel de Sola Pool papers (MC-0440), MIT Libraries, Department of Distinctive Collections, https://archivesspace.mit.edu/repositories/2/archival_objects/226074.

3. "Guetzkow project on simulation."

4. Meredith Broussard, *Artificial Unintelligence: How Computers Misunderstand the World* (Cambridge, MA: MIT Press, 2019).

5. "Guetzkow project on simulation."

6. "Guetzkow project on simulation."

7. "Guetzkow project on simulation."

8. For contrast, I recommend Paul Edwards' account of *system dynamics'* formulation preceding *The Limits to Growth* report. Whereas there were many ways that systems thinking encouraged thinking with computers, I focus on how political systems converged with computer systems. See: Paul N. Edwards, "The World in a Machine: Origins and Impacts of Early Computerized Global Systems Models," in *Systems, Experts, and Computers: The Systems Approach*, ed. Agatha C. Hughes and Thomas P. Hughes (Cambridge, MA: MIT Press, 2000).

9. Richard K. Ashley, "The Eye of Power: The Politics of World Modeling," *International Organization* 37, no. 3 (1983): 529–530, https://doi.org/10.1017/S0020818300032768.

10. My account, then, offers another history of where this view from nowhere came from, describing the situatedness of the situation-less. In doing so, this chapter follows on the work of Paul Edwards, most directly in thinking about the construction of a closed-world discourse in postwar America, as well as Jenny Andersson's work on future studies, Hunter Hayck's account of high modern social sciences, and Elgé Rindzevičiūtė on system-cybernetic rationality, all of which I discuss in turn.

11. Walter Clemens Jr., "A Propostional Analysis of the International Relations Theory in Temper—A Computer Simulation of Cold War Conflict," in *Simulation in the Study of Politics*, ed. William D. Coplin (Chicago: Markham, 1968), 59.

12. Harold Guetzkow, "Simulation in International Relations," in *Proceedings of The IBM Scientific Computing Symposium on Simulation Models and Gaming* (White Plains, NY: IBM Data Processing Division, 1966), 260.

13. "Guetzkow project on simulation."

14. Guetzkow shared a paper by influential international relations scholar Sidney Verba that I have not mentioned in this section to keep my argument focused, but his article was key to my interpretation of the debates around prototype. By 1964, Verba was a major name in political science. He had just published his third book, *The Civic Culture*, coauthored with his supervisor Gabriel A. Almond. A landmark study of survey research, the book popularized the comparative study of political cultures. A year after its publication, Verba took the time to offer his review of another approach to comparative global politics, the emerging field of global political simulations. There, he discussed validity as a problem in the field, like Abt and Guetzkow. Validity, according to Verba, involved how an operating model corresponded to a referent system or observable universe. Sidney Verba, "Simulation, Reality, and Theory in International Relations," *World Politics* 16, no. 3 (1964): 490–519, https://doi.org/10.2307/2009585. How, in other words, did the simulation match its reality? Validity became a key test for all models. Validity raised the stakes for a field that, as Verba put it, had "a plethora of theories and hypotheses" that now could be tested to see if it predicted the state of the world. Sidney Verba, "Assumptions of Rationality and Non-Rationality in Models of the International System," *World Politics* 14, no. 1 (1961): 517, https://doi.org/10.2307/2009558.

15. cf. Eric Winsberg, *Science in the Age of Computer Simulation* (Chicago: University of Chicago Press, 2010), https://press.uchicago.edu/ucp/books/book/chicago/S/bo9003670.html; Naomi Oreskes et al., "Verification, Validation, and Confirmation of Numerical Models in the Earth Sciences," *Science* 263, no. 5147 (1994): 641–646.

16. Daniel Bessner, *Democracy in Exile: Hans Speier and the Rise of the Defense Intellectual* (Ithaca, NY: Cornell University Press, 2018).

17. Jenny Andersson, *The Future of the World: Futurology, Futurists, and the Struggle for the Post Cold War Imagination* (Oxford: Oxford University Press, 2018).

18. William T. R. Fox, "Pluralism, The Science of Politics, and the World System," *World Politics* 27, no. 4 (1975): 597, https://doi.org/10.2307/2010016; Angelo Vulpiani, "Lewis Fry Richardson: Scientist, Visionary and Pacifist," *Lettera Matematica* 2, no. 3 (2014): 121–128, https://doi.org/10.1007/s40329-014-0063-z.

19. Harold Guetzkow, "Recollections about the Inter-Nation Simulation (INS) and Some Derivatives in Global Modeling," *Simulation & Gaming*, August 18, 2016, 45, https://doi.org/10.1177/1046878195264007.

20. Andersson, *The Future of the World*, 93.

21. J. David Singer, "Parents of the Field," interview by Chris Mitchell, n.d., https://activity.scar.gmu.edu/sites/default/files/global-documents/PoF/Singer_Parents_Transcript.pdf.

22. Richard A. Brody, "Some Systemic Effects of the Spread of Nuclear Weapons Technology: A Study Through Simulation of a Multi-Nuclear Future," *Journal of Conflict*

Resolution 7, no. 4 (1963): 663–667, https://doi.org/10.1177/002200276300700401; John Macrae and Paul Smoker, "A Vietnam Simulation: A Report on the Canadian/English Joint Project," *Journal of Peace Research* 4, no. 1 (1967): 1–24, https://doi.org/10.1177/002234336700400101; Hayward Alker Jr. and Ronald D. Brunner, "Simulating International Conflict: A Comparison of Three Approaches," *International Studies Quarterly* 13, no. 1 (1969): 70, https://doi.org/10.2307/3013481; Dina A. Zinnes, "A Comparison of Hostile Behavior of Decision-Makers in Simulate and Historical Data," *World Politics* 18, no. 3 (1966): 474–502, https://doi.org/10.2307/2009766.

23. Richard A. Brody, "Questions of Generalizing: From Ins-8 to the Real World," *Journal of Conflict Resolution* 7, no. 4 (1963): 748.

24. Brody, "Questions of Generalizing," 748.

25. Stuart A. Bremer, *Simulated Worlds* (Princeton, NJ: Princeton University Press, 1977), 19.

26. Macrae and Smoker, "A Vietnam Simulation," 5.

27. Paul Smoker, "International Processes Simulation: A Description," in *Experimentation and Simulation in Political Science*, ed. J. A. Laponce and Paul Smoker (Toronto: University of Toronto Press, 1972), 315–366.

28. Charles Hermann, "Validation Problems in Games and Simulations with Special Reference to Models of International Politics," *Behavioral Science* 12, no. 3 (1967): 216.

29. Hermann, "Validation Problems," 216.

30. Hermann, 222.

31. Hermann, 223.

32. Alker and Brunner, "Simulating International Conflict," 77.

33. Alker and Brunner, 107.

34. Alker and Brunner, 108.

35. Alker and Brunner, 108.

36. Alker and Brunner, 108–109.

37. Alker and Brunner, 108.

38. Charles F. Hermann and Margaret G. Hermann, "An Attempt to Simulate the Outbreak of World War I," *American Political Science Review* 61, no. 2 (1967): 400–416, https://doi.org/10.2307/1953253.

39. Alker and Brunner, "Simulating International Conflict," 109.

40. Macrae and Smoker, "A Vietnam Simulation," 3.

41. J. David Singer, "Data-Making in International Relations," *Behavioral Science* 10, no. 1 (January 1, 1965): 69.

42. Singer, "Data-Making," 79.

43. Ulises A. Mejias and Nick Couldry, "Datafication," *Internet Policy Review* 8, no. 4 (November 29, 2019), https://policyreview.info/concepts/datafication.

44. I do not presume to offer a clear distinction of what counts as a political indicator. Certainly, these approaches built on early efforts to quantify the world economy. Michelle Murphy is brilliant in chronicling the racial and political significance associated with the prewar emergence of the "economy" as a macrological figure. Indeed, the figures here are another side of Murphy's focus on "U.S. Cold War quantitative practices that generated economy and population as objects of governance and intervention, tracking how figures of surplus life, and life not worth being born, became calculable." Michelle Murphy, *The Economization of Life* (Durham, NC: Duke University Press, 2017), 9. At its founding in 1920, the League of Nations began to coordinate international data leading to its economic surveys, which the United Nations continues to publish. Charles K. Nichols, "The Statistical Work of the League of Nations in Economic, Financial and Related Fields," *Journal of the American Statistical Association* 37, no. 219 (1942): 336–342, https://doi.org/10.2307/2279001. By the 1930s, global economic data were also a priority to business organizations and the nascent neoliberal movement. Quinn Slobodian, "How to See the World Economy: Statistics, Maps, and Schumpeter's Camera in the First Age of Globalization," *Journal of Global History* 10, no. 2 (2015): 313, https://doi.org/10.1017/S174002281500008X. During the 1960s and into the 1970s, when American quantitative international relations was developing, global measurement expanded to include social and development indicators to measure fulfilment of human needs instead of economic growth. Stephen Macekura, "Whither Growth? International Development, Social Indicators, and the Politics of Measurement, 1920s–1970s," *Journal of Global History* 14, no. 2 (2019): 261–279, https://doi.org/10.1017/S1740022819000068.

45. Paul N. Edwards, *A Vast Machine: Computer Models, Climate Data, and the Politics of Global Warming* (Cambridge, MA: MIT Press, 2010), 251.

46. Fox, "Pluralism, The Science of Politics"; Kalpana Shankar et al., "Studying the History of Social Science Data Archives as Knowledge Infrastructure," *Science & Technology Studies* 29, no. 2 (2016): 62–73, https://doi.org/10.23987/sts.55691; Colin Koopman, *How We Became Our Data: A Genealogy of the Informational Person* (Chicago: University of Chicago Press, 2019).

47. Joy Rohde, "Pax Technologica: Computers, International Affairs, and Human Reason in the Cold War," *Isis* 108, no. 4 (2017): 792–813, https://doi.org/10.1086/695679.

48. Karl W. Deutsch, "Shifts in the Balance of Communication Flows: A Problem of Measurement in International Relations," *Public Opinion Quarterly* 20, no. 1 (1956): 144;

David Easton, "1. Classification of Political Systems," *Political Research, Organization and Design* 1, no. 2 (1957): 3–4, https://doi.org/10.1177/000276425700100201.

49. Karl W. Deutsch, "Toward an Inventory of Basic Trends and Patterns in Comparative and International Politics," *American Political Science Review* 54, no. 1 (1960): 35, https://doi.org/10.2307/1952407.

50. Deutsch, "Toward an Inventory," 38.

51. Though unmentioned in the articles, there is some debate about the accuracy of these data. Interviewees mentioned that much of it had errors. Indeed, I would guess that errors would have been used to justify these research projects' continued existence.

52. Frank Whelon Wayman, "Rummel and Singer, DON and COW," in *R.J. Rummel: An Assessment of His Many Contributions*, ed. Nils Petter Gleditsch, SpringerBriefs on Pioneers in Science and Practice (Cham, Switzerland: Springer International Publishing, 2017), 83, https://doi.org/10.1007/978-3-319-54463-2_9.

53. J. David Singer, "The Relevance of the Behavioral Sciences to the Study of International Relations," *Behavioral Science* 6, no. 4 (1961): 324.

54. Wayman, "Rummel and Singer"; James Tobin, "Can Data Preserve Peace?," *Michigan Today*, January 23, 2020, https://michigantoday.umich.edu/2020/01/23/can-data-preserve-peace/; Singer, "Parents of the Field."

55. J. David Singer and Melvin Small, "National Alliance Commitments and War Involvement, 1818–1945," in *International Politics and Foreign Policy: A Reader in Research and Theory*, ed. James N. Rosenau (New York: Free Press, 1969), 513.

56. J. David Singer and Melvin Small, "Formal Alliances, 1815–1939: A Quantitative Description," *Journal of Peace Research* 3, no. 1 (1966): 1–31, https://doi.org/10.1177/002234336600300101.

57. Rudolph J. Rummel, "Dimensionality of Nations Project: Nation Attribute Data, 1950–1965," Inter-university Consortium for Political and Social Research [distributor], 1992-02-16. https://doi.org/10.3886/ICPSR05020.v1.

58. Rudolph J. Rummel, "Some Dimensions in the Foreign Behaviour of Nations," in *International Politics and Foreign Policy: A Reader in Research and Theory*, ed. James N Rosenau (New York: Free Press, 1969), 601.

59. For more on his controversial status, see Nils Petter Gleditsch, ed., *R.J. Rummel: An Assessment of His Many Contributions*, SpringerBriefs on Pioneers in Science and Practice (Cham, Switzerland: Springer International, 2017), https://doi.org/10.1007/978-3-319-54463-2_1; James Lee Ray, "Understanding Rummel," ed. R. J. Rummel, *Journal of Conflict Resolution* 26, no. 1 (1982): 161–187.

60. Nils Petter Gleditsch, "R.J. Rummel—A Multi-Faceted Scholar," in *R.J. Rummel: An Assessment of His Many Contributions*, ed. Nils Petter Gleditsch, SpringerBriefs on

Pioneers in Science and Practice (Cham: Springer International, 2017), 8–10, https://doi.org/10.1007/978-3-319-54463-2_1.

61. Rohde, "Pax Technologica," 798–799.

62. Edward E. Azar, "The Conflict and Peace Data Bank (COPDAB) Project," *Journal of Conflict Resolution* 24, no. 1 (1980): 146, https://doi.org/10.1177/002200278002400106.

63. Rohde, "Pax Technologica," 798.

64. Bernard Berelson, *Content Analysis in Communication Research*, Content Analysis in Communication Research (New York: Free Press, 1952); Richard C. Gilman, "The General Inquirer: A Computer Approach to Content Analysis. Philip J. Stone, Dexter C. Dunphy, Marshall S. Smith, Daniel M. Ogilvie," *American Journal of Sociology* 73, no. 5 (1968): 634–635, https://doi.org/10.1086/224539; Philip J. Stone et al., *The General Inquirer: A Computer Approach to Content Analysis* (Cambridge: MIT Press, 1966), https://mitpress.mit.edu/books/general-inquirer; Charles Kadushin et al., "Literary Analysis with the Aid of the Computer: Review Symposium," *Computers and the Humanities* 2, no. 4 (1968): 177–202; Philip J. Stone et al., "The General Inquirer: A Computer System for Content Analysis and Retrieval Based on the Sentence as a Unit of Information," *Behavioral Science* 7, no. 4 (1962): 484–498; Erwin K. Scheuch and Philip J. Stone, "The General Inquirer Approach to an International Retrieval System for Survey Archives," *American Behavioral Scientist* 7, no. 10 (1964): 23–28, https://doi.org/10.1177/000276426400701006.

65. Fenwick McKelvey, "The Other Cambridge Analytics: Early 'Artificial Intelligence' in American Political Science," in *The Cultural Life of Machine Learning: An Incursion into Critical AI Studies*, ed. Jonathan Roberge and Michael Castelle (London: Palgrave Macmillan, 2021), 117–142, https://doi.org/10.1007/978-3-030-56286-1

66. Thanks to Richard Chadwick. Four interviews with him helped elaborate this larger history.

67. Lincoln E. Moses et al., "Scaling Data on Inter-Nation Action: A Standard Scale Is Developed for Comparing International Conflict in a Variety of Situations," *Science* 156, no. 3778 (1967): 1054–1059, https://doi.org/10.1126/science.156.3778.1054; Charles Hermann et al., "CREON: A Foreign Events Data Set," in *Sage Professional Papers in International Studies*, vol. 2, 024 vols. (Beverly Hills, CA: Sage, 1973).

68. Harold Guetzkow and Lloyd Jensen, "Research Activities on Simulated International Processes," *Background* 9, no. 4 (1966): 267–268.

69. Brody, "Some Systemic Effects," 665.

70. M. Mitchell Waldrop, *The Dream Machine: J.C.R. Licklider and the Revolution That Made Computing Personal* (New York: Penguin Books, 2002); Fenwick McKelvey,

Internet Daemons: Digital Communications Possessed, Electronic Mediations 56 (Minneapolis: University of Minnesota Press, 2018).

71. Joseph Carl Robnett Licklider, "Man-Computer Symbiosis," *Human Factors in Electronics, IRE Transactions On* HFE-1, no. 1 (1960): 5.

72. Peter Louis Galison, "The Ontology of the Enemy: Norbert Wiener and the Cybernetic Vision," *Critical Inquiry* 21, no. 1 (1994): 228–266"; Orit Halpern, *Beautiful Data: A History of Vision and Reason Since 1945*, Experimental Futures (Durham, NC: Duke University Press, 2014).

73. Charles F. Hermann, "Validation Problems in Games and Simulations with Special Reference to Models of International Politics," *Behavioral Science* 12, no. 3 (1967): 217, https://doi.org/10.1002/bs.3830120306.

74. Thanks to Nick Seaver for the advice here.

75. CRISISCOM is also interesting as another example of the overlapping fields of national and world simulation as well as funders. ARPA and the Naval Research Laboratory sponsored the project. Research was undertaken by the Simulmatics Corporation and the Center for International Studies at MIT. Project MAC at MIT provided computer access.

76. Ithiel de Sola Pool and Allan Kessler, "The Kaiser, the Tsar, and the Computer: Information Processing in a Crisis," *American Behavioral Scientist* 8, no. 9 (1965): 32.

77. A. R. Kessler and I. D. Sola Pool, "Crisiscom: A Computer Simulation of Human Information Processing During a Crisis," *IEEE Transactions on Systems Science and Cybernetics* 1, no. 1 (1965): 56, https://doi.org/10.1109/TSSC.1965.300061.

78. Pool and Kessler, "The Kaiser, the Tsar, and the Computer," 32.

79. Hermann, "Validation Problems in Games," 1967, 226.

80. Steve Holloway, "The Upper Arlington High School Class of 1969," 2009, http://www.ua69.com/PhotoCollections/SteveHolloway.htm.

81. Brian Dear, *The Friendly Orange Glow: The Untold Story of the PLATO System and the Dawn of Cyberculture* (New York: Pantheon, 2017).

82. Goldstein, Gordon, ed. 1966. "PLATO." *Digital Computer Newsletter* 18 (1): 26–33.

83. The POLIS Laboratory ran the ICONS Project (International Communication & Negotiation Simulations Project). Started in 1982 by Dr. Jonathan Wilkenfeld and Dr. Richard Brecht, the ICONS Project is still running at the University of Maryland. For more, see its website: https://www.icons.umd.edu/about/mission. For more about POLIS, see the small literature on the influential project: Jonathan Wilkenfeld and Joyce Kaufman, "Political Science: Network Simulation in International Politics," *Social Science Computer Review* 11, no. 4 (1993): 464–476, https://doi.org

/10.1177/089443939301100405; Robert C. Noël, "The Polis Laboratory," *American Behavioral Scientist* 12, no. 6 (1969): 30–35; Jean Dickinson, "Games Political Scientists Play," *Change: The Magazine of Higher Learning* 8, no. 6 (1976): 56–59, https://doi.org/10.1080/00091383.1976.10568913.

84. Friedrich Kittler, "Gramophone, Film, Typewriter," trans. Dorothea von Mücke and Philippe L. Similon, *October* 41 (1987): 116, https://doi.org/10.2307/778332.

85. The breakdown is well documented in the work of Katherine Hayles and Orit Halpern but can also be found in attempts to develop mathematical theories of politics; see, for example, Hayward R. Alker et al., eds., *Mathematical Approaches to Politics* (San Francisco: Jossey-Bass, 1973).

86. Defense Technical Information Center, *DTIC AD0647051: Demonstration of Two Simulations of Internal Revolutionary Conflict: Politica and Agile-Coin*, 1967, 28, http://archive.org/details/DTIC_AD0647051.

87. As an aside, patronage may be a murkier reason for political science modeling being overshadowed by the Club of Rome. The American orientation of even the peace researchers likely contributed to the embrace of more neutral system-dynamics models. Just as the club convinced the Volkswagen foundation to provide funding, Harold Guetzkow was at the UN. Guetzkow worked at the UN from 1970 to 1971 in New York City. The time was "much less productive" than in past because Guetzkow was "unable to establish a non-Central Intelligence Agency Status. The ever-present and obvious interest of Russian State Security Committee (KGB) agents in my work in simulation, being funded by the US military, undermined my credibility as an American scholar." Guetzkow, "Recollections About the Inter-Nation," 457–458.

88. Pablo Jacovkis and Rodrigo Castro, "Computer-Based Global Models: From Early Experiences to Complex Systems," *Journal of Artificial Societies and Social Simulation* 18, no. 1 (2015): 13; Hayward R. Alker, "Global Modeling Alternatives: The First Twenty Years," in *Theories, Models, and Simulations in International Relations: Essays and Research in Honor of Harold Guetzkow*, ed. Michael D. Ward (Boulder, CO: Westview Press, 1985), 9–38; Ashley, "The Eye of Power"; Michael Don Ward and Harold Guetzkow, "Toward Integrated Global Models: From Economic Engineering to Social Science Modeling," *Journal of Policy Modeling* 1, no. 3 (1979): 445–464, https://doi.org/10.1016/0161-8938(79)90008-5; Harold Guetzkow and Joseph J. Valadez, eds., *Simulated International Processes: Theories and Research into Global Modelling* (London: SAGE, 1981).

89. The Club of Rome's start is described in its early reports: Donella H. Meadows et al., *The Limits to Growth: A Report for the Club of Rome's Project on the Predicament of Mankind* (Falls Church, VA: Potomac Associates, 1972); Hasan Ozbekhan, University of Pennsylvania, and Management and Behavioral Science Center, *The Club of Rome: The Predicament of Mankind, Quest for Structured Responses to Growing World-Wide Complexities and Uncertainties—A Proposal.* (Philadelphia: Management and

Behavioral Science Center, University of Pennsylvania, 1970). See also a growing historical literature: Fernando Elichirigoity, *Planet Management: Limits to Growth, Computer Simulation, and the Emergence of Global Spaces* (Evanston, IL: Northwestern University Press, 1999); Matthias Schmelzer, "'Born in the Corridors of the OECD': The Forgotten Origins of the Club of Rome, Transnational Networks, and the 1970s in Global History," *Journal of Global History* 12, no. 1 (2017): 26–48, https://doi.org/10.1017/S1740022816000322; Jason L. Churchill, "The Limits to Influence: The Club of Rome and Canada, 1968 to 1988" (Diss., University of Waterloo, 2006), https://uwspace.uwaterloo.ca/handle/10012/747; Elodie Vieille Blanchard, "Modelling the Future: An Overview of the 'Limits to Growth' Debate," *Centaurus* 52, no. 2 (2010): 91–116, https://doi.org/10.1111/j.1600-0498.2010.00173.x; Edwards, "The World in a Machine; Andersson, *Future of the World*.

90. Schmelzer, "'Born in the Corridors of the OECD,'" 27.

91. Elichirigoity, *Planet Management*, 75–81.

92. Andersson, *Future of the World*, 186.

93. Churchill, "The Limits to Influence," 125–136.

94. Martin Shubik, "Modeling on a Grand Scale," *Science* 174, no. 4013 (1971): 1014.

95. William D. Nordhaus, "World Dynamics: Measurement Without Data," *The Economic Journal* 83, no. 332 (1973): 1157, https://doi.org/10.2307/2230846.

96. Marie Jahoda, *Models of Doom: A Critique of the Limits to Growth*, ed. H. S. D. Cole et al. (New York: Universe Books, 1973).

97. Mihajli Mesarovic and Eduard Pestel, *Mankind at the Turning Point: The Second Report to the Club of Rome* (New York: Reader's Digest Press, 1974).

98. Amílcar O. Herrera et al., *Catastrophe or New Society? A Latin American World Model* (Ottawa: IDRC, 1976), https://idl-bnc-idrc.dspacedirect.org/handle/10625/213.

99. Amílcar Herrera, "Introduction and Basic Assumptions of the Model," in *Latin American World Model: Proceedings of the Second IIASA Symposium on Global Modelling [Baden, Austria] October 7–10, 1974*, ed. Gerhart Bruckmann (Laxenburg, Austria: International Institute for Applied Systems Analysis, 1976), 5.

100. Sun-ha Hong, "Technofutures in Stasis: Smart Machines, Ubiquitous Computing, and the Future That Keeps Coming Back," *International Journal of Communication* 15, no. 0 (2021): 1941.

101. Herrera et al., *Catastrophe or New Society?*; Pablo Pryluka, "'Una futura Heidelberg argentina': El itinerario de la Fundación Bariloche (1963–1978)," *Pasado Abierto* 6, no. 11 (2020): 56–75; Gilberto C. Gallopin, "The Latin American World Model (a.k.a. the Bariloche Model): Three Decades Ago," *Futures* 33, no. 1 (2001): 77–89, https://doi.org/10.1016/S0016-3287(00)00055-0

102. For an excellent review of the criticism, see Blanchard, "Modelling the Future." Reactions from the time include Douglass B. Lee Jr., "Requiem for Large-Scale Models," *Journal of the American Institute of Planners* 39, no. 3 (1973): 163–178, https://doi.org/10.1080/01944367308977851; Shubik, "Modeling on a Grand Scale"; Carl Kaysen, "The Computer That Printed Out W*O*L*F*," *Foreign Affairs* 50, no. 4 (1972): 660, https://doi.org/10.2307/20037939; R. Gillette, "The Limits to Growth: Hard Sell for a Computer View of Doomsday," *Science* 175, no. 4026 (1972): 1088–1092, https://doi.org/10.1126/science.175.4026.1088; Johan Galtung, "'The Limits to Growth' and Class Politics," *Journal of Peace Research* 10, no. 1 (1973): 110–114; Nordhaus, "World Dynamics"; Robert Golub and Joe Townsend, "Malthus, Multinationals and the Club of Rome," *Social Studies of Science* 7, no. 2 (1977): 201–222, https://doi.org/10.1177/030631277700700204; Peter Passell et al., "The Limits to Growth," *New York Times*, April 2, 1972, sec. BR; Jahoda, *Models of Doom*; Hayward R. Alker and Ann Tickner, "Some Issues Raised by Previous Models," in *Problems of World Modeling: Political and Social Implications*, ed. Karl Wolfgang Deutsch et al. (Cambridge, MA: Ballinger, 1977), 17–32.

103. Churchill, "The Limits to Influence," 136–137.

104. Golub and Townsend, "Malthus, Multinationals and the Club of Rome."

105. Richard Buckminster Fuller, "Accommodating Human Unsettlement," *Town Planning Review* 49, no. 1 (1978): 52.

106. Galtung, "'The Limits to Growth'," 110.

107. For some context, Rachel Carson's 1972 book *Silent Spring* encouraged growing debate about human sustainability, encouraging neo-Malthusian thinking such as Paul R. Ehrlich's 1968 *The Population Bomb*. The US's first Earth Day was April 22, 1970. By the 1970s, the American environmentalist movement was in full swing. For more, see Riley E. Dunlap and Angela G. Mertig, *American Environmentalism: The US Environmental Movement, 1970–1990* (London: Taylor & Francis, 2014).

108. For a broader history of futurism, see Andersson, *Future of the World*; Richard B. Halley and Harold G. Vatter, "Technology and the Future as History: A Critical Review of Futurism," *Technology and Culture* 19, no. 1 (1978): 53–82, https://doi.org/10.2307/3103308; Kaya Tolon, "Futures Studies: A New Social Science Rooted in Cold War Strategic Thinking," in *Cold War Social Science: Knowledge Production, Liberal Democracy, and Human Nature*, ed. Mark Solovey and Hamilton Cravens (New York: Palgrave Macmillan US, 2012), 45–62, https://doi.org/10.1057/9781137013224_3; Christian Dayé, *Experts, Social Scientists, and Techniques of Prognosis in Cold War America* (Cham, Switzerland: Palgrave Macmillan, 2020).

109. Harold Guetzkow, "Six Continuing for Global Modelers: A Self-Critique," in *Simulated International Processes: Theories and Research into Global Modelling*, ed. Harold Guetzkow and Joseph J. Valadez (London: SAGE, 1981), 333.

110. Smoker, "International Processes Simulation."

111. Bremer, *Simulated Worlds*.

112. Guetzkow, "Recollections About the Inter-Nation," 457.

113. Daniel del Solar, "How We Planned a Coup," *Berkeley Bard*, September 14, 1973.

114. Donna Haraway, "Situated Knowledges: The Science Question in Feminism and the Privilege of Partial Perspective," *Feminist Studies* 14, no. 3 (1988): 581, https://doi.org/10.2307/3178066.

115. David Gilbert, "The UN Hired an AI Company to Untangle the Israeli-Palestinian Crisis," *Wired*, November 2, 2023, https://www.wired.com/story/culturepulse-ai-israeli-palestinian-crisis/.

116. Gilbert, "The UN Hired."

117. Katherine O'Lone et al., "Employing Multi-Agent AI to Model Conflict and Cooperation in Northern Ireland," *New England Journal of Public Policy* 36, no. 1 (2024): 12, https://scholarworks.umb.edu/nejpp/vol36/iss1/6.

118. "CulturePulse," accessed February 7, 2024, https://www.culturepulse.ai/.

119. Justin E. Lane, "How CulturePulse AI Helped Cambridge University Understand Conflict in Northern Ireland, the Balkans, and South Sudan," Culturepulse, April 2, 2023, https://culturepulse.ai/blog/how-culture-pulse-ai-helped-cambridge-university-understand-conflict.

120. Gilbert, "The UN Hired."

121. "CulturePulse."

122. O'Lone et al., "Employing Multi-Agent AI," 3.

123. Gilbert, "The UN Hired."

124. Catherine D'Ignazio and Lauren F. Klein, *Data Feminism*, Strong Ideas Series (Cambridge: MIT Press, 2020).

125. Carol Cohn, "Sex and Death in the Rational World of Defense Intellectuals," *Signs* 12, no. 4 (1987): 687–718; Jon Guice, "Controversy and the State: Lord ARPA and Intelligent Computing," *Social Studies of Science* 28, no. 1 (2016): 103–138, https://doi.org/10.1177/030631298028001004; Manan Ahmed Asif, "Technologies of Power: From Area Studies to Data Sciences," *Spheres: Journal for Digital Cultures* 5 (2019), http://spheres-journal.org/technologies-of-power-from-area-studies-to-data-sciences/; Robert Vitalis, *White World Order, Black Power Politics: The Birth of American International Relations*, reprint ed. (Ithaca, NY: Cornell University Press, 2017); Michael C. Desch, *Cult of the Irrelevant: The Waning Influence of Social Science on National Security* (Princeton, NJ: Princeton University Press, 2019), chap. 4, http://muse.jhu.edu/book/62654.

126. Armond R. Towns, "Toward a Black Media Philosophy," *Cultural Studies* 34, no. 6 (2020): 862, https://doi.org/10.1080/09502386.2020.1792524.

127. Lucy Suchman, "Imaginaries of Omniscience: Automating Intelligence in the US Department of Defense," *Social Studies of Science*, 53, no. 5 (2022): 3, https://doi.org/10.1177/03063127221104938.

Chapter 8

1. Armand Mattelart, *Networking the World, 1794–2000* (Minneapolis: University of Minnesota Press, 2000); Fernando Elichirigoity, *Planet Management: Limits to Growth, Computer Simulation, and the Emergence of Global Spaces* (Evanston, IL: Northwestern University Press, 1999).

2. Joy Rohde, "Pax Technologica: Computers, International Affairs, and Human Reason in the Cold War," *Isis* 108, no. 4 (2017): 792–813, https://doi.org/10.1086/695679.

3. Hayward R. Alker, "Global Modeling Alternatives: The First Twenty Years," in *Theories, Models, and Simulations in International Relations: Essays and Research in Honor of Harold Guetzkow*, ed. Michael D. Ward (Boulder, CO: Westview Press, 1985); A. Vág, "The Short History and the Plausible Future of World Modelling," *Acta Oeconomica* 55, no. 1 (2005): 63–88; Sam Cole, "Global Models: A Review of Recent Developments," *Futures* 19, no. 4 (1987): 403–430, https://doi.org/10.1016/0016-3287(87)90003-6.

4. Eglė Rindzevičiūtė, *The Power of Systems: How Policy Sciences Opened Up the Cold War World* (Ithaca, NY: Cornell University Press, 2016).

5. For some examples of modelling review articles, see John M. Richardson Jr., "A Decade of Global Modelling," *Futures* 14, no. 2 (1982): 136–145, https://doi.org/10.1016/0016-3287(82)90087-8. D. Meadows et al., *Groping in the Dark: The First Decade of Global Modelling* (Chichester, UK: John Wiley & Sons, 1982), http://pure.iiasa.ac.at/id/eprint/1829/; UNESCO, "Perceptions and Analyses of World Problems: Major Programme 1," 1986, https://unesdoc.unesco.org/ark:/48223/pf0000068817; Richard B. Halley and Harold G. Vatter, "Technology and the Future as History: A Critical Review of Futurism," *Technology and Culture* 19, no. 1 (1978): 53–82, https://doi.org/10.2307/3103308; Nathan Keyfitz, "Understanding World Models," *Sociological Methodology* 9 (1978): 1–19, https://doi.org/10.2307/270801.

6. Meadows et al., *Groping in the Dark*; Karl Wolfgang Deutsch et al., eds., *Problems of World Modeling: Political and Social Implications* (Cambridge, MA: Ballinger, 1977).

7. Eduard Pestel, "Modellers and Politicians," *Futures* 14, no. 2 (April 1982): 122–128, https://doi.org/10.1016/0016-3287(82)90085-4; Donella H. Meadows, "Lessons from Global Modelling and Modellers," *Futures* 14, no. 2 (1982): 111–121, https://doi.org/10.1016/0016-3287(82)90084-2.

8. Meadows, "Lessons from Global Modelling," 116.

9. Meadows, 116.

10. "Institute for the Future Formed in USA," *Futures* 1, no. 1 (1969): 66–68, https://doi.org/10.1016/S0016-3287(69)80009-1.

11. The threat of the USSR and its political approach to planning was an explicit enemy of more open futures research; for more, see Jenny Andersson, *The Future of the World: Futurology, Futurists, and the Struggle for the Post Cold War Imagination* (Oxford: Oxford University Press, 2018), 70–74.

12. Erich Jantsch, "The Organization of Technological Forecasting in the Soviet Union: Notes from a Brief Visit," *Technological Forecasting* 1, no. 1 (1969): 83–86, https://doi.org/10.1016/0099-3964(69)90008-8; Andersson, *Future of the World*; Jenny Andersson, "The Future of the Western World: The OECD and the Interfutures Project," *Journal of Global History* 14, no. 1 (2019): 126–144, https://doi.org/10.1017/S1740022818000384; Peter Brecke, "The Soviet Global Model: SIMIGDP," *Simulation & Gaming*, August 18, 2016, https://doi.org/10.1177/1046878195261002.

13. Charles F. Hermann and Margaret G. Hermann, "An Attempt to Simulate the Outbreak of World War I," *American Political Science Review* 61, no. 2 (1967): 400–416, https://doi.org/10.2307/1953253; Charles F. Hermann, *Crises in Foreign Policy: A Simulation Analysi* (Indianapolis: Bobbs-Merrill, 1969).

14. Rohde, "Pax Technologica"; Charles A. McClelland, *Crisis and Threat in the International Setting: Some Relational Concepts* (Fort Belvoir, VA: Defense Technical Information Center, 1975), https://doi.org/10.21236/ADA011913.

15. Rohde, "Pax Technologica," 806.

16. Stephen J. Andriole et al., "A Framework for the Comparative Analysis of Foreign Policy Behavior," *International Studies Quarterly* 19, no. 2 (1975): 161, https://doi.org/10.2307/2600267.

17. Stephen J. Andriole and Robert A. Young, "Toward the Development of an Integrated Crisis Warning System," *International Studies Quarterly* 21, no. 1 (1977): 115, https://doi.org/10.2307/2600149.

18. Richard Smith Beal, "Systems Analysis of International Crisis: Event Analysis of Nine Pre-Crisis Threat Situations, 1948–1962" (PhD diss., University of Southern California, 1977), https://www.proquest.com/pqdtglobal/docview/1645432592/citation/FE8D37E95A504A4APQ/2.

19. Richard Smith Beal, *Systems Analysis of International Crises* (Washington, DC: University Press of America, 1979), http://archive.org/details/systemsanalysiso0000beal.

20. Sidney Blumenthal, "Marketing the President," *New York Times*, September 13, 1981; Richard Pearson, "Richard Beal, Special Aide to Reagan, Dies," *Washington Post*,

November 4, 1984, https://www.washingtonpost.com/archive/local/1984/11/04/richard-beal-special-aide-to-reagan-dies/71b0e75d-0cf8-4c20-a63b-8308f9ebb515/; Wolfgang Saxon, "Richard Smith Beal Dies at 38," *New York Times*, November 4, 1984, sec. Obituaries, https://www.nytimes.com/1984/11/04/obituaries/richard-smith-beal-dies-at-38.html.

21. For more on Deutsch, see Charles Lewis Taylor and Bruce M. Russett, "Biography of Karl Wolfgang Deutsch (1912–1992)," in *Karl W. Deutsch: Pioneer in the Theory of International Relations: With a Preface by Charles Lewis Taylor and Bruce M. Russett*, ed. Charles Lewis Taylor and Bruce M. Russett (Cham, Switzerland: Springer International, 2020), 3–14, https://doi.org/10.1007/978-3-319-02910-8_1; Orit Halpern, *Beautiful Data: A History of Vision and Reason Since 1945*, Experimental Futures (Durham, NC: Duke University Press, 2014).

22. Nicholas D. Kristof, "The Best Political Scientist in the World Goes on Half-Time, Still an Optimist," *The Harvard Crimson*, May 23, 1979, https://www.thecrimson.com/article/1979/5/23/the-best-political-scientist-in-the/.

23. Kristof, "The Best Political Scientist."

24. Halpern, *Beautiful Data*.

25. Fenwick McKelvey, "The Other Cambridge Analytics: Early 'Artificial Intelligence' in American Political Science," in *The Cultural Life of Machine Learning: An Incursion into Critical AI Studies*, ed. Jonathan Roberge and Michael Castelle (Cham, Switzerland: Springer International, 2021), 117–142, https://doi.org/10.1007/978-3-030-56286-1_4.

26. Markus Ramsauer, "Endogenizing Politics: The GLOBUS World Model," Preprints, February 2, 2024, 5, https://doi.org/10.20944/preprints202402.0100.v1.

27. Karl Wolfgang Deutsch, "Foreword," in *The Globus Model: Computer Simulation of Worldwide Political and Economic Developments.*, ed. Stuart A Bremer (Boulder, CO: Westview Press, 1987), xiv, https://public.ebookcentral.proquest.com/choice/publicfullrecord.aspx?p=5893287.

28. Karl W. Deutsch, "Toward Drift and Steering Models," in *Problems of World Modeling: Political and Social Implications*, ed. Karl Wolfgang Deutsch et al. (Cambridge, MA: Ballinger, 1977), 5–10.

29. "Toward Drift," Deutsch, 7.

30. Deutsch, 9.

31. Deutsch, 9.

32. Deutsch, "Foreword," xiv.

33. Guetzkow and others claim that the US government stopped supporting global modeling. He reflects, "When my more conservative US government disallowed

further funding of global modeling (with its emphasis on politico-economic components), the West Berlin government picked up the thrust in global modeling through its Wissenschaftszentrum." Harold Guetzkow, "Recollections About the Inter-Nation Simulation (INS) and Some Derivatives in Global Modeling," *Simulation & Gaming*, August 18, 2016, 465, https://doi.org/10.1177/1046878195264007.

34. Guetzkow, "Recollections About the Inter-Nation," 463.

35. Harold Guetzkow and Joseph J. Valadez, *Simulated International Processes: Theories and Research into Global Modelling* (London: SAGE, 1981).

36. Stuart A. Bremer, *Simulated Worlds* (Princeton, NJ: Princeton University Press, 1977), 197.

37. Bremer, *Simulated Worlds*, 209.

38. GLOBUS Workshop Welcome Package, July 7–11, 1985, GLOBUS Model Folder, Das Wissenschaftszentrum Berlin für Sozialforschung (WZB), Berlin, Germany.

39. Hayward Alker Jr., "From Political Cybernetics to Global Modeling," in *From National Development to Global Community: Essays in Honor of Karl W. Deutsch*, ed. Richard L. Merritt and Bruce M. Russett (London: Allen & Unwin, 1981), 353–378.

40. Peter Brecke, interview by author, online, August 24, 2022.

41. Bremer, *The Globus Model*, 8.

42. Deutsch quoted in Bremer, *The Globus Model*, 12.

43. Bremer, 12.

44. Stuart Bremer, "Globale Modellierung am Wissenschaftszentrum," IIVG/pre 80–124 (Berlin: Wissenschaftszentrum Berlin für Sozialforschung, 1980).

45. GLOBUS Model: List of Publications, No Date, GLOBUS Model Folder, Das Wissenschaftszentrum Berlin für Sozialforschung (WZB), Berlin, Germany.

46. Stuart A. Bremer, ed., *Weltmodellstudien: Wachstumsprobleme u. Lösungsmöglichkeiten*, Schriften des Wissenschaftszentrums Berlin (Königstein/Ts.: Hain, 1980), http://www.dandelon.com/isearch/intelligentSEARCH_CLASSICS.nsf/alldocs/C1257680005BA284C125703E0053B967/$File/000000066579.PDF?OpenElement.

47. Mihajli Mesarovic and Eduard Pestel, *Mankind at the Turning Point the Second Report to the Club of Rome* (New York: Reader's Digest Press, 1974), 32–54.

48. Bremer, "Globale Modellierung am Wissenschaftszentrum," 2.

49. Deutsch, "Foreword," xv.

50. Barry Hughes, interview by author, online, November 2, 2022.

51. Bremer, *The Globus Model*, 577–591.

52. Bremer, 23.

53. Bremer, 777.

54. Bremer, 780.

55. Barry Hughes, interview by author, online, November 2, 2022.

56. GLOBUS ran, at least, on a Cray 1M, a Control Data 175, and a Control Data 170–35.

57. GLOBUS Workshop Welcome Package.

58. Peter Brecke, interview by author, online, August 24, 2022.

59. Deutsch, "Foreword," xvii.

60. GLOBUS included Argentina, Brazil, Canada, China, Czechoslovakia, East Germany, Egypt, France, India, Indonesia, Iran, Italy, Japan, Mexico, Nigeria, Pakistan, Poland, Saudia Arabia, South Africa, USSR, Turkey, United Kingdom, United States, Venezuela, and West Germany. Bremer, *The Globus Model*, 25.

61. Ramsauer, "Endogenizing Politics."

62. Bremer, *The Globus Model*, 24.

63. Bremer, 666–667.

64. Bremer, 666–667.

65. Bremer, 5–6.

66. Sharon Ghamari-Tabrizi, "Simulating the Unthinkable: Gaming Future War in the 1950s and 1960s," *Social Studies of Science* 30, no. 2 (2000): 163–223, https://doi.org/10.1177/030631200030002001.

67. Please contact me for a working copy of GLOBUS, as I have successfully recovered all five disks. That quest will probably be another book and a eulogy for my aspirations to be a FORTRAN programmer.

68. John K. Wildgen, "Software Reviews: MICRO GLOBUS: A Computer Model of Long-Term Global Political and Economic Processes Reviewed by John K. Wildgen, University of New Orleans Publisher: Edition Sigma, Heimstr. 14, D-1000 Berlin 61, Federal Republic of Germany (Telephone: 030 693–4396) Year of Publication: 1988 Version Reviewed: 1.0 Materials: Five 5.25-Inch Disks, 307-Page Manual with Index and Appendixes Price: By Arrangement with the Wissenschaftszentrum Berlin Für Sozialforschung, Reichpietschufer 50, D-1000 Berlin 30, Federal Republic of Germany," *Social Science Computer Review* 7, no. 2 (July 1, 1989): 227, https://doi.org/10.1177/089443938900700212.

69. Registered Micro GLOBUS Users Box, Das Wissenschaftszentrum Berlin für Sozialforschung (WZB), Berlin, Germany.

70. Wildgen, "Software Reviews," 227.

71. Barry Hughes, interview by author, online, November 2, 2022.

72. Stuart A. Bremer and Walter Gruhn, *Micro Globus: A Computer Model of Long-Term Global Political and Economic Processes*, 1988, 1–8, https://bibliothek.wzb.eu/fulltext/toc_text/2017/iw-79761.pdf.

73. Peter Brecke, interview by author, online, August 24, 2022.

74. Barry B. Hughes and Glenn Palmer, "Stuart A. Bremer: In Memoriam," *PS—Political Science & Politics* 36, no. 2 (2003): 325.

75. Quoted in Gerald O. Barney, *The Global 2000 Report to the President of the United States* (New York: Pergamon Press, 1980), vii.

76. Barney, *The Global 2000 Report.*

77. Quoted in Michael Lerner et al., "The Influence of Limits to Growth and Global 2000 on U.S. Environmental Governance," *International Journal of Social Science Studies* 4, no. 8 (June 29, 2016): 52–63, https://doi.org/10.11114/ijsss.v4i8.1674.

78. Guetzkow, "Recollections about the Inter-Nation," 465.

79. Ramsauer, "Endogenizing Politics," 14.

80. Ramsauer, 14–15.

81. Sun-ha Hong, "Technofutures in Stasis: Smart Machines, Ubiquitous Computing, and the Future That Keeps Coming Back," *International Journal of Communication* 15, no. 0 (2021): 1941.

82. Hong, "Technofutures in Stasis," 1954.

83. For a comparable point about Jay Forrester's legacy in urban planning, see Kevin Baker, "Model Metropolis," *Logic Magazine*, January 1, 2019, https://logicmag.io/play/model-metropolis/.

84. Robert Schulman, "A World in Flux Means Steady Work for Risk Analysts," *New York Times*, November 4, 1990, sec. Business, https://www.nytimes.com/1990/11/04/business/a-world-in-flux-means-steady-work-for-risk-analysts.html.

85. Paul Erickson, *The World the Game Theorists Made* (University of Chicago Press, 2015), 204.

86. Erickson, *World the Game Theorists Made*, 189–98.

87. Harald Hagemann et al., "Game Theory Modeling for the Cold War on Both Sides of the Iron Curtain," *History of the Human Sciences* 29, no. 4–5 (2016): 99–124, https://doi.org/10.1177/0952695116666012; S. M. Amadae and Bruce Bueno de Mesquita, "The Rochester School: The Origins of Positive Political Theory," *Annual Review of*

Political Science 2, (1999): 269–295, https://doi.org/10.1146/annurev.polisci.2.1.269; Jonathan Cohn, "Irrational Exuberance," *The New Republic*, October 25, 1999, https://newrepublic.com/article/78956/political-science-irrational-exuberance; Stephen M. Walt, "Rigor or Rigor Mortis?: Rational Choice and Security Studies," *International Security* 23, no. 4 (1999): 5–48; Kellie Maske and Garey Durden, "The Contributions and Impact of Professor William H. Riker," *Public Choice* 117, no. 1 (2003): 191–220, https://doi.org/10.1023/A:1026117828869; Iain McLean, "William H. Riker and the Invention of Heresthetic(s)," *British Journal of Political Science* 32, no. 3 (2002): 535–558, https://doi.org/10.1017/S0007123402000224.

88. William D. Coplin, ed., *Simulation in the Study of Politics* (Chicago: Markham, 1968).

89. Harold Guetzkow, "Comment on Andriole, Wilkenfeld, and Hopple: 'A Framework for the Comparative Analysis of Foreign Policy Behavior,'" *International Studies Quarterly* 20, no. 2 (1976): 333, https://doi.org/10.2307/2600122.

90. William D. Coplin and Michael Kent O'Leary, *Everyman's Prince: A Guide to Understanding Your Political Problems* (Belmont, CA: Duxbury Press, 1972), 14.

91. Coplin and O'Leary, *Everyman's Prince*, chap. 3.

92. Coplin and O'Leary, 160.

93. William D. Coplin and Michael Kent O'Leary, *Introduction to Political Risk Analysis* (Croton-on-Hudson, NY: Policy Studies Associates, 1983).

94. Prince's use in the CIA is unclear. Coplin is mentioned in the Agency's public archives, but there are considerable gaps in the public record. The Syracuse University student newspaper lost an eight-year court case to release details about the Agency's covert activities on campus in 1985, a blow to disclosure request. The case did result in eighteen thousand pages of documents involving activities between the university and the Agency. See https://www.cia.gov/readingroom/docs/CIA-RDP90-00806R000200970115-6.pdf.

95. William D. Coplin and Michael Kent O'Leary, *Political Analysis Through the Prince System* (Croton-on-Hudson, NY: Policy Studies Associates, 1983), 1–5.

96. Schulman, "A World in Flux."

97. Frank Uhle, "Frost & Sullivan, Inc.," in *International Directory of Company Histories*, ed. Tina Grant, vol. 43 (Detroit: St. James Press, 2003), 142–144, http://archive.org/details/internationaldir0000unse_v5o3.

98. William D. Coplin and Michael K. O'Leary, *Power Persuasion: A Surefire System to Get Ahead in Business* (Reading, MA: Addison-Wesley, 1985), http://archive.org/details/powerpersuasions00copl.

99. Mark Abdollahian et al., "Senturion: Predictive Political Simulation Model" (Washington, DC: Center for Technology and National Security Policy, National Defense University, 2006), 32.

100. Amadae and Bueno de Mesquita, "The Rochester School."

101. A note of curiosity: Many of the histories in the intelligence agencies attribute the tool's origin to only Bueno de Mesquita despite the three founders listed on the incorporation documents.

102. A. F. K. Organski and Jacek Kugler, *The War Ledger* (Chicago: University of Chicago Press, 1981), https://press.uchicago.edu/ucp/books/book/chicago/W/bo5955354.html.

103. Guetzkow reviewed the book, praising it while ignoring the dramatic differences between his work and Bueno de Mesquita's expected utility approach and, instead, claiming *The War Trap* was part of a trend in which "the glowing promises of the pioneers in quantitative international politics—of the Deutsches, the McClellands, and the Singers—are now being redeemed in hard work undertaken in the construction and testing of substantive models." See Harold Guetzkow, review of *The War Trap*, by Bruce Bueno de Mesquita, *Review of Politics* 44, no. 4 (1982): 627.

104. "Policon Corporation," OpenCorporates, January 12, 2024, https://opencorporates.com/companies/us_mi/800228046.

105. Details about Policon are scarce. Most evidence comes from a declassified article originally published in 1987 in the CIA's private journal, *Studies in Intelligence*. Feder, Stanley A. 2002. "Forecasting for Policy Making in the Post-Cold War Period." *Annual Review of Political Science* 5 (1): 111–25. https://doi.org/10.1146/annurev.polisci.5.102601.115116; Feder, Stanley. 1997. "FACTIONS and Policon: New Ways to Analyze Politics." In *Inside CIA's Private World: Declassified Articles from the Agency's Internal Journal, 1955-1992*, edited by H. Bradford Westerfield. Yale University Press.

106. Rob Johnston, *Analytic Culture in the United States Intelligence Community: An Ethnographic Study* (Washington, DC: Center for the Study of Intelligence, CIA, 2005), 72.

107. Feder, "FACTIONS and Policon: New Ways to Analyze Politics," 274.

108. The report was published by the Joint Military Intelligence College, now the National Intelligence University, originally founded by the Department of Defence in 1963.

109. Russell George Swenson, ed., *Bringing Intelligence About: Practitioners Reflect on Best Practices* (Washington, DC: Joint Military Intelligence College, 2003), 73.

110. Feder, "FACTIONS and Policon: New Ways to Analyze Politics," 275.

111. Feder, 275.

112. The first step of Policon is similar to Prince in this way.

113. It is telling that Policon's calculations came from French mathematician Marquis de Condorcet, who was noted for his faith in mathematics as a precise instrument to understand reality. See Massimo Mazzotti, *Reactionary Mathematics: A Genealogy of Purity* (Chicago: University of Chicago Press, 2023), 20.

114. Feder, "FACTIONS and Policon: New Ways to Analyze Politics," 279.

115. Feder, 284.

116. DECISION INSIGHTS, INCORPORATED, Plaintiff—Appellant, v. SENTIA GROUP, INCORPORATED; THOMAS H. SCOTT; MARK ABDOLLAHIAN; JACEK KUGLER; BRIAN EFIRD, No. 09–2300 (United States Court of Appeals for the Fourth Circuit March 15, 2011).

117. Decision Insights, Incorporated, Plaintiff—Appellant, V. Sentia Group, Incorporated; Thomas H. Scott; Mark Abdollahian; Jacek Kugler; Brian Efird.

118. Bruce Bueno de Mesquita, "A New Model for Predicting Policy Choices: Preliminary Tests," *Conflict Management and Peace Science* 28, no. 1 (2011): 65–87, https://doi.org/10.1177/0738894210388127.

119. Abdollahian et al., "Senturion," 4.

120. Erickson, *World the Game Theorists Made*, 189–198; Pablo Jacovkis and Rodrigo Castro, "Computer-Based Global Models: From Early Experiences to Complex Systems," *Journal of Artificial Societies and Social Simulation* 18, no. 1 (2015): 13"; Rainer Hegselmann, "Thomas C. Schelling and James M. Sakoda: The Intellectual, Technical, and Social History of a Model," *Journal of Artificial Societies and Social Simulation* 20, no. 3 (2017): 15, https://doi.org/10.18564/jasss.3511.

121. Philip Mirowski, *Machine Dreams: Economics Becomes a Cyborg Science* (Cambridge, UK: Cambridge University Press, 2002).

122. Stuart A. Bremer, "Computer Modeling in Global and International Relations: The State of the Art," *Social Science Computer Review* 7, no. 4 (1989): n3, https://doi.org/10.1177/089443938900700406.

123. Bruce Bueno de Mesquita, *The Invention of Power: Popes, Kings, and the Birth of the West* (New York: PublicAffairs, 2022).

124. "Integrated Crisis Early Warning System," Lockheed Martin, accessed September 5, 2023, https://www.lockheedmartin.com/en-us/capabilities/research-labs/advanced-technology-labs/icews.html.

125. Rohde, "Pax Technologica," 812.

126. Sean P. O'Brien, "Crisis Early Warning and Decision Support: Contemporary Approaches and Thoughts on Future Research," *International Studies Review* 12, no. 1 (2010): 93.

127. Jim Gasperini, interview by author, online, May 11, 2020.

128. Dorfman quoted in Jim Gasperini, "The Political Subtext of Computer Games," *Journal of Computer Game Design*, October 1989, http://www.erasmatazz.com/library/the-journal-of-computer/jcgd-volume-3/volume-3-number-1-octoberno.html.

129. Jim Gasperini, interview by author, online, May 11, 2020.

130. Jim Gasperini, "Culture, Idealism, and the Real World," *Journal of Computer Game Design*, May 1989, http://www.erasmatazz.com/library/the-journal-of-computer/jcgd-volume-2/volume-2-number-4-aprilmay.html.

131. Jim Gasperini, interview by author, online, May 11, 2020.

132. Gasperini's also influenced the *Sim City* game discussed by Kevin Baker. See Baker, "Model Metropolis."

133. *Suzanne Seggerman Interview*, 2008, https://www.youtube.com/watch?v=JIkjmSt-gYo.

Chapter 9

1. Norbert Wiener, *God & Golem, Inc.: A Comment on Certain Points Where Cybernetics Impinges on Religion* (Cambridge: MIT Press, 1964), 24–25.

2. Wiener, *God & Golem*, 17.

3. Wiener, 87–89.

4. While Weiner had fellow critics of game theory and computation, I want to highlight that these concerns are contemporary as well. My guide has been looking at what communications scholar Alessandra Renzi described as countermodeling. Describing citizen-led mobilization against formal urban plans in Jakarta, Renzi explains that these formal modelling plans "seal[ed] the separation between the kota, the planned city, and the kampung, its informal counterpart." This separation can be both the way that the *kota* diverges from the *kampung*, not unlike Vietnamese villagers modeled in simulations in the last chapters. There is also a politics of agency, not only how residents of kampung are both presented in the kota, but their access to the kota and how the model stands in for their own agency in the planning process. Thinking along these lines, to Renzi, is a "politics of counter-modelling" that "not only plays out at the level of the prototype (the new design for the kampung) but also at the level of the system, reorganizing the potential of the kampung to produce potential." Far from the kampung, countermodeling introduces how to

think about the computational imaginary of politics to its limits and other ways to work within its domain. For more, see Alessandra Renzi, "Entangled Data: Modelling and Resistance in the Megacity," Online Open, February 20, 2017, https://onlineopen.org/entangled-data-modelling-and-resistance-in-the-megacity.

5. Calvin Tomkins, "Buckminster Fuller, Intellectual Outlaw," *The New Yorker*, January 8, 1966.

6. Elizabeth Kolbert, "Dymaxion Man," *The New Yorker*, June 9, 2008.

7. Quoted in Donella H. Meadows and J. M. Robinson, *The Electronic Oracle: Computer Models and Social Decisions* (Chichester, UK: Wiley, 1985), 1.

8. Buckminister Fuller, "World Game," Smithsonian Folkways Recordings, accessed March 16, 2021, https://folkways.si.edu/r-buckminster-fuller/world-game/oral-history-biography/track/smithsonian.

9. The whole magazine is available online thanks to Google Books: https://books.google.ca/books?id=WlEEAAAAMBAJ&q=March+1,+1943+Life&pg=PA41&redir_esc=y#v=snippet&q=March%201%2C%201943%20Life&f=false.

10. Tim Stott, *Buckminster Fuller's World Game and Its Legacy*, Routledge Focus on Art History and Visual Studies (New York: Routledge, 2021), 5.

11. Orit Halpern, *Beautiful Data: A History of Vision and Reason Since 1945*, Experimental Futures (Durham, NC: Duke University Press, 2014).

12. Jonathan Massey, "Buckminster Fuller's Cybernetic Pastoral: The United States Pavilion at Expo 67," *Journal of Architecture* 21, no. 5 (2016): 795–815, https://doi.org/10.1080/13602365.2016.1207433; Janine Marchessault, *Ecstatic Worlds: Media, Utopias, Ecologies*, Leonardo Book Series (Cambridge, MA: MIT Press, 2017).

13. Massey, "Buckminster Fuller's Cybernetic Pastoral," 808.

14. Marchessault, *Ecstatic Worlds*, 212.

15. Medard Gabel, interview by author, online, October 13, 2020.

16. US Congress Senate Government Operations, *Establish a Select Senate Committee on Technology and the Human Environment: Hearings Before the Subcommittee on Intergovernmental Relations . . . 91–1, on S. Res. 78, March 4–6, April 24, and May 7, 1969*, 1969, 3.

17. Sylvia Doughty Fries, "Expertise Against Politics: Technology as Ideology on Capitol Hill, 1966–1972," *Science, Technology, & Human Values* 8, no. 2 (1983): 6–15.

18. Medard Gabel, interview by author, online, October 13, 2020.

19. Fred Turner, *From Counterculture to Cyberculture: Stewart Brand, the Whole Earth Network, and the Rise of Digital Utopianism* (Chicago: University of Chicago Press, 2006).

20. Fred Turner, "Why Study New Games?," *Games and Culture* 1, no. 1 (2006): 108, https://doi.org/10.1177/1555412005281823..

21. Turner, "Why Study New Games?," 109.

22. Medard Gabel, interview by author, online, October 13, 2020.

23. Medard Gabel, interview by author, online, October 13, 2020.

24. Medard Gabel, "Global Recall and Networld Game: Global Access to Global Model," in *Integrated Global Models of Sustainable Development*, vol. 1, *World3 and Strategem: History, Goals, Assumptions, Implications*, ed. Akira Onishi, vol. 3, (Oxford: Eolss, 2009); Howard A. Kurtz, "Software Reviews: Global Recall," *Social Science Computer Review* 9, no. 2 (1991): 338–339, https://doi.org/10.1177/089443939100900214.

25. Turner, *From Counterculture to Cyberculture*.

26. Jenny Andersson, *The Future of the World: Futurology, Futurists, and the Struggle for the Post Cold War Imagination* (Oxford: Oxford University Press, 2018), 168–70.

27. Richard A. Falk, *A Study of Future Worlds* (New York: Simon and Schuster, 1975), 7.

28. Falk, *Study of Future Worlds*, 7.

29. For an excellent history of WOMP, see Aaron McKeil, "Revisiting the World Order Models Project: A Case for Renewal?," *Global Policy* 13, no. 4 (2022): 417–426, https://doi.org/10.1111/1758-5899.13070.

30. James A. Yunker, *The Idea of World Government: From Ancient Times to the Twenty-First Century* (New York: Taylor & Francis, 2011); Thomas G. Weiss, "What Happened to the Idea of World Government," *International Studies Quarterly* 53, no. 2 (2009): 253–271, https://doi.org/10.1111/j.1468-2478.2009.00533.x.

31. Israel Shenker, "World Federalist Group Marks 30th Year and Tries to Put It All Together," *New York Times*, August 1, 1977, sec. Archives, https://www.nytimes.com/1977/08/01/archives/world-federalist-group-marks-30th-year-and-tries-to-put-it-all.html.

32. Grenville Clark, "The Dublin Declaration," *World Affairs* 108, no. 4 (1945): 265–270.

33. Richard A. Falk, *Public Intellectual: The Life of a Citizen Pilgrim* (Atlanta: Clarity Press, 2021).

34. World Policy Institute, "History: World Policy," 2018, https://web.archive.org/web/20210303080407/http://worldpolicy.org/about_us/history/.

35. Falk, *Public Intellectual*.

36. George A. Lipsky, "The Theory of International Relations of Harold D. Lasswell," *Journal of Politics* 17, no. 1 (1955): 43–58, https://doi.org/10.2307/2126403.

37. Richard Falk, interview by author, online, May 10, 2021.

38. Cord Meyer, *Facing Reality: From World Federalism to the CIA* (New York: Harper & Row, 1980), http://archive.org/details/facingrealityfro00meye.

39. Falk, *Public Intellectual.*

40. Daniel Ellsberg, *The Doomsday Machine: Confessions of a Nuclear War Planner* (New York: Bloomsbury USA, 2017), 8.

41. Richard Falk, interview by author, online, May 10, 2021.

42. Harold D. Lasswell, "The Promise of the World Order Modelling Movement," *World Politics* 29, no. 3 (1977): 425, https://doi.org/10.2307/2010004.

43. Richard A. Falk and Saul H. Mendlovitz, eds., "The Problem, the Plan, and Some Preliminary Considerations," in *The Strategy of World Order* (New York: World Law Fund, 1966), 1, http://archive.org/details/strategyofworldo01falk.

44. Saul Mendlovitz, "General Introduction," in *A Study of Future Worlds* (New York: Simon and Schuster, 1975), xvii–xxvii.

45. Richard Falk, interview by author, online, May 10, 2021.

46. Rajni Kothari, *Footsteps into the Future: Diagnosis of the Present World and a Design for an Alternative* (New York: Free Press, 1975), http://archive.org/details/footstepsintofut00rajn.

47. Ali Al'Amin Mazrui, *A World Federation of Cultures: An African Perspective* (New York: Free Press, 1976), 495, http://archive.org/details/worldfederationo00mazr.

48. Falk, *A Study of Future Worlds*, 7.

49. Paul N. Edwards, *A Vast Machine: Computer Models, Climate Data, and the Politics of Global Warming* (Cambridge, MA: MIT Press, 2010), 251.

50. Richard Falk, interview by author, online, May 10, 2021.

51. Myres S. McDougal et al., "The Intelligence Function and World Public Order," *Temple Law Quarterly* 46, no. 3 (1973): 365–449; Lasswell, "Promise of the World Order."

52. Richard Falk, "The World Order Models Project and Its Critics: A Reply," *International Organization* 32, no. 2 (1978): 532.

53. Tom J. Farer, "The Greening of the Globe: A Preliminary Appraisal of the World Order Models Project: (WOMP)," *International Organization* 31, no. 1 (1977): 130.

54. Richard Falk, interview by author, online, May 10, 2021.

55. Aaron McKeil, "Revisiting the World Order Models Project: A Case for Renewal?," *Global Policy* 13, no. 4 (2022): 417–426, https://doi.org/10.1111/1758-5899.13070.

56. For example, Walidah Imarisha et al., eds., *Octavia's Brood: Science Fiction Stories from Social Justice Movements* (Oakland, CA: AK Press, 2015).

57. Wendy Hui Kyong Chun, "On Hypo-Real Models or Global Climate Change: A Challenge for the Humanities," *Critical Inquiry* 41, no. 3 (2015): 703, https://doi.org/10.1086/680090.

58. Nick Srnicek and Alex Williams, *Inventing the Future: Postcapitalism and a World Without Work* (New York: Verso, 2015).

59. Fredric Jameson, *Valences of the Dialectic* (London: Verso, 2010), 415.

60. Jameson, *Valences of the Dialectic*, 434.

61. Louise Amoore, *Cloud Ethics: Algorithms and the Attributes of Ourselves and Others* (Durham, NC: Duke University Press, 2020), 158.

62. Jim Gasperini, "The Political Subtext of Computer Games," *Journal of Computer Game Design*, October 1989, http://www.erasmatazz.com/library/the-journal-of-computer/jcgd-volume-3/volume-3-number-1-octoberno.html.

63. Ian Bogost, *Persuasive Games: The Expressive Power of Videogames* (Cambridge, MA: MIT Press, 2007).

64. Timothy M. Lenton et al., "Life on Earth Is Hard to Spot," *Anthropocene Review* 7, no. 3 (2020): 249, https://doi.org/10.1177/2053019620918939.

65. Lenton et al., "Life on Earth," 249.

66. Amoore, *Cloud Ethics*, 166.

67. Amoore, 171.

68. Amoore, 172.

69. Harvey, Samantha. *Orbital*. Grove Press, 2023.

Chapter 10

1. Some of my inspiration includes Johannes Bruder and Orit Halpern, "Optimal Brain Damage: Theorizing Our Nervous Present," *Culture Machine* (blog), September 5, 2021, https://culturemachine.net/vol-20-machine-intelligences/optimal-brain-damage-theorizing-the-nervous-present-johannes-bruder-orit-halpern/; Fenwick McKelvey and Jonathan Roberge, "Recursive Power," in *Handbook of Critical Studies of Artificial Intelligence*, ed. Simon Lindgren (Northampton, UK: Edward Elgar, 2023), 21–32; Louise Amoore et al., "A World Model: On the Political Logics of Generative AI," *Political Geography* 113 (2024): 1, https://doi.org/10.1016/j.polgeo.2024.103134; Lucy Suchman, "Imaginaries of Omniscience: Automating Intelligence in the US Department of Defense," *Social Studies of Science*, 53, no. 5 (2022): 030631272211049,

https://doi.org/10.1177/03063127221104938; Mike Ananny, "Making Generative Artificial Intelligence a Public Problem. Seeing Publics and Sociotechnical Problem-Making in Three Scenes of AI Failure," *Javnost—The Public* 31, no. 1 (2024): 89–105, https://doi.org/10.1080/13183222.2024.2319000.

2. Jungsuk Han et al., "A Review of DAO Governance: Recent Literature and Emerging Trends," *Journal of Corporate Finance* 91 (2025): 102734, https://doi.org/10.1016/j.jcorpfin.2025.102734.

3. Neil Sahota, "The AI Factor in Political Campaigns: Revolutionizing Modern Politics," *Forbes*, January 12, 2024, https://www.forbes.com/sites/neilsahota/2024/01/12/the-ai-factor-in-political-campaigns-revolutionizing-modern-politics/.

4. "CulturePulse," accessed February 7, 2024, https://www.culturepulse.ai/; David Gilbert, "The UN Hired an AI Company to Untangle the Israeli-Palestinian Crisis," *Wired*, November 2, 2023, https://www.wired.com/story/culturepulse-ai-israeli-palestinian-crisis/.

5. Sasha Issenberg, "Project Narwhal: How a Top-Secret Obama Campaign Program Could Change the 2012 Race," *Slate Magazine*, February 15, 2012, http://www.slate.com/articles/news_and_politics/victory_lab/2012/02/project_narwhal_how_a_top_secret_obama_campaign_program_could_change_the_2012_race_.single.html.

6. Suchman, "Imaginaries of Omniscience," 19.

7. Rachel Boynton. *Our Brand Is Crisis*, Documentary (Boynton Films Production, British Broadcasting Corporation (BBC), Films Transit International, 2005); Christian Schafferer, "The Globalization of Political Marketing: An Introduction," in *Election Campaigning in East and Southeast Asia* (Routledge, 2006).

8. Author Katharine Dommett et al., *Data-Driven Campaigning and Political Parties: Five Advanced Democracies Compared*, Journalism and Political Communication Unbound (Oxford: Oxford University Press, 2024); Fenwick McKelvey and Jill Piebiak, "Porting the Political Campaign: The NationBuilder Platform and the Global Flows of Political Technology," *New Media & Society* 20, no. 3 (2018): 901–918, https://doi.org/10.1177/1461444816675439.

9. Eitan D. Hersh, *Hacking the Electorate: How Campaigns Perceive Voters* (New York: Cambridge University Press, 2015).

10. Manan Ahmed Asif, "Technologies of Power: From Area Studies to Data Sciences," *Spheres: Journal for Digital Cultures* 5 (2019), http://spheres-journal.org/technologies-of-power-from-area-studies-to-data-sciences/; Joy Rohde, "Pax Technologica: Computers, International Affairs, and Human Reason in the Cold War," *Isis* 108, no. 4 (2017): 792–813, https://doi.org/10.1086/695679.

11. Michael C. Desch, *Cult of the Irrelevant: The Waning Influence of Social Science on National Security* (Princeton, NJ: Princeton University Press, 2019), 241, http://muse.jhu.edu/book/62654.

12. William McKibben, "The End of Nature," *The New Yorker*, September 3, 1989, https://www.newyorker.com/magazine/1989/09/11/the-end-of-nature.

13. I will leave this comment as an endnote for fear of having to write another book. Modeling's trading zone—treating all computational approaches as similar—seems to have led to scientific climate models being *politically* dismissed as akin to political models based on expert opinions. The specificity of models—indeed, the strangeness of political modeling—must stand distinct from other attempts at modeling. Now, I am often left wondering what would have happened to modeling if it had not tried to cross into the unfathomable waters of politics, if it did not stretch so far.

14. Sarah T. Roberts and Mél Hogan, "Left Behind: Futurist Fetishists, Prepping and the Abandonment of Earth," *B2o: An Online Journal* 4, no. 2 (2019), https://escholarship.org/uc/item/8sr8n99w.

15. Whether a government agency used computer simulation to plot the coup against Allende is a contested historical point. One of its designers alleges a tool was used. See Daniel del Solar, "How We Planned a Coup," *Berkeley Bard*, September 14, 1973.

16. Carlos Eduardo Martins, "Herrera, Amílcar," in *Enciclopédia Latinoamericana*, July 8, 2017, https://latinoamericana.wiki.br/es/entradas/h/herrera-amilcar; Eden Medina, *Cybernetic Revolutionaries: Technology and Politics in Allende's Chile* (Cambridge, MA: MIT Press, 2011).

17. Desch, *Cult of the Irrelevant.*

18. Asif, "Technologies of Power."

19. Andrew Pickering, "Cyborg History and the World War II Regime," *Perspectives on Science* 3, no. 1 (1995): 1–48; Donna J. Haraway, "Manifesto for Cyborgs: Science, Technology, and Socialist Feminism in the 1980s," *Socialist Review*, no. 80 (1985): 65–108; Philip Mirowski, *Machine Dreams: Economics Becomes a Cyborg Science* (Cambridge, UK: Cambridge University Press, 2002).

20. Erving Goffman, "On Cooling the Mark Out," *Psychiatry* 15, no. 4 (1952): 451–463, https://doi.org/10.1080/00332747.1952.11022896.

21. Erving Goffman, *The Presentation of Self in Everyday Life* (Garden City, NY: Doubleday, 1959), 88.

22. Heather Timmons, "If Cambridge Analytica Is So Smart, Why Isn't Ted Cruz President?," Quartz, March 21, 2018, https://qz.com/1234364/cambridge-analytica-worked-for-mercer-backed-ted-cruz-before-trump.

23. Michael L. Butterworth, "Nate Silver and Campaign 2012: Sport, the Statistical Frame, and the Rhetoric of Electoral Forecasting," *Journal of Communication* 64, no. 5 (2014): 895–914, https://doi.org/10.1111/jcom.12113.

24. Carol Cohn, "Sex and Death in the Rational World of Defense Intellectuals," *Signs* 12, no. 4 (1987): 687–718.

25. Suchman, "Imaginaries of Omniscience," 19.

26. See: https://forensic-architecture.org/.

27. Vincent Mosco, *The Digital Sublime: Myth, Power, and Cyberspace* (Cambridge, MA: MIT Press, 2004); Daniel Kreiss, "The 2012 Obama Campaign, the Technological Sublime, and the Limits of Big Data," *Culture Digitally* (blog), February 18, 2012, http://culturedigitally.org/2012/02/the-2012-obama-campaign-the-technological-sublime-and-the-limits-of-big-data/; David E. Nye, *American Technological Sublime* (Cambridge, MA: MIT Press, 1994); James W. Carey and John J. Quick, "The Mythos of the Electronic Revolution," *American Scholar* 39, no. 3 (1970): 395–424

28. Paolo Gerbaudo, *The Digital Party: Political Organisation and Online Democracy* (London: Pluto Press, 2019).

29. Patrick Burkart, *Pirate Politics: The New Information Policy Contests* (Cambridge: MIT Press, 2014).

30. Adi Robertson, "They Spent $3 Million on a Dune Script Bible: Now What?," The Verge, February 28, 2022, https://www.theverge.com/2022/2/28/22950868/spice-dao-crypto-jodorowsky-dune-bible-collective-writing-contest.

31. Louise Amoore, *Cloud Ethics: Algorithms and the Attributes of Ourselves and Others* (Durham, NC: Duke University Press, 2020), 110.

32. Beth Coleman, "Technology of the Surround," *Catalyst: Feminism, Theory, Technoscience* 7, no. 2 (2021): 11, https://doi.org/10.28968/cftt.v7i2.35973.

33. Coleman, "Technology of the Surround," 10.

34. Richard K. Ashley, "The Eye of Power: The Politics of World Modeling," *International Organization* 37, no. 3 (1983): 529–530, https://doi.org/10.1017/S0020818300032768.

35. Marc Andreessen, "The Techno-Optimist Manifesto," Andreessen Horowitz, October 16, 2023, https://a16z.com/the-techno-optimist-manifesto/.

36. Coleman, "Technology of the Surround," 11.

37. Coleman, 11.

38. Jason Edward Lewis et al., "Making Kin with the Machines," *Journal of Design and Science*, July 16, 2018, https://doi.org/10.21428/bfafd97b.

39. Lewis et al., "Making Kin."

40. Claude Lefort, *Democracy and Political Theory*, trans. David Macey (Oxford: Polity, 1988), 17.

41. I am directly thinking with and around theories of posthuman democracy best popularized by Bruno Latour and Isabel Stengers. See Bruno Latour, *Politics of Nature: How to Bring the Sciences into Democracy* (Cambridge: Harvard University Press, 2004);

Isabelle Stengers, "Including Nonhumans in Political Theory: Opening Pandora's Box?," in *Political Matter*, ed. Bruce Braun and Sarah J. Whatmore (Minneapolis: University of Minnesota Press, 2010), 3–34; John Cheney-Lippold, *We Are Data: Algorithms and the Making of Our Digital Selves* (New York: New York University Press, 2017).

42. Jason Edward Lewis et al., "Making Kin with the Machines," *Journal of Design and Science* 3 (2018): 687, https://doi.org/10.21428/bfafd97b.

43. Amoore, *Cloud Ethics*, 158.

44. Lewis et al., "Making Kin."

45. I am building on Paul Patton's conclusion that Deleuzian possibilities invite the encounters with decolonial and indigenous epistemologies. Paul Patton, *Deleuze and the Political* (London: Routledge, 2000).

46. Lewis et al., "Making Kin."

47. Andrew Culp, *Dark Deleuze* (Minneapolis: University of Minnesota Press, 2016).

48. Fredric Jameson, *Valences of the Dialectic* (London: Verso, 2010), 434.

49. Jorge Luis Borges, "Of Exactitude in Science," in *A Universal History of Infamy*, ed. Jorge Luis Borges (New York: Dutton, 1972), 141.

Bibliography

Abdollahian, Mark, Michael Baranick, Brian Efird, and Jacek J. Kugler. "Senturion: Predictive Political Simulation Model." Washington, DC: Center for Technology and National Security Policy, National Defense University, 2006.

Abt, Clark C. *Serious Games*. New York: Viking Press, 1970.

Acland, Charles R. *American Blockbuster: Movies, Technology, and Wonder*. Duke University Press, 2020. https://doi.org/10.1215/9781478012160.

Agar, Jon. *The Government Machine: A Revolutionary History of the Computer*. History of Computing. Cambridge, MA: MIT Press, 2003.

Alker, Hayward R. "Global Modeling Alternatives: The First Twenty Years." In *Theories, Models, and Simulations in International Relations: Essays and Research in Honor of Harold Guetzkow*, edited by Michael D. Ward, 9–38. Boulder, CO: Westview Press, 1985.

Alker, Hayward R., Karl Wolfgang Deutsch, and Antoine Stoezel, eds. *Mathematical Approaches to Politics*. San Francisco: Jossey-Bass, 1973.

Alker, Hayward R., and Ann Tickner. "Some Issues Raised by Previous Models." In *Problems of World Modeling: Political and Social Implications*, edited by Karl Wolfgang Deutsch, Bruno Fritsch, Hélio Jaguaribe, and Andrei S Markovits, 17–32. Cambridge, MA: Ballinger, 1977.

Alker, Hayward, Jr. "From Political Cybernetics to Global Modeling." In *From National Development to Global Community: Essays in Honor of Karl W. Deutsch*, edited by Richard L. Merritt and Bruce M. Russett, 353–378. London: Allen & Unwin, 1981.

Alker, Hayward, Jr. and Ronald D. Brunner. "Simulating International Conflict: A Comparison of Three Approaches." *International Studies Quarterly* 13, no. 1 (1969): 70. https://doi.org/10.2307/3013481.

Allen, T. "The Evolution of Wargaming: From Chessboard to Marine Doom." *War and Games* 3 (2002): 231.

Amadae, S. M. *Prisoners of Reason: Game Theory and Neoliberal Political Economy*, reprint edition. New York: Cambridge University Press, 2016.

Amadae, S. M. *Rationalizing Capitalist Democracy: The Cold War Origins of Rational Choice Liberalism.* Chicago: University of Chicago Press, 2003.

Amadae, S. M., and Bruce Bueno de Mesquita. "The Rochester School: The Origins of Positive Political Theory." *Annual Review of Political Science* 2 (1999): 269–295. https://doi.org/10.1146/annurev.polisci.2.1.269.

Amoore, Louise. *Cloud Ethics: Algorithms and the Attributes of Ourselves and Others.* Durham, NC: Duke University Press, 2020.

Amoore, Louise. "Machine Learning Political Orders." *Review of International Studies*, 49, no. 1 (2023), 1–17. https://doi.org/10.1017/S0260210522000031.

Amoore, Louise, Alexander Campolo, Benjamin Jacobsen, and Ludovico Rella. "A World Model: On the Political Logics of Generative AI." *Political Geography* 113 (2024): 103134. https://doi.org/10.1016/j.polgeo.2024.103134.

Ananny, Mike. "Making Generative Artificial Intelligence a Public Problem. Seeing Publics and Sociotechnical Problem-Making in Three Scenes of AI Failure." *Javnost—The Public* 31, no. 1 (2024): 89–105. https://doi.org/10.1080/13183222.2024.2319000.

Anderson, C. W. *Apostles of Certainty: Data Journalism and the Politics of Doubt.* Oxford Studies in Digital Politics. New York: Oxford University Press, 2018.

Anderson, H. L. "Scientific Uses of the MANIAC." *Journal of Statistical Physics* 43, no. 5 (1986): 731–748. https://doi.org/10.1007/BF02628301.

Andersson, Jenny. "The Future of the Western World: The OECD and the Interfutures Project." *Journal of Global History* 14, no. 1 (2019): 126–144. https://doi.org/10.1017/S1740022818000384.

Andersson, Jenny. *The Future of the World: Futurology, Futurists, and the Struggle for the Post Cold War Imagination.* Oxford: Oxford University Press, 2018.

Andreessen, Marc. "The Techno-Optimist Manifesto." Andreessen Horowitz. October 16, 2023. https://a16z.com/the-techno-optimist-manifesto/.

Andriole, Stephen J., Jonathan Wilkenfeld, and Gerald W. Hopple. "A Framework for the Comparative Analysis of Foreign Policy Behavior." *International Studies Quarterly* 19, no. 2 (1975): 160–198. https://doi.org/10.2307/2600267.

Andriole, Stephen J., and Robert A. Young. "Toward the Development of an Integrated Crisis Warning System." *International Studies Quarterly* 21, no. 1 (1977): 107–150. https://doi.org/10.2307/2600149.

Ashley, Richard K. "The Eye of Power: The Politics of World Modeling." *International Organization* 37, no. 3 (1983): 495–535. https://doi.org/10.1017/S0020818300032768.

Asif, Manan Ahmed. "Technologies of Power: From Area Studies to Data Sciences." *Spheres: Journal for Digital Cultures* 5 (2019). http://spheres-journal.org/technologies-of-power-from-area-studies-to-data-sciences/.

Atanasoski, Neda, and Kalindi Vora. *Surrogate Humanity: Race, Robots, and the Politics of Technological Futures*. Perverse Modernities. Durham, NC: Duke University Press, 2019.

Atlas, Mark. "Gambling with Elections: The Problems of Geodemographics." *Campaigns & Elections*, 1981.

Azar, Edward E. "The Conflict and Peace Data Bank (COPDAB) Project." *Journal of Conflict Resolution* 24, no. 1 (1980): 143–152. https://doi.org/10.1177/002200278002400106.

Baker, Kevin. "Model Metropolis." *Logic Magazine*, January 1, 2019. https://logicmag.io/play/model-metropolis/.

Baldwin-Philippi, Jessica. "Data Campaigning: Between Empirics and Assumptions." *Internet Policy Review* 8, no. 4 (2019): 1–18. https://doi.org/10.14763/2019.4.1437.

Baldwin-Philippi, Jessica. "The Myths of Data-Driven Campaigning." *Political Communication* 34, no. 4 (2017): 627–633. https://doi.org/10.1080/10584609.2017.1372999.

Baldwin-Philippi, Jessica. *Using Technology, Building Democracy: Digital Campaigning and the Construction of Citizenship*. Oxford: Oxford University Press, 2015.

Ball, Moya A. *Vietnam-on-the-Potomac*. New York: Praeger, 1992.

Barabba, Vincent. "Basic Information Systems: P.I.P.S." In *The New Style in Election Campaigns*, edited by Robert Agranoff, 224–236. Boston: Holbrook Press, 1972.

Barabba, Vincent. "Oral History." Interview by Barbara Milton and David Pemberton, August 7, 1983. https://www2.census.gov/prod2/2003pubs/oh-Barabba.pdf.

Barber, Benjamin R. "The Politics of Political Science: 'Value-Free' Theory and the Wolin–Strauss Dust-Up of 1963." *American Political Science Review* 100, no. 4 (2006): 539–545.

Barkan, Joel D., and James E. Bruno. "Operations Research in Planning Political Campaign Strategies." *Operations Research* 20, no. 5 (1972): 925–941.

Barney, Gerald O. *The Global 2000 Report to the President of the United States*. New York: Pergamon Press, 1980.

Barrow, Clyde W. "The Intellectual Origins of New Political Science." *New Political Science* 30, no. 2 (2008): 215–244. https://doi.org/10.1080/07393140802082598.

Barrow, Clyde W. "The Political and Intellectual Origins of New Political Science." *New Political Science* 39, no. 4 (2017): 437–472. https://doi.org/10.1080/07393148.2017.1378297.

Bartels, Larry M. "The Study of Electoral Behavior." In *The Oxford Handbook of American Elections and Political Behavior*, edited by Jan E. Leighley and George C. Edwards III, 239–261. Oxford: Oxford University Press, 2010.

Baudrillard, Jean. *Simulacra and Simulation*. Cambridge, MA: Semiotext (e), 1983.

Beal, Richard Smith. *Systems Analysis of International Crises*. Washington, DC: University Press of America, 1979. http://archive.org/details/systemsanalysiso0000beal.

Beal, Richard Smith. "Systems Analysis of International Crisis: Event Analysis of Nine Pre-Crisis Threat Situations, 1948–1962." PhD diss., University of Southern California, 1977. https://www.proquest.com/pqdtglobal/docview/1645432592/citation/FE8D37E95A504A4APQ/2.

Bean, Louis H. *How to Predict Elections*. New York: A.A. Knopf, 1948.

Benjamin, Ruha. *Race After Technology: Abolitionist Tools for the New Jim Code*. Medford, MA: Polity, 2019.

Benson, Oliver. "A Simple Diplomatic Game." In *International Politics and Foreign Policy: A Reader in Research and Theory*, edited by James N. Rosenau, 504–511. New York: Free Press, 1961.

Ben-Yehuda, Hemda. *All the World's a Stage: The Theater of Political Simulations*. International Studies Intensives. New York: Routledge, 2021.

Berelson, Bernard. *Content Analysis in Communication Research*. Content Analysis in Communication Research. New York: Free Press, 1952.

Berelson, Bernard R., Paul F. Lazarsfeld, and William N. McPhee. *Voting: A Study of Opinion Formation in a Presidential Campaign*. Chicago: University of Chicago Press, 1954.

Bessner, Daniel. *Democracy in Exile: Hans Speier and the Rise of the Defense Intellectual*. Ithaca, NY: Cornell University Press, 2018.

Beville, Hugh Malcolm. *Audience Ratings: Radio, Television, and Cable*. Hillsdale, NJ: Lawrence Erlbaum Associates, 1988.

Blanchard, Elodie Vieille. "Modelling the Future: An Overview of the 'Limits to Growth' Debate." *Centaurus* 52, no. 2 (2010): 91–116. https://doi.org/10.1111/j.1600-0498.2010.00173.x.

Bloomfield, Lincoln P., and Norman J. Padelford. "Teaching Note: Three Experiments in Political Gaming." *American Political Science Review* 53, no. 4 (1959): 1105–1115. https://doi.org/10.2307/1952078.

Blumenthal, Sidney. "Marketing the President." *New York Times*, September 13, 1981.

Bock, Hans-Hermann. "Clustering Methods: A History of k-Means Algorithms." In *Selected Contributions in Data Analysis and Classification*, edited by Paula Brito, Guy

Cucumel, Patrice Bertrand, and Francisco de Carvalho, 161–172. Studies in Classification, Data Analysis, and Knowledge Organization. Berlin: Springer, 2007. https://doi.org/10.1007/978-3-540-73560-1_15.

Bogost, Ian. *Persuasive Games: The Expressive Power of Videogames*. Cambridge, MA: MIT Press, 2007.

Bohrnstedt, George W. "Borgatta, Edgar F." In *SAGE Research Methods Foundations*, edited by Paul Atkinson, Sara Delamont, Alexandru Cernat, Joseph W. Sakshaug, and Richard A. Williams. London: SAGE, 2020. https://doi.org/10.4135/9781526421036926258.

Bone, Hugh A. "Campaign Methods of Today." *Annals of the American Academy of Political and Social Science* 283, no. 1 (1952): 127–140. https://doi.org/10.1177/000271625228300115.

Boocock, Sarane S. "An Experimental Study of the Learning Effects of Two Games with Simulated Environments." *American Behavioral Scientist* 10, no. 2 (1966): 8–17. https://doi.org/10.1177/000276426601000203.

Boocock, Sarane S., and James S. Coleman. "Games with Simulated Environments in Learning." *Sociology of Education* 39, no. 3 (1966): 215. https://doi.org/10.2307/2111969.

Borgatta, Edgar F. "The Coincidence of Subtests in Four Personality Inventories." *Journal of Social Psychology* 56, no. 2 (1962): 227–244. https://doi.org/10.1080/00224545.1962.9919393.

Borgatta, Edgar F. "Mood, Personality, and Interaction." *Journal of General Psychology* 64, no. 1 (1961): 105–137. https://doi.org/10.1080/00221309.1961.9920431.

Borgatta, Edgar F., and Robert F. Bales. "Interaction of Individuals in Reconstituted Groups." *Sociometry* 16, no. 4 (1953): 302. https://doi.org/10.2307/2785935.

Borges, Jorge Luis. "Of Exactitude in Science." In *A Universal History of Infamy*, edited by Jorge Luis Borges, 141. New York: Dutton, 1972.

Bostrom, Nick. "Are You Living in a Computer Simulation?" *Philosophical Quarterly* 53, no. 211 (2003): 243–255.

Boynton, Rachel. *Our Brand Is Crisis*. Documentary. Boynton Films Production, British Broadcasting Corporation (BBC), Films Transit International, 2005.

Braman, Sandra. *Change of State: Information, Policy, and Power*. Cambridge, MA: MIT Press, 2007.

Brecke, Peter. "The Soviet Global Model: SIMIGDP." *Simulation & Gaming*, August 18, 2016. https://doi.org/10.1177/1046878195261002.

Bremer, Stuart. "Globale Modellierung am Wissenschaftszentrum." IIVG/pre 80–124. Berlin: Wissenschaftszentrum Berlin für Sozialforschung, 1980.

Bremer, Stuart A. "Computer Modeling in Global and International Relations: The State of the Art." *Social Science Computer Review* 7, no. 4 (1989): 459–478. https://doi.org/10.1177/089443938900700406.

Bremer, Stuart A., ed. *The Globus Model: Computer Simulation of Worldwide Political and Economic Developments*. Boulder, CO: Westview Press, 1987. https://public.ebookcentral.proquest.com/choice/publicfullrecord.aspx?p=5893287.

Bremer, Stuart A. *Simulated Worlds*. Princeton, NJ: Princeton University Press, 1977.

Bremer, Stuart A., ed. *Weltmodellstudien: Wachstumsprobleme u. Lösungsmöglichkeiten*. Schriften des Wissenschaftszentrums Berlin. Königstein/Ts.: Hain, 1980. http://www.dandelon.com/isearch/intelligentSEARCH_CLASSICS.nsf/alldocs/C1257680005BA284C125703E0053B967/$File/000000066579.PDF?OpenElement.

Bremer, Stuart A., and Karl W. Deutsch, eds. "Foreword." In *The Globus Model: Computer Simulation of Worldwide Political and Economic Developments*, vii–xiii. Boulder, CO: Westview Press, 1987. https://public.ebookcentral.proquest.com/choice/publicfullrecord.aspx?p=5893287.

Bremer, Stuart A., and Walter Gruhn. "Micro Globus: A Computer Model of Long-Term Global Political and Economic Processes." 1988. https://bibliothek.wzb.eu/fulltext/toc_text/2017/iw-79761.pdf.

Brindley, T. S., and J. W. Raine. "Social Area Analysis and Planning Research." *Urban Studies* 16, no. 3 (1979): 273–289.

Broder, David S. "How They Rehearsed the Election." *Washington Post*, November 16, 1980. https://www.washingtonpost.com/archive/opinions/1980/11/16/how-they-rehearsed-the-election/92f4c395-47ed-4c9a-ad14-cd7d83b047f7/.

Brody, Richard A. "Questions of Generalizing: From Ins-8 to the Real World." *Journal of Conflict Resolution* 7, no. 4 (1963): 747–748.

Brody, Richard A. "Some Systemic Effects of the Spread of Nuclear Weapons Technology: A Study Through Simulation of a Multi-Nuclear Future." *Journal of Conflict Resolution* 7, no. 4 (1963): 663–667. https://doi.org/10.1177/002200276300700401.

Broussard, Meredith. *Artificial Unintelligence: How Computers Misunderstand the World*. Cambridge, MA: MIT Press, 2019.

Brown, Wendy. *Undoing the Demos: Neoliberalism's Stealth Revolution*. New York: Zone Books, 2015.

Bruder, Johannes, and Orit Halpern. "Optimal Brain Damage: Theorizing Our Nervous Present." *Culture Machine* (blog). September 5, 2021. https://culturemachine.net/vol-20-machine-intelligences/optimal-brain-damage-theorizing-the-nervous-present-johannes-bruder-orit-halpern/.

Bueno de Mesquita, Bruce. "A New Model for Predicting Policy Choices: Preliminary Tests." *Conflict Management and Peace Science* 28, no. 1 (2011): 65–87. https://doi.org/10.1177/0738894210388127.

Burkart, Patrick. *Pirate Politics: The New Information Policy Contests*. Cambridge, MA: MIT Press, 2014.

Burnham, David. *The Rise of the Computer State*. New York: Random House, 1983.

Burton, Marion. "Kaye Lundgren Interview with Marion Burton." October 25, 2019. https://arstudies.contentdm.oclc.org/digital/collection/p1532coll1/id/16627/rec/1.

Butterworth, Michael L. "Nate Silver and Campaign 2012: Sport, the Statistical Frame, and the Rhetoric of Electoral Forecasting." *Journal of Communication* 64, no. 5 (2014): 895–914. https://doi.org/10.1111/jcom.12113.

Caffrey, Matthew B. *On Wargaming: How Wargames Have Shaped History and How They May Shape the Future*. Naval War College Newport Papers 43. Newport, RI: Naval War College Press, 2019.

Campbell, Angus, Philip E. Converse, Warren E. Miller, and Donald E. Stokes. *The American Voter*. Chicago: University of Chicago Press, 1960. https://press.uchicago.edu/ucp/books/book/chicago/A/bo24047989.html.

Cannon, James M. *Politics U.S.A.* New York: Doubleday, 1960.

Carey, James W., and John J. Quick. "The Mythos of the Electronic Revolution." *American Scholar* 39, no. 3 (1970): 395–424.

Carey, James W., and John J. Quirk. "The Mythos of the Electronic Revolution." *American Scholar* 39, no. 2 (1970): 219–241.

Carlisle, Johan. "Marketing Reagan." *Propaganda Review* 88 (1987): 9–13.

Carlos Eduardo Martins. "Herrera, Amílcar." In *Enciclopédia Latinoamericana*, July 8, 2017. https://latinoamericana.wiki.br/es/entradas/h/herrera-amilcar.

Carmi, Elinor. *Media Distortions: Understanding the Power Behind Spam, Noise, and Other Deviant Media*. New York: Peter Lang, 2020. https://library.oapen.org/handle/20.500.12657/42373.

Case, Andrew N. "'The Solid Gold Mailbox': Direct Mail and the Changing Nature of Buying and Selling in the Postwar United States." *History of Retailing and Consumption* 1, no. 1 (2015): 28–46. https://doi.org/10.1080/2373518X.2015.1012863.

de Chadarevian, Soraya, and Nick Hopwood. *Models: The Third Dimension of Science*. Stanford, CA: Stanford University Press, 2004.

Chartrand, Robert Lee. *Computers and Political Campaigning*. New York: Spartan Books, 1972.

Cheney-Lippold, John. *We Are Data: Algorithms and the Making of Our Digital Selves*. New York: New York University Press, 2017.

Cherryholmes, Cleo, and Michael Shapiro. *Representatives and Roll Calls: A Computer Simulation of Voting in the Eighty-Eighth Congress*. Indianapolis, IN: Bobbs-Merrill, 1969.

Chinoy, Ira. "Battle of the Brains: Election-Night Forecasting at the Dawn of the Computer Age." Dissertation, University of Maryland, 2010. http://drum.lib.umd.edu/handle/1903/10504.

Chun, Wendy Hui Kyong. *Discriminating Data: Correlation, Neighborhoods, and the New Politics of Recognition*. Cambridge, MA: MIT Press, 2021.

Chun, Wendy Hui Kyong. "On Hypo-Real Models or Global Climate Change: A Challenge for the Humanities." *Critical Inquiry* 41, no. 3 (2015): 675–703. https://doi.org/10.1086/680090.

Churchill, Jason L. "The Limits to Influence: The Club of Rome and Canada, 1968 to 1988." Dissertation, University of Waterloo, 2006. https://uwspace.uwaterloo.ca/handle/10012/747.

Clark, Grenville. "The Dublin Declaration." *World Affairs* 108, no. 4 (1945): 265–270.

Clarke, Adele E., Carrie Friese, and Rachel Washburn. *Situational Analysis: Grounded Theory After the Interpretive Turn*, 2nd ed. Los Angeles: Sage, 2017.

Clemens, Walter, Jr. "A Propositional Analysis of the International Relations Theory in Temper: A Computer Simulation of Cold War Conflict." In *Simulation in the Study of Politics*, edited by William D. Coplin, 59–101. Chicago: Markham, 1968.

Clotworthy, Orrin. 1962. "Some Far-out Thoughts on Computers." *Studies in Intelligence* 6 (4): 5–16.

Cohen, Bernard C. "Political Gaming in the Classroom." *Journal of Politics* 24, no. 2 (1962): 367–381.

Cohen-Cole, Jamie. "Cybernetics and the Machinery of Rationality." *British Journal for the History of Science* 41, no. 1 (2008): 109–114. https://doi.org/10.1017/S0007087407000015.

Cohen-Cole, Jamie. *The Open Mind: Cold War Politics and the Sciences of Human Nature*. Chicago: University of Chicago Press, 2014.

Cohn, Carol. "Sex and Death in the Rational World of Defense Intellectuals." *Signs* 12, no. 4 (1987): 687–718.

Cohn, Jonathan. "Irrational Exuberance." *The New Republic*, October 25, 1999. https://newrepublic.com/article/78956/political-science-irrational-exuberance.

Cole, Sam. "Global Models: A Review of Recent Developments." *Futures* 19, no. 4 (1987): 403–430. https://doi.org/10.1016/0016-3287(87)90003-6.

Coleman, Beth. "Technology of the Surround." *Catalyst: Feminism, Theory, Technoscience* 7, no. 2 (2021). https://doi.org/10.28968/cftt.v7i2.35973.

Coleman, James, Ernest Heau, Robert Peabody, and Leo Rigsby. "Computers and Election Analysis: *The New York Times* Project." *Public Opinion Quarterly* 28, no. 3 (1964): 418. https://doi.org/10.1086/267264.

Coleman, James S. "Analysis of Social Structures and Simulation of Social Processes with Electronic Computers." *Educational and Psychological Measurement* 21, no. 1 (1961): 203–218. https://doi.org/10.1177/001316446102100121.

Coleman, James S. "Introduction: In Defense of Games." *American Behavioral Scientist* 10, no. 2 (1966): 3–4. https://doi.org/10.1177/000276426601000201.

Coleman, James S. *Simulation Games and Social Theory*. Baltimore, MD: The Johns Hopkins University, 1968. http://archive.org/details/ERIC_ED017237.

Coleman, James S. "The Use of Electronic Computers in the Study of Social Organization." *European Journal of Sociology / Archives Européennes de Sociologie / Europäisches Archiv Für Soziologie* 6, no. 1 (1965): 89–107.

Colvin, Jeff, Matt Stirling, and Jessica Raines. *The Untold Story of the ZIP Code*. Washington, DC: US Postal Service Office of Inspector General, 2013.

Coplin, William D., ed. *Simulation in the Study of Politics*. Chicago: Markham, 1968.

Coplin, William D., and Michael K. O'Leary. *Power Persuasion: A Surefire System to Get Ahead in Business*. Reading, MA: Addison-Wesley, 1985. http://archive.org/details/powerpersuasions00copl.

Coplin, William D., and Michael Kent O'Leary. *Everyman's Prince: A Guide to Understanding Your Political Problems*. Belmont, CA: Duxbury Press, 1972.

Coplin, William D., and Michael Kent O'Leary. *Introduction to Political Risk Analysis*. Croton-on-Hudson, NY: Policy Studies Associates, 1983.

Coplin, William D., and Michael Kent O'Leary. *Political Analysis Through the Prince System*. Croton-on-Hudson, NY: Policy Studies Associates, 1983.

Cotter, Kelley, Mel Medeiros, Chankyung Pak, and Kjerstin Thorson. "'Reach the Right People': The Politics of 'Interests' in Facebook's Classification System for Ad Targeting." *Big Data & Society* 8, no. 1 (2021): 2053951721996046. https://doi.org/10.1177/2053951721996046.

CrimethInc Ex-Workers Collective. "CrimethInc: Up against the Wall, Motherfucker—The Game? Revisiting a Simulation of the 1968 Occupation of Columbia University." CrimethInc., March 14, 2019. https://crimethinc.com/2019/03/14/up-against-the-wall-motherfucker-the-game-revisiting-a-simulation-of-the-1968-occupation-of-columbia-university.

Crowther-Heyck, Hunter. *Herbert A. Simon: The Bounds of Reason in Modern America.* Baltimore: Johns Hopkins University Press, 2005.

Crowther-Heyck, Hunter. "Patrons of the Revolution: Ideals and Institutions in Postwar Behavioral Science." *Isis* 97, no. 3 (2006): 420–446. https://doi.org/10.1086/508075.

Culp, Andrew. *Dark Deleuze.* Minneapolis: University of Minnesota Press, 2016.

CulturePulse. "AI Powered Insights for Better Decisions." Accessed February 7, 2024. https://www.culturepulse.ai/.

Dahl, Robert A. "The Behavioral Approach in Political Science: Epitaph for a Monument to a Successful Protest." *American Political Science Review* 55, no. 4 (1961): 763–772.

Daley, David. "The Secret Files of the Master of Modern Republican Gerrymandering." *The New Yorker*, September 6, 2019. https://www.newyorker.com/news/news-desk/the-secret-files-of-the-master-of-modern-republican-gerrymandering.

Daston, Lorraine, and Peter Galison. *Objectivity.* New York: Zone Books, 2010.

David, Easton. *The Political System.* New York: Alfred A. Knopf, 1953. http://archive.org/details/dli.ernet.507692.

Davies, William. "Neoliberalism: A Bibliographic Review." *Theory, Culture & Society* 31, no. 7–8 (2014): 309–317. https://doi.org/10.1177/0263276414546383.

Davis, Aeron, and Catherine Walsh. "Distinguishing Financialization from Neoliberalism." *Theory, Culture & Society* 34, no. 5–6 (2017): 27–51. https://doi.org/10.1177/0263276417715511.

Davis, Bob. "Grand Old Party Tunes Up New Technology to Battle Democrats in Next Year's Elections." *Wall Street Journal*, August 19, 1987.

Dayé, Christian. *Experts, Social Scientists, and Techniques of Prognosis in Cold War America.* Cham, Switzerland: Palgrave Macmillan, 2020.

Dayé, Christian. "'A Fiction of Long Standing': Techniques of Prospection and the Role of Positivism in US Cold War Social Science, 1950–65." *History of the Human Sciences* 29, no. 4–5 (2016): 35–58. https://doi.org/10.1177/0952695116664838.

Dayé, Christian. "How to Train Your Oracle: The Delphi Method and Its Turbulent Youth in Operations Research and the Policy Sciences." *Social Studies of Science* 48, no. 6 (2018): 846–868. https://doi.org/10.1177/0306312718798497.

De Groot, Gerard J. *Selling Ronald Reagan: The Emergence of a President.* London: I.B. Tauris, 2015.

Dear, Brian. *The Friendly Orange Glow: The Untold Story of the PLATO System and the Dawn of Cyberculture.* New York: Pantheon, 2017.

Decision Insights, Incorporated, Plaintiff—Appellant, V. Sentia Group, Incorporated; Thomas H. Scott; Mark Abdollahian; Jacek Kugler; Brian Efird, No. 09–2300 (United States Court of Appeals for the Fourth Circuit March 15, 2011).

Defense Technical Information Center. *DTIC AD0647051: Demonstration of Two Simulations of Internal Revolutionary Conflict: Politica and Agile-Coin*, 1967. http://archive.org/details/DTIC_AD0647051.

Defense Technical Information Center. *DTC AD0653606: Temper As a Model of International Relations: An Evaluation for the Joint War Games Agency Department of Defense*, 1966. http://archive.org/details/DTIC_AD0653606.

Deleuze, Gilles. "Postscript on the Societies of Control." *October* 59, no. 1 (1992): 3–7.

Desch, Michael C. *Cult of the Irrelevant: The Waning Influence of Social Science on National Security*. Princeton, NJ: Princeton University Press, 2019. http://muse.jhu.edu/book/62654.

Desrosières, Alain. *The Politics of Large Numbers: A History of Statistical Reasoning*. Cambridge, MA: Harvard University Press, 2011.

Deutsch, Karl W. *The Nerves of Government*. New York: Free Press, 1963.

Deutsch, Karl W. "Shifts in the Balance of Communication Flows: A Problem of Measurement in International Relations." *Public Opinion Quarterly* 20, no. 1 (1956): 143–160.

Deutsch, Karl W. "Toward an Inventory of Basic Trends and Patterns in Comparative and International Politics." *American Political Science Review* 54, no. 1 (1960): 34–57. https://doi.org/10.2307/1952407.

Deutsch, Karl W. "Toward Drift and Steering Models." In *Problems of World Modeling: Political and Social Implications*, edited by Karl Wolfgang Deutsch, Bruno Fritsch, Hélio Jaguaribe, and Andrei S Markovits, 5–10. Cambridge, MA: Ballinger, 1977.

Deutsch, Karl Wolfgang. "Foreword." In *The Globus Model: Computer Simulation of Worldwide Political and Economic Developments*, edited by Stuart A. Bremer, 7–23. Boulder, CO: Westview Press, 1987. https://public.ebookcentral.proquest.com/choice/publicfullrecord.aspx?p=5893287.

Deutsch, Karl Wolfgang, Bruno Fritsch, Hélio Jaguaribe, and Andrei S. Markovits, eds. *Problems of World Modeling: Political and Social Implications*. Cambridge, MA: Ballinger, 1977.

Deutsch, K. W., J. Platt, and D. Senghaas. "Conditions Favoring Major Advances in Social Science." *Science* 171, no. 3970 (1971): 450–459. https://doi.org/10.1126/science.171.3970.450.

Dhaliwal, Ranjodh Singh. "On Addressability, or What Even Is Computation?" *Critical Inquiry* 49, no. 1 (2022): 1–27. https://doi.org/10.1086/721167.

Dickinson, Jean. "Games Political Scientists Play." *Change: The Magazine of Higher Learning* 8, no. 6 (1976): 56–59. https://doi.org/10.1080/00091383.1976.10568913.

D'Ignazio, Catherine, and Lauren F. Klein. *Data Feminism*. Strong Ideas Series. Cambridge, MA: MIT Press, 2020.

Dommett, Author Katharine, Glenn Kefford, and Simon Kruschinski. *Data-Driven Campaigning and Political Parties: Five Advanced Democracies Compared*. Journalism and Political Communication Unbound. Oxford: Oxford University Press, 2024.

Downs, Anthony. *An Economic Theory of Democracy*. New York: Harper & Row, 1957.

Dunlap, Riley E., and Angela G. Mertig. *American Environmentalism: The US Environmental Movement, 1970–1990*. London: Taylor & Francis, 2014.

Easton, David. "1. Classification of Political Systems." *Political Research, Organization and Design* 1, no. 2 (1957): 3–4. https://doi.org/10.1177/000276425700100201.

Easton, David. "Harold Lasswell; Policy Scientist for a Democratic Society." *Journal of Politics* 12, no. 3 (1950): 450–477. https://doi.org/10.2307/2126297.

Easton, David. *The Political Systems*. New York: Alfred A. Knopf, 1953.

Edwards, Paul N. *The Closed World: Computers and the Politics of Discourse in Cold War America*. Cambridge, MA: MIT Press, 1996.

Edwards, Paul N. *A Vast Machine: Computer Models, Climate Data, and the Politics of Global Warming*. Cambridge, MA: MIT Press, 2010.

Edwards, Paul N. "The World in a Machine: Origins and Impacts of Early Computerized Global Systems Models." In *Systems, Experts, and Computers: The Systems Approach*, edited by Agatha C. Hughes and Thomas P. Hughes, 221–254. Cambridge, MA: MIT Press, 2000.

Edwards, Phil. "6 Myths About the Ides of March and Killing Caesar." Vox, March 15, 2015. https://www.vox.com/2015/3/15/8214921/ides-of-march-caesar-assassination.

Elichirigoity, Fernando. *Planet Management: Limits to Growth, Computer Simulation, and the Emergence of Global Spaces*. Evanston, IL: Northwestern University Press, 1999.

Ellsberg, Daniel. *The Doomsday Machine: Confessions of a Nuclear War Planner*. New York: Bloomsbury USA, 2017.

Elmer, Greg, Ganaele Langlois, and Fenwick McKelvey. *The Permanent Campaign: New Media, New Politics*. Digital Formations, vol. 81. New York: Peter Lang, 2012.

Ensmenger, Nathan. "Is Chess the Drosophila of AI? A Social History of an Algorithm." *Social Studies of Science*, 2011, 0306312711424596.

Erickson, Paul. *The World the Game Theorists Made*. Chicago: University of Chicago Press, 2015.

Erickson, Paul, Judy L. Klein, Lorraine Daston, Rebecca Lemov, Thomas Sturm, and Michael D. Gordin. *How Reason Almost Lost Its Mind: The Strange Career of Cold War Rationality*. Chicago: University of Chicago Press, 2013.

Ertel, James. *How to Run for Office*. New York: Sterling, 1960.

Etheredge, Lloyd S., ed. *Humane Politics and Methods of Inquiry*. New Brunswick, NJ: Transaction, 2016.

Ezrahi, Yaron. "Dewey's Critique of Democratic Visual Culture and Its Political Implications." In *Sites of Vision: The Discursive Construction of Sight in the History of Philosophy*, edited by David Kleinberg-Levin, 315–336. Cambridge, MA: MIT Press, 1999.

Faber, Harold, and James Reston. *The New York Times Election Handbook 1964*. New York: McGraw-Hill, 1964.

Falk, Richard. "The World Order Models Project and Its Critics: A Reply." *International Organization* 32, no. 2 (1978): 531–545.

Falk, Richard A. *Public Intellectual: The Life of a Citizen Pilgrim*. Atlanta, GA: Clarity Press, 2021.

Falk, Richard A. *A Study of Future Worlds*. New York: Simon and Schuster, 1975.

Farer, Tom J. "The Greening of the Globe: A Preliminary Appraisal of the World Order Models Project: (WOMP)." *International Organization* 31, no. 1 (1977): 129–147.

Farr, James, Jacob S. Hacker, and Nicole Kazee. "The Policy Scientist of Democracy: The Discipline of Harold D. Lasswell." *American Political Science Review* 100, no. 4 (2006): 579.

Feder, Stanley. 1997. "FACTIONS and Policon: New Ways to Analyze Politics." In *Inside CIA's Private World: Declassified Articles from the Agency's Internal Journal, 1955-1992*, edited by H. Bradford Westerfield. Yale University Press.

Feder, Stanley A. "Forecasting for Policy Making in the Post-Cold War Period." *Annual Review of Political Science* 5 (2002): 111–125. https://doi.org/10.1146/annurev.polisci.5.102601.115116.

Feld, Scott L. "Simulation Games in Theory Development." *Sociological Forum* 12, no. 1 (1997): 103–115. https://doi.org/10.1023/A:1024608707275.

Fellow, Anthony R. "Computers and Politics: Innovation and the Role of Uncertainty in Political Campaign Organizations." *Social Science Computer Review* 10, no. 1 (1992): 29–41. https://doi.org/10.1177/089443939201000102.

Fishel, Murray, David Gopoian, and J. Michael Stacey. *On the Campaign Trail.* Washington, DC: Campaigns & Elections, 1987.

Foucault, Michel. *The Birth of Biopolitics: Lectures at the College de France, 1978–79.* New York: Palgrave Macmillan, 2008.

Foucault, Michel. *Security, Territory, Population: Lectures at the College de France, 1977–78.* Edited by Michel Senellart. Translated by Graham Burchell. New York: Palgrave Macmillan, 2007.

Fox, William T. R. "Pluralism, The Science of Politics, and the World System." *World Politics* 27, no. 4 (1975): 597–611. https://doi.org/10.2307/2010016.

Fries, Sylvia Doughty. "Expertise Against Politics: Technology as Ideology on Capitol Hill, 1966–1972." *Science, Technology, & Human Values* 8, no. 2 (1983): 6–15.

Fuller, Buckminister. "World Game." Smithsonian Folkways Recordings. Accessed March 16, 2021. https://folkways.si.edu/r-buckminster-fuller/world-game/oral-history-biography/track/smithsonian.

Fuller, Richard Buckminster. "Accommodating Human Unsettlement." *Town Planning Review* 49, no. 1 (1978): 51–60.

Gabel, Medard. "Global Recall and Networld Game: Global Access to Global Model." In *Integrated Global Models of Sustainable Development,* vol. 1. *World3 and Strategem: History, Goals, Assumptions, Implications,* edited by Akira Onishi, vol. 3. Oxford: Eolss, 2009.

Galison, Peter. "Computer Simulations and the Trading Zone." In *From Science to Computational Science,* edited by Gabriele Gramelsberger, 118–157. Zurich: Diaphanes, 2011. http://medientheorie.com/doc/galison_simulation.pdf.

Galison, Peter Louis. "The Ontology of the Enemy: Norbert Wiener and the Cybernetic Vision." *Critical Inquiry* 21, no. 1 (1994): 228–266.

Gallopin, Gilberto C. "The Latin American World Model (a.k.a. the Bariloche Model): Three Decades Ago." *Futures* 33, no. 1 (2001): 77–89. https://doi.org/10.1016/S0016-3287(00)00055-0.

Galtung, Johan. "'The Limits to Growth' and Class Politics." *Journal of Peace Research* 10, no. 1 (1973): 110–114.

Gamson, William A., and Russell J. Stambaugh. "Simulation Review Essay: Democracy." *Simulation & Gaming* 5, no. 4 (1974): 433–439.

Gandy, Oscar H., Jr. *The Panoptic Sort: A Political Economy of Personal Information,* 2nd ed. New York: Oxford University Press, 2021.

Garson, G. David. "Social Science Computer Simulation: Its History, Design, and Future." *Social Science Computer Review* 12, no. 1 (1994): 55–82. https://doi.org/10.1177/089443939401200104.

Gary, Brett. "Communication Research, the Rockefeller Foundation, and Mobilization for the War on Words, 1938–1944." *Journal of Communication* 46, no. 3 (1996): 124–148. https://doi.org/10.1111/j.1460-2466.1996.tb01493.x.

Gasperini, Jim. "Culture, Idealism, and the Real World." *Journal of Computer Game Design*, May 1989. http://www.erasmatazz.com/library/the-journal-of-computer/jcgd-volume-2/volume-2-number-4-aprilmay.html.

Gasperini, Jim. "The Political Subtext of Computer Games." *Journal of Computer Game Design*, October 1989. http://www.erasmatazz.com/library/the-journal-of-computer/jcgd-volume-3/volume-3-number-1-octoberno.html.

Geoghegan, Bernard Dionysius. *Code: From Information Theory to French Theory*. Sign, Storage, Transmission. Durham, NC: Duke University Press, 2023.

Gerbaudo, Paolo. *The Digital Party: Political Organisation and Online Democracy*. London: Pluto Press, 2019.

Gerovitch, Slava. *From Newspeak to Cyberspeak: A History of Soviet Cybernetics*. Cambridge, MA: MIT Press, 2004.

Ghamari-Tabrizi, Sharon. "Simulating the Unthinkable: Gaming Future War in the 1950s and 1960s." *Social Studies of Science* 30, no. 2 (April 1, 2000): 163–223. https://doi.org/10.1177/030631200030002001.

Giere, Ronald N. "Is Computer Simulation Changing the Face of Experimentation?" *Philosophical Studies* 143, no. 1 (2009): 59–62.

Gilbert, David. "The UN Hired an AI Company to Untangle the Israeli-Palestinian Crisis." *Wired*, November 2, 2023. https://www.wired.com/story/culturepulse-ai-israeli-palestinian-crisis/.

Gillette, R. "The Limits to Growth: Hard Sell for a Computer View of Doomsday." *Science* 175, no. 4026 (1972): 1088–1092. https://doi.org/10.1126/science.175.4026.1088.

Gilman, Richard C. "The General Inquirer: A Computer Approach to Content Analysis. Philip J. Stone, Dexter C. Dunphy, Marshall S. Smith, Daniel M. Ogilvie." *American Journal of Sociology* 73, no. 5 (1968): 634–635. https://doi.org/10.1086/224539.

Gitlin, Todd. "Media Sociology: The Dominant Paradigm." *Theory and Society* 6, no. 2 (1978): 205–253. https://doi.org/10.1007/BF01681751.

Gleditsch, Nils Petter, ed. *R.J. Rummel: An Assessment of His Many Contributions*. SpringerBriefs on Pioneers in Science and Practice. Cham, Switzerland: Springer International, 2017. https://doi.org/10.1007/978-3-319-54463-2_1.

Gleditsch, Nils Petter. "R.J. Rummel—A Multi-Faceted Scholar." In *R.J. Rummel: An Assessment of His Many Contributions*, edited by Nils Petter Gleditsch, 1–16. SpringerBriefs on Pioneers in Science and Practice. Cham, Switzerland: Springer International, 2017. https://doi.org/10.1007/978-3-319-54463-2_1.

Goffman, Erving. "On Cooling the Mark Out." *Psychiatry* 15, no. 4 (1952): 451–463. https://doi.org/10.1080/00332747.1952.11022896.

Goffman, Erving. *The Presentation of Self in Everyday Life*. Garden City, NY: Doubleday, 1959.

Goldhamer, Herbert, and Hans Speier. "Some Observations on Political Gaming." *World Politics* 12, no. 1 (1959): 71–83. https://doi.org/10.2307/2009213.

Goldstein, Gordon, ed. 1966. "PLATO." *Digital Computer Newsletter* 18 (1): 26–33.

Golub, Robert, and Joe Townsend. "Malthus, Multinationals and the Club of Rome." *Social Studies of Science* 7, no. 2 (1977): 201–22. https://doi.org/10.1177/030631277700700204.

Gorden, Morton. "Burdens for the Designer of a Computer Simulation of International Relations." In *Computers and the Policy-Making Community: Applications to International Relations*, edited by Davis B. Bobrow and Judah L. Schwartz. Englewood Cliffs, NJ: Prentice-Hall, 1968.

Gorden, Morton. "Comments on Clemens' Paper." In *Simulation in the Study of Politics*, edited by William D. Coplin, 101–104. Chicago: Markham, 1968.

de Grazia, Alfred. "Social Research with the Computer." *American Behavioral Scientist* 8, no. 9 (1965): 2–2. https://doi.org/10.1177/000276426500800901.

Green, Donald, and Ian Shapiro. *Pathologies of Rational Choice Theory: A Critique of Applications in Political Science*. New Haven, CT: Yale University Press, 1996.

Green, Lloyd. "Use of Games in College as a Means of Teaching." *Ottawa Citizen*, July 11, 1966.

Greene, Jay R., and Roger L. Sisson. *Dynamic Management Decision Games, Including Seven Non-Computer Games*. New York: Wiley, 1959.

Grofman, Bernard. "Anthony Downs (1930—)." In *Readings in Public Choice and Constitutional Political Economy*, edited by Charles K. Rowley and Friedrich G. Schneider, 91–95. Boston, MA: Springer US, 2008. https://doi.org/10.1007/978-0-387-75870-1_6.

Groves, Robert, and Eleanor Singer. "Survey Methodology." In *A Telescope on Society: Survey Research and Social Science at the University of Michigan and Beyond*, edited by Eleanor Singer, James S. House, F. Thomas Juster, Robert L. Kahn, and Howard Schuman, 21–64. Ann Arbor: University of Michigan Press, 2004.

Guetzkow, Harold. "Comment on Andriole, Wilkenfeld, and Hopple: 'A Framework for the Comparative Analysis of Foreign Policy Behavior.'" *International Studies Quarterly* 20, no. 2 (1976): 331–334. https://doi.org/10.2307/2600122.

Guetzkow, Harold. "Recollections about the Inter-Nation Simulation (INS) and Some Derivatives in Global Modeling." *Simulation & Gaming*, 26, no. 4 (2016): 453–470. https://doi.org/10.1177/1046878195264007.

Guetzkow, Harold. "Review of *The War Trap*, by Bruce Bueno de Mesquita." *Review of Politics* 44, no. 4 (1982): 626–628.

Guetzkow, Harold. "Simulation in International Relations." In *Proceedings of The IBM Scientific Computing Symposium on Simulation Models and Gaming*, 249–278. White Plains, NY: IBM Data Processing Division, 1966.

Guetzkow, Harold. "Six Continuing for Global Modelers: A Self-Critique." In *Simulated International Processes: Theories and Research into Global Modelling*, edited by Harold Guetzkow and Joseph J. Valadez, 331–358. London: SAGE, 1981.

Guetzkow, Harold. "A Use of Simulation in the Study of Inter-Nation Relations." *Behavioral Science* 4, no. 3 (1959): 183–191. https://doi.org/10.1002/bs.3830040302.

Guetzkow, Harold, and Lloyd Jensen. "Research Activities on Simulated International Processes." *Background* 9, no. 4 (1966): 261–274. https://doi.org/10.2307/3013650.

Guetzkow, Harold, and Joseph J. Valadez, eds. *Simulated International Processes: Theories and Research into Global Modelling*. London: SAGE, 1981.

Guice, Jon. "Controversy and the State: Lord ARPA and Intelligent Computing." *Social Studies of Science* 28, no. 1 (2016): 103–138. https://doi.org/10.1177/030631298028001004.

Gunnell, John G. "The Reconstitution of Political Theory: David Easton, Behavioralism, and the Long Road to System." *Journal of the History of the Behavioral Sciences* 49, no. 2 (2013): 190–210. https://doi.org/10.1002/jhbs.21593.

Hacking, Ian. "Making Up People." In *Reconstructing Individualism: Autonomy, Individuality, and the Self in Western Thought*, edited by Thomas C. Heller and Christine Brooke-Rose, 161–171. Stanford, CA: Stanford University Press, 1986.

Hagemann, Harald, Vadim Kufenko, and Danila Raskov. "Game Theory Modeling for the Cold War on Both Sides of the Iron Curtain." *History of the Human Sciences* 29, no. 4–5 (2016): 99–124. https://doi.org/10.1177/0952695116666012.

Hall, Wynton C. "The Invention of 'Quantifiable Safe Rhetoric': Richard Wirthlin and Ronald Reagan's Instrumental Use of Public Opinion Research in Presidential Discourse." *Western Journal of Communication* 66, no. 3 (2002): 319. https://doi.org/10.1080/10570310209374740.

Halley, Richard B., and Harold G. Vatter. "Technology and the Future as History: A Critical Review of Futurism." *Technology and Culture* 19, no. 1 (1978): 53–82. https://doi.org/10.2307/3103308.

Halpern, Orit. *Beautiful Data: A History of Vision and Reason Since 1945*. Experimental Futures. Durham, NC: Duke University Press, 2014.

Han, Jungsuk, Jongsub Lee, and Tao Li. "A Review of DAO Governance: Recent Literature and Emerging Trends." *Journal of Corporate Finance* 91 (2025): 102734. https://doi.org/10.1016/j.jcorpfin.2025.102734.

Haraway, Donna. "Situated Knowledges: The Science Question in Feminism and the Privilege of Partial Perspective." *Feminist Studies* 14, no. 3 (1988): 575–599. https://doi.org/10.2307/3178066.

Haraway, Donna J. "Manifesto for Cyborgs: Science, Technology, and Socialist Feminism in the 1980s." *Socialist Review*, no. 80 (1985): 65–108.

Haraway, Donna J. *Staying with the Trouble: Making Kin in the Chthulucene*. Experimental Futures: Technological Lives, Scientific Arts, Anthropological Voices. Durham, NC: Duke University Press, 2016.

Harrigan, Pat, and Matthew G. Kirschenbaum, eds. *Zones of Control: Perspectives on Wargaming*. Game Histories. Cambridge, MA: The MIT Press, 2016.

Hauptmann, Emily. "The Ford Foundation and the Rise of Behavioralism in Political Science." *Journal of the History of the Behavioral Sciences* 48, no. 2 (2012): 154–173. https://doi.org/10.1002/jhbs.21515.

Hausrath, Alfred Hartmann. *Venture Simulation in War, Business, and Politics*. New York: McGraw-Hill, 1972.

Hayles, N. Katherine. *How We Became Posthuman: Virtual Bodies in Cybernetics, Literature, and Informatics*. Chicago: University of Chicago Press, 1999.

Hayles, N. Katherine. "Self-Reflexive Metaphors in Maxwell's Demon and Shannon's Choice: Finding the Passages." In *Literature and Science: Theory & Practice*, edited by Stuart Peterfreund, 209–238. Boston: Northeastern University Press, 1990.

Hegselmann, Rainer. "Thomas C. Schelling and James M. Sakoda: The Intellectual, Technical, and Social History of a Model." *Journal of Artificial Societies and Social Simulation* 20, no. 3 (2017): 15. https://doi.org/10.18564/jasss.3511.

Hellman, Geoffrey T. "Lord's Politics." *The New Yorker*, May 23, 1952. https://www.newyorker.com/magazine/1952/05/31/lords-politics.

Helmreich, Stefan. *Silicon Second Nature: Culturing Artificial Life in a Digital World, Updated with a New Preface*. Berkeley: University of California Press, 2000.

Hermann, Charles. "Validation Problems in Games and Simulations with Special Reference to Models of International Politics." *Behavioral Science* 12, no. 3 (1967): 216–231.

Hermann, Charles, Maurice East, Margaret G. Hermann, Barbara G. Salmore, and Stephen A. Salmore. "CREON: A Foreign Events Data Set." In *Sage Professional Papers in International Studies*, vol. 2. Beverly Hills, CA: Sage, 1973.

Hermann, Charles F. *Crises in Foreign Policy: A Simulation Analysis*, 1st ed. Indianapolis, IN: Bobbs-Merrill, 1969.

Hermann, Charles F. "Validation Problems in Games and Simulations with Special Reference to Models of International Politics." *Behavioral Science* 12, no. 3 (1967): 216–231. https://doi.org/10.1002/bs.3830120306.

Hermann, Charles F., and Margaret G. Hermann. "An Attempt to Simulate the Outbreak of World War I." *American Political Science Review* 61, no. 2 (1967): 400–416. https://doi.org/10.2307/1953253.

Herrera, Amílcar. "Introduction and Basic Assumptions of the Model." In *Latin American World Model: Proceedings of the Second IIASA Symposium on Global Modelling [Baden, Austria] October 7–10, 1974*, edited by Gerhart Bruckmann, 3–8. Laxenburg, Austria: International Institute for Applied Systems Analysis, 1976.

Herrera, Amílcar O., Hugo D. Scolnik, Graciela Chichilnisky, Gilberto C. Gallopin, and Jorge E. Hardoy. *Catastrophe or New Society? A Latin American World Model*. IDRC, Ottawa, 1976. https://idl-bnc-idrc.dspacedirect.org/handle/10625/213.

Hersh, Eitan D. *Hacking the Electorate: How Campaigns Perceive Voters*. New York: Cambridge University Press, 2015.

Hersh, Eitan D., and Brian F. Schaffner. "Targeted Campaign Appeals and the Value of Ambiguity." *Journal of Politics* 75, no. 2 (2013): 520–534. https://doi.org/10.1017/s0022381613000182.

Heyck, Hunter. *Age of System: Understanding the Development of Modern Social Science*. Baltimore: Johns Hopkins University Press, 2015.

Heyck, Hunter. "Producing Reason." In *Cold War Social Science: Knowledge Production, Liberal Democracy, and Human Nature*, edited by Mark Solovey and Hamilton Cravens, 99–116. New York: Palgrave Macmillan US, 2012. https://doi.org/10.1057/9781137013224_6.

von Hilgers, Philipp. *War Games: A History of War on Paper*. MIT Press, 2012.

Holbrook, Morris B. "Market Clustering Goes Graphic: The Weiss Trilogy and a Proposed Extension." *Psychology & Marketing* 18, no. 1 (2001): 67–85. https://doi.org/10.1002/1520-6793(200101)18:1<67::AID-MAR4>3.0.CO;2-1.

Holloway, Steve. "The Upper Arlington High School Class of 1969." 2009. http://www.ua69.com/PhotoCollections/SteveHolloway.htm.

Hong, Sun-ha. "Technofutures in Stasis: Smart Machines, Ubiquitous Computing, and the Future That Keeps Coming Back." *International Journal of Communication* 15, no. 0 (2021): 21.

Howard, Philip N. 2015. *Pax Technica: How the Internet of Things May Set Us Free or Lock Us Up*. Yale University Press.

Howard, Philip N. *New Media Campaigns and the Managed Citizen*. Cambridge, UK: Cambridge University Press, 2006.

Howe, Quincy, and Arthur Schlesinger, Jr., eds. *Guide to Politics 1954*. New York: Dial Press, 1954.

Hrach, Thomas J. "An Incitement to Riot." *Journalism History* 37, no. 3 (2011): 163–171. https://doi.org/10.1080/00947679.2011.12062856.

Hughes, Barry B., and Glenn Palmer. "Stuart A. Bremer—In Memoriam." *PS—Political Science & Politics* 36, no. 2 (2003): 325.

Hwang, Tim. *Subprime Attention Crisis: Advertising and the Time Bomb at the Heart of the Internet*, 1st ed. FSG Originals x Logic. New York: FSG Originals, 2020.

Hyman, Sidney. "If Computers Called the Tune; THE 480. By Eugene Burdick. 313 Pp. New York: McGraw-Hill Book Cam-pany. $5." *New York Times*, June 28, 1964, sec. BR.

IBM Archives. "IBM 1311 Disk Storage Drive." TS200, January 23, 2003. https://web.archive.org/web/20190403052229/www.ibm.com/ibm/history/exhibits/storage/storage_1311.html.

Igo, Sarah Elizabeth. *The Averaged American: Surveys, Citizens, and the Making of a Mass Public*. Cambridge, MA: Harvard University Press, 2007.

Imarisha, Walidah, Adrienne Maree Brown, Sheree R. Thomas, and Institute for Anarchist Studies, eds. *Octavia's Brood: Science Fiction Stories from Social Justice Movements*. Oakland, CA: AK Press, 2015.

"Institute for the Future Formed in USA." *Futures* 1, no. 1 (1969): 66–68. https://doi.org/10.1016/S0016-3287(69)80009-1.

Isaac, Joel. "Tool Shock: Technique and Epistemology in the Postwar Social Sciences." *History of Political Economy* 42, no. Suppl. 1 (2010): 133–164. https://doi.org/10.1215/00182702-2009-075.

Issenberg, Sasha. "Project Narwhal: How a Top-Secret Obama Campaign Program Could Change the 2012 Race." *Slate*, February 15, 2012. http://www.slate.com/articles/news_and_politics/victory_lab/2012/02/project_narwhal_how_a_top_secret_obama_campaign_program_could_change_the_2012_race_.single.html

Issenberg, Sasha. *The Victory Lab: The Secret Science of Winning Campaigns*. New York: Crown, 2012.

Jacovkis, Pablo, and Rodrigo Castro. "Computer-Based Global Models: From Early Experiences to Complex Systems." *Journal of Artificial Societies and Social Simulation* 18, no. 1 (2015): 13.

Jahoda, Marie. *Models of Doom: A Critique of The Limits to Growth*. Edited by H. S. D. Cole, Christopher Freeman, and Keith Pavitt. New York: Universe Books, 1973.

Jameson, Fredric. *Valences of the Dialectic*. London: Verso, 2010.

Jansen, Sue Curry. "Forgotten Histories: Another Road Not Taken—The Charles Merriam-Walter Lippmann Correspondence." *Communication Theory* 20, no. 2 (2010): 127–146. https://doi.org/10.1111/j.1468-2885.2010.01357.x.

Jansiewicz, Donald R. *The New Alexandria Simulation: A Serious Game of State and Local Politics*. San Francisco: Canfield Press, 1973. http://archive.org/details/newalexandriasim00jans.

Jantsch, Erich. "The Organization of Technological Forecasting in the Soviet Union: Notes from a Brief Visit." *Technological Forecasting* 1, no. 1 (1969): 83–86. https://doi.org/10.1016/0099-3964(69)90008-8.

Jasanoff, Sheila, and Sang-Hyun Kim. *Dreamscapes of Modernity: Sociotechnical Imaginaries and the Fabrication of Power*. Chicago: University of Chicago Press, 2015.

Johnson, Dennis W. *Democracy for Hire: A History of American Political Consulting*. New York: Oxford University Press, 2016.

Johnson, Paul. "Simulation Modeling in Political Science." *American Behavioral Scientist* 42, no. 10 (1999): 1509–1530.

Johnson, Paul E. "Formal Theories of Politics: The Scope of Mathematical Modelling in Political Science." *Mathematical and Computer Modelling* 12, no. 4–5 (1989): 397–404. https://doi.org/10.1016/0895-7177(89)90412-3.

Johnston, Rob. *Analytic Culture in the United States Intelligence Community: An Ethnographic Study*. Washington, DC: Center for the Study of Intelligence, CIA, 2005.

Jones, Bryan D. "Bounded Rationality." *Annual Review of Political Science* 2, (1999): 297–321. https://doi.org/10.1146/annurev.polisci.2.1.297.

Kadushin, Charles, Joseph Lovett, and James D. Merriman. "Literary Analysis with the Aid of the Computer: Review Symposium." *Computers and the Humanities* 2, no. 4 (1968): 177–202.

Karpf, David. *Analytic Activism: Digital Listening and the New Political Strategy*. Oxford Studies in Digital Politics. New York: Oxford University Press, 2016.

Karpf, David, Daniel Kreiss, Rasmus Kleis Nielsen, and Matthew Powers. "The Role of Qualitative Methods in Political Communication Research: Past, Present, and Future." *International Journal of Communication* 9 (2015): 1888–1906.

Kaysen, Carl. "The Computer That Printed Out W*O*L*F*." *Foreign Affairs* 50, no. 4 (1972): 660. https://doi.org/10.2307/20037939.

Kelley, Stanley, and Thad W. Mirer. "The Simple Act of Voting." *American Political Science Review* 68, no. 2 (1974): 572–591. https://doi.org/10.2307/1959506.

Kelty, Christopher. *Two Bits: The Cultural Significance of Free Software*. Durham, NC: Duke University Press, 2008.

Kessel, John H. Review of *Review of Candidates, Issues and Strategies.*, by Robert P. Abelson, Samuel Popkin, and Ithiel de Sola Pool. *Midwest Journal of Political Science* 10, no. 4 (1966): 515–518. https://doi.org/10.2307/2108932.

Kessler, A. R., and I. D. Sola Pool. "Crisiscom: A Computer Simulation of Human Information Processing During a Crisis." *IEEE Transactions on Systems Science and Cybernetics* 1, no. 1 (1965): 52–58. https://doi.org/10.1109/TSSC.1965.300061.

Keyfitz, Nathan. "Understanding World Models." *Sociological Methodology* 9 (1978): 1–19. https://doi.org/10.2307/270801.

Kim, K. W. "The Limits of Behavioural Explanation in Politics." *Canadian Journal of Economics and Political Science / Revue Canadienne d'Economique et de Science Politique* 31, no. 3 (1965): 315–327. https://doi.org/10.2307/139732.

Kirk, John A. *An Epitaph for Little Rock: A Fiftieth Anniversary Retrospective on the Central High Crisis*. Fayetteville: University of Arkansas Press, 2010.

Kirk, John A. *Winthrop Rockefeller: From New Yorker to Arkansawyer, 1912–1956*. Fayetteville: University of Arkansas Press, 2022. https://muse.jhu.edu/book/98968/.

Kittler, Friedrich. "Gramophone, Film, Typewriter." Translated by Dorothea von Mücke and Philippe L. Similon. *October* 41 (1987): 101–118. https://doi.org/10.2307/778332.

Knowles, Scott G., and Stuart W. Leslie. "'Industrial Versailles': Eero Saarinen's Corporate Campuses for GM, IBM, and AT&T." *Isis* 92, no. 1 (2001): 1–33. https://doi.org/10.1086/385038.

Koch, Nadine S. "Winning Is Not the Only Thing 'On the Campaign Trail': An Evaluation of a Micro-Computer Campaign Simulation." *PS: Political Science and Politics* 24, no. 4 (1991): 694–98. https://doi.org/10.2307/419407.

Kolbert, Elizabeth. "Dymaxion Man." *The New Yorker*, June 9, 2008.

Koopman, Colin. *How We Became Our Data: A Genealogy of the Informational Person*. Chicago: University of Chicago Press, 2019.

Kothari, Rajni. *Footsteps into the Future: Diagnosis of the Present World and a Design for an Alternative*. New York: Free Press, 1975. http://archive.org/details/footstepsintofut00rajn.

Krapp, Peter. *Computing Legacies: Digital Cultures of Simulation*. Cambridge, MA: MIT Press, 2024.

Kraus, Rebecca. "Statistical Déjà Vu: The National Data Center Proposal of 1965 and Its Descendants." *Journal of Privacy and Confidentiality* 5, no. 1 (2013). https://doi.org/10.29012/jpc.v5i1.624.

Kreiss, Daniel. *Prototype Politics: Technology-Intense Campaigning and the Data of Democracy*. Oxford Studies in Digital Politics. New York: Oxford University Press, 2016.

Kreiss Daniel, and Shannon C. McGregor, "The 'Arbiters of What Our Voters See': Facebook and Google's Struggle with Policy, Process, and Enforcement Around Political Advertising," *Political Communication* 36, no. 4 (2019): 499–522

Kreiss, Daniel. "The 2012 Obama Campaign, the Technological Sublime, and the Limits of Big Data." *Culture Digitally* (blog), 2012. http://culturedigitally.org/2012/02/the-2012-obama-campaign-the-technological-sublime-and-the-limits-of-big-data/.

Kristof, Nicholas D. "The Best Political Scientist in the World Goes on Half-Time, Still an Optimist." *Harvard Crimson*, May 23, 1979. https://www.thecrimson.com/article/1979/5/23/the-best-political-scientist-in-the/.

Kugel, Peter. 1962. "Computers and Political Strategy." *Computers and Automation* 11, no. 5: 17–22.

Kurtz, Howard A. "Software Reviews: Global Recall." *Social Science Computer Review* 9, no. 2 (1991): 338–339. https://doi.org/10.1177/089443939100900214.

Lane, Justin E. "How CulturePulse AI Helped Cambridge University Understand Conflict in Northern Ireland, the Balkans, and South Sudan." *Culturepulse*, April 2, 2023. https://culturepulse.ai/blog/how-culture-pulse-ai-helped-cambridge-university-understand-conflict.

Langlois, Ganaele, and Greg Elmer. "Impersonal Subjectivation from Platforms to Infrastructures." *Media, Culture & Society* 41, no. 2 (2019): 236–251. https://doi.org/10.1177/0163443718818374.

Larson, Erik. *The Naked Consumer*. New York: H. Holt, 1992. http://archive.org/details/nakedconsumerhow00lars.

Lasswell, Harold D. "Introduction: The Shape of the Future." *American Behavioral Scientist* 8, no. 9 (1965): 3. https://doi.org/10.1177/000276426500800902.

Lasswell, Harold D. "The Political Science of Science: An Inquiry into the Possible Reconciliation of Mastery and Freedom." *American Political Science Review* 50, no. 4 (1956): 961–979.

Lasswell, Harold D. "The Promise of the World Order Modelling Movement." *World Politics* 29, no. 3 (1977): 425–437. https://doi.org/10.2307/2010004.

Lasswell, Harold D. "Technique of Decision Seminars." *Midwest Journal of Political Science* 4, no. 3 (1960): 213–236. https://doi.org/10.2307/2108975.

Latour, Bruno. *Politics of Nature: How to Bring the Sciences into Democracy*. Cambridge, MA: Harvard University Press, 2004.

Lee, Douglass B., Jr. "Requiem for Large-Scale Models." *Journal of the American Institute of Planners* 39, no. 3 (1973): 163–178. https://doi.org/10.1080/01944367308977851.

Lefort, Claude. *Democracy and Political Theory*. Translated by David Macey. Oxford: Polity, 1988.

Lenton, Timothy M., Sébastien Dutreuil, and Bruno Latour. "Life on Earth Is Hard to Spot." *Anthropocene Review* 7, no. 3 (2020): 248–272. https://doi.org/10.1177/2053019620918939.

Lepore, Jill. *If Then: How Simulmatics Corporation Invented the Future*. New York: Liveright, 2020.

Lerner, Michael, Ryo Fujikura, Mikiyasu Nakayama, and Manami Fujikura. "The Influence of Limits to Growth and Global 2000 on U.S. Environmental Governance." *International Journal of Social Science Studies* 4, no. 8 (2016): 52–63. https://doi.org/10.11114/ijsss.v4i8.1674.

Lewis, Jason Edward, Noelani Arista, Archer Pechawis, and Suzanne Kite. "Making Kin with the Machines." *Journal of Design and Science*, July 16, 2018. https://doi.org/10.21428/bfafd97b.

Lewis, Jeremy R. T. "Software Reviews: Political Science Simulations: A Review Essay." *Social Science Computer Review* 7, no. 3 (1989): 369–377. https://doi.org/10.1177/089443938900700313.

Licklider, JCR. "Man-Computer Symbiosis." *IRE Transactions on Human Factors in Electronics* HFE-1, no. 1 (1960): 4–11.

Light, Jennifer S. *From Warfare to Welfare: Defense Intellectuals and Urban Problems in Cold War America*. Baltimore: Johns Hopkins University Press, 2005.

Light, Jennifer S. "Taking Games Seriously." *Technology and Culture* 49, no. 2 (2008): 347–375.

Lippman, Theo, Jr. "First One 'Inside the Beltway' Politics." *Baltimore Sun*, April 16, 1997. https://web.archive.org/web/20210622164118/https://www.baltimoresun.com/news/bs-xpm-1997-04-16-1997106020-story.html.

Lipsky, George A. "The Theory of International Relations of Harold D. Lasswell." *Journal of Politics* 17, no. 1 (1955): 43–58. https://doi.org/10.2307/2126403.

Livingston, Samuel A. "Effects of a Legislative Simulation Game on the Political Attitudes of Junior High School Students." *Simulation & Gaming* 3, no. 1 (1972): 41–51. https://doi.org/10.1177/104687817200300104.

Lockheed Martin. "Integrated Crisis Early Warning System." Accessed September 5, 2023. https://www.lockheedmartin.com/en-us/capabilities/research-labs/advanced-technology-labs/icews.html.

Lowi, Theodore. "Foreword." In *Disenchanted Realists: Political Science and the American Crisis, 1884–1984*, edited by Raymond Seidelman, vii–xix. Albany: State University of New York Press, 1985.

Macekura, Stephen. "Whither Growth? International Development, Social Indicators, and the Politics of Measurement, 1920s–1970s." *Journal of Global History* 14, no. 2 (July 2019): 261–279. https://doi.org/10.1017/S1740022819000068.

MacLean, Nancy. *Democracy in Chains: The Deep History of the Radical Right's Stealth Plan for America*. New York: Viking, 2017.

Macrae, John, and Paul Smoker. "A Vietnam Simulation: A Report on the Canadian/English Joint Project." *Journal of Peace Research* 4, no. 1 (1967): 1–24. https://doi.org/10.1177/002234336700400101.

Malcolm, D. G. "Bibliography on the Use of Simulation in Management Analysis." *Operations Research* 8, no. 2 (1960): 169–177. https://doi.org/10.1287/opre.8.2.169.

Marchessault, Janine. *Ecstatic Worlds: Media, Utopias, Ecologies*. Leonardo Book Series. Cambridge, MA: MIT Press, 2017.

Mari, Will. *Newsrooms and the Disruption of the Internet: A Short History of Disruptive Technologies, 1990–2010*. Disruptions. London: Routledge, 2022.

Marsden, Peter V. "The Sociology of James S. Coleman." *Annual Review of Sociology* 31, (2005): 1–24. https://doi.org/10.1146/annurev.soc.31.041304.122209.

Maske, Kellie, and Garey Durden. "The Contributions and Impact of Professor William H. Riker." *Public Choice* 117, no. 1 (2003): 191–220. https://doi.org/10.1023/A:1026117828869.

Massey, Jonathan. "Buckminster Fuller's Cybernetic Pastoral: The United States Pavilion at Expo 67." *The Journal of Architecture* 21, no. 5 (2016): 795–815. https://doi.org/10.1080/13602365.2016.1207433.

Mattelart, Armand. *Networking the World, 1794–2000*. Minneapolis: University of Minnesota Press, 2000.

Maxa, Rudy. "Can Matt Reese and a System Called Claritas Answer the Prayers of Democrats Everywhere? The Search for Votes Is Never Ending." *Washington Post*, July 22, 1979.

Mazrui, Ali Al'Amin. *A World Federation of Cultures: An African Perspective*. New York: Free Press, 1976. http://archive.org/details/worldfederationo00mazr.

Mazzotti, Massimo. *Reactionary Mathematics: A Genealogy of Purity*. Chicago: University of Chicago Press, 2023.

McClelland, Charles A. *Crisis and Threat in the International Setting: Some Relational Concepts*. Fort Belvoir, VA: Defense Technical Information Center, 1975. https://doi.org/10.21236/ADA011913.

McClelland, Charles A. "The Function of Theory in International Relations." *Journal of Conflict Resolution* 4, no. 3 (1960): 303–336.

McDougal, Myres S., Harold D. Lasswell, and W. Michael Reisman. "The Intelligence Function and World Public Order." *Temple Law Quarterly* 46, no. 3 (1973): 365–449.

McGrath, Patrick J. *Scientists, Business, and the State, 1890–1960*. Chapel Hill: University of North Carolina Press, 2012.

McGuigan, Lee. "Automating the Audience Commodity: The Unacknowledged Ancestry of Programmatic Advertising." *New Media & Society* 21, no. 11–12 (2019): 2366–2385. https://doi.org/10.1177/1461444819846449.

McGuigan, Lee. *Selling the American People: Advertising, Optimization, and the Origins of Adtech*. Distribution Matters. Cambridge, MA: MIT Press, 2023.

McHugh, Francis. "Fundamentals of War Gaming, Third Edition." AD686108. Newport: US Naval War College, 1966. https://apps.dtic.mil/sti/pdfs/AD0686108.pdf.

McIlwain, Charlton D. *Black Software: The Internet and Racial Justice, from the AfroNet to Black Lives Matter*. New York: Oxford University Press, 2020.

McKeil, Aaron. "Revisiting the World Order Models Project: A Case for Renewal?" *Global Policy* 13, no. 4 (2022): 417–426. https://doi.org/10.1111/1758-5899.13070.

McKelvey, Fenwick. "Book Review: If Then: How the Simulmatics Corporation Invented the Future." *International Journal of Press/Politics*, January 16, 2021, 194016122198921S. https://doi.org/10.1177/194016122198921S.

McKelvey, Fenwick. *Internet Daemons: Digital Communications Possessed*. Electronic Mediations 56. Minneapolis: University of Minnesota Press, 2018.

McKelvey, Fenwick. "The Other Cambridge Analytics: Early 'Artificial Intelligence' in American Political Science." In *The Cultural Life of Machine Learning: An Incursion into Critical AI Studies*, edited by Jonathan Roberge and Michael Castelle, 117–142. London: Palgrave Macmillan, 2021. https://doi.org/10.1007/978-3-030-56286-1.

McKelvey, Fenwick. "When the New Magic Was New: The Claritas Corporation and the Clustering of America." *IEEE Annals of the History of Computing* 44, no. 4 (2022): 44–56. https://doi.org/10.1109/MAHC.2022.3214223.

McKelvey, Fenwick, and Jill Piebiak. "Porting the Political Campaign: The NationBuilder Platform and the Global Flows of Political Technology." *New Media & Society* 20, no. 3 (2018): 901–918. https://doi.org/10.1177/1461444816675439.

McKelvey, Fenwick, and Jonathan Roberge. "Recursive Power." In *Handbook of Critical Studies of Artificial Intelligence*, edited by Simon Lindgren, 21–32. Northampton, UK: Edward Elgar, 2023.

McKibben, William. "The End of Nature." *The New Yorker*, September 3, 1989. https://www.newyorker.com/magazine/1989/09/11/the-end-of-nature.

McLean, Iain. "William H. Riker and the Invention of Heresthetic(s)." *British Journal of Political Science* 32, no. 3 (2002): 535–558. https://doi.org/10.1017/S0007123402000224.

McPhee, William N. "Note on a Campaign Simulator." *Public Opinion Quarterly* 25, no. 2 (1961): 184–193. https://doi.org/10.1086/267013.

McPhee, William N., and James Coleman. "A Program of Research in 'Mass Dynamics.'" *American Behavioral Scientist* 1, no. 4 (1958): 6–10. https://doi.org/10.1177/000276425800100403.

McPhee, William N., and Robert B. Smith. "A Model for Analyzing Voting Systems." In *Public Opinion and Congressional Elections*, edited by William N. McPhee and William A. Glaser, 123–154. Glencoe, IL: Free Press, 1962.

Meadows, D., J. Richardson, and G. Bruckmann. *Groping in the Dark: The First Decade of Global Modelling*. Chichester, UK: John Wiley & Sons, 1982. http://pure.iiasa.ac.at/id/eprint/1829/.

Meadows, Donella H. "Lessons from Global Modelling and Modellers." *Futures* 14, no. 2 (1982): 111–121. https://doi.org/10.1016/0016-3287(82)90084-2.

Meadows, Donella H., Dennis L. Meadows, Jørgen Randers, and William W. Behrens III. *The Limits to Growth: A Report for the Club of Rome's Project on the Predicament of Mankind*. Falls Church, VA: Potomac Associates, 1972.

Meadows, Donella H., and J. M. Robinson. *The Electronic Oracle: Computer Models and Social Decisions*. Chichester, UK: Wiley, 1985.

Medina, Eden. *Cybernetic Revolutionaries: Technology and Politics in Allende's Chile*. Cambridge, MA: MIT Press, 2011.

Mejias, Ulises A., and Nick Couldry. "Datafication." *Internet Policy Review* 8, no. 4 (2019). https://policyreview.info/concepts/datafication.

Mendlovitz, Saul. "General Introduction." In *A Study of Future Worlds*, xvii–xxvii. New York: Simon and Schuster, 1975.

Mesarovic, Mihajli, and Eduard Pestel. *Mankind at the Turning Point: The Second Report to the Club of Rome*. New York: Reader's Digest Press, 1974.

de Mesquita, Bruce Bueno. *The Invention of Power: Popes, Kings, and the Birth of the West*. New York: PublicAffairs, 2022.

Metropolis, Nicholas. "The Beginning of the Monte Carlo Method." *Los Alamos Science* 15, no. 584 (1987): 125–130.

Meyer, Cord. *Facing Reality: From World Federalism to the CIA*. New York: Harper & Row, 1980. http://archive.org/details/facingrealityfro00meye.

Meyer, D. Swing. *The Winning Candidate: How to Defeat Your Political Opponents*. New York: Heinemann, 1966.

Miller, Gary J. "The Impact of Economics on Contemporary Political Science." *Journal of Economic Literature* 35, no. 3 (1997): 1173–1204.

Mirowski, Philip. "A Brief History of Neoliberalism, David Harvey. Oxford University Press, 2005, VII+247 Pages." *Economics and Philosophy* 24, no. 1 (2008): 111–117.

Mirowski, Philip. *Machine Dreams: Economics Becomes a Cyborg Science*. Cambridge, UK: Cambridge University Press, 2002.

Mirowski, Philip. "Postface: Defining Neoliberalism." In *The Road from Mont Pèlerin*, edited by Philip Mirowski and Dieter Plehwe, 417–456. Cambridge, MA: Harvard University Press, 2009. https://doi.org/10.4159/9780674054264-013.

Mockus, Joseph. 1980. "Geodemographics II: Targeting Your Turnout." *Campaigns & Elections* 1 (2): 55–66.

Monea, Alexander, and Jeremy Packer. "Media Genealogy: Technological and Historical Engagements of Power—Introduction." *International Journal of Communication* 10 (2016): 3141–3159.

Morgan, Mary S., and Margaret Morrison, eds. *Models as Mediators: Perspectives on Natural and Social Science*. Ideas in Context. Cambridge, UK: Cambridge University Press, 1999. https://doi.org/10.1017/CBO9780511660108.

Morgan, Thomas Bruce. "The People-Machine." *Harper's Magazine*, January 1961.

Morgenthau, Hans. *Politics Among Nations*. New York: Alfred A. Knopf, 1948. http://archive.org/details/in.ernet.dli.2015.237473.

Moriyama, Takahito. *Empire of Direct Mail: How Conservative Marketing Persuaded Voters and Transformed the Grassroots*. Lawrence: University Press of Kansas, 2022.

Morrison, Margaret. *Reconstructing Reality: Models, Mathematics, and Simulations*. Oxford: Oxford University Press, 2015.

Mosco, Vincent. *The Digital Sublime: Myth, Power, and Cyberspace*. Cambridge, MA: MIT Press, 2004.

Moses, Lincoln E., Richard A. Brody, Ole R. Holsti, Joseph B. Kadane, and Jeffrey S. Milstein. "Scaling Data on Inter-Nation Action: A Standard Scale Is Developed for Comparing International Conflict in a Variety of Situations." *Science* 156, no. 3778 (1967): 1054–1059. https://doi.org/10.1126/science.156.3778.1054.

Mouffe, Chantal. *On the Political*. New York: Routledge, 2005.

Mukerji, Chandra. *A Fragile Power: Scientists and the State*. Princeton, NJ: Princeton University Press, 1989.

Muldoon, James P., Jr. "The Model United Nations Revisited." *Simulation & Gaming*, August 18, 2016. https://doi.org/10.1177/1046878195261003.

Murphy, Michelle. *The Economization of Life*. Durham, NC: Duke University Press, 2017.

Myers, Natasha. *Rendering Life Molecular: Models, Modelers, and Excitable Matter*. Durham, NC: Duke University Press, 2015. https://doi.org/10.1215/9780822375630.

Newman, Jake. "Data Firms Mining Gold from Census Information." *Washington Post*, June 7, 1982, sec. Business.

Nichols, Charles K. "The Statistical Work of the League of Nations in Economic, Financial and Related Fields." *Journal of the American Statistical Association* 37, no. 219 (1942): 336–342. https://doi.org/10.2307/2279001.

Nicholson, Michael. "Lewis Fry Richardson and the Study of the Causes of War." *British Journal of Political Science* 29, no. 3 (1999): 541–563.

Nielsen, Rasmus Kleis. *Ground Wars: Personalized Communication in Political Campaigns*. Princeton, NJ: Princeton University Press, 2012.

Nielsen, Rasmus Kleis. "Mundane Internet Tools, Mobilizing Practices, and the Coproduction of Citizenship in Political Campaigns." *New Media & Society* 13, no. 5 (2011): 755–771. https://doi.org/10.1177/1461444810380863.

Niemelä, Jari. *Urban Ecology: Patterns, Processes, and Applications*. Edited by Jürgen H. Breuste, Thomas Elmqvist, Glenn Guntenspergen, Philip James, and Nancy E. McIntyre. Oxford: Oxford University Press, 2011. https://doi.org/10.1093/acprof:oso/9780199563562.001.0001.

Noël, Robert C. "The Polis Laboratory." *American Behavioral Scientist* 12, no. 6 (1969): 30–35.

Nordhaus, William D. "World Dynamics: Measurement Without Data." *Economic Journal* 83, no. 332 (1973): 1156–1183. https://doi.org/10.2307/2230846.

Nye, David E. *American Technological Sublime*. Cambridge, MA: MIT Press, 1994.

O'Brien, Lawrence. *The Democratic Campaign Manual*. Washington, DC: Democratic National Committee, 1964.

O'Brien, Sean P. "Crisis Early Warning and Decision Support: Contemporary Approaches and Thoughts on Future Research." *International Studies Review* 12, no. 1 (2010): 87–104.

Odegard, Peter. Review of *Review of The Pre-Election Polls of 1948 and The Polls and Public Opinion*, by Frederick Mostelle, Herbert Hyman, Philip J. McCarthy, Eli S. Marks, David B. Truman, Norman C. Meier, and Harold W. Saunders. *American Political Science Review* 44, no. 2 (1950): 459–464. https://doi.org/10.2307/1950284.

O'Lone, Katherine, Michael Gantley, Justin Lane, and F. Shults. "Employing Multi-Agent AI to Model Conflict and Cooperation in Northern Ireland." *New England Journal of Public Policy* 36, no. 1 (2024). https://scholarworks.umb.edu/nejpp/vol36/iss1/6.

O'Neil, Cathy. *Weapons of Math Destruction: How Big Data Increases Inequality and Threatens Democracy*, 1st ed. New York: Crown, 2016.

Onlinejournalismsymp. "Suzanne Seggerman Interview," 2008. https://www.youtube.com/watch?v=JIkjmSt-gYo.

OpenCorporates. "Policon Corporation." January 12, 2024. https://opencorporates.com/companies/us_mi/800228046.

Oren, Ido. *Our Enemies and US: America's Rivalries and the Making of Political Science*. Cornell, NY: Cornell University Press, 2003.

Oreskes, Naomi, Kristin Shrader-Frechette, and Kenneth Belitz. "Verification, Validation, and Confirmation of Numerical Models in the Earth Sciences." *Science* 263, no. 5147 (1994): 641–646.

Organski, A. F. K., and Jacek Kugler. *The War Ledger*. Chicago: University of Chicago Press, 1981. https://press.uchicago.edu/ucp/books/book/chicago/W/bo5955354.html.

Ozbekhan, Hasan, University of Pennsylvania, and Management and Behavioral Science Center. *The Club of Rome: The Predicament of Mankind, Quest for Structured Responses to Growing World-Wide Complexities and Uncertainties—A Proposal*. Philadelphia: Management and Behavioral Science Center, University of Pennsylvania, 1970.

Özden-Schilling, Tom. "Authors of Misfortune: Interpretation and Expertise in a Model Disaster." *Journal of the Royal Anthropological Institute*, 30 no. 1 (2024): 75–96. https://doi.org/10.1111/1467-9655.14047.

Page, Scott E. *The Model Thinker: What You Need to Know to Make Data Work for You*. New York: Basic Books, 2018.

Passell, Peter, Marc Roberts, and Leonard Ross. "The Limits to Growth." *New York Times*, April 2, 1972, sec. BR.

Patel, Samir R. "What Can AI Teach Brands About Customer-Centric Marketing?" Blue State, May 18, 2018. https://www.bluestate.co/news/ai-customer-marketing/.

Patton, Paul. *Deleuze and the Political*. London: Routledge, 2000.

Pearson, Richard. "Ithiel de Sola Pool, Communication Theorist, Dies." *Washington Post*, March 13, 1984. https://www.washingtonpost.com/archive/local/1984/03/13/ithiel-de-sola-pool-communication-theorist-dies/1ec2df79-f36a-452b-b0b4-31a55d8d86e6/.

Pearson, Richard. "Richard Beal, Special Aide to Reagan, Dies." *Washington Post*, November 4, 1984. https://www.washingtonpost.com/archive/local/1984/11/04/richard-beal-special-aide-to-reagan-dies/71b0e75d-0cf8-4c20-a63b-8308f9ebb515/.

Pepper, David. *Laboratories of Autocracy: A Wake-Up Call from Behind the Lines*. Cincinnati, OH: St. Helena Press, 2021.

Perry, James M. *The New Politics: The Expanding Technology of Political Manipulation*. New York: Clarkson N. Potter, 1968.

Perry, Ravi K., and D. LaRouth Perry. *The Little Rock Crisis*. New York: Palgrave Macmillan US, 2015. https://doi.org/10.1057/9781137521347.

Pestel, Eduard. "Modellers and Politicians." *Futures* 14, no. 2 (1982): 122–128. https://doi.org/10.1016/0016-3287(82)90085-4.

Peters, Benjamin. *How Not to Network a Nation: The Uneasy History of the Soviet Internet.* Cambridge, MA: MIT Press, 2016.

Peters, Benjamin. "Normalizing Soviet Cybernetics." *Information & Culture: A Journal of History* 47, no. 2 (2012): 145–175. https://doi.org/10.1353/lac.2012.0009.

Petrison, Lisa A., Robert C. Blattberg, and Paul Wang. "Database Marketing: Past, Present, and Future." *Journal of Direct Marketing* 11, no. 4 (1997): 109–125. https://doi.org/10.1002/(SICI)1522-7138(199723)11:4<109::AID-DIR12>3.0.CO;2-G.

Pias, Claus. "On the Epistemology of Computer Simulation." *Zeitschrift für Medien- und Kulturforschung,* 2011, 29–54. https://doi.org/10.25969/MEDIAREP/18462.

Pickering, Andrew. "Cyborg History and the World War II Regime." *Perspectives on Science* 3, no. 1 (1995): 1–48.

Pickering, Andrew, and Katherine Hayles. *Cybernetics for the 21st Century,* vol. 1. *Epistemological Reconstruction.* Edited by Yuk Hui. Kwai Chung, New Territories, Hong Kong: Hanart Press, 2024.

Pool, Ithiel de Sola. "Use of Available Sample Surveys in Comparative Research." *Social Science Information* 2, no. 2 (1963): 16–35. https://doi.org/10.1177/053901846300200202.

Pool, Ithiel de Sola. "Automation: New Tool for Decision Makers." *Challenge* 11, no. 6 (1963): 26–27. https://doi.org/10.1080/05775132.1963.11469546.

Pool, Ithiel de Sola, and Robert Abelson. "The Simulmatics Project." *Public Opinion Quarterly* 25, no. 2 (1961): 167–183. https://doi.org/10.1086/267012.

Pool, Ithiel de Sola, Robert P. Abelson, and Samuel L. Popkin. *Candidates, Issues, and Strategies: A Computer Simulation of the 1960 Presidential Election.* Cambridge, MA: MIT Press, 1964.

Pool, Ithiel de Sola, Robert P. Abelson, and Samuel L. Popkin. "A Postscript on the 1964 Election." *American Behavioral Scientist* 8, no. 9 (1965): 39–44. https://doi.org/10.1177/000276426500800910.

Pool, Ithiel de Sola, and Allan Kessler. "The Kaiser, the Tsar, and the Computer: Information Processing in a Crisis." *American Behavioral Scientist* 8, no. 9 (1965): 31–38.

Pooley, Jefferson. "A 'Not Particularly Felicitous' Phrase: A History of the 'Behavioral Sciences' Label." *SocArXiv,* April 21, 2020. https://doi.org/10.31235/osf.io/uzqdj.

Pooley, Jefferson, and Mark Solovey. "Marginal to the Revolution: The Curious Relationship Between Economics and the Behavioral Sciences Movement in Mid-Twentieth-Century America." *History of Political Economy* 42, no. Suppl. 1 (2010): 199–233. https://doi.org/10.1215/00182702-2009-077.

Popkin, Samuel L. "Computer Simulations of Voting Behavior. By William R. Shaffer. (New York: Oxford University Press, 1972. Pp. 164. $7.50, Cloth; $2.95, Paper.)." *American Political Science Review* 68, no. 4 (1974): 1747–1749. https://doi.org/10.2307/1959973.

Porter, Theodore M. *Trust in Numbers: The Pursuit of Objectivity in Science and Public Life*. Princeton, NJ: Princeton University Press, 1995.

Powell, Alison B. *Undoing Optimization: Civic Action in Smart Cities*. New Haven, CT: Yale University Press, 2021.

Pryluka, Pablo. "'Una futura Heidelberg argentina': el itinerario de la Fundación Bariloche (1963–1978)." *Pasado Abierto* 6, no. 11 (2020): 56–75.

Ramsauer, Markus. "Endogenizing Politics: The GLOBUS World Model." Preprints, February 2, 2024. https://doi.org/10.20944/preprints202402.0100.v1.

Ray, James Lee. "Understanding Rummel." Edited by R. J. Rummel. *Journal of Conflict Resolution* 26, no. 1 (1982): 161–187.

Reed, Stanley Foster. "Campaigns & Computers." *Campaigns & Elections*, Fall 1982.

Renshaw, J. R., and Annette Heuston. *The Game Monopologs*. Santa Monica, CA: RAND Corporation, January 1, 1957. https://www.rand.org/pubs/research_memoranda/RM1917-1.html.

Renzi, Alessandra. "Entangled Data: Modelling and Resistance in the Megacity." Online Open, February 20, 2017. https://onlineopen.org/entangled-data-modelling-and-resistance-in-the-megacity.

Republican National Committee. *Electronic Data Processing for the Political Executive*. Washington, DC: Republican National Committee, 1968.

Republican National Committee Committee on Data Processing. *Electronic Data Processing and Politics*." Washington, DC: Republican National Committee, 1966.

Restivo, Sal. "The Social Construction of Mathematics." In *Sociology, Science, and the End of Philosophy*, 253–281. London: Palgrave Macmillan, 2017. https://doi.org/10.1057/978-1-349-95160-4_7.

Richardson, John M., Jr. "A Decade of Global Modelling." *Futures* 14, no. 2 (1982): 136–145. https://doi.org/10.1016/0016-3287(82)90087-8.

Riker, William H., and Peter C. Ordeshook. "A Theory of the Calculus of Voting." *American Political Science Review* 62, no. 1 (1968): 25–42. https://doi.org/10.2307/1953324.

Rindzevičiūtė, Eglė. *The Power of Systems: How Policy Sciences Opened Up the Cold War World*. Ithaca, NY: Cornell University Press, 2016.

Robbin, Jonathan. "Geodemographics: The New Magic." *Campaigns & Elections* 1, no. 1: 25–45 (1980).

Robbin, Jonathan. *A Guide to the Use of Census Data for Political Campaign Planning and Management.* Rosslyn, VA: Claritas Corporation, 1972.

Robbin, Jonathan. "What Is Geodemography?" 2004. https://web.archive.org/web/20110515000000*/https://ricercar.com/gdef.html.

Roberts, Sarah T., and Mél Hogan. "Left Behind: Futurist Fetishists, Prepping and the Abandonment of Earth." *B2o: An Online Journal* 4, no. 2 (2019). https://escholarship.org/uc/item/8sr8n99w.

Robertson, Adi. "They Spent $3 Million on a Dune Script Bible: Now What?" The Verge, February 28, 2022. https://www.theverge.com/2022/2/28/22950868/spice-dao-crypto-jodorowsky-dune-bible-collective-writing-contest.

Robinson, William S. "Ecological Correlations and the Behavior of Individuals." *American Sociological Review* 15, no. 3 (1950): 351–357. https://doi.org/10.2307/2087176.

Rockmore, Dan. "How Much of the World Is It Possible to Model?" *The New Yorker*, January 15, 2024. https://www.newyorker.com/culture/annals-of-inquiry/how-much-of-the-world-is-it-possible-to-model.

Rohde, Joy. *Armed with Expertise: The Militarization of American Social Research During the Cold War.* Ithaca, NY: Cornell University Press, 2013.

Rohde, Joy. "The Last Stand of the Psychocultural Cold Warriors: Military Contract Research in Vietnam." *Journal of the History of the Behavioral Sciences* 47, no. 3 (2011): 232–250. https://doi.org/10.1002/jhbs.20509.

Rohde, Joy. "Pax Technologica: Computers, International Affairs, and Human Reason in the Cold War." *Isis* 108, no. 4 (2017): 792–813. https://doi.org/10.1086/695679.

Rosenof, Theodore. "The Legend of Louis Bean: Political Prophecy and the 1948 Election." *The Historian* 62, no. 1 (1999): 63–78. https://doi.org/10.1111/j.1540-6563.1999.tb01434.x.

Ross, Dorothy. *The Origins of American Social Science*. Cambridge, UK: Cambridge University Press, 1991.

Rummel, Rudolph J. "Some Dimensions in the Foreign Behaviour of Nations." In *International Politics and Foreign Policy: A Reader in Research and Theory,* edited by James N. Rosenau, 600–621. New York: Free Press, 1969.

Sabagh, Georges, Peter Orleans, Joseph B. Birdsell, Andreas Tietze, and Ralph Turner. "Eshref Shevky, Anthropology and Sociology: Los Angeles." December 1970.

http://texts.cdlib.org/view?docId=hb629006wb;NAAN=13030&doc.view=frames&chunk.id=div00040&toc.depth=1&toc.id=&brand=calisphere.

Sahota, Neil. "The AI Factor in Political Campaigns: Revolutionizing Modern Politics." *Forbes*, January 12, 2024. https://www.forbes.com/sites/neilsahota/2024/01/12/the-ai-factor-in-political-campaigns-revolutionizing-modern-politics/.

Saxon, Wolfgang. "Richard Smith Beal Dies at 38." *New York Times*, November 4, 1984, sec. Obituaries. https://www.nytimes.com/1984/11/04/obituaries/richard-smith-beal-dies-at-38.html.

Schaar, John H., and Sheldon S. Wolin. "Essays on the Scientific Study of Politics: A Critique." *American Political Science Review* 57, no. 1 (1963): 125–50. https://doi.org/10.2307/1952724.

Schafferer, Christian. "The Globalization of Political Marketing: An Introduction." In *Election Campaigning in East and Southeast Asia*. London: Routledge, 2006.

Schechter, Neil. "Further Investigations of a Computer Simulation of Voting Behavior." *Political Methodology* 2, no. 4 (1975): 437–454.

Scheuch, Erwin K., and Philip J. Stone. "The General Inquirer Approach to an International Retrieval System for Survey Archives." *American Behavioral Scientist* 7, no. 10 (1964): 23–28. https://doi.org/10.1177/000276426400701006.

Schmelzer, Matthias. "'Born in the Corridors of the OECD': The Forgotten Origins of the Club of Rome, Transnational Networks, and the 1970s in Global History." *Journal of Global History* 12, no. 1 (2017): 26–48. https://doi.org/10.1017/S1740022816000322.

Schneider, Edward J. "Geodemographics Refined: An Alternative to Standardized Clustering." *Campaigns & Elections*, 3, no. 4 (1983): 62–73.

Schudson, Michael. "The Troubling Equivalence of Citizen and Consumer." *Annals of the American Academy of Political and Social Science* 608 (2006): 193–204.

Schulman, Robert. "A World in Flux Means Steady Work for Risk Analysts." *New York Times*, November 4, 1990, sec. Business. https://www.nytimes.com/1990/11/04/business/a-world-in-flux-means-steady-work-for-risk-analysts.html.

Schulte, Stephanie Ricker. "'The WarGames Scenario': Regulating Teenagers and Teenaged Technology (1980–1984)." *Television & New Media* 9, no. 6 (2008): 487–513. https://doi.org/10.1177/1527476408323345.

Schwartzman, Edward. *Campaign Craftmanship: A Professional's Guide to Campaigning for Elective Office*. New York: Universe Books, 1973.

Seaver, Nick. *Computing Taste: Algorithms and the Makers of Music Recommendation*. Chicago: University of Chicago Press, 2022. https://press.uchicago.edu/ucp/books/book/chicago/C/bo183892298.html.

Securities and Exchange Commission. "General Analytics Files for Offering and Secondary." *News Digest*, October 3, 1968, 68–194.

Shaffer, William R. *Computer Simulations of Voting Behavior*. Studies in Behavioral Political Science. New York: Oxford University Press, 1972.

Shaffer, William R., and Ronald E. Weber. "Computer Simulation of Voting: A Test of a Revised Model." *Political Methodology* 3, no. 2 (1976): 253–279.

Shankar, Kalpana, Kristin R. Eschenfelder, and Greg Downey. "Studying the History of Social Science Data Archives as Knowledge Infrastructure." *Science & Technology Studies* 29, no. 2 (2016): 62–73. https://doi.org/10.23987/sts.55691.

Shapiro, Michael J. "The House and the Federal Role: A Computer Simulation of Roll-Call Voting." *American Political Science Review* 62, no. 2 (1968): 494–517. https://doi.org/10.2307/1952944.

Sheingate, Adam. *Building a Business of Politics: The Rise of Political Consulting and the Transformation of American Democracy*. New York, NY: Oxford University Press, 2016.

Shenker, Israel. "World Federalist Group Marks 30th Year and Tries to Put It All Together." *New York Times*, August 1, 1977. https://www.nytimes.com/1977/08/01/archives/world-federalist-group-marks-30th-year-and-tries-to-put-it-all.html.

Shevky, Eshref, and Wendell Bell. *Social Area Analysis: Theory, Illustrative Application, and Computational Procedures*. Stanford Sociological Series 1. Stanford, CA: Stanford University Press, 1955.

Shevky, Eshref, and Marilyn Williams. *The Social Areas of Los Angeles: Analysis and Typology*. Berkeley: University of California Press, 1949.

Shubik, Martin. "Modeling on a Grand Scale." Edited by Jay W. Forrester. *Science* 174, no. 4013 (1971): 1014–1015.

Simonson, Peter. "Writing Figures into the Field: William McPhee and the Parts Played by People in Our Histories of Media Research." In *The History of Media and Communication Research: Contested Memories*, edited by David W. Park and Jefferson Pooley, 291–320. New York: Peter Lang, 2008.

Simpson, Christopher. *Science of Coercion: Communication Research and Psychological Warfare, 1945–1960*, reprint ed. New York: Oxford University Press, 1995.

Singer, J. David. "Data-Making in International Relations." *Behavioral Science* 10, no. 1 (1, 1965): 68–80.

Singer, J. David. Parents of the field. Interview by Chris Mitchell, 2013. https://www.youtube.com/watch?v=JY7v02RJOyk .

Singer, J. David. "The Relevance of the Behavioral Sciences to the Study of International Relations." *Behavioral Science* 6, no. 4 (1961): 324–335.

Singer, J. David, and Melvin Small. "Formal Alliances, 1815–1939: A Quantitative Description." *Journal of Peace Research* 3, no. 1 (1966): 1–31. https://doi.org/10.1177/002234336600300101.

Singer, J. David, and Melvin Small. "National Alliance Commitments and War Involvement, 1818–1945." In *International Politics and Foreign Policy: A Reader in Research and Theory*, edited by James N. Rosenau, 513–542. New York: Free Press, 1969.

Slobodian, Quinn. "How to See the World Economy: Statistics, Maps, and Schumpeter's Camera in the First Age of Globalization." *Journal of Global History* 10, no. 2 (2015): 307–332. https://doi.org/10.1017/S174002281500008X.

Smith, Terence. "Arkansas Victory Rockefeller's Own." *New York Times*, November 10, 1966.

Smoker, Paul. "International Processes Simulation: A Description." In *Experimentation and Simulation in Political Science*, edited by J. A. Laponce and Paul Smoker, 315–366. Toronto: University of Toronto Press, 1972.

del Solar, Daniel. "How We Planned a Coup." *Berkeley Bard*, September 14, 1973.

Solovey, Mark. "Cold War Social Science: Specter, Reality, or Useful Concept?" In *Cold War Social Science: Knowledge Production, Liberal Democracy, and Human Nature*, edited by Mark Solovey and Hamilton Cravens, 1–22. New York: Palgrave Macmillan US, 2012. https://doi.org/10.1057/9781137013224_1.

Solovey, Mark. "Project Camelot and the 1960s Epistemological Revolution: Rethinking the Politics-Patronage-Social Science Nexus." *Social Studies of Science* 31, no. 2 (2001): 171–206. https://doi.org/10.1177/0306312701031002003.

Solow, Robert M. "How Did Economics Get That Way and What Way Did It Get?" *Daedalus* 126, no. 1 (1997): 39–58.

Sovacool, Benjamin K., and David J. Hess. "Ordering Theories: Typologies and Conceptual Frameworks for Sociotechnical Change." *Social Studies of Science* 47, no. 5 (2017): 703–750. https://doi.org/10.1177/0306312717709363.

Srnicek, Nick, and Alex Williams. *Inventing the Future: Postcapitalism and a World Without Work*. New York: Verso, 2015.

Starr, Paul. "Seductions of Sim." *American Prospect*, 1994.

Steingart, Alma. *Axiomatics: Mathematical Thought and High Modernism*. Chicago: University of Chicago Press, 2023.

Stengers, Isabelle. "Including Nonhumans in Political Theory: Opening Pandora's Box?" In *Political Matter*, edited by Bruce Braun and Sarah J. Whatmore, 3–34. Minneapolis: University of Minnesota Press, 2010.

Stone, Philip J., Robert F. Bales, J. Zvi Namenwirth, and Daniel M. Ogilvie. "The General Inquirer: A Computer System for Content Analysis and Retrieval Based on the Sentence as a Unit of Information." *Behavioral Science* 7, no. 4 (1962): 484–498.

Stone, Philip J., Dexter Dunphy, Marshall S. Smith, and Daniel M. Ogilvie. *The General Inquirer: A Computer Approach to Content Analysis*. Cambridge, MA: MIT Press, 1966. https://mitpress.mit.edu/books/general-inquirer.

Stott, Tim. *Buckminster Fuller's World Game and Its Legacy*. Routledge Focus on Art History and Visual Studies. New York: Routledge, 2021.

Suchman, Lucy. "Imaginaries of Omniscience: Automating Intelligence in the US Department of Defense." *Social Studies of Science*, June 23, 2022, 030631272211049. https://doi.org/10.1177/03063127221104938.

Suchman, Lucy, Randall Trigg, and Jeanette Blomberg. "Working Artefacts: Ethnomethods of the Prototype." *British Journal of Sociology* 53, no. 2 (2002): 163–179. https://doi.org/10.1080/00071310220133287.

Swenson, Russell George, ed. *Bringing Intelligence About: Practitioners Reflect on Best Practices*. Washington, DC: Joint Military Intelligence College, 2003.

Tanjo. "TAP." Accessed February 23, 2021. https://web.archive.org/web/20180501000000*/https://www.tanjo.net/tap.

Taylor, Charles. "Modern Social Imaginaries." *Public Culture* 41, no. 1 (2002): 91–124.

Taylor, Charles Lewis, and Bruce M. Russett. "Biography of Karl Wolfgang Deutsch (1912–1992)." In *Karl W. Deutsch: Pioneer in the Theory of International Relations: With a Preface by Charles Lewis Taylor and Bruce M. Russett*, edited by Charles Lewis Taylor and Bruce M. Russett, 3–14. Cham, Switzerland: Springer International, 2020. https://doi.org/10.1007/978-3-319-02910-8_1.

"TEMPER Volume 1, Orientation Manual." Bedford, MA: Raytheon Company, July 9, 1965. https://apps.dtic.mil/sti/citations/AD0470375.

"TEMPER. Volume 2. The Theory of the Model." Bedford, MA: Raytheon Company, August 25, 1965. https://apps.dtic.mil/sti/citations/AD0471458.

Theophanidis, Philippe, Ghislain Thibault, and Dominique Trudel. "At the Margins of Cybernetics." *Canadian Journal of Communication* 42, no. 3 (2017): 397–405. https://cjc.utppublishing.com/doi/full/10.22230/cjc.2017v42n3e3304.

Thompson, Erica. *Escape from Model Land: How Mathematical Models Can Lead Us Astray and What We Can Do About It*. New York: Basic Books, 2022.

Timmons, Heather. "If Cambridge Analytica Is So Smart, Why Isn't Ted Cruz President?" Quartz, March 21, 2018. https://qz.com/1234364/cambridge-analytica-worked-for-mercer-backed-ted-cruz-before-trump.

Tobin, James. "Can Data Preserve Peace?" *Michigan Today*, January 23, 2020. https://michigantoday.umich.edu/2020/01/23/can-data-preserve-peace/.

Tolon, Kaya. "Futures Studies: A New Social Science Rooted in Cold War Strategic Thinking." In *Cold War Social Science: Knowledge Production, Liberal Democracy, and Human Nature*, edited by Mark Solovey and Hamilton Cravens, 45–62. New York: Palgrave Macmillan US, 2012. https://doi.org/10.1057/9781137013224_3.

Tomkins, Calvin. "Buckminster Fuller, Intellectual Outlaw." *The New Yorker*, January 8, 1966.

Towns, Armond R. "Toward a Black Media Philosophy." *Cultural Studies* 34, no. 6 (2020): 851–873. https://doi.org/10.1080/09502386.2020.1792524.

Tsing, Anna Lowenhaupt. "On Nonscalability: The Living World Is Not Amenable to Precision-Nested Scales." *Common Knowledge* 18, no. 3 (2012): 505–524. https://doi.org/10.1215/0961754X-1630424.

Turek, Maciej, and Paweł Laider, eds. "The Federal Election Campaign Act of 1971: 86 Stat. 3 (1972)." In *Basic Documents in Federal Campaign Finance Law*, edited by Paweł Laidler and Maciej Turek, 34–39. Kraków, Poland: Jagiellonian University Press, 2015.

Turner, Fred. *From Counterculture to Cyberculture: Stewart Brand, the Whole Earth Network, and the Rise of Digital Utopianism*. Chicago: University of Chicago Press, 2006.

Turner, Fred. "Prototype." In *Digital Keywords: A Vocabulary of Information Society and Culture*, edited by Benjamin Peters, 256–268. Princeton Studies in Culture and Technology. Princeton, NJ: Princeton University Press, 2016.

Turner, Fred. "Why Study New Games?" *Games and Culture* 1, no. 1 (2006): 107–110. https://doi.org/10.1177/1555412005281823.

Uhle, Frank. "Frost & Sullivan, Inc." In *International Directory of Company Histories*, edited by Tina Grant, 43:142–144. Detroit: St. James Press, 2003. http://archive.org/details/internationaldir0000unse_v5o3.

Ulam, Stanislaw M. "Monte Carlo Calculations in Problems of Mathematical Physics." *Modern Mathematics for the Engineers*, 1961, 261–281.

UNESCO. "Perceptions and Analyses of World Problems: Major Programme 1." 1986. https://unesdoc.unesco.org/ark:/48223/pf0000068817.

Urwin, Cathy Kunzinger. *Agenda for Reform: Winthrop Rockefeller as Governor of Arkansas, 1967–71*. Fayetteville: University of Arkansas Press, 1991.

US Census Bureau, Census History Staff. "UNIVAC I—History—U.S. Census Bureau." Accessed December 1, 2020. https://www.census.gov/history/www/innovations/technology/univac_i.html.

US Congress Senate Government Operations. *Establish a Select Senate Committee on Technology and the Human Environment: Hearings Before the Subcommittee on Intergovernmental Relations . . . 91–1, on S. Res. 78, March 4–6, April 24, and May 7, 1969*, 1969. Washington, DC: US GPO.

Vág, A. "The Short History and the Plausible Future of World Modelling." *Acta Oeconomica* 55, no. 1 (2005): 63–88.

Verba, Sidney. "Assumptions of Rationality and Non-Rationality in Models of the International System." *World Politics* 14, no. 1 (1961): 93–117. https://doi.org/10.2307/2009558.

Verba, Sidney. "Simulation, Reality, and Theory in International Relations." *World Politics* 16, no. 3 (1964): 490–519. https://doi.org/10.2307/2009585.

Vincent, Douglas F. "The Orgin and Development of Factor Analysis." *Applied Statistics* 2, no. 2 (1953): 107. https://doi.org/10.2307/2985729.

Vitalis, Robert. *White World Order, Black Power Politics: The Birth of American International Relations*, reprint ed. Ithaca, NY: Cornell University Press, 2017.

Vulpiani, Angelo. "Lewis Fry Richardson: Scientist, Visionary and Pacifist." *Lettera Matematica* 2, no. 3 (2014): 121–128. https://doi.org/10.1007/s40329-014-0063-z.

Waismel-Manor, Israel. "Spinning Forward: Professionalization Among Campaign Consultants." *Journal of Political Marketing* 10, no. 4 (2011): 350–371. https://doi.org/10.1080/15377857.2011.614556.

Waldrop, M. Mitchell. *The Dream Machine: J.C.R. Licklider and the Revolution That Made Computing Personal*. New York: Penguin Books, 2002.

Walker, George Harris. *A Study on the Simulation and Optimization of a Hypothetical Total Firm*. Ann Arbor, MI: University Microfilms, 1969.

Wallace, David. "Review of Candidates, Issues, and Strategies: A Computer Simulation of the 1960 and 1964 Presidential Elections. Pp. Xi, 193. Cambridge, Mass.: M.I.T. Press, 1965. $2.45." *Annals of the American Academy of Political and Social Science* 366, no. 1 (1966): 159–160. https://doi.org/10.1177/000271626636600130.

Walt, Stephen M. "Rigor or Rigor Mortis? Rational Choice and Security Studies." *International Security* 23, no. 4 (1999): 5–48.

Wang, Jackie. *Carceral Capitalism*. South Pasadena, CA: Semiotext, 2018.

Ward, John L. *The Arkansas Rockefeller*. Baton Rouge: LSU Press, 1978.

Ward, John L. *Winthrop Rockefeller, Philanthropist: A Life of Change*. Fayetteville: University of Arkansas Press, 2004.

Ward, Michael D., and Daniel Guetzkow. "Harold S. Guetzkow." *PS: Political Science & Politics* 42, no. 2 (2009): 413–414. https://doi.org/10.1017/S104909650922066X.

Ward, Michael Don, and Harold Guetzkow. "Toward Integrated Global Models: From Economic Engineering to Social Science Modeling." *Journal of Policy Modeling* 1, no. 3 (1979): 445–464. https://doi.org/10.1016/0161-8938(79)90008-5.

Warner, Bernhard. "Revealed: The 1962 CIA Paper That Predicts the Big Deal with Big Data." Bloomberg.com. March 14, 2013. https://www.bloomberg.com/news/articles/2013-03-13/revealed-the-1962-cia-paper-that-predicts-the-big-deal-with-big-data.

Wayman, Frank Whelon. "Rummel and Singer, DON and COW." In *R.J. Rummel: An Assessment of His Many Contributions*, edited by Nils Petter Gleditsch, 87–96. SpringerBriefs on Pioneers in Science and Practice. Cham, Switzerland: Springer International, 2017. https://doi.org/10.1007/978-3-319-54463-2_9.

Weaver, Warren, Jr. "Computers Counseling the Candidates." *New York Times*, October 30, 1970.

Weaver, Warren, Jr. "New Polling Technique Offers a Way to Reach Similar Voters over U.S.: Attitudes in 40 Classifications." *New York Times*, June 24, 1980, sec. Business & Finance.

Weaver, Warren, Jr. "A Pinpoint System Is Developed for Finding Voters for an Issue: Supposedly Reversed Opinion Old Method Computerized Other Factors Held Immeasurable." *New York Times*, February 3, 1979.

Weinberger, Sharon. *The Imagineers of War: The Untold Story of DARPA, the Pentagon Agency That Changed the World*. New York: Vintage, 2017.

Weintraub, E. Roy. "Game Theory and Cold War Rationality: A Review Essay." SSRN Scholarly Paper. Rochester, NY: Social Science Research Network, February 23, 2016. https://papers.ssrn.com/abstract=2737005.

Weisberg, Michael. *Simulation and Similarity: Using Models to Understand the World*. Oxford Studies in Philosophy of Science. New York: Oxford University Press, 2013.

Weiss, Michael J. *The Clustering of America*. New York: HarperCollins, 1988.

Weiss, Thomas G. "What Happened to the Idea of World Government." *International Studies Quarterly* 53, no. 2 (2009): 253–271. https://doi.org/10.1111/j.1468-2478.2009.00533.x.

White, Harrison. Review of Formal Theories of Mass Behavior. *American Sociological Review* 29, no. 5 (1964): 771–773. https://doi.org/10.2307/2091444.

White, Howard B. "The Processed Voter and the New Political Science." *Social Research* 28, no. 2 (1961): 127–150.

White, Howard B. "Rejoinder for the 'New Political Science' Reexamined: A Symposium." *Social Research* 29, no. 2 (1962): 142–156.

Wiener, Norbert. *God & Golem, Inc.: A Comment on Certain Points Where Cybernetics Impinges on Religion*. Cambridge, MA: MIT Press, 1964.

Wilcox, Clyde. "Election Simulations: President Elect (1988 Edition), Campaign Promises, and on the Campaign Trail." *Computers and the Humanities* 25, no. 4 (1991): 257–260.

Wildgen, John K. "Software Reviews: MICRO GLOBUS: A Computer Model of Long-Term Global Political and Economic Processes Reviewed by John K. Wildgen, University of New Orleans." *Social Science Computer Review* 7, no. 2 (July 1, 1989): 224–227. https://doi.org/10.1177/089443938900700212.

Wilkenfeld, Jonathan, and Joyce Kaufman. "Political Science: Network Simulation in International Politics." *Social Science Computer Review* 11, no. 4 (1993): 464–476. https://doi.org/10.1177/089443939301100405.

Winsberg, Eric. *Science in the Age of Computer Simulation*. Chicago: University of Chicago Press, 2010. https://press.uchicago.edu/ucp/books/book/chicago/S/bo9003670.html.

World Policy Institute. "History—World Policy." 2018. https://web.archive.org/web/20210303080407/http://worldpolicy.org/about_us/history/.

Young, Liam Cole. *List Cultures: Knowledge and Poetics from Mesopotamia to BuzzFeed*. Amsterdman: Amsterdam University Press, 2017. https://doi.org/10.2307/j.ctv5jxm7n.

Yunker, James A. *The Idea of World Government: From Ancient Times to the Twenty-First Century*. New York: Taylor & Francis, 2011.

Zinnes, Dina A. "A Comparison of Hostile Behavior of Decision-Makers in Simulate and Historical Data." *World Politics* 18, no. 3 (1966): 474–502. https://doi.org/10.2307/2009766.

Zuboff, Shoshana. "Big Other: Surveillance Capitalism and the Prospects of an Information Civilization." *Journal of Information Technology* 30, no. 1 (2015): 75–89. https://doi.org/10.1057/jit.2015.5.

Sources

Archives Consulted

Archives of Ontario
Center for Arkansas History and Culture
Columbia University Archives
Defense Technical Information Center
Gerald R. Ford Presidential Library
Harvard University Archives
Hoover Institution Library and Archives

John F. Kennedy Presidential Library
MIT Special Archives and Collections
RAND Corporation Archives
Ronald Reagan Presidential Library
University of Chicago Archives
University of Oklahoma Archives
University of Toronto Archives

Interviews

Adrian Robbin	July 7, 2021
Anonymous political technologist	December 12, 2013
Barry Hughes	November 2, 2020
Boyd Reilly	May 26, 2020
Brad Stock	April 28, 2020
Brad Wardell	September 29, 2020
Charlie Athanas	28, April 2020
Chris Crawford	June 1 and 9, 2020
Cliff Harris	October 5, 2020
Dave Miller	February 3, 2021
Dennis F. Kinsey	December 2, 2020
Donald R. Jansiewicz	May 18, 2020
Doug Dyment	May 11, 2020
Glenn Doren	April 28, 2020
Jacek Kugler	February 13, 2023
Jim Gasperini	May 11, 2020
Joel Billings	May 4, 2020
Kimball W. Brace	January 25, 2021
Medard Gabel	October 13, 2020
Murrary Fishel	30, July 2020
Nelson Hernandez	May 1 and 5, 2020
Phil Schrodt	February 11, 2021
Phil Smith	June 23, 2014
Richard Chadwick	October 10 and 24, 2020
Richard Falk	10, May 2021
Ronald Charnock	June 23, 2014
Ronald Friedman	20, May 2020
Sam Barton	December 5, 2020
Scott Bennett Jr.	November 23, 2021
William Coplin	May 25, 2021

Index

Page numbers in italics denote tables and figures. Endnotes are indicated by "n" followed by the endnote number.

Information Policy Series

Edited by Sandra Braman

Virtual Economies: Design and Analysis, Vili Lehdonvirta and Edward Castronova

Traversing Digital Babel: Information, e-Government, and Exchange, Alon Peled

Chasing the Tape: Information Law and Policy in Capital Markets, Onnig H. Dombalagian

Regulating the Cloud: Policy for Computing Infrastructure, edited by Christopher S. Yoo and Jean-François Blanchette

Privacy on the Ground: Driving Corporate Behavior in the United States and Europe, Kenneth A. Bamberger and Deirdre K. Mulligan

How Not to Network a Nation: The Uneasy History of the Soviet Internet, Benjamin Peters

Hate Spin: The Manufacture of Religious Offense and Its Threat to Democracy, Cherian George

Big Data Is Not a Monolith, edited by Cassidy R. Sugimoto, Hamid R. Ekbia, and Michael Mattioli

Decoding the Social World: Data Science and the Unintended Consequences of Communication, Sandra González-Bailón

Open Space: The Global Effort for Open Access to Environmental Satellite Data, Mariel John Borowitz

You'll See This Message When It Is Too Late: The Legal and Economic Aftermath of Cybersecurity Breaches, Josephine Wolff

The Blockchain and the New Architecture of Trust, Kevin Werbach

Digital Lifeline? ICTs for Refugees and Displaced Persons, edited by Carleen F. Maitland

Designing an Internet, David D. Clark

Reluctant Power: Networks, Corporations, and the Struggle for Global Governance in the Early 20th Century, Rita Zajácz

Human Rights in the Age of Platforms, edited by Rikke Frank Jørgensen

The Paradoxes of Network Neutralities, Russell Newman

Zoning China: Online Video, Popular Culture, and the State, Luzhou Li

Design Justice: Community-Led Practices to Build the World We Need, Sasha Costanza-Chock

Fake News: Understanding Media and Misinformation in the Digital Age, edited by Melissa Zimdars and Kembrew McLeod

Researching Internet Governance: Methods, Frameworks, Futures, edited by Laura DeNardis, Derrick L. Cogburn, Nanette S. Levinson, and Francesca Musiani

Red Lines: Cartoons and Political Censorship, Cherian George and Sonny Liew

Seeing Human Rights: Video Activism as a Proxy Profession, Sandra Ristovska

Farm Fresh Broadband: The Politics of Rural Connectivity, Christopher Ali

Cyberinsurance Policy: Rethinking Risk for the Internet Age, Josephine Wolff

Resistance to the Current: The Dialectics of Hacking, Johan Söderberg and Maxigas

Universal Access and its Asymmetries: The Untold Story of the Last 200 Years, Harmeet Sawhney and Hamid R. Ekbia

The Power of Partnership in Open Government? Reconsidering Multistakeholder Governance Reform, Suzanne J. Piotroswki, Daniel Berliner, and Alex Ingrams

Managing Meaning in Ukraine: Information, Communication, and Narration Since the Euromaidan Revolution, Göran Bolin and Per Ståhlberg

The Character of Consent: The History of Cookies and the Future of Technology Policy, Meg Leta Jones

Science Competes: Informing Policy in a Time of Distrust, Fracture, and Chaos, Barry Bozeman

Declaring Independence in Cyberspace: Internet Self-Governance and the End of U.S. Control of ICANN, Milton L. Mueller

Content Confusion: News Media, Native Advertising, and Policy in an Era of Disinformation, Michelle A. Amazeen

Digital Authoritarianism in the Making: Repression and Resistance on the Russian Internet, edited by Françoise Daucé, Benjamin Loveluck, and Francesca Musiani

SimPolitics: America's Quest to Solve Politics with Computers, Fenwick McKelvey

Publisher contact:
The MIT Press
Massachusetts Institute of Technology
77 Massachusetts Avenue, Cambridge, MA 02139
mitpress.mit.edu

EU Authorised Representative:
Easy Access System Europe, Mustamäe tee 50,
10621 Tallinn, Estonia
gpsr.requests@easproject.com

Printed by Integrated Books International,
United States of America